# California
# Police
# Officer
# Exam

## 2nd Edition

LEARNINGEXPRESS®

NEW YORK

Library of Congress Control Number: 2007921204

Printed in the United States of America

9 8 7 6 5 4 3

Second Edition

ISBN: 978-1-57685-588-1

For more information on LearningExpress, other LearningExpress products, or bulk sales, please write to us at:
   LearningExpress
   2 Rector Street
   26th Floor
   New York, NY 10006

Or visit us at:
   www.learnatest.com

# List of Contributors ▶

The following individuals contributed to the content of this book.

**Jan Gallagher**, PhD, is a test-development specialist, editor, and teacher living in Jersey City, New Jersey.

**Mary Hesalroad**, a former police officer for the Austin, Texas, Police Department, consults with police departments on recruiting efforts and is a freelance writer now living in Alameda, California.

**Lieutenant David McGill**, a 20-year veteran of the Los Angeles Police Department, has worked a variety of assignments, including patrol, juvenile officer, training officer, intelligence officer, and detective and field supervisor. In addition, he has worked at Internal Affairs, Antiterrorist Division, and as an administrative lieutenant and bureau chief adjutant. Currently, Lieutenant McGill is an officer-in-charge at Internal Affairs Group, Professional Standards Bureau; holds the position of vice president of the National Internal Affairs Investigators Association; and is on the Board of Directors of the California Peace Officers Association.

**Karen Petty** is a New York City–based writer specializing in career development issues.

**Judith F. Olson**, MA, is chairperson of the language arts department at Valley High School in West Des Moines, Iowa, where she also conducts test preparation workshops.

**Judith Robinovitz** is an independent educational consultant and director of Score at the Top, a comprehensive test preparation program in Vero Beach, Florida.

**Judith Schlesinger**, PhD, is a writer and psychologist whose background includes years of working with police officers in psychiatric crisis interventions.

**Jay Smith** is an exercise physiologist and director of physical fitness and health maintenance programs for the Massachusetts Criminal Justice Training Council.

# Contents

# CONTENTS

CHAPTER

# 1 ▶ Life behind the Badge: The Work of a Police Officer

## CHAPTER SUMMARY

Congratulations! You've decided to find out about police work as a possible career choice. This first chapter will tell you what police work involves, from the variety of tasks you can expect to be doing to the skills and traits a police officer needs. You'll also find out about the latest trends in police departments and long-term career opportunities.

**S**o you're in great shape. You can do multiple sit-ups with ease. You can run up and down stairs time and again and barely become winded. A wall climb or an obstacle course? No problem. Your vision is perfect, your heart sound, and you can hear a pin drop a block away. You'd pass any medical exam with flying colors.

If you want to join the police force, all that counts. Police work requires stamina, agility, and strength. But having a healthy body and 20/20 eyesight is only one measure of whether or not you're suited for the job.

It takes a lot to be a good police officer. To give you some idea, you'll need to be able to

- read human behavior.
- cope with high levels of stress.
- communicate with all types of people.
- develop a commanding presence and be able to make tough decisions.
- learn the law.
- have an eye for detail and a knack for paperwork.

- serve as a good leader, role model, negotiator, and problem solver.
- help people in a caring manner while keeping some emotional distance.
- be ready to put your life on the line at any time.

If it sounds like you need the qualities of a psychologist, air traffic controller, teacher, lawyer, accountant, politician, doctor, and firefighter all rolled up into one—well, yes, that's just about the size of it. What's more, you'll go through a rigorous and often lengthy process just to get accepted as a police recruit. That reality tests your level of motivation right off the bat. You have to really want this job to persevere and succeed at each part of the application process.

## ▶ Have You Got What It Takes?

Police departments use the application process to evaluate certain qualities that can make or break your competence as an officer. It's true that there's no exact science to measure such key traits as honesty and integrity. Yet the series of tests that police candidates are put through—written, oral, and physical exams—is designed by experts to offer departments a reliable indication of an applicant's general character and abilities.

For example, police departments are looking for candidates with emotional stability. They're looking for a sense of responsibility and a clear respect for authority. At the same time, they want to know that you are able to make decisions independently and exercise good judgment. An important point here is that departments want recruits who care about helping people *from all walks of life*—of every race, religion, sex, sexual preference, age, or socioeconomic class. This goes for the people you work with as well as the public you serve. Police officers are obliged to treat all people equally and equitably under the law. That same attitude and behavior are what police candidates need to express.

## ▶ Skills You'll Need

The qualifications just described have to do with a person's temperament, personality, and belief system. But police departments look for certain basic skills as well.

For example, you can expect your communication skills to be tested. You don't have to be the world's greatest public speaker or write like an English professor. However, police work does involve a constant processing of information, both spoken and written. As an officer, you'll need to prepare daily activity reports. You'll be interviewing witnesses, interrogating arrestees, and negotiating disputes. You'll have to understand orders and department policies handed down by superior officers clearly. You'll be settling disputes and calming down people in crisis situations. These and many other tasks call for an ability to express yourself effectively and to interact well with other people. That means the *way* you interact matters, too—for instance, being tactful, cooperative, and not condescending, even if you happen to be dealing with people who are disrespectful, hostile, or just plain aggravating. It'll be up to you to keep your cool.

Some skills that are desirable in a police officer can't necessarily be "taught," although they can be developed or improved through practice and focus. Having a good memory, good powers of observation, and reliable instincts about people and situations are examples. Part of the job, after all, is being able to do such things as recall what a fleeing suspect was wearing, discover evidence at a crime scene, and notice suspicious behavior. And part of the tests you'll take to become an officer will be aimed at measuring these kinds of abilities.

## ▶ Skills You'll Learn

Many skills will be taught to police officer candidates once they've made it through the application process and been accepted as a recruit. For instance, you don't need to know how to use firearms or administer first aid to pass the entrance exams. These are skills you'll learn as part of your professional training. You'll also be taught self-defense techniques, patrol and traffic control procedures, the use of police equipment and vehicles, emergency measures, and a variety of other strategies and tactics. On small or rural forces, new recruits often get the bulk of their professional training on the job, working closely with an experienced officer. Larger departments typically require a period of formal training, often weeks or months in a police academy or other academic setting. Classroom instruction is then followed by a period of on-the-job or field training.

You also won't need to have specific knowledge about laws or the legal system before you take the police entrance exams. Police departments include this kind of instruction in their training programs for new recruits. That's when they'll make sure that you are up to speed on state and local laws, constitutional rights, civil rights, and other areas relevant to law enforcement.

As you can see, police officers are highly trained professionals. And with good reason. As an officer, you'll be trusted with ensuring the safety and well-being of your community, while doing so within the boundaries of the Constitution and state and local laws. Because of that trust, you will face high expectations in performing your job and be held to the highest standards of behavior. An officer's work is demanding, difficult, and always potentially dangerous. All in all, there's a lot more to policing than enforcing the law. There's also a lot less glamour and excitement than most TV shows and movies portray. Still, it's a job that is highly honorable and carries many rewards for the right kind of person. Policing offers you a chance to do important and interesting work—and work that you can be proud of.

## ▶ The Police Officer: On the Job

If you like having a variety of responsibilities and duties, you'll get that with police work. This can be especially true with new officers, when one of the key purposes behind the assignments they are given is to expose them to different aspects of police work, both inside the station and out on the streets. Alternating between night shifts and day shifts, at any point in time you could find yourself directing traffic, monitoring the crowd at a rock concert, guarding a criminal suspect who is hospitalized—or guarding the front desk at the station house.

Once you have gone through basic training and become a full-fledged member of the force, you'll most likely start out as a patrol officer. While small police departments will naturally command small numbers of patrol officers, in large departments these individuals make up the majority of the force. Patrol officers do exactly what their title implies: patrol a designated area, usually by car or on foot, and in some cases by motorcycle, bicycle, or even on horseback.

### Just the Facts

The first-ever motorcycle cop came on the scene in 1909 in Pittsburgh, Pennsylvania. Vehicle of choice: a Harley.

The overall role of a police officer is to protect people and property, maintain order, enforce the law, and reduce the fear and incidents of crime, always within the scope of safeguarding every citizen's constitutional rights. Toward that goal, you'll be trained as an officer to watch for and investigate suspicious situations, illegal activities, and public safety hazards. When you're on patrol, this can run the gamut from observing driving and parking violations and reporting traffic lights that aren't working to responding to radio calls that take you to the scene of serious incidents, either reported or in progress, such as burglaries, assaults, murders, domestic abuse, rapes, and suicides.

## ▶ There Is No "Routine"

As an officer at a crime scene, you may need to identify and question suspects and witnesses, gather criminal evidence, and arrest and transport suspects to the police station for booking and detention. Depending on the nature of the crime, you may perform these duties at the direction of, or to assist, detectives also called to the scene. When suspects you've arrested are brought to trial, as the arresting officer you may be called upon to testify in court for the prosecuting attorney.

A large part of a police officer's job involves ensuring people's safety and maintaining order. As such, officers are often on hand for crowd and traffic control during large public gatherings—sporting events, parades, concerts, political rallies, demonstrations, and the like. They are called on to perform similar services in emergency situations, such as fires, natural disasters, and auto accidents, and are trained to provide basic medical care to aid accident or crime victims.

Police officers may work alone or with partners, often depending on the nature of a particular assignment or the size of the police force. Typically you'll work 40-hour weeks on rotating shifts. You can plan on working at night or during the day, weekends and holidays included. Plus, it's not unusual to work extra shifts and long hours because of department overload or during pressing criminal investigations or large-scale emergency situations.

## ▶ The Bottom Line

What you'll earn as a police officer varies, of course, from force to force. On a national level, the Bureau of Labor Statistics reports that the median salary of nonsupervisory police officers was approximately $45,000 a year in 2004. Those in the middle 50% earned between about $34,400 and $56,300. Those at the lowest end (10%) were paid less than $27,000, while the highest paid (also 10%) made more than $68,000 a year. Salaries tend to be higher in metropolitan areas with large police departments. But wherever you work, your salary can vary significantly based on the level of overtime pay and other benefits unique to the particular agency.

Your compensation package as a police officer usually includes standard employee benefits such as paid vacation days, sick leave, and health and life insurance. Most departments will supply you with required safety equipment—such as a weapon, ballistic vest, a baton, and handcuffs—and provide special allowances for you to purchase uniforms. Generous pension plans are a major benefit of police work. Many officers are able to retire at half-pay after 20 or 25 years of service, free to pursue second careers or other interests while still in their 40s or 50s.

## ▶ The Other Side of the Coin

There are real advantages to the profession of policing. It offers you the chance to do responsible, worthwhile work. Each day holds the promise of making a positive difference in people's lives, right on up to saving lives. Other pluses include the variety of duties, the personal challenges you'll face, and the flexible work schedules versus the nine-to-five office routine. It's also a profession known for a spirit of camaraderie and fellowship. On the practical side, the level of job security tends to be higher than that of many other occupations, not to mention the generally higher salaries and benefits that come with the territory.

Then there are the tough parts of the job. You know that police work can be risky. But it's a different thing to experience the risks in reality. You will face unruly crowds and criminals who can be angry, violent, armed, and irrational. The authority of your badge and the threat of physical force may not be heeded. You won't have a stunt expert doubling for you in physical altercations and car chases like in the movies. Cars collide. The bullets are real. And police officers sometimes get hurt.

## What Officers Earn

The following information is based on the Labor Relations Information System's 2004 Wage and Benefit Survey. The data represent an *average* of wages and benefits paid to officers in 322 cities nationwide with populations greater than 50,000. Keep in mind, therefore, that compensation may vary significantly among individual cities.

### Average Monthly Wages
Police Officer (entry level)—$3,004
Detective (basic wage)—$3,954
Sergeant—$5,061
Lieutenant—$5,829
Captain—$6,582
Chief—$8,870

Note: Figures listed (1) represent top level wages for each ranked position except police officer and detective, and (2) do not include any additional wages paid for longevity on force.

### Benefits
**Health Insurance Contribution**
- Percentage of full family premium paid by *employer*—83.58%
- Percentage of full family premium paid by *employee*—16.42%

**Retirement Plan Contribution**
- Percentage of salary paid toward plan by *employer*—11.89%
- Percentage of salary paid toward plan by *employee*—5.54%

**Plainclothes Allowance**
- $658/year

**Holidays**
- 97.1 hours/year

**Vacation after 10 Years**
- 141 hours/year

**Education Pay-Step Bonus**
- 2-year education—$112
- 4-year education—$199

## ▶ Serious Business

Doing this job means living in harm's way and dealing with human tragedies. That's true whether you're an urban cop or a rural cop, and whether your brushes with violent crime and tragic events are frequent or rare. But it's not only the potential dangers of the job that can take their toll. Stresses of the job can come from many sources. From the 1970s to the 1990s, suicides among police officers in many cities were well above the national average. Even today, more police officers are killed by their own hands than are murdered by an assailant. Although suicides among officers continue to be a serious issue, departments have made great strides in reducing them through employee assistance programs and on-staff psychological assistance.

## Just the Facts

Police officers are often referred to as "The Thin Blue Line"—the protective force positioned between law-abiding citizens on one side, and anarchy, where criminals and dangerous forces can be found.

Try to imagine the level of frustration officers experience when they arrest a criminal for rape or murder, are backed by an army of witnesses to testify against him—yet watch the guy go free on a technicality or a plea bargain. Try to picture—and later erase—the image of a three-year-old child who has just been brutally beaten or sexually abused by a parent. Try to grasp the sense of betrayal and disappointment when learning that fellow officers have been arrested for taking bribes or selling drugs. Even the most skilled and diligent police officers can find it difficult to cope with those kinds of emotions. Because such feelings are not easy to put aside when the shift ends, extra pressures can be brought home with them as well.

Other aspects of policing can generate more subtle levels of stress. Patrolling the same daily beat has its tedious side, both when there's no action on the streets and when you're dealing with the same kind of action time after time. The routine paperwork, reports to file, and bureaucratic red tape can become equally grueling. On the personal level, the downside of a changing schedule and lots of overtime is that these can disrupt your sleeping habits, family life, and social life.

## ▶ The Image

One of the more taxing elements of policing has to do with public perceptions. That can mean high expectations—living up to the image of an officer as a super-human being, always calm, cool, and collected, never making mistakes. Or it can mean hostility—dealing with people who blame cops for rising crime or hold the firm opinion that all cops are corrupt, racist, and power-hungry. And it's not just criminal suspects who can be belligerent. Even normally reasonable people can fly into a rage when they're a victim or perpetrator of a crime.

Police are also under intense scrutiny from the press and are frequently subjected to news reports on crooked cops, rogue cops, and department-wide scandals. In 1995, a police officer in New Orleans was charged with the murders of three people, one of them another officer. A group of New York City officers made national headlines for their lewd and disorderly conduct at the hotel they were staying at during a police convention. Officers in Philadelphia pleaded guilty to planting drug evidence, stealing money, and falsifying arrest reports. And is there anybody out there who hasn't heard of Detective Mark Fuhrman? How about the infamous Rampart scandal of the LAPD? These kind of stories not only are demoralizing to "good cops," but all too often have the effect of smearing the profession rather than just the lone offenders.

Those are some of the tough parts of policing. They are important factors for you to be aware of and consider when making a move to join the force. But consider, too, the kind of help and support that's available once you're there. Many police departments actively provide the kind of training and assistance officers need to handle the pressures of police work effectively, including stress management programs and confidential counseling services. Fellow officers can be a source of understanding and encouragement. Also on your side is the fact that plenty of citizens out there respect and are grateful for the work that police officers do. As virtually every person in this field will tell you with conviction—the majority of cops are good cops.

There is no better feeling in the world than going home after a shift, knowing you helped someone or put a bad person away for society's sake.

## ▶ The Application Process

If what you've read so far appeals to you, and you think you've got the "right stuff" to be a police officer, it's time to think about what's involved in applying for the job.

The basic requirements you need to be aware of include the following:

- A minimum age, usually between 18 and 21, and a maximum from 29 to 40
- Excellent health and good vision
- U.S. citizenship or, in some cities, resident alien status
- A high school diploma or its equivalent
- A valid driver's license for the state in which you are applying
- A clean criminal record

In Chapter 2, you'll find the specifics of how police officers are selected. But briefly, here's what you can expect:

- A written test
- A thorough medical exam
- Various tests of physical ability
- A psychological test or personality evaluation
- Drug testing and possibly a polygraph (lie detector) test
- A thorough background investigation
- An oral interview with one officer or a board of police officers and citizens

Because police departments frequently have more applicants than job openings, they pay attention to "extra" abilities or experiences that make you stand out from the crowd. Beyond meeting the basic requirements for becoming a police officer, having qualifications in these areas may help your cause:

- *Education:* Many departments have adopted or are moving toward higher educational standards for police recruits. Educational level has already been linked to *rank promotions* at several departments, for example, in New York City and Chicago. Most experts in the field believe that it's just a matter of time before a college degree becomes a minimum requirement across the country for *entry* to the force. This isn't yet the case, but as a rule of thumb there's an advantage in having completed at least some college (including junior colleges and universities); more of an advantage for earning a college degree in any field; and a greater advantage still in having taken courses or earned a degree in a directly relevant field such as police science, law enforcement, or criminal justice. The advantage may come not only in terms of the hiring process, but also in terms of a pay-step bonus in many departments.
- *Second Languages:* Being able to speak more than one language can also be an unofficial "plus." This is especially true in urban areas with large ethnic populations, where knowing Spanish, Korean, or Filipino could all come in handy, depending on the neighborhood. Being able to communicate with non-English-speaking people in their native languages can help enormously in resolving disputes, directing crowds, aiding crime victims, and conducting investigations. Most important, it also could save your life in certain threatening situations.
- *Computer Skills:* Knowing how to type on a keyboard is essential. Most reporting today is done on computers, and high-tech communications systems are becoming more and more a part of police work, right down to patrol officer duties. For example, most patrol cars today are equipped with a mobile digital terminal or notebook computer that allows officers to tap into state or national data bases to run driver, vehicle, weapon, and record checks, or to e-mail inquiries. Completing routine reports on a computer can also save a lot of time. Computers are often networked or linked to a mainframe at the department, so this "paperwork" can go directly into department "files" for storage.
- *Military Experience:* The self-discipline and life experiences developed during military service often make a candidate more attractive to police departments. Former military personnel easily fit into the workforce and adapt well to the police officer work environment.

## Just the Facts

Over 90% of local police departments in the United States. have fewer than 50 officers on their force. About half have fewer than ten officers.

Those are the basics of what's involved in applying for the job. You also need to be aware that the competition for police jobs tends to be steep. (Note also that new hires don't always come from current applications, but instead may be based on an eligibility list of applicants from previous years.)

The good news is that overall job prospects in the field are favorable. There are about 18,000 police agencies with roughly 600,000 police officers in the United

States today, and the U.S. Bureau of Labor Statistics (BLS) projects that employment of police officers will grow about as fast as the average for all occupations. In the post–9/11 world, the demand for competent law enforcement professionals will not diminish.

You can rest assured that the demand for top-notch candidates is strong at police departments across the country. To join the ranks, you'll need to show yourself as someone who possesses high moral character, is intelligent, can make decisions, and is willing and able to perform beyond the call of duty—exactly the kind of recruit that every department is looking for. The more you know about what goes into the selection of recruits, the better you can prepare yourself to fit the bill.

## ▶ Moving Up and Around

Leap ahead for a minute. You've passed the entrance requirements at your department of choice. You've gone through all the police officer training and really learned the ropes. You've been on the force for a while and proven yourself a commendable officer. Now where can you go from there?

To get some idea of where you can take your career as a police officer, you first need to have some notion of how police departments are organized. Police departments have many things in common in the way they're managed and operated: They have similar goals, serve similar functions, abide by similar laws, and are mostly all run under local city government and control. However, no single organizational chart fits every single police department. They are organized in a similar manner as the military.

That's mostly a matter of size. For example, it's typical to organize departments by breaking them down into divisions that are each responsible for a specific type of police work. The larger the department, the more divisions you'll find. In fact, the number of *divisions* on a large force is usually greater than the total number of *officers* in a small department. If you join a

rural police force, your department may have no formal divisions at all—among other differences from a large urban force (see the following sidebar "Policing in Rural Territory).

In a department that is organized by divisions, patrol officers generally make up one division. Other divisions carry names that are probably familiar to you and are related to the nature of the crimes investigated—homicide, burglary, traffic, and vice and narcotics, to name a few. Still other divisions are responsible for the administrative side of police work, such as internal affairs, personnel, records, and training.

The structure of the organization may not stop there. Especially in medium-sized and large departments, divisions may be grouped and operated under another organizational unit known as a "bureau." The vice and narcotics division, for instance, could be part of the investigative services bureau; patrol could be part of the field services bureau; and internal affairs could be part of the administrative services bureau.

Many police departments—and definitely those in large urban areas—operate highly specialized divisions or bureaus. These may be in charge of functions that are unique or appropriate to specific geographical locations, such as a harbor patrol, an aviation unit, or mounted police. Or they may perform functions that are necessary because of a high level of community need surrounding certain types of criminal activity, such as bomb squads, hostage negotiations, sex crime analysis, or juvenile services.

When you're checking out various police departments you may want to join, be aware that different departments may use slightly different titles for their various divisions and bureaus. The homicide and robbery division in one place may be called the "crimes against persons" division in another, just as an investigative services bureau may be referred to less formally as the detective bureau. Generally, the larger the department, the more able you are to move around to different jobs and to be promoted to higher levels.

On a big city police force, you could be one of one thousand, ten thousand, or more than 20 thousand sworn officers. At the other extreme, you could be one of ten or fewer officers serving a rural community. Along with answering to a much smaller roll call, outlined below are some of the differences you'd find working on a rural force. (Note that small departments aren't necessarily rural, although some of the same characteristics may apply.)

### The Daily Routine

Rural departments won't have all the specialized divisions of policing that a large force has. A rural officer tends to be more of a jack-of-all-trades, responsible for all different types of police work. Because overall crime rates are lower in rural communities, especially the level of violent crime, officers there face fewer dangerous events on a day-to-day basis. The pace is slower—and the standard of living generally higher—than in an urban environment. Rural officers also work directly with their superior officers (including the chief of police being right at hand) and tend to get more personal guidance and instruction as a result. Working closely with just a few fellow officers makes good teamwork essential. It also makes for less bureaucracy and fewer "layers of management" to wade through to make decisions and get the job done.

In larger urban police departments, the frequency of calls for service is higher, and officers are confronted with more dangerous events on a daily basis. Therefore, it is only natural that they tend to have more experience in all aspects of police work, and their training tends to be better and more frequent than other departments.

### Tools of the Trade

Limited operating budgets are common among rural departments. This can result in a force being understaffed. It often means less access to new or more sophisticated equipment and systems. And there may not be funds available to invest in officers through continued training and educational programs. (Take note, however, that the same can be true of large forces that have gotten the budget ax. In turn, rural departments in communities with a high tax base may have all the latest, greatest equipment at their disposal.)

### Adapting to the Territory

Rural and urban officers alike handle criminal matters such as property crimes, juvenile offenses, and domestic violence. But some kinds of criminal activity are unique to certain rural areas, such as illegal game or fish poaching; thefts of farm crops, livestock, or timber; or illegal immigration in border regions. Officers in most rural areas may deal less with cocaine and crack dealers, but instead may have to contend with liquor and tobacco trafficking or marijuana crops being grown and distributed. Regarding crimes related to substance abuse, alcohol is the drug that represents more of a problem throughout rural communities, especially incidents of DUI (driving under the influence) and DWI (driving while intoxicated).

### The Familiarity Factor

Police officers in rural areas tend to know or recognize the people involved in a crime. Likewise, the victims, witnesses, and perpetrators of crimes are more likely to be acquainted with one another. This level of familiarity can help officers identify and track suspects in a criminal investigation. Yet it can create a unique set of problems as well. Victims and witnesses in a small town may be less apt to press charges or point the finger at people they come into contact with on a regular basis. Rural officers, too, may find themselves having to investigate or arrest a local citizen who happens to be their neighbor's grandson, the upstanding local bank president, or their children's schoolteacher. Because of this "familiarity factor," rural officers often take a more personal approach and use less formal (but no less professional) procedures when conducting police business.

## ▶ Career Moves

It's clear that not all police forces are the same size or organized the same way. That being the case, you can assume that the opportunities for you to move up and around—to climb the ranks or try out different areas of police work—also won't be the same at every department. But some general guidelines do apply.

When it comes to "moving up," police departments tend to be more similar because the job titles used to show your rank or seniority on the force (sergeant, captain, etc.) are fairly standard everywhere. The differences among departments in this area have more to do with how many slots there are to fill, rather than with the types of promotions available. Where there are fewer slots to move up to, salary hikes may be awarded instead.

"Moving around" is another story. On a small force you won't do as much moving around the department because there simply won't be as many divisions to move around to; here you're more likely to be handling all kinds of police work on a regular basis. In larger departments, it's possible to do more moving around and concentrate on specific kinds of police work because that's where you can transfer in and out of specialized divisions.

The "Career Ladder Chart" gives you a look at how your career could progress within a large department based on rank. Going by job title alone, some positions obviously are higher in the pecking order—for example, a captain ranks higher than a sergeant. In addition, job titles may be assigned numerical rankings—such as Detective I, II, or III—to recognize a higher level of authority, experience, and expertise.

Keep in mind, of course, that a police force with a total of nine officers requires far fewer layers of command than those shown on the chart. And these exact career routes may not apply to every large or even medium-sized department. What the "ladder" in this particular chart shows is a *common* chain of command.

What isn't shown on the chart is that, at each level of command, the position you hold may be further classified based on the division you work in or your area of assignment—for example, homicide detective, records division sergeant, precinct captain, or identification and records commander. This kind of job classification would be used to identify not only your rank on the force, but also the types of duties you perform as part of a certain division. Officers with the same rank can have very different job duties.

For example, as a *patrol division lieutenant*, your duties could range from conducting a roll call of the patrol force, to inspecting police logbooks for conformance with regulations, to setting bail for prisoners held on nonfelony charges.

As a *traffic lieutenant*, however, you would be focused on traffic control activities, such as directing officers to remove illegally parked vehicles; recommending changes in traffic control devices and regulations in the community; and working with organizers of a parade to determine police staffing requirements, traffic rerouting plans, and crowd control procedures.

Yet as a *community relations lieutenant*, you would have another focus altogether, performing duties such as supervising police personnel in efforts to resolve community social problems; working with social service agencies to develop crime prevention programs; and lecturing to local civic, school, and community groups about the mission, functions, and resources of the police department.

## ▶ Moving Up

You can see that what you'll be doing in different jobs depends on a number of factors—most of all, on your rank and division and the department's size and operating structure. Still, if you're moving up the ladder, you can count on certain changes taking place. For one thing, you're likely to take on a supervisory role, guid-

# Career Ladder Chart

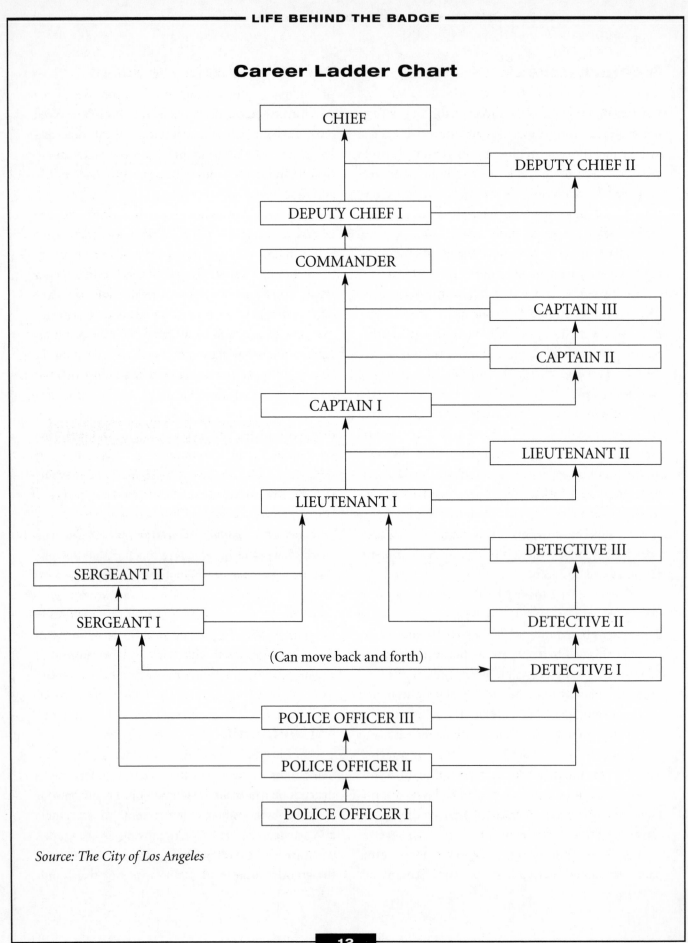

CHIEF

DEPUTY CHIEF II

DEPUTY CHIEF I

COMMANDER

CAPTAIN III

CAPTAIN II

CAPTAIN I

LIEUTENANT II

LIEUTENANT I

DETECTIVE III

SERGEANT II

SERGEANT I

DETECTIVE II

(Can move back and forth)     DETECTIVE I

POLICE OFFICER III

POLICE OFFICER II

POLICE OFFICER I

*Source: The City of Los Angeles*

ing the work of other police personnel. You'll probably have more administrative responsibilities, such as maintaining budgets, filing inspection reports, or conducting job performance evaluations of officers under your charge. Because moving up implies that you've gained a certain level of know-how about the department and the community it serves, you may become more involved in strategic planning and in setting department policies and goals. You'll also have more decision-making authority about matters of procedure, disciplinary measures, expenditures, and so forth.

To become eligible for promotion, officers typically must go through a probationary period. How long the probationary period is depends on an individual department's promotion policy and personnel needs, but you can figure around three years on average—sometimes more, sometimes less. Plan on taking a written exam for promotion to sergeant, lieutenant, and captain; exam scores plus a record of your on-the-job performance then determine your placement on a promotion list. If you need additional training or education to advance, many police departments are willing to foot part or all of the bill. This financial help could include tuition for you to take college courses or work toward a degree in a law enforcement–related field, often with an added incentive of boosting your salary if you end up earning the degree.

When you're thinking about how far you can go in a police organization, remember that moving up the ladder doesn't necessarily equal greater job satisfaction. Some officers aspire to one day occupy the police chief's office. Others feel at their best patrolling the beat. Once you're on the force, it will be up to you to decide where you want to go and to prove yourself capable of getting there. One of the best things you can do is take the initiative to learn new skills and knowledge and tackle different assignments. The more time you spend on the job, the better you'll be able to tell what kind of police work appeals to you most. Then you can navigate your career path accordingly.

## ▶ Changing with the Times

Back before automobiles and radio transmitters, you'd most likely find police officers either at the precinct station or out walking their beat. They were a fixture in the neighborhood; they knew the people and the people knew them.

Naturally, many things have changed over the years. One major shift occurred when foot patrol gave way to car patrol, allowing officers to cover more territory during their watch and to reach crime scenes faster. Patrol cars were also a visible and constant reminder of police presence, which was viewed in and of itself as a crime control strategy. The now common 911 dispatching system produced another shift in policing when it came along with its promise that the police were just a phone call away.

### Just the Facts

Back in 1895, the New York City Police Department formed a bicycle squad to slow down horse-drawn carriages. The two-wheeling, 29-officer squad made 1,366 arrests for speeding that year alone.

Go back for a moment to the example of how the patrol car influenced policing, but this time consider the downside. The simple act of being inside instead of outside a car separates an officer from people on the street. Yet these people might have vital information, valid complaints, and some good suggestions about how to reduce crime in their communities.

Think, too, of certain disadvantages of the 911 system. Besides being subject to overload and non-emergency reports, the system puts officers in a *reactive* position—constantly responding to calls about crimes that may or may not be in progress by the time they arrive. As a result, the chances of apprehending a criminal, much less preventing a crime, are reduced.

According to research reported by John E. Eck and William Spelman in *Problem Solving: Problem-Oriented Policing in Newport News,* fewer than 5% of all 911 calls in most cities bring an officer to a crime in progress, where he or she can intercede or make an arrest. In fact, the majority of 911 calls—anywhere from 50% to 90%—are not even about crime.

Another familiar strategy with some clear drawbacks is that of policing "by the numbers," through which your performance as an officer is be evaluated by the number of calls you've answered, arrests you've made or tickets you've issued, or even how many times you manage to circle a neighborhood in your patrol car during a shift. Needless to say, a lot determines whether or not you're doing a good job.

It's not that these and other common police procedures need to be thrown out altogether. But some of the weaknesses in these systems began to surface as early as the 1960s. At the same time that police departments were being expanded and loads of new equipment were being purchased, crime rates and citizens began to express greater levels of fear. Something wasn't working.

## ▶ In the Spotlight

The 1960s launched a time of major social upheaval and unrest. Decades of deeply imbedded prejudices were brought to the surface, authority was questioned. When it came to civil rights issues, the antiwar movement, and the corruption of government officials, police were often caught in the middle. They weren't used to the level of civil disobedience happening around them, nor the level of disrespect that came with being viewed as part of "the Establishment." Suddenly their job put them in direct confrontation with large groups of citizens. Their methods of policing were being scrutinized by the media and by the public. Meanwhile, they were trying to understand and adapt to the changes in society just like everyone else. You could argue that citizens' expectations of the police were unrealistically high. But from the people's point of view, if the police couldn't keep the peace, then who would?

The complicated issues and problems that were raised four decades ago live on today in some form, putting the methods and goals of policing under the microscope for close inspection. Slowly but surely, changes are underway, showing up in what the public is asking for from police departments across the country and in how police officers are being trained, in the demographic make-up of departments, and in the roles and responsibilities officers are being asked to take on.

Police departments today are focused on tailoring their tactics to the times. And despite the obvious

Since the infamous terrorist attacks on the United States on September 11, 2001, policing in this country has been forever changed. Although police officers will continue to be expected to reduce the fear and incidents of crime in every city throughout the United States, a new reality has emerged that has taxed the resources of every department in the nation.

Leaders in homeland security have long recognized that the police officers working the beat are, and will continue to be, the front line in the War on Terror. When the next incident occurs, it will be the police officer on patrol who will be there to maintain control of the situation, effect an arrest if possible, and help solve the crime. This tremendous responsibility cannot be taken lightly by any prospective officer. Better training, better intelligence gathering, and better cooperation among law enforcement agencies make this an exciting time in policing.

More and more task forces and cooperative working relationships among local law enforcement professional and state and federal agencies have been formed, and new, innovative means to detect and prevent terrorists from employing their deadly deeds have been deployed. Work among the Federal Bureau of Investigation, the Secret Service, Immigration and Customs Enforcement, and a host of other national and international agencies has led to better information sharing and the disruption of potential terrorist cells throughout the United States, most of which you never hear about.

Police officers today are on the front line, protecting America as best they can and trying to improve their skills to prevent the next incident before it occurs.

addition of high-speed cruisers and high-tech tools, some of the current changes in policing look suspiciously like "the good ol' days" when officers walked their beat.

## ▶ Trends and Opportunities

Certain major forces or trends are changing both the mission and methods of modern policing. As a potential police recruit, you should be aware of these forces. What's happening in policing now—and where it's headed—have a lot to do with your future in this profession.

One of these driving forces won't come as a surprise: The public has issued a mandate to *get tough on crime.* Another major force is directly linked to the first: Police departments are aware of the need to *get back in touch* with the communities they serve. Both of these trends affect the demand for police officers—and the demands being placed on officers.

Getting tough on crime centers on the fact that crime is a hot topic, one of the most serious social issues of the day. It's encouraging that most areas of the country have seen a decline in criminal activity in recent years. However, the public's cry for more police officers is still loud and strong.

The U.S. Justice Department's Bureau of Justice Statistics (BJS) revealed a whopping 24 million reported crimes in 2004—not all crimes actually committed. In the daily news are accounts of robberies, assaults, rapes, murders, drug-related crime, and gang-related crime. The incidence of violent crime is especially alarming: According to the BJS, violent crime is behind the conviction of 94% of state prisoners, many of whom are repeat offenders.

The general trend in lawmaking leans toward harsher sentencing in the courts, but it's slow going. Mostly because of overcrowded prisons and courtrooms, plea bargaining has become commonplace, resulting in large numbers of known criminal offenders being released on parole or probation. Some wind up becoming law-abiding citizens. Many don't. That's another reason for the current clamor for good police officers—and more of 'em.

Wanting, of course, doesn't always mean getting. Funds aren't always available to increase the size of any given police force. In addition, research has indicated that having more officers doesn't automatically mean having less crime. Other elements have to change as well. So along with hiring extra officers when they need to and can, many police departments are testing new methods of policing that focus on preventing crime, not just arresting criminals after the fact.

## Back to the Beat

That leads around to the need for police departments to get back in touch with the communities they serve. Many departments are adopting a strategy known as *community policing.* (Problem-oriented policing, strategic policing, neighborhood policing, and back-to-the-beat policing are other names used to refer to this and other strategies based on a similar philosophy.)

Giving more of a leadership role to patrol officers is a key element of community policing. According to supporters of this strategy, that's just common sense. Patrol officers are out in the community 24 hours a day, every day of the week. They have the closest contact with citizens' concerns and criminal activity on the street. So, the argument goes, if you're a patrol officer, naturally you should have some say in how departments go about enforcing the law and controlling crime.

Patrol officers now are being encouraged to do more than issue citations, make arrests, and hand in reports. They are being asked to use their firsthand knowledge of crime and its related problems in the community to help develop solutions that work.

## A Call for Teamwork

Community policing also asks patrol officers to seek the help of local citizens in keeping the peace. This takes getting to know the people on your beat—residents, store owners, church groups, schools. It takes effort to learn about people's fears and complaints and their ideas for creating a safer community. And it takes

time to develop a partnership with citizens and earn their trust. For example, instead of always being assigned to different beats, you may be regularly patrolling the same beat—by car and on foot—so that you become a familiar face to the people who live and work there. That's the aspect of community policing that looks a lot like "the good ol' days." As you become a part of the neighborhood, you have more of a stake in making things better.

Cities across the country—New York, Los Angeles, Houston, Chicago, Tampa, San Diego, and many more—have spent the last several years doing what it takes to put this strategy into action. The models they've developed are now making their way into departments in smaller cities and towns. The shift to community or problem-oriented policing isn't an overnight process. Police resources have to be used in different ways. Often more officers are needed, especially when increased foot patrol is part of the plan. Most of all, a shift in mind-set has to take place. Community policing calls for more teamwork at all levels of the department. It puts the focus on cleaning up neighborhoods and attacking crime at its root, not just treating the symptoms through one-at-a-time responses to 911 calls. And it includes sharing responsibility and working together with citizens to achieve these goals.

These goals are also being supported by many other actions on the part of police departments. The technical skills, interpersonal skills, and the philosophy behind community policing are now being incorporated into police officer training programs—both for new recruits and experienced officers. Departments are also taking advantage of advancements in technology. Sophisticated high-tech equipment is increasingly being used to help control crime, solve crimes, and work more effectively with other police departments and government agencies. In addition, departments are boosting their efforts to bring more women and members of diverse racial and ethnic groups onto the force, changing the traditional white male image of the police force to reflect better the demographic makeup of the population each department serves.

All of this influences your career as a police officer because it spells new opportunities. Think about it. Once you join the force, you'll start off as a patrol officer. Modern policing strategies value and rely on the patrol officer. How well an officer deals one-on-one with people on the street can make or break the goals of community policing. That's where your opportunities come in.

To wage a successful battle against crime, police departments need qualified, committed recruits more than ever before. They need your ability to be a leader, a problem solver, a negotiator, a decision maker, a role model, a team player and an independent thinker. Yes, the traditional chain of command still exists. No, the bureaucracy hasn't vanished. But the current trends in policing are designed to elevate both the role of the officer on patrol and the profession of policing as a whole.

## The Computer Age

Using computers to assist law enforcement is becoming more and more prevalent in police departments across the country. Crime statistics are downloaded into computer programs that allow analysts to detect trends. The better and more updated the crime statistics, the faster law enforcement managers can adjust resources to apprehend the criminals. Police work today means doing more with less and becoming as efficient and effective as possible with limited resources.

One of the newest trends emerging in law enforcement is COMPSTAT, which simply stands for "computerized statistics." Los Angeles Police Department Chief William J. Bratton used this technique effectively while police commissioner in New York in the late 1990s, and he brought it to the LAPD when he became chief in 2003. Monthly meetings are held with command officers in respective areas, during which crime events are depicted on large computer maps for all

to see. These statistics are only days old, which makes their relevance as close to "real time" as possible.

Managers are grilled about trends and patterns of criminal activity in their area and are asked how they are combating these issues. Innovative ways to deal with those crimes are brainstormed, and if successful, they are replicated in other areas of the city with similar identifiable issues. Resources are quickly directed to particular criminal issues, with great success. Los Angeles has quickly become the second-safest large city in the United States under Bratton. Computers are an important part of law enforcement today, and they will continue to be used to fight crime effectively and efficiently.

## Making the Commitment

The widespread and deep-seated problems of modern society make this an especially challenging time to be a police officer. You'll need a good dose of idealism and optimism about the ability of the police to enforce the law and keep the streets safe. Add to that, a realistic point of view about some of the difficulties you'll face while carrying out those tasks. No matter how well they do their job, police officers simply can't right all of society's wrongs. But as one old saying goes, if you're not part of the solution, you're part of the problem. Being a good cop is definitely part of the solution.

Now you need to get here from there. Set your course. Make your plan. Get yourself ready. Luckily, many paths are open for you to learn more about the profession and prepare yourself to become a top candidate for the force. To start you off in that direction, here are some actions you can take.

1. *Get fit.* If you're currently dedicated to a regular physical fitness program, that's great. Keep it up. If not, then now's the time to start. Every police department includes a physical performance test in the application process. You can ask in advance about what's involved—sit-ups, dummy drags, wall climbs, stair running, and so on. In general, know that you'll be tested for strength, agility,

quickness, and endurance. Tip: If you're not already doing so, you could get a head start by enrolling in martial arts classes. These disciplines are valuable not only for their practical techniques of self-defense, but also for the mind/body connection they foster, which is valuable for remaining centered and focused in stressful circumstances.

2. *Do some networking.* The best resource for advice and mentoring are people now working in the field. Maybe you have family, friends, or acquaintances involved in policing as officers or educators. Maybe you'll need to make some contacts on your own. In either case, it's a good idea to seek people out who have some firsthand knowledge. You can ask questions and get some helpful pointers. You might even make some friends on the force you want to join. The point is not about getting any special treatment—you'll have to pass all the same tests that any other applicant must pass. It's about getting information that you can factor into your decision and actions toward becoming a police officer.

3. *Conduct your own background investigation.* Along with talking to people in the field, do plenty of reading. Many police organizations and government agencies publish newsletters that are available to nonmembers. The criminal justice departments of colleges and universities are another source for newsletters, academic papers, research reports, and books. You may want to subscribe to various police magazines or review them at public or college libraries. (Note: They're not always available at newsstands.) Also, keep up to date through newspaper articles—not only about the police profession itself, but about social issues, legal issues and new laws, crime trends, and other topics that directly influence police work.On the Internet, you'll find a wealth of material on policing, including data provided by and about individual police departments. Plus, you can extend your networking contacts in chat rooms or on a social networking website.

4. *Research police departments you may want to join.* You'll be doing part of this homework if you focus some of your reading and networking efforts on individual departments. You'll also need to contact departments you're considering directly, by phone, mail, and/or with a personal visit. Compose a list of the basic facts you want to find out about a department—such as how many officers are on the force, how it's organized, and what kind of opportunities it offers. Very important are the specifics about a department's entry requirements. You need to know in advance, for example, about residential and educational requirements, in case meeting those would involve relocating or getting additional schooling. Tip: Research police forces of different sizes and in different locales. Even if you already think you know where you want to go, the people you meet and the information you get from another kind of place may just change your mind. There's also no substitute for "a good vibe"—when you visit a place and it just feels right to you.

5. *Find out when and how you can apply.* At this point, you'll already know the entry requirements for the department(s) you are considering. But you'll need to get a date, time, and location for taking the written exam. And you'll need to know what's next after you take the test. For example, if a department doesn't have immediate hiring needs, then once you pass the exam you may be put on an eligibility list and contacted later to move forward with the other steps in the applicant testing process. The personnel or recruiting division is usually the office to contact for these details. Also, ask about anything you may need to bring with you to the exam—for instance, pencils, notepads, a pocket calculator, paperwork, or documents (such as photo identification, a birth cer-

tificate, or a social security card). Keep in mind that departments can vary widely as to how often they give exams—anywhere from four times a week to once every two years.

6. **Prepare for the written exam.** It was mentioned earlier in this chapter that you don't need to know police regulations or the law of the land in order to take the entrance exam. But you can study and give yourself an advantage in other ways. In this book you'll find sample practice exams that have been designed to mimic those given by police departments in your city and state. These chapters also explain the rationale behind the exam (that is, what departments are trying to find out about the testtaker) and offer a variety of preparation and test-taking tips. In general, the written exam will gauge your skills in such areas as logical reasoning; good judgment; problem solving; observation and memory for details; basic grammar and writing skills; and reading comprehension. A multiple-choice format is typical. Questions often make use of police terms, procedures, scenarios, and passages from actual police manuals or other such documents. All the information you need to answer the questions will be there; the key lies in how you interpret and respond to the information presented.

7. **Prepare for the oral interview.** Some people get intimidated at the idea of being quizzed about their background, skills, and ambitions by seasoned police officers. It may help to think of it as any other job interview. And it may help to practice. Spend some time alone thinking about your reasons for wanting to become a police officer. Think about your goals. Think about your particular knowledge, abilities, and experience—what you can bring to the force. Once you've spent some time thinking or even writing about these topics, enlist a colleague or family member (or a friend you've made on the force) to give you a practice interview. Remember that you're not trying to come up with dry, rehearsed responses to any possible question. Instead, determine your choice, your potential, and your talents, and then simply to get a feel for the interview situation. When it's time for the real interview, the best thing you can do is be yourself and be honest.

8. **Get involved in your community.** Explore opportunities in your community to learn about this profession by participating in police-sponsored activities. Volunteer work is a good bet in practically any community. One route is to join neighborhood crime watch or cleanup groups that work in conjunction with local police precincts. Many departments sponsor juvenile sports and recreation programs, such as the Police Athletic League (PAL). The Police Explorers—Boy/Girl Scout troops sponsored by police departments—is another young people's program that often needs volunteers.

9. **Try out police work.** Local departments may have a police officer reserve program that would allow you to keep your regular job while committing time to working for the police department (similar to the National Guard setup). Or it may have internships available, either through the department or through a work/study arrangement with a college criminal justice program. Another possibility at some departments is a police cadet corps program or student worker program, which offers paid jobs to select college students between the ages of 18 and 21. Both internships and cadet programs give you the chance to try your hand at various types of police work. Completing the latter often takes cadets straight to the police academy if they've met the required performance standards.

10. **Develop your competitive edge.** If you've delved into the first nine steps with gusto, you definitely will have a competitive edge. But being the determined candidate that you are, you know there's always more you can do. In keeping with the pre-

vious sidebar "Your Competitive Edge," you can consider three more avenues for broadening your advantage. First, you could sign up for some college courses in police-related disciplines or other areas that you know would be useful for police work (such as classes in expository writing, psychology and sociology, or political science). Second, learn another language or take a refresher course in one you're already familiar with. (For this to be of real value, try to match your choice to the citizen population of the department.) Third, learn about computers. You could take a training class for popular software applications or just get yourself on a computer and learn by doing. With all three of these endeavors, it's important to set achievable goals for yourself and find appealing ways to meet them. You'll be more interested and engaged in the learning when the effort feels like something you *want* to do, not *have* to do.

Of course, at some point in the process of getting in shape, networking, investigating, preparing for tests, immersing yourself in the field, and learning new skills . . . you'll just have to take the plunge. Make the commitment, apply for the job, and show them what you've got.

# 2 ▶ How Police Officers Are Selected

## CHAPTER SUMMARY

Now that you have a better idea of what policing is really like, you need to know what you'll face if you try for a job as a police officer. This chapter provides a summary of the process of selecting police recruits, from finding out about openings to the swearing-in ceremony.

In order to become a police officer, you have to go through a selection process that takes anywhere from several months to two or even three years. Why such a long and complicated process? Because police work is tough. It requires a lot of positive character traits and varied skills, and the agency you want to work for needs to know that you're qualified.

In most places, many more people apply to be police officers than could ever be accepted. A large percentage of people who apply fail one or another part of the selection process: the written exam, the physical agility test, the background investigation, the oral interview board, or the medical or psychological exam. You don't want to be one of those people.

That's one reason you're reading this book: It will tell you what to expect, so you'll know exactly what the steps are in becoming a police officer. Knowing those steps, you'll have an edge on applicants coming in cold, and you can make a realistic assessment of your personality, your background, and your skills.

During this assessment, you may find things that make becoming a police officer unrealistic for you. However, you may instead find weaknesses that *you can correct*—and this book will help you make the changes you need to succeed in the police officer selection process. People who plan *now* are the ones who are most likely to rise to the top of the eligibility list.

## ▶ The Eligibility List

Most police departments establish a list of candidates in rank order. How ranks are determined varies from place to place; sometimes the rank is based solely on the written exam score, sometimes on the oral board, and sometimes on a combination of factors. The point is, even if you make it through the entire selection process, the likelihood that you will be hired as a police officer depends on *the quality of your performance* in one or more parts of the selection process.

Make a commitment now: You need to work hard, in advance, to do well on the written exam, the physical agility test, and the oral board, so that your name will stand out at the top of your agency's eligibility list.

First, though, you need information. You need to know about the police officer selection process. This chapter outlines the basic process of becoming a police officer. The majority of police departments use most of the steps presented here, although the order may vary and some departments may put more or less emphasis on certain steps.

## ▶ Basic Qualifications

The basic qualifications you need in order to even think about becoming a police officer vary from city to city, and it's worthwhile to find out what those qualifications are in the agency you want to serve. Some qualifications are pretty standard:

- A minimum age from 18 to 21. The maximum age varies by agency. Check with the respective agency you are interested in to find out.
- U.S. citizenship or, in a few cities, resident alien status
- A high school diploma or its equivalent and, increasingly, some college or even a college degree
- No felony convictions

- Excellent physical and mental health, including good vision and hearing and an appropriate weight-to-height ratio
- A valid driver's license and a satisfactory driving record

Many jurisdictions, but not all, require that you live in the jurisdiction or nearby. Most police departments give special consideration to veterans over civilians, a practice sometimes called a "Veteran's Preference" policy, whereby points are automatically added to the written exam. Is this unfair? No. Military personnel have already learned the discipline and many of the skills—such as use of firearms—that are vital to police work. Veterans are simply better qualified than most other people. Also, for older applicants, some departments subtract the number of years served in the military from an applicant's age to satisfy the upper age requirement.

### Automatic Disqualifiers

There are lots of things that can disqualify you, the most important being any trouble with the law in the past. Convicted felons are not welcome as police officers in any jurisdiction, no matter how much they may have reformed their lives since their conviction. Misdemeanors and even traffic tickets can disqualify applicants in some cities. People who use illegal drugs or abuse legal ones need not apply. See the section "The Personal History Statement and Background Investigation" later in this chapter for more information.

Police officers have to be in excellent physical and emotional shape. Disabilities that would not be a problem in other occupations can become disqualifying conditions for police officers. These disabilities do not have to be obvious or serious. For instance, many departments require perfect color vision; a simple and common condition such as blue-green color blindness can disqualify an applicant. So can being overweight. See the section "The Medical Exam" later in this chapter for more information on applicants with disabilities.

The qualifications necessary to become a police officer in some of your state's major cities are listed later in this book. For other jurisdictions, contact the recruiting or personnel office directly; it will provide you a list of qualifications and the steps you have to go through to apply.

## ▶ The Exam Announcement

Applying to be a police officer differs from applying for most other jobs. The differences begin with the exam announcement. You won't see openings in the police department advertised in the newspaper. Instead, a city or state starts recruiting police officers with a special announcement. This announcement will outline the basic qualifications to be a police officer as well as the steps you will have to go through in the selection process. It often tells you some of the duties police officers are expected to perform. It may give the date and place of the written exam, which is usually the first step in the selection process.

*Get a copy of this announcement.* The Internet is an excellent source for this information. Often your public library will have a copy, or you can get one directly from the agency or the city personnel department. If exams are held irregularly, the agency or personnel department may maintain a mailing list, so you can receive an exam announcement the next time an exam is scheduled. If exams are held frequently, you will sometimes be told simply to show up at the exam site on a given day of the week or month. In those cases, you usually get more information about the job and the selection process if you pass the written exam. *Study the exam announcement,* as well as any other material, such as brochures, that the department sends you. You need to be prepared for the whole selection process in order to be successful.

## ▶ The Application

Often the first step in the process of becoming a police officer is filling out an application. Sometimes this is a full application, asking for your education, employment experience, personal data, and so on. In this case, the application is really the personal history statement you'll read about later. Anyone whose application shows that he or she doesn't meet the basic qualifications will not be invited to participate in the selection process. Sometimes there's just an application to take the written test, with the full application form coming later for those who pass. Application forms for major cities in your state are reproduced in a later chapter.

When you call for an exam announcement or application, the person who answers the phone may conduct a brief prescreening to make sure that you meet the basic qualifications as to age, education, and so on. Answer briefly and politely, and don't launch into your life story. The person on the other end of the line may remember you when it comes time to select names from the eligibility list.

## ▶ The Written Exam

In most cities, taking a written exam is the next step in the application process, although in some cases a background interview comes first. (By putting the background interview first, agencies save themselves the expense of testing applicants who don't meet the basic qualifications.)

The written exam is usually your first opportunity to show that you have what it takes to be a police officer. As such, it's extremely important. People who don't pass the written exam don't go further in the selection process. Likewise, the written exam score often figures into an applicant's rank on the eligibility list; in some cases, this score by itself determines your rank, while in others, it is combined with other scores, such as physical agility or oral interview scores. In those cities, a person who merely passes the exam with a score of, say, 70, is unlikely to be hired when there are plenty of applicants with scores in the 90s. The exam bulletin usually specifies what the rank will be based on.

- Neatness and accuracy count. Filling in your apartment number in the blank labeled "city" reflects poorly on your ability to follow directions. **Type** your application.
- Most agencies don't want your resume. It goes straight into the circular file. Save your time and energy for filling out the application form the agency gives you.
- If you're mailing your application, take care to submit it to the proper address. It might go to the city personnel department rather than to the police department. Be careful to follow the directions exactly on the exam announcement.

## What the Written Exam Is Like

Most written exams simply test basic skills and aptitudes: how well you understand what you read, your writing ability, your ability to follow directions, your judgment and reasoning skills, and sometimes your memory or your math. In this preliminary written exam, *you will not be tested on your knowledge of police policies and procedures, the law, or any other body of knowledge specific to police work.* This test is designed *only* to see if you can read, write, reason, and do basic math.

In a few cities, taking the exam involves studying written materials in advance and then answering questions about them on the exam. Some of these written materials have to do with the law and police procedures—but all you have to do is study the guide you're given. You're still being tested just on your reading skills and memory, and there are good reasons for this.

Police officers have to be able to read, understand, and act on complex written materials such as laws, policy handbooks, and regulations. They have to write incident reports and other materials that have to be clear and correct enough to stand up in court. They have to be able to think independently, because a patrol officer gets little direct supervision. They have to be able to do enough math to add up the value of stolen material or compute the street price of a drug sold to a dealer. The basic skills the written exam tests for are skills police officers use every day.

Most exams are multiple-choice tests of the sort you've often encountered in school. You get an exam book and an answer sheet where you have to fill in little circles (bubbles) or squares with a Number 2 pencil.

Increasingly, cities are supplementing multiple-choice tests with other formats. Because writing is such an important part of a police officer's job, and because multiple-choice tests don't do a great job of assessing writing skills, some cities have applicants write an essay or mock report. You might be asked to write a page or so on a general topic, like something you may write about for a school assignment. Or you might be shown a videotape or slides and be told to write about what you see. In this case, the agency can assess both your writing skills and your short-term memory. By having you actually write something, the agency can assess your ability to relate facts in a logical order as well as your skills in grammar, punctuation, spelling, and the like.

## How to Prepare for the Written Exam

Pay close attention to any material the recruiting unit or city personnel department puts out about the exam. If there's a study guide, use it. Pay close attention to what you're going to be tested on and then find similar materials to practice with.

There are lots of books and Internet websites out there with practice test materials. Any test prep book that has basic skills questions in it, including reading comprehension, writing, and math, will help. For focused, specific preparation based on police exams actually given in your state, work through the practice police exams, sample exercises, and customized test instruction in this book.

## The Kinds of Questions You Can Expect

Police exams usually cover such subjects and skills as reading, writing, math, memory, and judgment. Sometimes your ability to read a map or graph is also tested. The exam bulletin or position announcement, available from your recruitment office, should tell you what subjects are on your exam.

## Reading Comprehension Questions

Reading comprehension is a part of almost every written police exam. These reading questions are like the ones you've probably encountered in school tests: You're given a paragraph or two to read and then are asked questions about it. Questions typically ask you about

- the main idea of the passage as a whole.
- specific facts or details contained in the passage.
- the meaning of words or phrases as they are used in the passage.
- inferences and conclusions you can draw from what is stated in the passage.

## Writing Questions

A few police departments test writing ability by having candidates write a short essay or report. More often, the exams use a multiple-choice format to test your language skills, including grammar, spelling, and vocabulary.

## Grammar Questions

Usually, a grammar question asks you to choose which of four versions of a sentence is most correct. The incorrect choices might contain

- incomplete sentences (fragments).
- two or more sentences put together as if they were one (run-ons).
- verbs that don't go with their subjects (*he think*) or that use the wrong tense (*yesterday she goes*).
- pronouns that don't match the noun they refer to (*a person . . . they*).

Sometimes grammar questions also test punctuation or capitalization, usually by giving you a sentence with punctuation marks or capital letters underlined and asking you to choose which one is wrong.

## Spelling Questions

Spelling questions might give you a sentence with a word missing and then ask you which of the choices is the correct spelling of the missing word. Or you might be given several different words and asked which one is spelled wrong.

## Vocabulary Questions

Vocabulary questions usually ask you to find a *synonym*—a word that means the same—or the *antonym*—a word that means the opposite—of a given word. If you're lucky, the other words in the sentence will help you guess its meaning. If you're less lucky, you'll just be given the word and have to choose a synonym or antonym without any help from the context.

Another way vocabulary is tested is to give you a sentence with a blank in it and ask you to choose the word that fits best in the sentence.

## Math Questions

Math is usually a minor part of a police exam, if it's included at all. The questions usually test basic arithmetic: just adding, subtracting, multiplying, and dividing whole numbers. Most often the math questions are word problems that present everyday situations: the total value of stolen property, that kind of thing.

Some tests might ask you to work with fractions, decimals, or percentages, but still in real-life situations: how much is left after one person eats half and another person eats a third; the amount of mileage on a car gauge after a certain number of trips; how much you have to pay for a shirt with a 15% discount; and so on.

## Memory Questions

Police officers have to be able to remember lots of details about things they see and read, so observation

- Ask for and use any material the police or personnel department puts out about the written test. Some agencies have study guides; some even conduct study sessions. Why let others get a vital advantage while you don't?
- Practice, practice, practice. And then practice some more.
- Try to find some people who have taken the exam in your city recently, and ask them what was on the exam. Their hindsight—"I wish I had . . ."—can be your foresight.
- Take the practice police exams in this book and study the instructional material.

and memory questions are often a part of police exams. You may be given a study booklet in advance of the exam and asked to answer questions about it during the exam without referring to the book. Or you may be given a picture to look at or a passage to read during exam and then have to answer questions about it, usually without referring to the picture or passage. You may even be shown a videotape and then asked questions about it later.

### Judgment Questions

Obviously police officers need to have good judgment, so some exams include multiple-choice questions designed to test your judgment and common sense. You may be given laws or police procedures and asked to apply them to a hypothetical situation, or you may be asked which hypothetical situation is most likely to indicate dangerous or criminal activity. Answering these questions requires both common sense and an ability to read carefully.

### Map Reading Questions

Map reading questions are pretty straightforward: You're given a small city map and told to find the quickest way to get from Point A to Point B without driving the wrong way down a one-way street or through a building. These questions test your ability to orient yourself on a map and read simple symbols such as one-way arrows.

### Finding Out How You Did

Applicants are generally notified in writing about their performance on the exam. The notification may simply say whether or not you passed, but it may tell you what your score was. It may also say when you should show up for the next step in the process, which is often a physical agility test.

## ▶ The Physical Ability Test

The physical ability test is usually the next step in the process after the written exam. You may have to bring a note from your doctor saying that you are in good enough shape to undertake this test before you will be allowed to participate. A few agencies give the medical exam before the physical ability test. They all want to make sure that no one has a heart attack in the middle of the test. This is a clue: expect the test to be tough.

Police work, after all, is physically demanding. Not to discourage you, but the physical ability test isn't even designed to find out whether you're in good enough shape to be a police officer. It assesses only whether you're in good enough shape to do well in the physical training at the police academy. It's the academy that whips recruits into the physical shape police officers need to be in.

Start exercising now. Yes, today. Work up to a 45-minute workout at least four times a week. If you smoke, stop. If you're overweight, diet along with your exercise. (No one said becoming a police officer would be easy!)

## What the Physical Ability Test Is Like

The exact events that make up the physical agility test vary from city to city, but there's usually a fair amount of running, some lifting or other upper-body strength requirements, and often a test of hand strength, which helps to determine whether you'll be able to handle a pistol. Some places use calisthenics like sit-ups and push-ups to assess your physical strength; others have an obstacle course. You can find out just what will be required by your agency from the exam announcement or related materials.

## How to Prepare for the Physical Ability Test

The physical ability test is one area in which advance preparation is almost guaranteed to pay off. No matter how good a shape you're in, start an exercise program *now*. You can design your program around the requirements listed in the exam announcement if you want, but any exercise that will increase your stamina, flexibility, and strength will help.

If you're *not* in great shape, consult a doctor before you begin. Start slow and easy and increase your activity as you go. And remember that you don't have to do all this work alone. Taking any kind of physical fitness class at a gym will help increase your stamina, and you can supplement such activities with ones that work on your strength.

For more information, see the chapter titled "The Physical Ability Test."

## ▶ The Personal History Statement and Background Investigation

Either at the beginning of the whole process or after the first couple of cuts are made, the hiring agency will have you fill out a long form about your personal history. You will usually be interviewed about this material by someone from the police or city personnel department. As the department begins to get serious about considering you, it will conduct an investigation into your background, using your personal history statement as a starting point.

This step may be the most important in the whole process, even though the results may not be reflected in your rank on the eligibility list. This is where the police department checks not only your experience and education, but also, and perhaps more important, your character. Do you have the integrity, the honesty, the commitment, the personal stamina, and the respect for authority and the law that a police officer must have? Police departments go to a lot of trouble and expense to find out.

## What the Personal History Statement Is Like

You take part in the investigation by filling out the personal history form and talking with the interviewer. The form will be long—up to 30 pages—and requires your serious attention and effort. Assume that everything you say will be double-checked by a trained, experienced police investigator. You'll be asked where you were born, where you have lived, where you went to school—including elementary school—what you've studied, where you've worked and what you did there, what organizations you have belonged to, and so on.

Your whole life will be laid out on paper. You'll have to supply names of teachers, employers, neighbors, and relatives, as well as the names of several additional people who can attest to your character and fitness to be a police officer.

### How to Fill Out the Personal History Statement

Fill the form out completely, looking up dates and places whenever you can rather than relying on your memory. Attach all documents, such as diplomas or transcripts, you're asked for. Neatness and accuracy count, but one thing counts even more: honesty.

Be completely honest in everything you write and everything you say to the interviewer. Covering up something in your past, even by just not mentioning it, will in itself be taken as evidence that you don't have the integrity it takes to be a police officer. Yes, past drug use, hospitalizations, scrapes with the law, family or financial difficulties, and such can hurt your chances, but not as much as not mentioning them and having them surface during the investigation. Better to acknowledge up front anything that might cause doubt about your fitness to be a police officer and deal with it. Convince the interviewer that, although you know you had difficulties in the past, you have since dealt with them and they will not affect your performance now or in the future. The interviewer may have suggestions about how to resolve past "blots" on your record. For more information, see the chapter entitled "The Personal History Statement."

### What the Background Investigation Is Like

Starting from your personal history statement, a background investigator from the police department will check you out. The investigator will verify what you've said about yourself: Do you in fact have a high school diploma, an honorable discharge, and five years' employment with the same firm?

And *then* the investigator will start asking the *real* questions. Your former teachers, landlords, employers, friends, and others will be asked by the investigator how long and how well they knew you and what kind of person they found you to be. Did you meet your obligations? How did you deal with problems? Do they know of anything that might affect your fitness to be a police officer? Your references will lead the investigator to other people who knew you, and when the investigator is finished, he or she will have a pretty complete picture of what kind of person you are.

### How to Prepare for the Personal History Statement and Background Investigation

As a candidate for the job of police officer, you can best improve your performance on the personal history statement by improving your personal history. You can't change the past, exactly, but you can use the present to improve your chances in the future. For example, you can take steps to make yourself more attractive to the police department by doing police work either as a volunteer, an intern, or as a paid cadet. Check out this and other suggestions on the list under "Making the Commitment" near the end of Chapter 1.

## ▶ The Lie Detector Test

Some jurisdictions require a polygraph, or lie detector, test as part of the background investigation process, although the polygraph, if required, is typically one of the last steps you will go through.

There really is no such thing as a lie detector. What the polygraph detects are changes in heart and respiratory rates, blood pressure, and galvanic skin resistance (basically a measure of how much you're perspiring). A cuff like the one your doctor uses to take your blood pressure will be wrapped around your arm. Rubber tubes around your trunk will measure your breathing, and clips on your fingers or palm will measure skin response. The theory is that people who are consciously lying get nervous, and their involuntary bodily responses give them away.

Don't worry about being betrayed by being nervous in the first place. Everyone's a little nervous when confronting a new technology. The polygraph examiner will explain the whole process to you. More important, the examiner will ask you a series of questions to establish a baseline both for when you're telling the truth and for when you're not. For instance, the examiner might tell you to answer "No" to every question and then ask you whether your name is George (if it isn't) and whether you drove to the examination today (if you did).

All questions for a polygraph exam have to be in yes-or-no form. You should be told in advance what every question will be. Some questions will be easy lobs such as whether you're wearing sneakers. The questions that really count will be ones that relate to your fitness to be a police officer: whether you've committed a crime, whether you have received speeding tickets, whether you've been arrested. You will probably have been over any problematic areas with the background investigator or other interviewers before, so just tell the truth and try to relax.

## ▶ The Oral Interview

The selection process in your chosen jurisdiction may include several oral interviews, none of which will be much like other job interviews you've had in the past. There may be an interview connected with your personal history statement, where the interviewer simply tries to confirm or clarify what you've written. An interview is usually part of the psychological evaluation. Most agencies also conduct an oral interview or board that continues the process of determining whether candidates will make good police officers.

### What the Oral Board Is Like
The oral board typically assesses such qualities as interpersonal skills, communication skills, judgment and decision-making abilities, respect for diversity, and adaptability. The board itself consists of two to five people, who may be sworn officers or civilians. There's usually some variety in the makeup of the board: sworn officers of various ranks and/or civilians from the city personnel department or from the community.

The way the interview is conducted depends on the practices of the individual department. You may be asked a few questions similar to those you would be asked at a normal employment interview: Why do you want to be a police officer? Why in this department? What qualities do you have that would make you a good officer? You may be asked questions about your personal history. Have answers prepared for such questions in case they come.

Instead of or in addition to such questions, you may be presented with hypothetical situations that you will be asked to respond to. A board member may simply tell you what the situation is and ask you what you would do, or one or more board members may role-play the situation, putting you in the place of the officer in charge. You may even see a video that the board members will ask you about after you've seen it.

Increasingly, cities have standardized the oral board questions. The same questions are asked of every candidate, and when the interview is over, the board rates each candidate on a standard scale. This procedure helps the interviewers reach a somewhat more objective conclusion about the candidates they have interviewed and may result in a score that is included in the factors used to generate the eligibility list. Indeed, some departments have decided that the oral board is so important that this score by itself determines candidates' rank on the list.

### How to Prepare
### for the Oral Board
If the police or city personnel department puts out any material about the oral board, study it carefully. It will tell you what the board is looking for. It might even give you some sample questions you can practice with. The chapter "The Oral Interview" in this book can help, too.

Think about your answers to questions you might be asked. You might even try to write your own oral board questions and situations. Write down your answers if you want. Practice saying them in front of a mirror until you feel comfortable, but don't memorize them. You don't want to sound like you're reciting from a book. Your answers should sound conversational even though you've prepared in advance.

Then, enlist friends or family to serve as a mock oral board. If you know a speech teacher, get him or her to help. Give them your questions, tell them about what you've learned, and then have a practice oral board. Start from the moment you walk into the room. Go through the entire session as if it were the real thing, and then ask your mock board for their feedback on your performance.

It may even help to videotape your mock board session. The camera can reveal things about your body language or habits that you don't even know about.

## ▶ The Psychological Evaluation

Before you get offended at having to go through a battery of psychological tests, consider: Do you want even one nutcase running around the city maintaining public order and safety with a gun?

Neither does the police department. OK, you're not a nutcase, and neither are most of the people applying with you. But remember, police work is one of the most stressful occupations there is. While no one can guarantee that a given individual won't "crack" under the stress, police departments want to weed out as many people with underlying instabilities as they can, in hopes that those remaining will be able to deal with the problems in healthy ways. Sometimes, too, the real purpose of the psychological evaluation is not so much to disclose instabilities as to determine applicants' honesty, habits, and other such factors.

## What the Written Psychological Evaluation Is Like

More often than not, the psychological evaluation begins with one or more written tests. These are typically standard tests licensed from a psychological testing company; they are often multiple-choice or true-false tests. The Minnesota Multiphasic Personality Inventory (MMPI) is one commonly used test. The tests may take one hour or several; the hiring agency will let you know approximately how much time to allot.

There's only one piece of advice we can offer you for dealing with a written psychological evaluation: *Don't try to psych out the test.* The people who wrote these tests know more about psyching out tests than you do. They designed the test so that one answer checks against another to find out whether test takers are lying. Just answer honestly, and don't worry about whether your answers to some of the questions seem to you to indicate that you might be nuts after all. They probably don't.

## What the Oral Psychological Evaluation Is Like

Whether or not there is a written psychological examination, there is usually an oral interview with a psychologist or psychiatrist, who may be either on the city's staff or an independent contractor. The psychologist may ask you questions about your schooling and jobs, your relationships with family and friends, your habits, your hobbies. Because there's such a broad range of things you could be asked about, there's really no way to prepare. In fact, the psychologist may be more interested in the way you answer—whether you come across as open, forthright, and honest—than in the answers themselves.

Once again, honesty is the best policy; there's no point in playing psychological games with someone who's better trained at it than you are. Try to relax, and

- Dress neatly and conservatively, as you would for a business interview.
- Be polite; say "please" and "thank you," "sir" and "ma'am."
- Remember, one-half of communication is listening. Look at board members as they speak to you, and listen carefully to what they say.
- Think before you speak. Nod or say "OK" to indicate that you understand the question, and then pause a moment to collect your thoughts before speaking.
- If you start to feel nervous, take a deep breath, relax, and just do your best.

answer openly. The psychologist is not trying to trick you and isn't really interested in your feelings about your mother unless they're so extreme that they're going to make you unfit to be a police officer. See the chapter "The Psychological Assessment" for more tips on dealing with the psychological evaluation.

## ▶ The Medical Examination

Before passage of the Americans with Disabilities Act (ADA), most police departments conducted a medical examination early in the process, before the physical agility test. Now, the ADA says it's illegal to do any examinations or ask any questions that could reveal an applicant's disability until after a conditional offer of employment has been made. That means that in most cities you will get such a conditional offer before you are asked to submit to a medical exam. Indeed, you may get such an offer before the polygraph examination, the psychological examination, or, in a few cases, even before the background investigation, precisely because all these components could reveal a disability.

### Drug Testing

Note, however, that a test for use of illegal drugs *can* be administered before a conditional offer of employment. If the test comes back positive because of an applicant's use of prescription drugs, the department can ask about and verify that prescription drug use but

cannot use the condition for which the drugs are prescribed to reject an applicant.

Yes, you'll have to pee in a cup. Being drug-free is a bona fide occupational qualification for a police officer.

### Physical Disabilities and the ADA

After the conditional offer of employment, applicants can be rejected for disabilities revealed in the medical or psychological exam, according to the ADA, as long as the disabilities are related to essential job functions and no reasonable accommodations exist that would make it possible for the applicant to function in the job. For instance, a potential police officer with a heart condition can reasonably be rejected on the basis of that disability. While officers don't spend their lives running down suspects, they may have to do so at a moment's notice, and the police department can't accommodate someone who can't safely run several blocks and still get the job done.

Departments have the right, even under the ADA, to reject applicants who have disabilities as minor as color blindness. Being able to provide descriptions of victims, suspects, vehicles, and so on, both for investigative purposes and in court, is an essential function of a police officer, and there isn't always someone else available to make the identification.

If you've gotten this far, you don't have any obvious or seriously disabling conditions. You got through the written exam, physical agility test, psychological evaluation, and oral interview. Any other conditions that you reveal at this point or that come up in the medical exam will probably have to be dealt with on a case-by-case basis. Even conditions such as diabetes or epilepsy need not disqualify you, if your condition is controlled so that you will be able to fulfill the essential functions of a police officer.

## What the Medical Exam Is Like

The medical exam itself is nothing to be afraid of. It will be just like any other thorough physical exam. The doctor may be on the staff of the police department or, in smaller departments, someone outside the department with his or her own practice, just like your own doctor. Your blood pressure, temperature, weight, and so on will be measured; your heart and lungs will be listened to and your limbs examined. The doctor will peer into your eyes, ears, nose, and mouth, and maybe some other body cavities . . . but it won't be that painful. You'll also have to donate some blood and some urine. Because of those tests, you won't know the results of the physical exam right away. You'll probably be notified in writing in a few weeks, after the test results come in.

## ▶ If at First You Don't Succeed, Part One

The selection process for police officers is a rigorous one. If you fail one of the steps, take time for some serious self-evaluation.

**If you fail the written test,** look at the reasons you didn't do well. Was it just that the format was unfamiliar? Well, now you know what to expect.

Do you need to brush up on some of the skills tested? There are lots of books and information out there to help people with reading, writing, and computation. You might start with the LearningExpress Skill Builders for Test Takers (order information at the back

of this book). Enlist a teacher or a friend to help you, or check out the inexpensive courses offered by local high schools and community colleges.

Many cities allow you to retest after a waiting period—a period you should use to improve your skills. If the exam isn't being offered again for years, consider trying some other police department.

**If you fail the physical agility test,** your course of action is clear. Increase your daily physical exercise until you *know* you can do what is required, and then retest or try another police department.

**If you fail the oral board,** try to figure out what the problem was. Do you think your answers were good, but perhaps you didn't express them well? Then you need some practice in oral communication. You can take courses or enlist your friends to help you practice.

Did the questions and situations throw you for a loop, so you made what now seem like inappropriate answers? Then try to bone up for the next time. Talk to candidates who were successful and ask them what they said. Talk with police officers you know about what might have been good answers for the questions you were asked. Even if your department doesn't allow you to redo the oral board, you can put what you learn to use in applying to another department.

**If the medical exam eliminates you,** you will usually be notified as to what condition caused the problem. Is the condition one that can be corrected? See your doctor for advice. A few minor conditions can eliminate you in one department but be acceptable in another. Contact the recruiting officer at a nearby police department to see if you can apply there.

**If you don't make the list and aren't told why,** the problem might have been the oral board or, more likely, the psychological evaluation or the background investigation. Now you really have to do some hard thinking.

Can you think of *anything* in your past that might lead to questions about your fitness to be a police officer? Could any of your personal traits or attitudes raise such questions? And then the hard question: Is there anything you can do to change these aspects of your past or your personality? If so, you might have a chance when you reapply or apply to another police department. If not, it's time to think about another field.

If you feel you were wrongly excluded, most departments have appeals procedures if it was on the basis of a psychological evaluation or background check. However, that word *wrongly* is very important. The psychologist or background investigator almost certainly had to supply a rationale in recommending against you. Do you have solid factual evidence that you can use in an administrative hearing to counter such a rationale? If not, you'd be wasting your time and money, as well as the police department's, by making an appeal. Move carefully and get legal advice before you take such a step.

## The Waiting Game

You went through the whole long process, passed all the tests, did the best you could, made the eligibility list—and now you wait. You *could* just sit on your hands. Or you could decide to *do* something with this time to prepare for what you hope is your new career. Even if you don't get called, even if your rank on the score doesn't get you a job this time, you'll be better qualified for the next try. There's a top-ten list of things you can do to prepare for police work in Chapter 1. Don't just sit there; do it!

Here's one thing you *don't* want to do while you're waiting: Don't call to find out what your chances are or how far down on the list they've gotten or when they might call you. You probably won't get to talk to the people making those decisions, so you'll just annoy some poor receptionist. If you did get through to the decision makers, you'd be in even worse shape: You'd be annoying *them*.

## ▶ If at First You Don't Succeed, Part Two

If you make the list, go through the waiting game, and finally aren't selected, don't despair. Think through all the steps of the selection process, and use them to do a critical self-evaluation.

Maybe your written, physical, or oral board score was high enough to pass but not high enough to put you near the top of the list. At the next testing, make sure you're better prepared.

Maybe you had an excellent score that should have put you at the top of the list, and you suspect that you were passed over for someone lower down. That means someone less well qualified was selected while you were not, right? Maybe, maybe not.

There were probably a lot of people on the list, and a lot of them may have scored high. One more point on the test might have made the difference, or maybe the department had the freedom to pick and choose on the basis of other qualifications. Maybe, in comparison with you, a lot of people on your list had more education or experience. Maybe there was a special need for people with particular skills, such as proficiency in Spanish or Cantonese or training in photography. And yes, members of minority groups may have been given preference in hiring. Whether or not you think that's fair, you can be assured that it was a conscious decision on the part of the police department; it may even have been mandated from above.

What can you do? You've heard or read about a lot of suits being brought against law enforcement agencies about their selection processes, particularly in large cities. That's a last resort, a step you would take only after getting excellent legal advice and thinking through the costs of time, money, and energy. You'd also have to think about whether you'd want to occupy a position you got as the result of a lawsuit and whether you'd be hurting your chances of being hired somewhere else.

Most people are better off simply trying again. And don't limit your options. There are lots of police departments all over the country; there are other careers available in law enforcement. Do your research. Find out what's available. Find out who's hiring. Start with the chapter "Law Enforcement Careers," and expand from there. Consider applying to smaller agencies in small towns or rural agencies, to sheriff's departments, to the state police. Being turned down by one department need not be the end of your law enforcement career.

## ▶ When You Do Succeed

Congratulations! The end of the waiting game for you is notification to attend the police academy. You're on the road to your law enforcement career.

The road is hardly over, though. In most jurisdictions, you're now hired as a police recruit. You'll be paid to go to the academy, usually at a lower rate than you'll make when you actually become a member of the force. Academies typically run some 14 to 30 weeks and include physical and firearms training as well as courses in the laws you'll be expected to enforce and in police techniques and procedures. In many jurisdictions, the academy is followed by a period of field training in the jurisdiction that hired you.

After your training, many states require you to pass a certification exam. The certification exam is usually directly related to the academy curriculum, so you'll know exactly what you need to study. And you *will* need to study; these exams are tough. But if you pass, your reward is the job you've been working and waiting for all this time. You can stand tall and proud as, in full dress uniform, you vow to protect the lives and property of the citizens of your community at your swearing-in ceremony.

# 3 ▶ The Police Officer Suitability Test

## CHAPTER SUMMARY

Wanting to be a police officer is one thing; being suited for it is something else. The following self-quiz can help you decide whether you and this career will make a good match.

**T**here is no one "type"of person who becomes a police officer. Cops are as varied as any other group of people in their personalities, experience, and styles. At the same time, there are some attitudes and behaviors that seem to predict success and satisfaction in this profession. They have nothing to do with your intelligence and ability—they simply reflect how you interact with other people and how you choose to approach the world.

These suitability factors were pulled from research literature and discussions with police psychologists and screeners across the country. They fall into five groups; each has ten questions spaced throughout this test.

The LearningExpress Police Officer Suitability Test is not a formal psychological test. For one thing, it's not nearly long enough; the MMPI (Minnesota Multiphasic Personality Inventory) test used in most psychological assessments has 11 times more items than you'll find here. For another, it does not focus on your general mental health.

Instead, the test should be viewed as an informal guide—a private tool to help you decide whether being a police officer would suit you, and whether you would enjoy it. It also provides the opportunity for greater self-understanding, which is beneficial no matter what you do for a living.

# ► The Police Officer Suitability Test

## Directions

You'll need about 20 minutes to answer the following 50 questions. It's a good idea to do them all at one sitting—scoring and interpretation can be done later. For each question, consider how often the attitude or behavior applies to you. You have a choice between Never, Rarely, Sometimes, Often, and Always; put the number for your answer in the space after each question. For example, if the answer is "sometimes," the score for that item is 10; "always" gets a 40, etc. How they add up will be explained later. If you try to outsmart the test or figure out the "right" answers, you won't get an accurate picture at the end. So just be honest.

**Please note:** Don't read the scoring sections before you answer the questions, or you'll defeat the whole purpose of the exercise!

How often do the following statements sound like you? Choose one answer for each statement.

| NEVER | RARELY | SOMETIMES | OFTEN | ALWAYS |
|-------|--------|-----------|-------|--------|
| 0 | 5 | 10 | 20 | 40 |

1. I like to know what's expected of me.

2. I am willing to admit my mistakes to other people.

3. Once I've made a decision, I stop thinking about it.

4. I can shrug off my fears about getting physically hurt.

5. I like to know what to expect.

6. It takes a lot to get me really angry.

7. My first impressions of people tend to be accurate.

8. I am aware of my stress level.

9. I like to tell other people what to do.

10. I enjoy working with others.

11. I trust my instincts.

12. I enjoy being teased.

13. I will spend as much time as it takes to settle a disagreement.

14. I feel comfortable in new social situations.

15. When I disagree with people, I let them know about it.

16. I'm in a good mood.

17. I'm comfortable making quick decisions when necessary.

18. Rules must be obeyed, even if you don't agree with them.

19. I like to say exactly what I mean.

20. I enjoy being with people.

21. I stay away from doing exciting things that I know are dangerous.

22. I don't mind when a boss tells me what to do.

23. I enjoy solving puzzles.

**24.** The people I know consult me about their problems.

**25.** I am comfortable making my own decisions.

**26.** People know where I stand on things.

**27.** When I get stressed, I know how to make myself relax.

**28.** I have confidence in my own judgment.

**29.** I make my friends laugh.

**30.** When I make a promise, I keep it.

**31.** When I'm in a group, I tend to be the leader.

**32.** I can deal with sudden changes in my routine.

**33.** When I get into a fight, I can stop myself from losing control.

**34.** I am open to new facts that might change my mind.

**35.** I understand why I do the things I do.

**36.** I'm good at calming people down.

**37.** I can tell how people are feeling even when they don't say anything.

**38.** I take criticism without getting upset.

**39.** People follow my advice.

**40.** I pay attention to people's body language.

**41.** It's important for me to make a good impression.

**42.** I remember to show up on time.

**43.** When I meet new people, I try to understand them.

**44.** I avoid doing things on impulse.

**45.** Being respected is important to me.

**46.** People see me as a calm person.

**47.** It's more important for me to do a good job than to get praised for it.

**48.** I make my decisions based on common sense.

**49.** I prefer to keep my feelings to myself when I'm with strangers.

**50.** I take responsibility for my own actions rather than blame others.

## ► Scoring

Attitudes and behaviors can't be measured in units, like distance or weight. Besides, psychological categories tend to overlap. As a result, the numbers and dividing lines between score ranges are approximate, and numbers may vary about 20 points either way. If your score doesn't fall in the optimal range, it doesn't mean a "failure"—only an area that needs focus.

It may help to share your test results with some of the people who are close to you. Very often, there are differences between how we see ourselves and how we actually come across to others.

### Group 1—Risk

**Add up scores for questions 4, 6, 12, 15, 21, 27, 33, 38, 44, and 46.**

TOTAL =

This group evaluates your tendency to be assertive and take risks. The ideal is in the middle, somewhere between timid and reckless: You should be willing to take risks, but not seek them out just for excitement. Being nervous, impulsive, and afraid of physical injury are all undesirable traits for a police officer. This group also reflects how well you take teasing and criticism, both of which you may encounter every day. And as you can imagine, it's also important for someone who carries a gun not to have a short fuse.

- A score between 360 and 400 is rather extreme, suggesting a kind of aggressive approach that could be dangerous in the field.
- If you score between 170 and 360, you are on the right track.
- If you score between 80 and 170, you may want to think about how comfortable you are with the idea of confrontation.
- A score between 0 and 80 indicates that the more dangerous and stressful aspects of the job might be difficult for you.

### Group 2—Core

**Add up scores for questions 2, 8, 16, 19, 26, 30, 35, 42, 47, and 50.**

TOTAL =

This group reflects such basic traits as stability, reliability, and self-awareness. Can your fellow officers count on you to back them up and do your part? Are you secure enough to do your job without needing praise? Because, in the words of one police psychologist, "If you're hungry for praise, you will starve to death." The public will not always appreciate your efforts, and your supervisors and colleagues may be too busy or preoccupied to pat you on the back.

It is crucial to be able to admit your mistakes and take responsibility for your actions, to be confident without being arrogant or conceited, and to be straightforward and direct in your communication. In a job where lives are at stake, the facts must be clear. Mood is also very important. While we all have good and bad days, someone who is depressed much of the time is not encouraged to pursue police work; depression affects one's judgment, energy level, and the ability to respond and communicate.

- If you score between 180 and 360, you're in the ballpark. Above 360 may be unrealistic.
- A score between 100 and 180 indicates you should look at the questions again and evaluate your style of social interaction.
- Scores between 0 and 100 suggest you may not be ready for this job—yet.

## Group 3—Judgment

Add scores for questions 3, 7, 11, 17, 23, 28, 37, 40, 43, and 48.

TOTAL =

This group taps how you make decisions. Successful police officers are sensitive to unspoken messages, can detect and respond to other people's feelings, and make fair and accurate assessments of a situation, rather than being influenced by their own personal biases and needs. Once the decision to act is made, second-guessing can be dangerous. Police officers must make their best judgments in line with accepted practices, and then act upon these judgments without hesitancy or self-doubt. Finally, it's important to know and accept that you cannot change the world single-handedly. People who seek this career because they want to make a dramatic individual difference in human suffering are likely to be frustrated and disappointed.

- A score over 360 indicates you may be trying too hard.
- If you scored between 170 and 360, your style of making decisions, especially about people, fits with the desired police officer profile.
- Scores between 80 and 170 suggest that you think about how you make judgments and how much confidence you have in them.
- If you scored between 80 and 170, making judgments may be a problem area for you.

## Group 4—Authority

Add scores for questions 1, 10, 13, 18, 22, 25, 31, 34, 39, and 45.

TOTAL =

This group contains the essential attributes of respect for rules and authority—including the "personal authority" of self-reliance and leadership—and the ability to resolve conflict and work with a team. Once again, a good balance is the key. Police officers must accept and communicate the value of structure and control without being rigid. And even though most decisions are made independently in the field, the authority of the supervisor and the law must be obeyed at all times. Anyone on a personal mission for justice or vengeance will not make a good police officer and is unlikely to make it through the screening process.

- A score between 160 and 360 indicates you have the desired attitude toward authority—both your own and that of your superior officers. Any higher is a bit extreme.
- If you scored between 100 and 160, you might think about whether a demanding leadership role is something you want every day.
- With scores between 0 and 100, ask yourself whether the required combination of structure and independence would be comfortable for you.

## Group 5—Style

**Add up scores for questions 5, 9, 14, 20, 24, 29, 32, 36, 41, and 49.**

TOTAL =

This is the personal style dimension that describes how you come across to others. Moderation rules here as well: Police officers should be seen as strong and capable, but not dramatic or heavy-handed; friendly, but not overly concerned with whether they are liked; patient, but not to the point of losing control of a situation. A good sense of humor is essential, not only in the field but among one's fellow officers. Flexibility is another valuable trait—especially given all the changes that can happen in one shift—but too much flexibility can be perceived as weakness.

- A score between 160 and 360 is optimal. Over 360 is trying too hard.
- Scores between 80 and 160 suggest that you compare your style with the previous description and consider whether anything needs to be modified.
- If you scored between 0 and 80, you might think about the way you interact with others and whether you'd be happy in a job where people are the main focus.

## ▶ Summary

The Police Officer Suitability Test reflects the fact that being a successful police officer requires moderation rather than extremes. Attitudes that are desirable in reasonable amounts can become a real problem if they are too strong. For example, independence is a necessary trait, but too much of it creates a "Dirty Harry" type of officer who takes the law into his or her own hands. Going outside accepted police procedure is a bad idea; worse, it can put other people's lives in jeopardy.

As one recruiter said, the ideal police officer is "low key and low maintenance." In fact, there's only one thing you can't have too much of, and that's common sense. With everything else, balance is the key. Keep this in mind as you look at your scores.

*This test was developed by Judith Schlesinger, PhD, a writer and psychologist whose background includes years of working with police officers in psychiatric crisis interventions.*

# Becoming a Police Officer in California

## CHAPTER SUMMARY

This chapter introduces POST, the California Commission on Peace Officer Standards and Training. It's useful to know something about this organization, which sets standards for hiring and training law enforcement officers in California. This chapter also provides a handy listing of recruiting contacts at the 25 largest police departments in the state and the 10 largest sheriff's departments in California.

From the paperwork to the testing to the training, there's a lot involved in becoming a police officer. In the next several chapters, you'll find a wealth of specific information about this process for each of eight major cities in California. These chapters will also give you a good indication of the employment requirements you can expect at police departments in other cities and towns across the state.

No matter where in California you'd like to work, an organization you need to be aware of is the Commission on Peace Officer Standards and Training (POST). That's because all 345 cities that maintain police departments in this state follow certain requirements established by the POST Commission for both hiring and training peace officers. (The term *peace officers* is used by this agency to include police officers as well as other law enforcement professionals, such as sheriffs and marshals, who participate in POST programs.)

Your first contact with POST comes in the selection process. The age you need to be, the education you need to have, the background investigation and interviews you need to undergo—these and other minimum employment requirements are set by POST and applied by police departments statewide.

Once you've been selected by a department, you'll have another key encounter with this agency. That's when newly appointed officers are required to complete a course of POST-certified training called the Basic Course or Academy. California has 38 Basic Police Academies throughout the state. Some police departments sponsor their own Basic Police Academy; selected applicants are considered employees while they attend and costs are paid by the department.

You'll face more POST requirements after you've made it through this training and completed a probationary period of at least one year. Before you can be officially empowered as a full-fledged officer, you have to obtain a POST Basic Certificate, which shows that you've acquired the knowledge and skills you need to perform the job.

Through the POST Commission, police departments throughout California can ensure that officers are selected and trained according to the same high-quality standards. Both new officers and time-tested veterans must satisfy a certain level of POST-certified training throughout their careers. Numerous certified courses are available through government agencies, police officer associations, educational institutions, and private sector organizations. Individual departments make use of the agency's state-of-the-art video and computer-based training courses and live satellite TV broadcasts.

Also, beyond the Basic Certificate, the POST Commission awards Intermediate, Advanced, Supervisory, Management, and Executive Certificates. Extra pay and promotions are typical ways that police departments recognize officers who earn these professional certificates.

As you can see, the POST Commission can really influence your career as a police officer in California. You'll have to meet its standards to even join a department. Then you'll be able to take advantage of the different opportunities it offers to grow and develop as an officer—and that's important to police departments everywhere.

## ▶ Recruiting Contacts at the 25 Largest Police Departments in California

### Anaheim Police Department
Human Resources Department
200 South Anaheim Boulevard #332
Anaheim, CA 92805
714-765-5111
www.anaheim.net

### Bakersfield Police Department
Human Resources
1501 Truxtun Avenue
Bakersfield, CA 93301
661-326-3981
www.BakersfieldPD.us

### Chula Vista Police Department
Human Resources Department
276 Fourth Avenue
Chula Vista, CA 91910
619-691-5096
www.chulavistapd.org

### City of Berkeley
Human Resources Department
2180 Milvia Street, First Floor
Berkeley, CA 94704
510-981-6800
www.ci.berkley.ca.usfpolice

### Fremont Police Department
Human Resources
3300 Capitol Avenue, Bldg. B
Fremont, CA 94537-5006
510-494-4660
www.fremontpolice.org

**Fresno Police Department**
City of Fresno Department of Personnel
2600 Fresno Street, First Floor
Fresno, CA 93721-1575
559-621-6950
www.ci.fresno.ca.us/fpd

**Glendale Police Department**
Human Resources
613 E. Broadway, Room 100
Glendale, CA 91206-4392
818-548-2110
www.police.ci.glendale.us

**Huntington Beach Police Department**
Human Resources
2000 Main Street
Huntington Beach, CA 92468
714-536-5492
www.hbpd.org

**Long Beach Police Department**
Civil Service Department
333 West Ocean Boulevard
Long Beach, CA 90802
310-570-6555
www.longbeach.gov/police

**Los Angeles Police Department**
Personnel Department
700 E. Temple Street
Los Angeles, CA 90012
213-847-9240
www.joinlapd.org

**Modesto Police Department**
Personnel Department
P.O. Box 642
Modesto, CA 95354
209-577-5402
www.modestopolice.com

**Oakland Police Department**
Background and Recruitment Unit
250 Frank H. Ogawa Plaza #D
Oakland, CA 94612
510-238-3339
www.oaklandpolice.com

**Ontario Police Department**
Human Resources Department
303 East B Street
Ontario, CA 91764
909-395-2442
www.ontariopolice.org

**Oxnard Police Department**
Human Resources Department
300 West Third Street, First Floor
Oxnard, CA 93030
805-385-7590
www.oxnardpd.org

**City of Pasadena**
Human Resources
117 E. Colorado Blvd.
Pasadena, CA 91109
626-774-4366
www.ci.pasadena.ca.us/police

**Pomona Police Department**
Human Resources Department
505 South Garey Avenue
Pomona, CA 91766
909-620-2291
www.ci.pomona.ca.us/city_departments/police

**Riverside Police Department**
Humand Resources
3780 Market Street
Riverside, CA 92501
951-826-5808
www.riversideca.gov/rpd

**Sacramento Police Department**
Human Resources
915 I Street, Plaza Level
Sacramento, CA 95814-2604
916-808-5726
www.sacpd.org

**San Bernardino Police Department**
Human Resources
300 North D Street, Second Floor
San Bernardino, CA 92418
909-384-5104
www.ci.san-bernardino.ca.us/depts/police_departments

**San Diego Police Department**
Recruiting Unit
1401 Broadway, Mail Stop #769
San Diego, CA 92101-5729
619-531-2547
www.sandiego.gov/police

**San Francisco Police Department**
Human Resources
44 Gough Street
San Francisco, CA 94103-1233
415-553-1999
www.sfgov.org/site/police

**San Jose Police Department**
Human Resources
200 E. Santa Clara Street
San Jose, CA 95113
408-535-1285
www.sjpd.org

**Santa Ana Police Department**
Personnel Services
240 Civic Center Plaza
Santa Ana, CA 92701
714-647-5340
www.ci.santa-ana.ca.us/pd

**Santa Monica Police Department**
Human Resources Department
1685 Main Street
Santa Monica, CA 90407
310-458-8697
www.santamonicapd.org

**Stockton Police Department**
Human Resources
22 East Weber Avenue #150
Stockton, CA 95202
209-937-8233
www.ci.stockton.ca.us/police

**Torrance Police Department**
Human Resources
3231 Torrance Blvd.
Torrance, CA 90503
310-618-2324
www.tornet.com/TPD

## ▶ Recruiting Contacts at the Ten Largest Sheriff's Departments in California

**Alameda County Sheriff**
Background & Recruiting
6289 Madigan Road
Dublin, CA 94268
925-551-6874
www.alamedacountysheriff.org

**Fresno County Sheriff**
Personnel Department
2220 Tulare Street
Fresno, CA 93721
559-488-3364
www.fresnosheriff.org

**Kern County Sheriff**
Personnel Department
1115 Truxen Avenue
Bakersfield, CA 93301
661-868-3480
www.co.kern.ca.us/sheriff

**Los Angeles County Sheriff**
Sheriff's Department Training Bureau
11515 South Colima Road
Whittier, CA 90604
800-233-7889
*or*
Mira Loma Facility
45100 60th Street West
Lancaster, CA 93536
661-949-3877
www.la-sheriff.org
www.lasd.org

**Orange County Sheriff**
Personnel Department
550 North Flower Street
Santa Ana, CA 92702
714-647-1881
www.ocsd.org

**Riverside County Sheriff**
Human Resources
4095 Lemon Street
Riverside, CA 92502
951-955-3500
www.riversidesheriff.org

**Sacramento County Sheriff**
Personnel Services Department
609 Ninth Street
Sacramento, CA 95814
916-874-6771
www.sacsheriff.com

**San Bernardino County Sheriff**
County of San Bernardino
Human Resources
157 West Fifth Street
San Bernardino, CA 92415-0440
909-387-8304
www.co.san-bernardino.ca.us/sheriff

**San Diego County Sheriff**
Recruiting Office
9621 Ridgehaven Ct.
San Diego, CA 92123
619-974-2400
www.sdsheriff.net

**Ventura County Sheriff**
Personnel Department
800 South Victoria Avenue
Ventura, CA 93009
805-654-2000
www.vcsd.org

# 5 ▶ Becoming a Police Officer in Fresno

## CHAPTER SUMMARY

This chapter describes in detail the selection process for becoming a police officer in Fresno. It offers the applicant useful information in such key areas as training, requirements and procedure, benefits, and initial assignment.

The City of Fresno Police Department, known as the FPD, is the eighth-largest police department in the state of California employing 700 sworn officers. The Fresno Police Department believes that reaching its citizens early and often is a key to controlling crime in its district. With a widely diverse population, which includes a growing Hmong community and thousands of seasonal workers who come to the San Joaquin valley at harvest time, the Fresno Police Department is investing time and effort in establishing solid relationships with citizen leaders.

At the Citizens Police Academy, officers train community representatives and keep them current on police activities and goals. These classes are offered to citizens in three languages—English, Spanish, and Hmong—to ensure that communication problems will not prevent the message of unity from being heard.

The police department encourages police officers to interact with the community's children. Through the Police Activities League, youngsters get a chance to work with police officers in a fun and informative setting. The department sponsors field trips, camping weekends, and even puppetry in an effort to become an early, positive force in young citizens' lives.

The Fresno Police Department also welcomes citizen involvement through a ride along program that lets volunteers join officers on the beat, generating a greater understanding of the department's job functions and goals.

The FPD has developed the following statement of its goals as a police department and its mission to the community of Fresno:

*Vision Statement: We are a model law enforcement agency, nationally accredited, and viewed internally and externally as professional, enthusiastic, and trustworthy. We reward our employees for creativity, hard work, and being responsive to the needs of our community. We treat our employees and our citizens with dignity and respect, continually meeting their needs. We operate with fiscal prudence as we effectively manage our resources, while providing the highest level of service and protection to our citizens.*

*Mission Statement: The mission of the Fresno Police Department is to provide a professional, effective, and timely response to crime and disorder and to enhance traffic safety in our community.*

## ▶ Applying to Become a Police Officer in Fresno

### Minimum Requirements

There are two routes to becoming a police officer with the FPD. If you have no prior police training or experience, you would apply for an **academy trainee** position. This is your classification as you attend the police academy and earn a California Basic Peace Officer Standards and Training (POST) Certificate. Upon successful completion of academy training, you are sworn in as a **police officer recruit**.

You may also apply to the FPD as a police officer recruit. Candidates who follow this procedure must either have a) graduated from a POST-approved California Law Enforcement Basic Academy no more than three years prior to applying with the FPD, or b) been

employed within the last three years as a police officer with a department whose minimum requirements include graduation from a Basic POST Academy.

In either case, to meet the following minimum qualifications, candidates must

- have a high school diploma or General Equivalency Diploma (GED).
- be 21 years of age.
- be a U.S. citizen or permanent resident alien who is eligible and has applied for citizenship at least one year prior to applying for the position of academy trainee or police officer recruit.
- have a valid California driver's license at the time of appointment.

The police department may give special consideration to bilingual candidates based on the needs of the Fresno community.

## ▶ Selection Process

If you meet the minimum requirements previously listed, you are eligible to begin a selection process, which consists of the following steps:

1. The Application
2. Written Examination
3. Oral Examination
4. Background Investigation and Polygraph
5. Chief's Interview
6. Medical Exam
7. Psychological Evaluation

### Step One: The Application

Your first step is to file an application for employment with the city of Fresno Department of Personnel. Applications for academy trainee and police officer recruit positions are accepted on an ongoing basis. The same application is used for either classification; indicate on the form the position you are applying for.

**To apply**
City of Fresno Human Resources Department
2600 Fresno Street, First Floor
Fresno, CA 93721
559-621-6950

**Police Academy**
Fresno City College
Regional Training Academy
1101 East University Avenue
Fresno, CA 93741
559-442-8264 (recorded information)
559-442-8277

If you file an application when no written exam has been scheduled, the Department of Personnel will notify you by mail of the date and location of the next scheduled exam.

As part of Step One, you are also required to fill out a police officer recruit/academy trainee supplemental application. This application provides the Department of Personnel with information on your prior training, experience, and bilingual skills (if any). Your employment application cannot be processed without a completed supplemental application.

## Step Two: Written Examination

This exam tests your reading comprehension, map reading skills, memory, and basic mathematical skills. Your logic and ability to understand illustrated material are also tested. The exam may include a writing exercise, which is evaluated by the oral board panel as part of the oral examination. You must score at least 70 out of 100 to pass this exam. You are notified by mail of your test results.

## Step Three: Oral Examination

The oral examination is conducted by a panel from the Fresno Human Resources Department. The panel asks you about your personal traits, training, and experience and evaluates your readiness for a police officer position. This interview counts as 100% of your final score in the examination process. You are notified by mail of your interview results.

Candidates who have a combined score of 70 or better on both the written and oral examinations are placed on an eligibility list. As openings occur in the police department, names are taken from this list to fill the positions. However, before you are appointed as an academy trainee or police officer recruit, you must complete additional screenings in the selection process.

## Step Four: Background Investigation and Polygraph

Each candidate who is considered for employment by the FPD must undergo a full background investigation. Background investigators consider your educational, work, financial, driving, and criminal history. Information you provide is verified in a polygraph (lie detector) test. The FPD also takes a candidate's fingerprints at this time.

Background factors that may disqualify a candidate from the selection process are

- recent and/or prolonged use of illegal controlled substances.
- associations with drug dealers.
- felony convictions.
- drunk driving convictions.

If you have worked for another police department, background investigators will want to know your reasons for leaving that department.

## Step Five: Chief's Interview

All candidates are interviewed by a staff member from the personnel department. You are asked questions that relate to your readiness for a career in law enforcement, such as why you are choosing police work as a career and how you have prepared yourself for this career choice.

## Step Six: Medical Exam

Before being hired, you must pass an extensive medical examination in which you are screened for overall fitness and physical problems, such as spinal abnormalities or heart conditions, that may prevent your performing the duties of a police officer. This exam includes a drug test.

Your vision is tested at this time and must conform to the following standards:

- If you wear glasses or hard contacts, your vision must be corrected to 20/20; uncorrected vision must be no worse than 20/40.
- If you wear soft contacts, your vision must be corrected to 20/20, and you must a) have successfully worn soft contacts for at least six months and b) agree to replace them every six months to one year or if they become uncomfortable or difficult to wear.

## Step Seven: Psychological Evaluation

This evaluation gives the department a profile of a candidate's psychological makeup and determines whether he or she is suitable for the job. Your results from a written and oral psychological exam form the basis of this investigation.

Applicants who successfully pass all the steps of the selection process are placed on an official eligibility list. If your name is chosen from this list, you are sent to the police academy to begin your training.

## ▶ Training

If you are hired by the city of Fresno as an academy trainee, you are automatically accepted into the academy. This is a salaried position and training is paid for by the city. Applicants who have not been hired by the city may still attend the police academy, but they must pay their own tuition and uniform and equipment fees. Because class space is limited, recruits sponsored by a law enforcement agency have first priority. Nonaffiliated recruits are accepted based primarily on their scores from the written examination; they must have also passed all the phases of the selection process previously listed.

For information on attending the police academy as a nonaffiliated recruit, contact the Fresno City College Regional Training Academy (Fresno's police academy) at the number listed at the beginning of this chapter.

Fresno's police academy is located at Fresno City College. The program provides all the necessary training for California police officers and covers all topics mandated by the Commission on Peace Officer Standards and Training (POST), the state of California's certifying agency. Areas of study include the following:

- Criminal Justice System
- Crisis Intervention
- Juvenile Law and Procedure
- Vehicle Operations
- Investigative Report Writing
- Traffic Enforcement
- Preliminary Investigation
- Firearms
- Community Relations

## Initial Assignment

After graduating from the academy, you begin an 18-month probation period. You are assigned to work with a field training officer and complete 17 weeks of on-the-job training, during which you get the necessary experience in all areas of your work.

## ▶ Salary and Benefits

The accompanying chart lists monthly and annual salary for different ranks within the police department.

## Foreign Language Incentive

Officers with bilingual skills are paid an additional foreign language incentive per month.

## Educational Incentives

After completing your probation period and upon approval by the chief of police and the chief administration officer, you can be paid either a) 2% above your base pay for completion of three semester units at an accredited college or university, b) 3% above your base pay for a bachelor's degree, or c) 5% above base pay for a master's or doctorate.

## Holidays

You are entitled to 13 holidays per year, including your birthday and two floating holidays.

## Vacation

Vacation is earned as follows:

- One to five years of service = 12 days vacation
- Five to ten years of service = 13 days vacation
- 10–20 years of service = 15 days vacation
- Over 20 years of service = 20 days vacation

## Uniform Allowance

You receive a yearly uniform allowance, paid in semi-annual installments.

## Sick Leave

Officers are granted 8 hours of sick leave per month.

## Health Coverage

Police officers receive a monthly allowance to help cover the cost of health benefits.

## Retirement

You may retire at age 50 and claim 2% of your average pay for each year of service. If you retire after 50, the percentage you are paid increases to a maximum of 2.7% at age 55. The maximum compensation for retirement is 75% of your average pay.

| SALARY: AT A GLANCE | | |
| --- | --- | --- |
| POSITION | MONTHLY SALARY | AVERAGE ANNUAL SALARY |
| Deputy Police Chief | $10,961 | $131,532 |
| Police Officer Recruit | $3,861 – 4,057 | $47,490 |
| Police Officer | $4,460 – 5,247 | $58,242 |
| Sergeant | $5,470 – 6,326 | $64,302 |
| Lieutenant | $6,746 – $8,476 | $91,332 |
| Captain | $7,768 – 9,762 | $105,180 |

Note: *Figures supplied by the city of Fresno Personnel Office.*

# Becoming a Police Officer in Long Beach

## CHAPTER SUMMARY

This chapter describes in detail the selection process for becoming a police officer in Long Beach. It offers the applicant useful information in such key areas as training, requirements and procedure, benefits, and initial assignment.

The city of Long Beach Police Department, known as the LBPD, is the fifth-largest police department in the state of California employing 903 sworn officers. With citizens of numerous ethnic origins, including strong African American, Hispanic, and Cambodian communities, Long Beach is a true melting pot. To address the policing requirements of such a diverse population, the Long Beach Police Department has been a leader in providing cultural awareness training for its officers.

All department employees take part in the cultural awareness training program. Phase One of the program began in 1989 and primarily focused on familiarizing officers and administrative employees with the various cultures that make up Long Beach. Phase Two, completed in 1993, included an updated curriculum with special emphasis on hate crimes.

Phase Three of the cultural awareness program was completed in the mid-1990s. All officers completed a three-day program geared toward building a working partnership with various groups in the communities. Through these citizen meetings and other such measures, Long Beach is taking strides toward building mutual trust and respect between members of the police force and the community it serves.

The LBPD's motto is "One Team, One Mission" and its mission is "to become California's safest large city." The LBPD has developed the following statement to define its goals as a police department and its mission to the community of Long Beach:

*Crime Reduction: Impact violent crime through the identification of crime trends and the application of innovative strategies to reduce criminal activity and improve quality of life. Professional Service: Leverage the use of Long Beach Police Department assets and resources to maximize organizational efficiency.*

*Public Trust: Establish a closer and more effective working relationship with the community to improve information exchange, enhance transparency, and empower joint problem solving.*

## Applying to Become a Police Officer in Long Beach

### Minimum Requirements

At the time of filing an application for the position of **police recruit** in Long Beach, an individual must

- have a high school diploma or a General Equivalency Diploma (GED).
- be 20 years of age or older.
- have a valid driver's license.
- be a U.S. citizen or have applied for citizenship.
- have his or her weight proportionate to height, muscular development, and skeletal structure.
- have vision correctable to 20/20 and have no color blindness.
- have normal hearing.
- have no felony convictions or convictions that would a) be a felony in any other state, or b) prevent your carrying, possessing, or control of a firearm.

The Long Beach Police Department values reading comprehension and writing skills, the ability to communicate effectively, and sound decision making. The job of police officer demands both strenuous physical activity and the ability to interact with people.

The department stresses that recent college credits in law enforcement–related subject areas are considered a plus. The city of Long Beach gives special consideration to candidates who have bilingual skills in English/Spanish or English/Southeast Asian languages.

## Selection Process

The selection process of the Long Beach Police Department consists of the following steps, in two phases:

I. Civil Service Department Testing Process
1. Civil Service Application
2. Written and Video Scenario Examination
II. Police Department Review and Selection Process
3. Police Recruit Orientation
4. Physical Ability Test
5. Psychological Test
6. Background Assessment Interview and Investigation
7. Medical Exam

### Step One: The Application

The testing process for the LBPD begins with the application, which should be filled out completely and turned in by the close of the filing period. Written applications should be sent to the City of Long Beach, Civil Service Department, 333 W. Ocean Blvd., Seventh Floor, Long Beach, California, 90802. Candidates may also apply online via http://agency.governmentjobs.com/longbeach.

### Step Two: Written and Video Scenario Examination

Candidates meeting the minimum requirements to file an application will be invited to the written and video scenario examination, which are conducted in one day. You

**To apply**
Long Beach Civil Service Commission
City Hall
333 West Ocean Boulevard, Seventh Floor
Long Beach, CA 90802
310-570-6555
www.longbeach.gov/civilservice

For recorded job opening announcements, directions to City Hall, and Civil Service Commission offers, call 310-570-6201. If you are hearing impaired, the TDD number is 310-570-6638.

are not required to have prior knowledge or experience in law or police procedure to complete this test successfully. The written examination is a general knowledge test that measures your ability to learn and apply police information, to remember details, to complete reports, to interpret maps and accident diagrams, and to use judgment and logic. The video scenario places candidates in police-related situations and measures human interaction skills, unbiased enforcement, situational judgments, social maturity, and appropriate use of force.

The written exam is 100% of your total score. The video scenario is pass or fail. Candidates must receive a minimum score of 70 to be considered eligible to continue to the second phase of the selection process.

## Step Three: Police Recruit Orientation

The next phase of the selection process begins when a candidate receives a certified letter of invitation to attend a police recruit orientation held at the Long Beach Police Academy.

The police recruit orientation marks the beginning of the evaluation process by the police department. Candidates invited to the orientation should be aware that police department academy staff begins the screening and selection process as soon as they see a candidate enter the orientation room. Candidates should keep this in mind and conduct themselves accordingly. The following outline provides a preview of the orientation:

- A description of the police department review and selection process, including a discussion of selection standards, tentative hiring dates, the number of vacancies, and a description of the background investigation.
- Instructions on completing essential forms that include a background questionnaire, an extensive police recruit application form that requests information on present and past employers, educational history, and other personal history data forms.
- An explanation of the tests administered by the police department: the psychological written examination and the physical ability test. In short, candidates should be prepared to spend the whole day (usually a Saturday or Sunday) at the Long Beach Police Academy and should be mentally and physically ready to start the process.

## Step Four: The Physical Ability Test

The physical ability test is given the day of the police recruit orientation and requires each candidate to perform the following obstacle course within a specified time:

- run 300 feet
- scale a six-foot wall (two attempts)
- walk a balance beam (two attempts)
- run another 300 feet

- squeeze a gripping device
- mandatory rest of 30 seconds
- run 50 feet to a dummy
- drag a 165-pound dummy 50 feet

Applicants will then be required to perform as many push-ups as they are able (25–40 is desirable).

Applicants will then be required to run $1\frac{1}{2}$ miles in less than 15 minutes. Failure to complete this run under the required time will disqualify you from advancing to the next testing process.

Candidates unable to complete the physical ability test may retake the test within a week and may schedule practice sessions. Practice sessions may also be arranged with the academy staff before attending the orientation. Interested individuals must present their letters of invitation to the orientation to schedule a practice session. For information on arranging practice sessions, call the Long Beach Police Academy at 562-570-5890.

Following the police recruit orientation, the psychological examination, and the physical ability test, applicants are scheduled for the next steps in the selection process.

## Step Five: Psychological Examination

This examination is by a qualified psychologist. Candidates are urged to answer all questions (written or oral) honestly.

## Step Six: Background Assessment Interview and Investigation

The background assessment interview is called the "chief's interview" and is conducted by background investigators who represent the chief of police. The background investigators review each candidate's responses on the background questionnaire, the extensive police recruit application, and other forms completed during the police recruit orientation. Information gathered during the background assessment interview will be checked and verified during other stages of the overall background investigation. It is expected that candidates will be candid and honest with the background investigator during this interview.

During the background investigation, candidates will take a polygraph examination that will inquire about illegal activity, recent or prolonged involvement with illegal drugs, and other possible unlawful behavior. Information obtained from the personal history document, polygraph, and any other relevant documents will be compiled during the course of the background investigation.

Criminal inquiries will be made at the local, county, state, national, and, if necessary, the international level. Driver history inquiries will be made where appropriate. Candidates will take a polygraph examination that will inquire about illegal activity, recent or prolonged involvement with illegal drugs, and other possible unlawful behavior.

Information obtained from the personal history document, polygraph, and any other relevant documents will be compiled during the course of the background investigation. Criminal inquiries will be made at the local, county, state, national, and, if necessary, the international level. Driver history inquiries will be made where appropriate.

- Personal: Name, aliases, birth date, Social Security number, tattoos, citizenship, etc.
- Relatives and Acquaintances: Reference checks related to your suitability to be a police officer.
- Education: High school(s), college(s), trade school(s), etc., and any other sources of diplomas, certificates, or degrees received or in progress.
- Residence: Residences for the last ten years.
- Experience and Employment: History of employment and volunteer services; job-related inquiries with past and current employers and coworkers.
- Military Service: Registration with the Selective Service System and evaluation of military service record, if applicable.
- Financial: Inquiries relative to responsibility, dependability, and liability as these relate to meeting financial obligations. You will be asked to

submit an Experion Credit Report with other required documentation.

- Legal: Investigation of all possible and actual criminal conduct; arrests and or convictions evaluated on a case-by-case basis. (A misdemeanor conviction in and of itself is not necessarily a disqualifying factor.)
- Motor Vehicle Operation: Behavior as it relates to driving ability and required automobile insurance.

### Step Seven: Medical Exam

Candidates are required to pass a medical examination and drug-screening test.

## ▶ Training

The police department selects names of new recruits from the eligibility list maintained by the civil service department and sends these recruits to the police academy.

Once accepted by the academy, you become a paid employee of the city of Long Beach. Your 18-month probation period begins when you enter the academy and ends upon completion of your field training.

Police academy training lasts six months and covers areas required by the California Police Officer Standards and Training (POST) guidelines, including the following:

- Criminal Investigation
- Traffic Laws
- Force and Weaponry
- Patrol Procedures
- Investigative Report Writing
- First Aid
- Vehicle Operations
- Laws of Arrest
- Physical Fitness and Stress Management

### Initial Assignment

Upon graduation from the academy, you begin a five-month field training program under the close supervision of an experienced field training officer. This training gives you hands-on experience in the duties of an officer. Your probation period ends when you complete field training. At this time, you receive a California Basic POST certificate.

## ▶ Salary and Benefits

The accompanying chart lists monthly and annual salary for different ranks within the police department.

### Vacation

As a police officer, you receive 12 working days of paid vacation a year. After five years of service on the force, you begin to earn additional vacation days, up to 20 working days a year after 20 years of service.

### Holidays

Officers are entitled to nine holidays per year and can take four more days a year for personal holiday leave.

### Educational Incentive

Officers with an associate's or bachelor's degree receive a percent increase in the base salary of their classification.

### POST Incentive

If you hold an intermediate POST certificate, you are paid an additional $48 biweekly ($ 0.60 per hour). Officers with an advanced certification receive an additional $119 biweekly ($1.49 per hour).

(After earning a basic POST Certificate, officers who meet additional requirements are eligible for an intermediate or advanced certificate. An intermediate certificate is awarded to officers with a minimum of two years' patrol experience and a bachelor's degree, or four years' experience and an associate's degree. Advanced certificates are earned with a) at least four years' experience and a master's degree, b) six years' experience and a bachelor's degree, or c) nine years' experience and an associate's degree. Officers who do not have college degrees may earn these certificates on the basis of training, patrol experience, and related education.)

## Sick Leave

Paid sick leave is accumulated at the rate of one day per month.

## Health Coverage

The city of Long Beach pays for the health and dental coverage of its employees and their dependents. Additional coverage plans are available at group rates.

## Retirement

Police officer retirement benefits are provided by the Public Employees Retirement System (PERS) into which the city of Long Beach pays the employee's contribution. Officers may retire at the age of 55 and receive 3% of their base pay for each year served on the force.

| SALARY: AT A GLANCE | | |
| --- | --- | --- |
| POSITION | MONTHLY SALARY | AVERAGE ANNUAL SALARY |
| Police Recruit | $3,922 | NA |
| Police Officer | $4,357 – $5,396 | $58,518 |
| Sergeant | $5,538 – $7,048 | $75,516 |
| Lieutenant | $6,568 – $8,106 | $88,044 |
| Captain | $7,390 – $9,122 | $99,072 |

Note: *Figures supplied by the city of Fresno Personnel Office.*

# Becoming a Police Officer in Los Angeles

## CHAPTER SUMMARY

This chapter describes in detail the selection process for becoming a police officer in Los Angeles. It also offers the applicant useful information in such key areas as requirements and procedures, training, salary and benefits, and initial assignments.

The city of Los Angeles Police Department, known as the LAPD, is the largest police department in the state of California with more than 9,000 sworn officers. Officers of the LAPD seem to carry out their duties under a national spotlight. A series of high-profile, racially charged incidents served to divide city residents and generate a rash of negative press for the department. In response, the LAPD is focused on improving its effectiveness, revitalizing its reputation, and strengthening public support.

Changes underway at the LAPD include a reorganization of basic patrol services and a citywide implementation of community policing initiatives. The goal is to serve neighborhood needs better and to partner with local residents in efforts to reduce crime. As part of this "back to the beat" strategy, the LAPD has gained the city's commitment to increase the size of the force, ultimately up to 10,000 officers. In addition, the department's technological capabilities are being upgraded to improve its policing operations further.

The LAPD is divided into 19 divisions and each division operates in a semiautonomous fashion, particularly when it comes to specialized training. Two more divisions are anticipated in the near future. Division captains are responsible for the day-to-day operations and crime reduction within their district.

At times, the entire LAPD force is brought together for specialized training. For example, following the riots that ensued after the Rodney King verdict in 1991, all sworn personnel received three days of training on riot and mob control.

The LAPD has developed the following statement to describe what it sees as its mission:

*Motto: To Protect and to Serve*

*Mission: It is the mission of the Los Angeles Police Department to safeguard the lives and property of the people we serve, to reduce the incidence and fear of crime, and to enhance public safety while working with the diverse communities to improve their quality of life. Our mandate is to do so with honor and integrity, while at all times conducting ourselves with the highest ethical standards to maintain public confidence.*

The department states its core values as

- service to the communities of Los Angeles.
- reverence for the law.
- commitment to leadership.
- integrity in action and speech.
- respect for people.
- quality though continuous improvement.

## ▶ Applying to Become a Police Officer in Los Angeles

### Minimum Requirements

To apply for the entry-level position of **police recruit** in Los Angeles, you must meet certain minimum requirements.

### Age Limitations

At the time of hire, you must be at least 21 years of age. You may take the written examination if you are $20\frac{1}{2}$ years old by the written test date. Candidates 35 and older will not be eligible to apply for police officer.

### Education

The Los Angeles Police Department values applicants with some college education, but it is not a requirement. You must have a U.S. high school diploma or a General Equivalency Diploma (GED) equivalent to a U.S. diploma. A degree from an accredited two- or four-year school may be substituted for a high school diploma. You are eligible for a higher starting salary if you have prior peace officer experience and/or postsecondary (college) education.

### Citizenship

U.S. citizenship is not required for employment with the LAPD; however, you must have applied for citizenship by the time the selection process begins. If you do not show documentation that you have applied for citizenship, you will be disqualified from the process. California state law requires that you become a U.S. citizen within three years of application for employment.

### Health

Your health must be excellent, with no conditions that would limit your capacity to complete police training and perform the functions of police work.

### Vision

Your visual acuity must be no worse than 20/40 uncorrected. Waivers may be granted if you have worn soft contact lenses for at least one year. You must have normal functional color vision. Candidates who have had refractive surgery are subject to deferral from consideration for six months or more from the date of surgery. Candidates with functional monocular vision because of vision loss or strabismus may be subject to medical disqualification.

# Important Addresses and Phone Numbers

**Recruitment Station**
700 East Temple; Room B28
Los Angeles, CA 90012
213-485-3617
Monday through Friday
between 8:30 A.M. and 5:00 P.M.
www.joinlapd.com

**Police Academy**
Los Angeles Police Recruit Training Center
5651 West Manchester Avenue
Los Angeles, CA 90045

**Written Exam Sites**
Saturday testing is held at 8:00 A.M. (except holiday weekends) at the following location:

**Personnel Building**
700 East Temple Street, Room #115-B
Los Angeles, CA 90012

Evening testing takes place on various nights (excluding holidays) at the following times and locations:

**First Monday of every month—7:00 P.M.**
Constituent Services Center
8475 South Vermont Avenue
Los Angeles, CA 90044

**Third Monday of every month—6:00 P.M.**
Baldwin Hills Crenshaw Plaza
Community Room
3650 West Martin Luther King Boulevard
Los Angeles, CA 90008

**Every Monday—7:00 P.M.**
San Pedro Municipal Building
Conference Room #452
638 South Beacon Street
San Pedro, CA 90731

**Every Tuesday—7:00 P.M.**
Marvin Braude Constituent Center
Conference Room #1A
6262 Van Nuys Boulevard
Van Nuys, CA 90401

**Every Wednesday—7:00 P.M.**
Personnel Department Building
Room #115-B
700 East Temple Street
Los Angeles, CA 90012

**Every Thursday—7:00 P.M.**
Hollywood Neighborhood City Hall
Community Room
6501 Fountain Avenue
Los Angeles, CA 90028

## Hearing
You must have normal hearing ability and be able to 1) understand speech in noisy areas, 2) localize sounds, and 3) understand soft-spoken speech.

## Driver's License
You must obtain a California driver's license prior to appointment.

## Height/Weight
There is no minimum or maximum height or weight limit. However, your weight must be appropriate for height and build.

## ▶ Selection Process

To become a police officer in Los Angeles, you must complete a nine-step selection process. You must successfully complete each step before continuing to the next.

The selection process consists of several tests, interviews, and skill assessments, in this order:

1. Preliminary Background Application and Job Preview Questionnaire
2. Written Examination
3. Personal Qualifications Essay
4. Physical Abilities Test
5. Background Investigation
6. Polygraph
7. Department Interview
8. Medical Exam and Psychological Evaluation
9. Certification and Appointment

Note that the period for which test results remain valid varies according to the test.

### Step One: Preliminary Background Application and Job Preview Questionnaire

All applicants must complete the online, interactive Preliminary Background Application (PBA) and Job Preview Questionnaire (JPQ). The online PBA will identify issues that you should resolve before beginning the selection process and will tell you if you have a realistic chance of success in the background investigation portion of the selection process. The online JPQ includes questions designed to help you better understand the nature of police officer work. Bring the printed results with you to the test site.

### Step Two: Multiple-Choice Written Examination

The qualifying multiple-choice written exam measures reading comprehension and English usage. The test is scored pass/fail. If you fail, you may retake the written exam after six months.

### Step Three: Personal Qualifications Essay

The Personal Qualifications Essay (PQE) consists of essay questions related to judgment and decision making and behavioral flexibility. Your written communication skills will also be evaluated. The passing score you receive will determine your placement on the eligible list. If you fail, you may retake the PQE after six months.

### Step Four: Physical Abilities Test

The Physical Abilities Test (PAT) consists of two portions. The first portion is designed to measure strength, agility, and endurance. The second portion measures aerobic capacity and will usually be administered at the time of the medical evaluation. It is a pass/fail test. Many applicants train for this test either by participating in the free Candidate Assistance Program offered by the LAPD or by training on their own. The physical fitness program at the academy is intensely rigorous, and passing the Physical Abilities Test does not guarantee that you will be fit enough to pass the academy program. This is why most dedicated applicants will continue to train after the PAT, in preparation for the academy.

As part of the police officer examination, you will be required to pass the physical abilities test, which currently consists of two portions. The first portion of the test consists of three events designed to measure endurance, strength, and agility. The second portion of the test consists of a measure of aerobic capacity. The first test portion is taken after placement on the eligible list and is administered at the City of Los Angeles Personnel Department Building, 700 East Temple Street, First Floor, Los Angeles, CA 90012. It consists of three events designed to measure endurance, strength, and agility. A passing score will be based upon the cumulative score of all three test events. The first two events will each be performed more than once; the average of the attempts is used in the cumulative score.

The Physical Abilities Test (Part I) consists of the following three events, administered in the following order:

**SIDE STEP (AGILITY)**—You will have ten seconds to move from one side of the center line to the other side as many times as possible. Performed twice.

**CABLE PULL (STRENGTH)**—You will have five seconds to pull horizontally as hard as possible while gripping a pair of handles. Performed three times.

**STATIONARY BICYCLE (ENDURANCE)**—You will have two minutes to pedal as many revolutions as possible against a preset resistance. Performed once.

The second portion of the test consists of one event designed to measure aerobic capacity. For candidate safety, it will be administered usually at the time of the medical evaluation after appropriate medical screening at the City of Los Angeles Medical Services Division Building, 432 East Temple Street, Los Angeles, CA 90012.

**TREADMILL (AEROBIC CAPACITY)**—This test measures aerobic capacity. The treadmill is programmed to simulate running 1.5 miles in 14 minutes on a track. During the test, the speed and incline of the machine will vary, and as a result, the actual test time is 10 minutes 20 seconds. The pass/fail score for this test is based upon your completion of this test for the specified period.

Passing the Physical Abilities Test indicates only the minimum level of fitness required to begin academy training. Once in the academy as a recruit, you will be required to perform physically at much higher levels.

If you are unable to perform any one of these exercises, you should initiate a regular physical fitness program to prepare yourself for the academy. It is recommended that you receive a medical examination from your own physician before beginning. Remember, you do not achieve excellent physical fitness overnight, and it does take physical and mental effort.

The LAPD has designed a program called the Candidate Assistance Program (CAD) to assist you in preparing for the Physical Abilities Test and the rigorous physical demands of the police academy. Female candidates are especially encouraged to participate in this program.

Physical training classes are offered free to all police candidates on Tuesday and Thursday evenings from 6:00 P.M. to 9:00 P.M. at the old Los Angeles Police Academy, 1880 North Academy Drive, Los Angeles. Participants are required to wear athletic supportive clothing, workout gear, and suitable running shoes. Call Employee Opportunity and Development Division (EODD) for more information at 213-485-6345. Times and locations are subject to change.

## Important

The Los Angeles Police Department strongly urges candidates to participate in this program. It will greatly enhance your chance of success in the selection process leading to a career with the Los Angeles Police Department. However, this class is not mandatory and is to assist police officer candidates. Your participation in the program does not automatically qualify you to be hired. All candidates must pass the official civil service examinations.

## Step Five: Background Investigation

The background investigation begins with completion of a personal history form (which requires compilation of extensive biographical information) and additional questionnaires, fingerprinting, and an interview with a background investigator. If you meet the city's standards, a thorough background investigation will be conducted. It will include checks of employment, police, financial, education, and military records and interviews with family members, neighbors, supervisors, coworkers, and friends.

### Step Six: Polygraph

The polygraph examination is conducted to confirm information obtained during your background interview.

### Step Seven: Department Interview

The department interview will be conducted by a panel to assess your personal accomplishment, job motivation, continuous learning orientation, instrumentality, interpersonal skills, and oral communication skills. Only those candidates who are selected during this part of the process will move forward in the selection process

### Step Eight: Medical Exam and Psychological Evaluation

The medical exam is thorough, and it is essential that you be in excellent health with no conditions that would restrict your ability to safely do police work. Written psychological tests and the second portion of the PAT will also be administered at this time. The medical exam also includes a psychological evaluation that consists of an individual oral interview and evaluation by a city psychologist on factors related to successful performance in the difficult and stressful job of police officer. The information evaluated includes the written psychological tests as well as the background findings.

### Step Nine: Certification and Appointment

The certification and appointment/preemployment substance screening are the final steps in the selection process. To be considered for hiring, you must have successfully completed all the steps in the selection process. When a candidate is appointed will depend on the next available class date, selection by LAPD management, and accordance with provisions of the Consent Decree.

## ▶ Training

Candidates who successfully complete all the steps in the selection process are placed on a civil service eligibility list prepared by the personnel department. Appointments to the police academy are made from this list. As noted, your rank on the eligibility list is determined by a variety of tests.

Recruit officer training lasts eight months and covers a variety of subjects. Recruit officers receive full-time pay while at the academy. Classes are held eight hours a day, five days a week, and cover all areas of police work, including the following:

- Applications of Police Law and Procedure
- Report Writing
- Investigation Procedures
- Cultural Diversity and Human Relations
- Physical Training
- Firearms and Police Equipment Training
- Police Driving
- Police Tactics

The academy provides recruit officers extra help with their studies if they need it.

### Initial Assignment

Upon graduation from the police academy, you are sworn in as a Police Officer I and assigned to a patrol division. The Los Angeles Police Department's total training/probationary period lasts 18 months, with your eight months at the academy considered Phase One of the training. Phase Two, structured field training, lasts 24 weeks. During this period, you are given basic patrol-car assignments in which you are partnered with a field training officer and given close supervision and biweekly reviews.

After successfully completing Phase Two, you enter Phase Three, which lasts 16 weeks. During Phase Three, advanced field training, you are given more varied assignments, including single-man units, specialized units, and desk assignments. You are allowed to take on tasks that require minimal assistance or supervision, and reviews are reduced from biweekly to monthly.

Upon completion of advanced field training, you are promoted to Police Officer II and your probationary period ends. You are then reassigned to a different location and are free to apply to different departments and specialized units. At this point, you become eligible for higher California Peace Officer Standards and Training (POST) certification.

## ▶ Crime Academy Trainee Program

Qualified female police officer candidates who have successfully completed all steps in the police officer selection process are eligible for the Crime Academy Trainee (AT) Program. This program prepares female recruits for the police academy and increases their chances for success in crucial areas of recruit training. The AT program consists of various academic subjects, psychological preparation, physical conditioning, and practical instruction in drill and police equipment maintenance. Recruits gain hands-on experience in such areas as investigation, patrol, and administrative duties. It also offers psychological preparation, such as stress management, assertiveness training, developing support networks, and job expectations. ATs receive a monthly salary for this program, which usually runs for about five weeks.

## ▶ Lateral Entry Program

The LAPD offers lateral entry for applicants with a valid California Basic Peace Officer Standards and Training (POST) Certificate. This program allows recruits a shortened academy training. With the exception of the written examinations, all other police officer requirements must be met. For further information, call 213-485-3617.

## ▶ Consent Decree

The city of Los Angeles has voluntarily agreed to a federal court-approved decree that gives greater employment opportunity to minority and female candidates. The city also seeks to increase its Asian-Pacific police officer numbers; applicants who speak an Asian-Pacific and/or other foreign language(s) may be entitled to selective certification and bonus pay.

## ▶ Salary and Benefits

The accompanying chart lists monthly and annual salaries for different ranks within the police department.

### Family and Domestic Partner Health and Dental Plans
Officers may choose from several health and dental plans for themselves and eligible dependents. All plans are partially subsidized by the city of Los Angeles.

### Pension/Retirement Plan
The city of Los Angeles offers an independent pension system to which both employee and the city contribute. Employees contribute 8% of their gross salary. Participation in the plan is automatic and a condition of employment. Under this plan, you may retire after you reach the age of 50, if you have at least ten years of service with the LAPD at a rate based on the number of years served. This plan also provides disability benefits in case of injury, as well as survivor benefits to qualified spouses and children.

A deferred compensation plan (similar to a 401K) is also provided to all members of the LAPD. You may make regular contributions to the plan that are not taxable until withdrawal.

### Sick Leave and Disability Benefits
Upon your hire as a sworn police officer, you are entitled to 12 days of 100% paid sick leave, five days at

75%, and five days at 50%. You may accumulate up to 100 days at 100%, 75%, and 50% paid sick leave. If you must retire because of a service-related disability, there is no waiting period for retirement pay.

## Vacation and Holidays

After one year of service, you receive 15 days of vacation; after 10 years, you are allowed 23 days. Sworn employees of the LAPD are given 13 paid floating holidays per year, one day every four weeks.

## Longevity Pay

Police officers receive an additional $165.30 per month after ten years of service; $332.34 per month after 15 years; and $497.64 per month after 20 years.

## Court Pay

Officers are compensated for attending court while on off-duty status.

## Education Pay

Police officers who hold an associate's or bachelor's degree earn an additional education pay per month.

## Foreign Language Pay

Officers who speak an Asian-Pacific language or other foreign language are eligible for additional pay.

## Uniform and Equipment Allowance

Each officer is allotted $900 yearly to cover the cost of uniforms and equipment.

## Field Bonus

Officers assigned to field duties, such as patrol, receive an additional 25% pay.

| SALARY: AT A GLANCE | |
| --- | --- |
| **POSITION** | **AVERAGE ANNUAL SALARY** |
| Police Officer I | $51,114 to $68,612 |
| Police Officer II (automatic increase after 18 months) | $55,248 to $72,391 |
| Police Officer III (FTO) | $58,318 to $76,546 |
| Detective I–III | $72,391 to $100,328 |
| Sergeant I–II | $80,764 to $95,025 |
| Lieutenant I–II | $95,025 to $111,750 |
| Police Captain I–III | $111,708 to $146,557 |
| CMOR | $138,768 to $163,302 |
| Deputy Chief I–II | $151,129 to $220,493 |

Note: *Figures supplied by the city of Los Angeles Personnel Department.*

# CHAPTER

# 8 ▶ Becoming a Police Officer in Oakland

## CHAPTER SUMMARY

This chapter describes in detail the selection process for becoming a police officer in Oakland. It offers the applicant useful information in such key areas as requirements and procedures, training, salary and benefits, and initial assignment.

The city of Oakland Police Department, known as the OPD, is the seventh-largest police department in the state of California with about 750 sworn officers. Few cities span as broad a range of urban cultures and economic scales as Oakland. The city is made up of literally hundreds of "communities," including strong African American and Asian American populations. In turn, each community has its own list of crime priorities, prompted by its own demographic composition. To help police officers better understand the makeup and expectations of these neighborhoods, the Oakland Police Department has implemented a number of community policing programs that put officers directly in touch with their beats.

A mandatory 40-hour class called Advanced Officers School (AOS) deals exclusively with community policing. AOS turns the broad problems into specifics by highlighting areas of concentrated crime. For instance, business districts may have complaints about skateboarders, while urban residential areas may be concerned with drug dealing. The Oakland Police Department wants its officers to understand what problems are occurring, and where, so that they can approach each problem appropriately.

The department also enlists the help of non-sworn citizens called Neighborhood Service Coordinators to help officers better understand their beats. Other community policing efforts include the formation of various

## Important Addresses and Phone Numbers

Oakland Police Department
Background and Recruitment Unit
250 Frank H. Ogawa Plaza #D
Oakland, CA 94612
510-238-3339
www.oaklandpolice.com

*Respect: We value respect; the respect for ourselves, each other, and all members of the community; showing an understanding and appreciation for our similarities and differences.*

*Service: We value the opportunity to provide service which is courteous, responsive, firm, and sensitive to the needs of the community.*

*Teamwork: We value teamwork and cooperation in combining our diverse backgrounds, skills, and beliefs to achieve a common goal.*

ethnic councils and interaction with community organizations who help police actually solve crimes. A newsletter, *Police Community Beat*, supports this effort.

The City of Oakland Police Department has developed the following statement of values that reflects its mission, vision, and values to the Oakland community:

*Mission: The mission of the Oakland Police Department is to provide competent, effective, public safety services to all persons, with the highest regard for human dignity through efficient, professional, and ethical law enforcement and crime prevention practices.*

*Vision: Our vision is to enhance our status as a premier law enforcement agency as championed by our customers and benchmarked by our counterparts. As such, we will be recognized as a high-performance team of empowered professionals capable of responding to new challenges as they occur within the city of Oakland and throughout the police profession.*

*"F.I.R.S.T. Commitment"*

*Fairness: We value fairness and strive to deliver services, provide assistance, and make decisions that are impartial, unbiased, and without prejudice.*

*Integrity: We value the trust and confidence placed in us by the public we serve and will not compromise ourselves or allow personal benefit to influence our decision in serving the community.*

## ▶ Applying to Become a Police Officer in Oakland

### Minimum Requirements

To apply for the entry-level position of **police officer trainee** in Oakland, you must meet the following minimum requirements:

- You must be at least 20 years and 6 months old at the time of the written examination.
- You must be a high school graduate or have a General Equivalency Diploma (GED).
- Your vision must be corrected to 20/20 in one eye and 20/30 in the other eye. You will also be screened for color blindness.
- You must be a U.S. citizen or be eligible to work in the U.S. and eligible to apply for citizenship.
- You must have a clean criminal record.
- Your weight must be proportionate to your height.
- You must have good basic reading and writing skills.

## ▶ Selection Process

The selection process for becoming a police officer trainee consists of six steps, each of which assesses a certain area of your abilities and character. You must successfully complete each step, which usually follow in this order:

1. Application
2. Written Multiple-Choice Test
3. Oral Interview
4. Physical Agility Test
5. Background Investigation and Polygraph
7. MedicaL Exam and Psychological Evaluation

The Police Recruiting Unit and the City Personnel Office's Employment Information Desk provide a study guide to help you prepare for all the stages of the selection process.

If you pass each step of the selection process, your name is placed on an eligibility list. The police department takes names from this list to fill vacancies as they occur.

## Step One: The Application

The first step in the selection process is the completion of an application and supplemental questionnaire. Applications and supplemental questionnaires will be distributed to and completed by candidates at the written test. Photo identification and a Social Security number are required to complete the application and take the test.

The city of Oakland advises that, in compliance with federal, state, and local laws, it will employ and promote qualified individuals without regard to disability. The city is committed to making reasonable accommodations in the examination process and in the work environment for the disabled. Individuals requesting reasonable accommodation in the examination process must do so no later than five working days after the final filing date for receipt of applications; otherwise, it may not be possible to arrange accommodations for the selection process. For further information, please contact the Office of Personnel Resource Management, 150 Frank H. Ogawa Plaza, 2nd Floor, Oakland, CA 94612. You may also phone the office at 510-238-3112 or TDD 510-238-3724 for the hearing impaired.

## Step Two: Written Multiple-Choice Test

This test, which is known as the Police Trainee Written Examination, evaluates such basic skills as reading comprehension, inductive reasoning, memory, and arithmetic. You must bring photo identification to be admitted to the exam site. Candidates must have a score of 70 or better to pass the exam. Candidates who pass the written exam take the physical agility test on the same day. Bring loose-fitting, comfortable clothes, and athletic shoes for the physical agility test.

If you have recently taken and passed the written test as part of the process for becoming an Oakland police cadet or an OPD reserve officer, or if you have taken the Post-Entry-Level Test Battery in other jurisdictions within the last 12 months, this test may be waived with the written consent of the Oakland Police Department and the Office of Personnel Resource Management.

## Step Three: Oral Interview

Successful candidates will participate in an interview that is designed to evaluate job-related skills and abilities such as oral communication, interpersonal skills, and judgment. In addition to general questions, candidates will be presented with hypothetical scenarios (either orally or on videotape) and asked to explain how they would respond to each situation.

After the scheduled interview, candidates will be given the Personal History Questionnaire (PHQ), which is a 31-page document to be completed by all candidates prior to their background investigation. The completed PHQ must be submitted to the Oakland Police Recruiting and Background Investigation Unit at the scheduled physical agility test.

Candidates who pass the oral interview will be placed on the eligibility list for further employment consideration, subject to successful completion of the remaining stages.

Entry-level/lateral police officer is an unclassified position and, therefore, is not subject to the traditional conventions of the civil service rules. The Office of Personnel will provide OPD with the names of all qualified individuals for further processing.

The Personal History Questionnaire (PHQ) is the foundation for an extensive background investigation conducted by the department. The PHQ is a detailed summary of your education, work experience, residences, financial history, references, and other information. It is the foundation of an extensive background investigation conducted by the police department.

You submit a Personal History Questionnaire and then discuss its contents with background investigators. This interview is crucial; at any point in the selection process, you may be disqualified for background factors that the OPD considers unacceptable.

The background investigation considers many aspects of your behavior. The department gives favorable consideration to candidates who

- demonstrate strong moral character and good judgment.
- have a stable work and education history.
- have had little or no involvement in criminal activities, particularly with narcotics and other controlled substances.
- maintain a reasonably good driving record.
- handle personal finances responsibly.
- complete the Personal History Questionnaire fully and truthfully.

You may be asked to take a polygraph examination in connection with your background investigation. Your fingerprints are also taken.

## Important

The background investigation is very thorough and time-consuming for both the candidate and the department. If you have any concerns or questions about events in your past, the Oakland Police Department suggests that you contact a recruiting officer at 510-238-3339.

### Step Four: Physical Agility Test

The physical agility test measures your balance, coordination, strength, and agility and is scored on a pass/fail basis. The test is comprised of eight consecutive events, performed in an "obstacle course" fashion. You have two-and-a-half minutes to complete all eight of the following exercises, which include a mandatory 30-second rest period:

- run 300 feet
- scale a six-foot wall
- walk the length of a standard balance beam
- run 300 feet
- grasp and squeeze with one hand a grip strength device (qualifying is 75 pounds)
- run 50 feet
- drag 140-pound dummy 50 feet
- place 140-pound dummy on top of two-foot high platform

A voluntary practice physical agility test is offered prior to the examination. To find out the location and time of the practice test, contact the Recruiting Unit at 510-238-3339.

### Step Five: Background Investigation and Polygraph

Prior to a conditional job offer, candidates will be assessed for background and psychological suitability. The psychological assessment is designed to measure job-related traits and characteristics that are important for successful performance as a police officer, such as conscientiousness and the ability to work as part of a team.

During the background investigation, investigators will contact references, friends, family, former employers, and other contacts to verify the information provided. The background investigation will also check for a criminal record, obtain a copy of each candidate's driving record, and check credit references.

Applicants may be rejected for background factors at any step of the selection process, and providing fraudulent information at any stage of the selection process may be grounds for removal from the process. Candidates will also be required to submit to a polygraph examination in connection with the investigation.

### Step Six: Medical Exam and Psychological Evaluation

Prior to your actual appointment with the department, you must pass a comprehensive medical exam and psychological evaluation.

The medical exam verifies that you have no conditions that would physically prevent you from performing all your duties as an officer or that would be susceptible to the stress of the job. Such problems may be a cardiac problem, a bad back, or any ailment that restricts your physical movement. The city physician's decision related to this examination is final.

Because police work requires mental stability and strong moral character, you must pass a series of psychological tests before you can be hired by the OPD. A psychological exam is conducted by a staff psychologist and involves a series of tests, which profiles your personality type and evaluates your suitability for a career in law enforcement.

### ▶ Training

Candidates who successfully complete all phases of the process and are chosen from the eligibility list begin their training at Oakland's police academy.

As a police officer trainee, you will attend 20 weeks of recruit academy training. Class hours are Monday to Friday from 8:00 A.M. to 4:30 P.M. This schedule may be adjusted to allow for completion of classes and exercises. Recruits are paid for required overtime.

The police academy training is extensive and covers such areas as the following:

- History and Principles of Law Enforcement
- Criminal Justice System
- Community Relations
- Criminal Law
- Laws of Arrest
- Search and Seizure Law
- Vehicle Operation
- Investigative Report Writing
- Patrol Techniques
- Traffic
- Investigation
- Physical Fitness and Stress Management
- First Aid

### Initial Assignment

After graduating from the academy, a trainee works for 15 weeks under the direct supervision of a field training officer, followed by one year of probationary service. Once a trainee has completed probation, he or she is eligible for promotion to the position of police officer.

### ▶ Reserve Officers

Citizens of Oakland who are already on a career track, but have an interest in contributing to the safety of their community, may serve as sworn OPD reserve officers. These officers perform the duties and obligations of a sworn full-time officer but serve on a part-time, volunteer basis. To be eligible for a reserve officer position, you must meet the same minimum requirements listed in this chapter for police officer trainee candidates.

The Oakland Police Department places much value on the diverse career experience that each reserve officer brings to the force. At the same time, serving as a reserve officer provides an opportunity to someone who may want to explore police work before considering it as a full-time career. While keeping their full-time jobs, reserve officers fulfill at least 20 hours of duty per month, providing services in the city's commercial, industrial, and residential areas. At times, they assist the regular police force during emergencies or special events.

If you should decide to apply for a position as an Oakland police recruit, the training and experience you gain as a reserve officer benefits you in the competitive selection process. The police department gives additional consideration to applicants who either a) are employees or volunteers of the city of Oakland, or b) have prior police training and experience.

The reserve officer training program is an abridged version of the police academy that adds up to more than 320 hours of instruction. It addresses all aspects of law enforcement, such as the following:

- Police Community Relations
- Criminal Law and Investigations
- Laws of Evidence
- Patrol Procedures
- Vehicle Operation
- Report Writing and Court Testimony
- Defensive Tactics and Weaponry

This program is held in the evenings and on Saturdays.

## ▶ Police Cadet Program

The Oakland Police Department offers a police cadet program to give young adults between the ages of $17\frac{1}{2}$ and $20\frac{1}{2}$ the opportunity to develop their interest in police work. To qualify, you must meet the age requirement and you must either a) attend an accredited college or university while completing a minimum of six quarter units per term and maintaining a grade point average of at least 2.0, or b) currently attend high school as a senior and have been accepted by an accredited college or university. You may not have any felony convictions, and while you are employed by the OPD, you must maintain a valid, unrestricted California driver's license.

To become an OPD police cadet, you must follow the same application and selection procedure as for

police officer trainees. As a cadet, you are a paid, part-time employee and can work up to 19.5 hours per week. Your schedule depends upon departmental demand and your school commitments. Depending on departmental needs, you may be assigned a variety of police tasks, including community policing, traffic, recruiting, training, and crime analysis. While working in these areas, you receive close supervision, training, counseling, and evaluation by trained police officers.

## ▶ Job Opportunities

As you progress in your career as an Oakland police officer, you have opportunities to take on specialized assignments in police work, among which are the following:

- Vice Patrol
- Canine Handler
- Horse Patrol
- Recruiting Unit
- Motorcycle Patrol
- Helicopter Patrol
- Narcotics Enforcement
- Youth Services Division
- Community Services Division
- Criminal Investigations Division

You must take competitive examinations to be promoted to higher positions within the department.

## ▶ Salary and Benefits

The following chart lists monthly and annual salary for different ranks within the police department.

### Longevity Pay

Officers are eligible for additional longevity pay beginning with their seventh year of service.

## Educational Incentives

After you successfully complete your 12-month probationary period, the city of Oakland provides tuition reimbursement to officers completing approved, accredited college courses. You will also receive additional pay based on the level of degree you have completed.

## Vacation

Annual paid vacations range from three to four weeks per year.

## Holidays

Officers are compensated for 12 holidays a year.

## Military Leave

Officers are allowed 15 working days annually for such commitments as National Guard and Army Reserve service.

## Uniform and Equipment Allowance

You receive an annual allowance for uniforms and equipment. Upon appointment to the department, you receive an allowance that goes toward the purchase of initial equipment or uniform-related necessities.

## Sick Leave

Sixty days at full pay and 60 days at half pay are provided for each non-job-related illness.

## Bonus Days

Officers earn one bonus day after each calendar-year quarter of perfect attendance.

## Health Coverage

Members of the police department are offered a choice of several health plans. The city pays 100% of the least expensive premium or makes a substantial contribution toward an alternate plan. Dental insurance is also provided for officers and their dependents.

## Retirement

You may retire at any age after 20 years of service with the OPD. Retirement benefits are provided through the Public Employee's Retirement System (PERS). These benefits include disability retirement as well as 25-year service retirement as early as age 50 with 50% of salary, basic, and special death benefits. The city of Oakland pays the full PERS contribution (9%) on behalf of the employee.

| SALARY: AT A GLANCE | | |
|---|---|---|
| **POSITION** | **MONTHLY SALARY** | **AVERAGE ANNUAL SALARY** |
| Police Officer Trainee | $5,185 | $62,220 |
| Police Officer | $6,352 – $7,613 | $76,224 – $91,356 |
| Sergeant | $8,790 | $105,480 |
| Lieutenant | $10,161 | $121,932 |
| Captain | $12,379 | $148,548 |

Note: *Figures supplied by the Oakland Police Department Recruiting Office.*

# 9 ▶ Becoming a Police Officer in Sacramento

## CHAPTER SUMMARY

This chapter describes in detail the selection process for becoming a police officer in Sacramento. It offers the applicant useful information in such key areas as requirements and procedures, training, salary and benefits, and initial assignment.

The city of Sacramento Police Department, known as the SPD, is the sixth-largest police department in the state of California employing 664 sworn officers. Along with being the capital of the most populous state in the country, Sacramento is one of the fastest-growing cities in America. These facts combine to present the Sacramento Police Department with a number of policing challenges.

Keeping the peace during demonstrations and protests is one of those challenges. All officers undergo training on crowd incidents and civil disobedience procedures to help calm politically charged situations before trouble can arise. The SPD works closely with the state police to identify potential "hot" issues and government locations. Crowd psychologists and political groups are other resources tapped to help officers coordinate crowd control.

With rapid growth resulting in dramatic demographic change, the SPD is also reaching out to new subcommunities. Through its Indo-Chinese Outreach Program, for example, officers rely on ethnic business, cultural and religious leaders to help them understand the traditions and perspectives of a burgeoning Southeast Asian community.

Reducing youth crimes is another priority of the SPD. An aggressive campaign has been implemented by the force to handle graffiti, curfew violations, and other "soft" crimes committed by adolescents. The intention is to create a sense of responsibility among juveniles and change their attitude toward petty criminal behaviors, which often lead to harder crime.

The SPD has also established a high-tech task force to take advantage of Sacramento's strong technology business community. Its goals include determining ways to help officers apply from technological advances, as well as identifying crime associated with the industry, such as computer chip and component theft.

The SPD has developed the following statement that reflects its goals as a police department and its mission to the community of Sacramento:

*The mission of the Sacramento Police Department is to work in partnership with the community to protect life and property, solve neighborhood problems, and enhance the quality of life in our city.*

## ▶ Applying to Become a Police Officer in Sacramento

### Minimum Requirements
In order to meet the minimum qualifications for the entry-level position of **police cadet** in Sacramento, you must

- be at least 21 years of age.
- be a high school graduate or have a General Equivalency Diploma (GED).
- have earned at least 60 *semester* units or 90 *quarter* units from an accredited college or university (continue reading for more information on this requirement).
- have a valid Class "C" driver's license.
- have no felony convictions.
- have no history of abuse of illegal controlled substances or alcohol as an adult.
- be a U.S. citizen or a resident alien who is eligible for and has applied for citizenship.
- reside within 35 air miles of Sacramento within one year of appointment.

Because the job requires use of respiratory protection equipment at times, men may be asked to remove facial hair.

The Sacramento Police Department encourages applications from people who have an interest in progressive types of police work, such as community, neighborhood, and problem-oriented policing.

If the college credits or degree you cite on your application were earned from an institution outside of the United States, you must have them evaluated and translated by a credentialing agency before submitting them to the Sacramento Human Resources Department. Credits or degrees that are not translated cannot be accepted to meet the minimum qualifications.

Transcript evaluation can take several weeks to complete, so begin the process as soon as possible to ensure that the documentation is ready when you apply. Refer to the addresses and phone numbers on page 77 for agencies that offer this service.

## ▶ Selection Process

Becoming a police cadet involves passing a series of examinations and evaluations, which determine an applicant's suitability for a job in law enforcement. This process consists of the following:

1. Application
2. Written Examination
3. Physical Agility Test
4. Oral Interview
5. Background Investigation
6. Medical Exam and Psychological Evaluation

### Step One: The Application
Applications for the position of police cadet are accepted at any time. If you meet the minimum qualifications previously listed, you can obtain a police cadet application from the city of Sacramento Human Resources Department. This can be done in person, or you can request an application by phone.

Sacramento Police Department
Human Resources
915 I Street, Plaza Level
Sacramento, CA 95814-2604
916-808-5726
www.sacpd.org

College Credentialing Services
(for college credit evaluation):

Educational Records Evaluation Service
U.S. Bank Plaza
601 University Avenue #127
Sacramento, CA 95825
916-921-0798
edu@eres.com

International Education Research Foundation, Inc.
Credentials Evaluation Service
P.O. Box 3665
Culver City, CA 90231
310-258-9451

Center for Applied Research, Evaluation,
and Education, Inc.
P.O. Box 18358
Anaheim, CA 92817
714-237-9272
www.iescaree.com

Accreditation documentation must accompany your application; otherwise, you may not be eligible to apply for the position of police cadet.

### Step Two: Written Examination

The written examination is administered whenever the police department has positions available. If you have submitted an application for police cadet to the Sacramento Human Resources Department, you will be notified by mail when a written examination is scheduled.

The exam is an entry-level California Peace Officer Standards and Training (POST) written test that is designed to evaluate your reading, grammar, vocabulary, spelling, and writing skills.

Successful completion of this exam qualifies you for a place on an eligibility list, which the police department consults to fill vacancies in the police cadet position.

### Step Three: Physical Agility Test

This test, which is scored on a pass/fail basis, evaluates candidates on various physical maneuvers. You should be in good physical condition to attempt the physical agility test. It is recommended that you begin a physical training program in order to prepare for the physical agility test and the demands of police work; however, it is a good idea to check with your physician before starting such a program. The following events comprise the test:

- *Operating a Handgun*
- *Operating a Shotgun from Both Shoulders*
- *Body Drag*
  Lift a 165-pound dummy and drag it as quickly as possible for 32 feet (two attempts)
- *Obstacle Course*
  Run 99 yards going around or over obstacles, such as six-inch-by-six-inch pylons and a 34-inch sawhorse, which may be cleared by climbing, jumping, or vaulting (two attempts)
- *Chain-link Fence Climb*
  Run five yards, then scale a six-foot chain-link fence as quickly as possible, and then run an additional 25 yards (two attempts)
- *Solid Fence Climb*
  Run five yards, scale a six-foot solid wood fence as

quickly as possible, and then run an additional 25 yards. This fence may be scaled in any fashion except by use of the fence supports (two attempts)

- *500-Yard Run*
  Run 500 yards as quickly as possible on a standard track (one trial)

You should wear loose-fitting, comfortable clothing and athletic shoes for this test. Candidates who pass the physical agility test are eligible to continue the selection process.

## Step Four: Oral Interview

The oral examination is conducted in front of a board of one or two sworn officers (who could be any rank) and usually a civilian. Research the Sacramento Police Department and the city of Sacramento regarding pertinent information useful for your interview. For example, who is the chief of police? What is the city's population? What are the current issues/operations/press releases involving that department and the public? A good research tool is the Internet, especially the department's website.

## Step Five: Background Investigation

A background investigation is conducted based on references you supply on a personal history questionnaire. A thorough check is done of your financial, employment, military, driving, and criminal history. Your relatives, friends, and acquaintances may be contacted and asked to comment on your suitability for police work.

The information you give on the employment application about prior drug use is subject to verification through a polygraph and a drug screening test. The Sacramento Police Department specifies the standards for substance use as a) no felony use as an adult, and/or b) no prolonged use or abuse of any substance.

Your driving record is also examined, and if you have four or more points of negligent driving on your record *or* an invalid license, you cannot be considered for appointment.

## Step Six: Medical Exam and Psychological Evaluation

To be appointed as a police cadet, you must pass a psychological evaluation, which is conducted by a city-appointed psychologist. The exam involves a written test and an oral interview and evaluates your readiness for a career in law enforcement.

You must also take a complete medical exam, which determines if you are healthy enough to perform all aspects of police work on a regular basis. A vision test is performed during the medical exam. Your vision must conform to the standards set by the Sacramento Police Department, which are as follows:

- If you wear glasses or hard contact lenses, your uncorrected vision must be no worse than 20/80 and must be correctable to 20/30.
- If you wear soft contact lenses, there is no limit on uncorrected vision; however, you must provide documentation that you have successfully worn soft contact lenses for at least six months prior to application. Soft contact lens wearers are requested to submit proof that their vision is correctable to 20/30.

## ▶ Training

If you successfully complete all the steps in the selection process, you are eligible for the position of police cadet. Once accepted by the academy, you become a paid employee of the city of Sacramento.

Police academy training lasts 22 weeks and covers all aspects of police work, including the following:

- Traffic Laws
- Vehicle Operations
- Laws of Arrest
- Patrol Procedures
- Use and Maintenance of Firearms
- Investigative Report Writing

- Criminal Investigation
- Search and Seizure
- Physical Fitness and Stress Management

## Initial Assignment

Upon graduation from the academy, you begin an 18-month probationary period of employment. For the first six to nine months, you work under the direct supervision of a field training officer, gaining hands-on, practical experience in all the relevant areas of police work. Following field training, you receive a certificate of completion, and after one year of employment, you earn a California basic POST certificate.

## ▶ Salary and Benefits

The accompanying chart lists monthly and annual salaries for different ranks within the police department.

## Vacation

You are allowed ten days of paid vacation per year during your first through fifth year on the force. You receive 15 days of paid vacation during your sixth through 15th year, and after 16 years, you receive 20 days of paid vacation yearly.

## Educational and Certification Incentives

Officers who have completed the 18-month probation period are eligible for educational and training incentives. If you have a bachelor's degree from an accredited college or university, you receive an additional 5% of their base salary. Officers who have an intermediate POST certificate receive an additional 7.5% of their base salary; an advanced certification earns officers an additional 15% of their base pay.

(After earning a basic POST certificate, officers who meet additional requirements are eligible for an intermediate or advanced certificate. An intermediate certificate is awarded to officers with a minimum of two years' patrol experience and a bachelor's degree, or four years' experience and an associate's degree. Advanced certificates are earned with a) at least four years' experience and a master's degree, b) six years' experience and a bachelor's degree, or c) nine years' experience and an associate's degree. Officers who do not have college degrees may earn these certificates on the basis of training, patrol experience and related education.)

## Tuition Reimbursement

You are awarded a 5% educational benefit if you hold a bachelor's degree and have completed a probation term.

## Longevity Pay

After 20 years of service, you receive an additional longevity pay each July. After 25 years of service, officers' longevity pay increases.

## Night Differential

For each hour worked between 6:00 P.M. and 6:00 A.M., you are paid an additional percentage of your hourly wage.

## Holidays

Officers are entitled to 12 to 14 paid holidays per year, depending on date of hire and years of service. If you work on a holiday, you are paid time-and-a-half for that day.

## Uniform and Equipment Allowance

You are paid a uniform and equipment allowance biweekly for uniform needs. If you have a work assignment that requires safety shoes, the city of Sacramento pays an allowance per pair of shoes.

## Parental Leave

You are eligible for up to four weeks of paid parental leave per year.

## Sick Leave

Paid sick leave days are accumulated at approximately one day per month. You may have up to 12 days a year of paid sick leave.

## Education

A 5% education benefit is awarded to those employees who hold a bachelor's degree.

## Field Training Officer Pay

An extra 8% pay is allotted to those appointed to the field training officer (FTO) position.

## Health Coverage

The city offers medical, dental, vision, and life insurance benefits. Officers also receive a basic life insurance policy upon hire. If an officer is assigned to an Emergency Ordinance Demolition Unit, he or she is covered for up to $200,000 for death or dismemberment.

## Retirement

A police officer's retirement is covered under the Public Employee Retirement System (PERS), into which the city of Sacramento makes the contribution. You may also set up a deferred compensation plan in addition to the PERS fund; you contribute to this fund from your own paycheck. Unused portions of your monthly medical/dental/life allotment can be placed in this fund.

| SALARY: AT A GLANCE | | |
|---|---|---|
| POSITION | MONTHLY SALARY | AVERAGE ANNUAL SALARY |
| Police Cadet | $3,057 | NA |
| Police Officer | $4,015 – $4,880 | $50,592 – $61,500 |
| Sergeant | $5,043 – $6,130 | $64,812 – $78,780 |
| Lieutenant | $6,947 – 10,420 | $83,364 – $125,040 |
| Captain | $7,642 – $11,462 | $91,704 – $137,544 |

Note: *Figures supplied by the city of Sacramento Human Resources Department. For officer, sergeant, and lieutenant, range includes educational and certification incentives.*

# 10 ▶ Becoming a Police Officer in San Diego

## CHAPTER SUMMARY

This chapter describes in detail the selection process for becoming a police officer in San Diego. It offers the applicant useful information in such key areas as training, requirements and procedure, benefits, and initial assignment.

The city of San Diego Police Department, known as the SDPD, is the third-largest police department in the state of California. The San Diego Police Department has 2,064 sworn officers who believe responding to public demands takes more than just bandaging up chronic neighborhood crime problems. Instead, the department has opted to coordinate its own efforts with those of local citizens, community organizations, and governmental agencies to get to the roots of those problems. This philosophy has made the SDPD a forerunner in community policing.

In 1988, the Bureau of Justice selected San Diego as one of five cities to participate in a series of field studies using community policing in association with drug enforcement. One year later, the SDPD received an Innovation Award from the National League of Cities, applauding the police department's drug enforcement program.

Today, San Diego police officers seek to build trust and a rapport within the seven city districts by rotating traditional patrol squads with neighborhood police officers. Many local residents, groups, and agencies have partnered with the SDPD to prioritize and address community problems, including fire inspectors, the housing commission, the district attorney's office, churches, private businesses, and the parks and recreation department.

San Diego police officers face a challenging workload. In fact, the SDPD has one of the lowest officer per capita ratios in the nation. No longer are number of arrests, citations, and contacts the measure of an officer's performance. True to the SDPD's brand of problem-oriented policing, officers are encouraged and trained to direct their attention to looking for and solving existing beat problems.

The SDPD has developed the following definition of its vision as a police department and its mission to the community of San Diego:

*Vision: We are committed to working together, within the department, in a problem-solving partnership with communities, government agencies, private groups, and individuals to fight crime and improve the quality of life for the people of San Diego.*

*Mission: Our mission is to maintain peace and order by providing the highest quality police services in response to community needs by*

- *apprehending criminals.*
- *developing partnerships.*
- *respecting individuals.*

The principles of the San Diego Police Department are the following:

- Protection of Human Life
- Ethics
- Crime Fighting
- Valuing People
- Loyalty
- Open Communication
- Fairness
- Diversity

## ▶ Applying to Become a Police Officer in San Diego

### Minimum Requirements
To apply for the entry-level position of **police recruit** in San Diego, you must meet certain minimum requirements.

### Age
Candidates must be at least $20\frac{1}{2}$ years old at the time of the written examination and 21 at the time of graduation from the police academy.

### Citizenship
You must be a U.S. citizen or a permanent resident alien who is eligible and has applied for U.S. citizenship prior to filing an application with the SDPD.

### Driver's License
By the time of appointment, you must have obtained a valid California Class C (Class 3) driver's license.

### Education
You must have either a) a U.S. or U.S. territory high school diploma, b) a General Equivalency Diploma (GED), c) passed the California High School Exit Examination, or d) a two- or four-year degree from an accredited college or university.

### Vision
Candidates must have no visual conditions that would restrict their duties as a police officer. Specifically, you must have vision in both eyes, normal visual fields, normal binocular fusion, and no color vision deficiencies.

If you wear hard contacts, your uncorrected vision must be no worse than 20/70. If you wear soft contacts, there is no limit on uncorrected vision, but you must show documentation from your private eye doctor that you have successfully worn soft contacts for at least six months. In both cases, your vision must be correctable to 20/20.

Note that if you have had radial keratotomy or a similar procedure, you cannot be considered for a police officer position until one year has elapsed from your last surgery or "touch-up" procedure.

## ▶ Selection Process

To qualify for the position of **police recruit**, you must meet the minimum requirements, and successfully complete all the phases of the selection process:

1. The Application
2. Written Test

## Important Addresses and Phone Numbers

San Diego Police Department
1401 Broadway
San Diego, CA 92101-5729
619-531-2000
Note: Call the SDPD to get a mail stop number before sending correspondence to a particular unit within the department.

SDPD Recruiting
1401 Broadway,
Mail Stop #769
San Diego, CA 92101
619-531-2547

City of San Diego Personnel Department
Employment Information Center
1200 Third Avenue, Suite 300
San Diego, CA 92101-4107
619-236-6467
Monday, Wednesday, and Friday, 8:00 A.M. to 5:00 P.M.

Places to apply:
Employment Information Center
Civic Center Plaza
1200 Third Avenue, Suite 101-A
San Diego, CA 92101
619-236-6400
Monday, Wednesday, and Friday, 8:00 A.M. to 5:00 P.M.

San Diego Police Department
Personnel Office and Recruiting Unit
1401 Broadway, Mail Stop #769
San Diego, CA 92101
619-531-2547
Monday through Friday, 8:00 A.M. to 4:00 P.M.

For police department information, call
619-531-2677 (531-COPS).
For 24-hour job information, call 619-682-1011.
This recording is updated every two weeks.

---

3. Personal History Statement
4. Physical Ability Test
5. Background Investigation
6. Medical Exam and Psychological Evaluation

After all criteria have been met, candidates are placed on an eligibility list. It is from this list that the police academy selects new recruits.

The SDPD holds a recruiting seminar for candidates beginning the application process. This seminar provides an opportunity for you to ask questions about the written exam, the background investigation, and job opportunities with the department. You are given additional materials and information for the selection process, such as a personal history statement form, which forms the basis of the background investigation. For further information about the seminar, contact the recruiting unit.

### Step One: The Application

The San Diego Police Department does not have an open application procedure. You may apply for the position of police recruit only when a written examination has been scheduled. This exam has been administered on a monthly basis in the past, and applicants are advised to contact the SDPD recruiting unit for test dates and locations.

When you take the written test, you receive a packet that includes a personal history questionnaire. You submit this form to the department in lieu of a job application.

### Step Two: Written Test

The written test, when offered, is administered to applicants on a walk-in basis. It is recommended that you arrive at the test location two hours prior to test time. If you cannot get into the test because of a high number of other applicants, you can reserve a spot for yourself in the next exam by requesting a written test reservation card from the recruiting unit. This card is available approximately one month prior to the scheduled test date and is distributed on a first-come, first-served basis. The availability of these cards may be discontinued with a five-day notice, so it is recommended that you apply for the card promptly.

If you need to obtain a written test card by mail, send your request and a business-sized, self-addressed stamped envelope to the city of San Diego Personnel Office's Employment Information Center at the address previously listed.

The written test is a general aptitude assessment, which requires no prior knowledge of police work or law enforcement.

Part one of the test evaluates your logic, observation, and map reading skills. You are asked to recall specific details of information that is presented visually; to identify important elements in a situation and to choose a course of action based on general guidelines and policies; and to locate map destinations, follow written directions, and determine routes using a map or map index.

Part two tests your ability to read, understand, and interpret information presented in various written formats. It also evaluates your written communication skills, such as English grammar, spelling, punctuation, and written expression.

Parts one and two are graded separately, but applicants must pass both parts to qualify for the eligibility list. You will receive a police recruit *Notice of Test Results* by mail. If you do not pass the written test, you may apply to be retested six months after the date of your test.

If you pass the written test and your eligibility expires, you do not need to take the police recruit written test again. To be reinstated on the eligibility list, you may submit a written test waiver application along with a copy of your *Notice of Test Results* from your written exam to the recruiting unit.

If you already have a California basic POST certificate, you may be waived from the written exam by submitting a waiver application with a copy of your certificate. (A California basic POST certificate verifies

that you have graduated from a police academy and, in most cities, have successfully completed a field training program and probationary period. Some police departments in California require two years' patrol experience for certification.)

## Step Three: Personal History Statement

You are provided with the personal history statement form and instructions on how to complete it during the police department's recruiting seminar. It asks you to provide a summary of your employment, financial, driving, educational, and related history, and forms the basis of the background investigation. However, you will need to complete the personal history statement only if you have passed or have been waived from the written test. Note that the personal history statement is not the same document as the personal history questionnaire.

If the review of your personal history statement results in a positive recommendation, you may continue to the next phases of the application process.

## Step Four: Physical Ability Test

This test simulates the physical demands of police work. It consists of an obstacle course, which evaluates your ability to perform maneuvers that would be required in pursuit of a suspect. The course is 500 yards long and consists of the following:

- dodging low-hanging objects
- climbing ladders and stairs
- running through a series of pylons
- jumping, stepping, and/or climbing over three-foot, four-foot, and six-foot fences
- lifting and dragging a 155-pound dummy

You must wear a three-pound vest while performing the physical ability test. Wear comfortable athletic shoes with gripping rubber soles and shorts or loose-fitting clothing that does not restrict movement.

If you are not in good physical condition, the SDPD recommends that you undertake a program to improve the areas in which you will be tested. The SDPD also suggests that candidates visit their physician prior to beginning a physical exercise program.

If you do not pass the physical ability test, you may ask to be retested at a later date. Unless you pass the physical test, you will not be allowed to complete the selection process.

After the physical ability test, you will be given a preinvestigative questionnaire (PIQ), which is the beginning of the background investigation.

### Step Five: Background Investigation

During the selection process, an investigation is conducted on your personal, credit, employment, criminal, and driving history. This investigation is based on the personal history statement you are given at the recruiting seminar. You are asked to give individuals and organizations permission to release and verify relevant information about you. The background investigator contacts references and names you have provided of relatives and prior employers. An in-depth background interview with a police department investigator follows during which you are fingerprinted. The answers you provide in the background investigation are verified in a polygraph test.

If you have questions about aspects of your background, San Diego Police Recruiting Unit recommends that you contact the Background Investigation Unit for further assistance.

### Step Six: Medical Exam and Psychological Evaluation

Before you are hired as a police recruit, you must pass a complete medical examination, which includes a drug screening. The medical exam verifies that you are in good enough health to perform all aspects of police work on a regular basis. Your vision is also tested at this time.

If you successfully complete all phases of the selection process, your name is placed on an eligibility list. The police department consults this list for new recruits as positions open in the department.

## ▶ Training

As a police recruit, you attend the San Diego Regional Law Enforcement Training Center (police academy), located on the Miramar College campus. Once accepted by the police academy, you become a paid employee of the city of San Diego. You earn 20 college semester units by completing this training.

The academy training totals 32 weeks. The curriculum consists of classroom lectures on law enforcement, demonstrations, and six weeks of field training. You are required to read textbooks and articles on police work, complete homework assignments, write reports, and pass tests on academy materials. Among the subjects covered in the training are the following:

- Principles of Law Enforcement
- Criminal Law
- Rules of Evidence
- Search and Seizure
- Laws of Arrest
- Traffic Laws
- Juvenile Laws
- Control Methods
- First Aid
- Use and Maintenance of Firearms
- Patrol Theory and Methods
- Criminal Justice System
- Physical Conditioning
- Self-Defense

### Initial Assignment

Upon graduation from the academy, you are sworn in as a police officer I. Graduates immediately begin a 12-week field training program under the supervision of experienced field training officers. You must complete a one-year probationary period, at the end of which you receive a basic California POST certificate.

## ▶ Salary and Benefits

The chart that follows lists monthly and annual salaries for different ranks within the police department.

### Foreign Language Incentive

If you have bilingual skills, you are paid an additional foreign language incentive.

### Educational Incentives

Officers who hold an Intermediate California POST certificate receive an additional educational incentive per month; an advanced certificate earns you a larger educational incentive per month.

(After earning a basic POST certificate, officers who meet additional requirements are eligible for an intermediate or advanced certificate. An intermediate certificate is awarded to officers with a minimum of two years' patrol experience and a bachelor's degree, or four years' experience and an associate's degree. Advanced certificates are earned with a) at least four years' experience and a master's degree, b) six years' experience and a bachelor's degree, or c) nine years' experience and an associate's degree. Officers who do not have college degrees may earn these certificates on the basis of training, patrol experience, and related education.)

### Vacation

During your first through fifth year of service, you are allowed 17 paid vacation days; from the sixth to 15th year, you have 22 days paid vacation; after 16 years on the force, you are given 27 days of paid vacation. Vacation time includes all absences, personal days, and sick days.

### Holidays

Officers are given 12 holidays per year.

### Uniform and Equipment Allowance

A basic uniform and equipment allowance is allotted for the year.

### Health Coverage

The city of San Diego offers a "cafeteria-style" plan, from which officers may choose medical, life, dental, and vision care.

### Retirement

You may retire at the age of 50 with at least 20 years of service, or at the age of 55 with at least ten years of service. Officers contribute to their own retirement fund. The annual retirement compensation you receive is calculated based on your age, years of service, and salary level while on the force.

| SALARY: AT A GLANCE | | |
| --- | --- | --- |
| **POSITION** | **MONTHLY SALARY** | **AVERAGE ANNUAL SALARY** |
| Police Recruit | $3,103 – $3,738 | NA |
| Police Officer I | $3,646 – $4,400 | $48,276 |
| Police Officer II | $4,651 – $5,620 | $61,626 |
| Police Agent | $4,875 – $5,896 | $64,626 |
| Sergeant | $5,646 – $6,825 | $74,826 |
| Lieutenant | $7,221 – $8,648 | $95,214 |
| Captain | $8,575 – $10,272 | $113,082 |

Note: *Figures supplied by the San Diego Personnel Office.*

# 11 ▶ Becoming a Police Officer in San Francisco

## CHAPTER SUMMARY

This chapter describes in detail the selection process for becoming a police officer in San Francisco. It offers the applicant useful information in such key areas as training, requirements and procedures, salary and benefits, and initial assignment.

**T**he city of San Francisco Police Department, known as the SFPD, is the second-largest police department in the state of California with 2,227 sworn officers. San Francisco is the quintessential urban environment, with high population density and cultural and economic diversity. The goal of the San Francisco Police Department is to stay current and proactive on the trends affecting the city's residents.

As with many cities, homelessness has long been a problem in San Francisco. San Francisco police were used to enforce the "no camping" policy in Golden Gate Park. In order to implement the policy fully while remaining sensitive to the needs of the homeless population, officers received training from the various governmental and private agencies that serve and provide benefits to homeless citizens. As a result, police officers are now capable of referring homeless men and women to organizations that can help provide housing, food, and temporary employment.

The issue of gangs and gang violence is also near the top of the department's priority list. San Francisco was one of the first cities in the nation to investigate gangs as organized crime entities, and today the department provides intensive training to officers to allow them to stay abreast of constantly changing and evolving gang crime techniques and methodology.

The SFPD also turned its attention to the growing problem of domestic violence. Officers receive training on spotting "hot" situations and how to prevent heated domestic arguments from turning into more serious crimes. The department credits the concentrated effort and community involvement of several women's advocacy groups for helping formulate new domestic violence policies.

The San Francisco Police Department has developed the following statement of purpose to express its commitment to serving the community:

*We, the members of the San Francisco Police Department, are committed to excellence in law enforcement and are dedicated to the people, traditions, and diversity of our city. In order to protect life and property, prevent crime, and reduce the fear of crime, we will provide service with understanding, response with compassion, performance with integrity, and law enforcement with vision.*

## ▶ Applying to Become a Police Officer in San Francisco

### Minimum Requirements

To be appointed as a San Francisco police officer, you must meet the following minimum requirements.

### Age

You must be at least 20 years old on or before the date of the written examination and 21 to be accepted into the police academy. There is no maximum age limit.

### Citizenship

If you are a permanent resident alien, you may participate in the selection process, but you must be a U.S. citizen to be appointed as a police officer.

### Driver's License

You must have a valid California driver's license by the time of your appointment as a police officer. You are requested to give a summary of your driving history on your application and background forms. For disqualifying driving offenses, see step seven "Background Investigation."

### Criminal Record

According to the California Penal Code and the Police Officer Standards and Training (POST) administrative manual, you must not have been convicted of a) a felony in the state of California or have committed an act that would be a felony in any other state, or b) any misdemeanor that would prevent your carrying, possessing, or control of a firearm.

### Education

You must have a high school diploma or a General Equivalency Diploma (GED). The minimum acceptable score on the GED is an overall score of 45, with no single score under 35.

### Use of Illegal Controlled Substances

Any use of illegal controlled substances after you have begun the application process is mandatory cause for rejection. Your prior use is explored in detail in the background investigation and reviewed during the polygraph examination. Any abuse of illegal controlled substances, prescribed medications, or alcohol is unacceptable. See step seven, "Background Investigation," for additional drug-related factors that may disqualify you from the process.

### Health and Medical

Both your present and past medical conditions are evaluated to determine that you meet the necessary standards to perform police duties. Because of the physical demands and stress of the job, you must be free from such problems as spinal abnormalities and cardiac conditions. Your height/weight proportions must conform to the guidelines set by the SFPD and police surgeon.

## ▶ Selection Process

The selection process for becoming a San Francisco police officer is comprised of a three-part examination and a background investigation. These evaluate a candidate's abilities and suitability for law enforcement

Police Department of the City
and County of San Francisco
Thomas J. Cahill Hall of Justice
850 Bryant Street
San Francisco, CA 94103
General number 415-553-1551

Recruitment and Retainment
850 Bryant Street Room 577-17
San Francisco, CA 94103
415-401-4470

City and County of San Francisco
Civil Service Commission
Recruitment and Selection Division
44 Gough Street
San Francisco, CA 94103
415-557-4800

Note: The city and county of San Francisco are one and the same. San Francisco is a municipality whose city limits coincide with the boundary of San Francisco County.

---

work. You do not need prior police or legal knowledge any part of the process. Candidates who pass the written examination and the oral interview are placed on an eligibility list. Their place on that list is *not official* until all phases of the selection process have been successfully completed. The final eligibility list may be in rank order or in alphabetical order. Police academy recruits are selected from this eligibility list.

The steps of the selection process occur in this order:

1. The Application
2. Written Examination
3. Oral Interview
4. Physical Agility Test
5. Psychological Evaluation
6. Medical Exam
7. Background Investigation

The recruitment and retention unit offers pre-examination practice sessions for all stages of the application process. You may contact a representative in this division at the phone number and address listed at the beginning of this chapter.

### Step One: The Application

Your first step in the selection process is to obtain a pre-application interest card and pre-application checklist. These are available from the recruitment and retention

unit. Mail the completed card and checklist to the SFPD Examination Unit. You are notified by mail of the date and location of the next written examination and the application deadline.

You might find it easier to apply online. You can find detailed instructions and the online application form at wwwsfgov.org/site/police_index.asp?id=27860.

### Step Two: Written Examination

This is a standardized California POST exam, which evaluates your reading comprehension and writing skills, English grammar, spelling, and vocabulary. It may be scored on a pass/fail or weighted basis. If you pass the written test, you are scheduled for your oral interview. Applicants who do not pass the written test are disqualified and must wait at least one year before taking the test again.

At the time of the written test, you receive a personal history questionnaire to fill out. This form provides information to the police department for your background investigation.

### Step Three: Oral Interview

The oral interview assesses such communication skills as listening and speaking. It also tests your ability to make common-sense decisions in hypothetical, police-like scenarios. Your responses determine your score in this interview, which may be either pass/fail or weighted.

## Step Four: Physical Agility Test

The physical ability test determines your ability to perform the physical maneuvers necessary for police work. You will be notified prior to the test of what this exam involves. In general, it measures your manual dexterity and your ability to run, jump, and lift. The physical ability test is scored on a pass/fail basis. If you do not pass the physical ability test, your name will remain on the eligibility list, and you will have two more chances to take the test.

If you are pregnant or temporarily disabled, you may request a deferral to take the physical ability test at a later time. Medical verification of your condition must be provided to be deferred.

The police department does not guarantee that the physical agility test will be offered more than three times within the application period.

Candidates who successfully complete the three-part examination continue into the next phases of the selection process.

## Step Five: Psychological Evaluation

This evaluation determines if your personality is compatible with a career in law enforcement. Candidates take a series of written tests and attend a clinical interview with a department-appointed psychologist. The interview is based on results from the written psychological tests and factors from your background.

## Step Six: Medical Exam

A complete medical exam is conducted by the Center for Municipal Occupational Safety and Health. You must meet the standards of the medical examination to be considered for the position of police officer.

Your vision is also tested in this exam. All candidates must have entirely full visual fields and no color blindness. If you wear eyeglasses or hard contact lenses, your uncorrected binocular vision must be at least 20/100. If you have successfully worn soft contact lenses for at least six months, there is no minimum uncorrected vision standard to be met. In either case, your vision must be correctable to at least 20/30.

## Step Seven: Background Investigation

A thorough investigation is conducted on your employment, educational, financial, criminal, and driving history. You are also required to take a polygraph test. Before this investigation begins, you must complete the personal history questionnaire given to you when you take the written exam.

According to the office of the chief of police, the SFPD places special emphasis on an applicant's prior drug use in the background investigation. The information you give in the background investigation is verified in a polygraph test. The office of the chief has compiled a list of factors that disqualify applicants who have had prior involvement with controlled substances. You will be disqualified for the following:

- use of an illegal controlled substance other than marijuana within five years of filing an application for peace officer with the SFPD
- use of marijuana within one year of filing application
- use of a mind-altering hallucinogenic drug or any of its derivatives more than ten times and/or within five years of filing application
- use of heroin, its derivatives, or any type of synthetic heroin
- use of cocaine more than ten times and/or within five years of filing application
- use of amphetamines or any of their derivatives without prescription more than ten times and/or within five years of filing application
- use of any nonprescription anabolic steroids within five years of filing application and/or had prolonged use of them
- history or pattern of extensive use or abuse of controlled substances
- history of extensive use or abuse of alcohol without corresponding evidence of rehabilitation
- sale, furnishing, or distribution of any illegal controlled substance or anabolic steroids
- cultivation or manufacture any controlled substance

- use, sale, or transportation of an illegal controlled substance at their place of employment within five years of filing application

Other factors that may disqualify you from the selection process are as follows:

- withholding information on, misstating, or lying about your background
- felony conviction or convictions that the state of California categorizes as felonies
- conviction of drunk driving or hit-and-run driving with personal injury or property damage over $25
- three moving violations in the last three years or two moving violations within the last two years
- a driver's license that has been suspended within one year of the written test, or if you are on negligent operator probation or have been convicted of operating a vehicle unsafely

When the psychological evaluation, medical exam, and background investigation are successfully completed, an employment recommendation is made to the department hiring committee. If the committee approves your recommendation, you may be offered an appointment to the police academy.

## ▶ Special Notes on the Selection Process

1. If you are disqualified, you may reapply for the position of police officer, although you must wait at least one year after the date of your written examination with the following exceptions:
   - If you are disqualified from the process based on background information or the psychological evaluation, you must wait two years from the date of disqualification before applying to take the written examination.
   - If your disqualification is because of medical problems that cannot be corrected, an unacceptable criminal record, or substance abuse problems, you cannot reapply to become a police officer.

2. Candidates must pass the written and oral examinations.

3. The medical exam, vision testing, psychological screening, polygraph, and background investigation may not be administered to all candidates. In order to fill police academy classes, a random selection process may be used to choose among candidates who have passed the written and oral examinations.

4. The police department may specify that certain positions be offered only to candidates who meet specific bilingual requirements.

5. The consent decree division reserves the right to limit or prohibit the use of waivers. (A consent decree is an instance where an applicant is hired under a certain set of guidelines, usually by court order and to fill a quota of minority employees.)

6. The eligibility list created by the examination process is valid for two years from its date of inception; however, the list may be subject to cancellation if the pool of minority candidates is exhausted before the list's expiration date.

7. If you are disabled and require special accommodation during any phase of the examination, it is recommended that you contact the SFPD Examination Unit as soon as possible at 415-553-1805.

8. If you have a change in your name or address, you must submit the appropriate form to the examination unit. Failure to inform the department of these changes may result in disqualification.

9. Military veterans who served before 1973 and received their first separation within the last ten years may claim veteran's preference. Veterans may receive additional consideration from the department. You must submit a copy of your

DD214 (proof of service) form to claim veterans' preference.

## ▶ Training

When you have successfully completed all phases of the selection process and are chosen from the eligibility list, you then begin training at the police academy. While attending the academy, you hold a paid, temporary position of recruit officer with the city of San Francisco.

The police academy is located in San Francisco. The training lasts 18 weeks, and classes are held eight hours a day, five days a week. It covers all areas of police work, including the following:

- Applications of Police Law and Procedure
- Report Writing
- Investigation Procedures
- Physical Fitness
- Firearms and Police Equipment Training
- Police Driving
- Cultural Diversity

The academy provides recruits extra help with their studies if they need it.

### Initial Assignment

Upon graduation from the police academy, you are sworn in as a police officer. You then complete 12 weeks of field training at various stations in San Francisco, gaining practical patrol experience with other officers. After you successfully complete your field training, you are given a regular patrol assignment as a full-duty police officer. Your probation ends after you have served one year as a full-duty officer, and at that time you receive your basic POST certificate.

## ▶ Salary and Benefits

The chart on page 93 lists monthly and annual salaries for different ranks within the police department.

### Vacation

Officers are entitled to ten paid vacation days a year during their first five years of service and 15 days per year for the next 10 years. After 15 years of service, officers receive 20 days of paid vacation.

### Uniform and Equipment Allowance

You receive an annual allowance of $630 for uniforms and equipment.

### Sick Leave

Officers earn 13 paid sick days per year.

### Health Coverage

You may choose from a variety of health plans.

### Retirement

Employees of the city and county of San Francisco are covered under San Francisco's retirement plan. You may retire after 25 years of service with 50% of your salary. If you choose to stay on the force beyond 25 years, your retirement benefits will include an extra 3% of your salary for each additional year. The maximum amount paid for retirement is 70% of your salary.

If you serve at least five years on the force, you are eligible for retirement benefits from the city. You have the option to leave that money in the system until the age of 50, with the principle amount increasing by 2% each year. This plan also reinstates your health insurance at the age of 50.

| SALARY: AT A GLANCE | | |
| --- | --- | --- |
| **POSITION** | **MONTHLY SALARY** | **AVERAGE ANNUAL SALARY** |
| Recruit Officer | $4,808 – $6,619 | $68,562 |
| Police Officer 2 | $5,001 – $6,881 | $71,292 |
| Police Officer 3 | $5,100 – $7,018 | $72,708 |
| Inspector | $7,770 – $8,145 | $95,490 |
| Sergeant | $7,770 – $8,145 | $95,490 |
| Lieutenant | $8,873 – $9,302 | $109,050 |
| Captain | $10,417 – $10,920 | $128,022 |

Note: *Figures supplied by the San Francisco Police Personnel Payroll Office.*

# 12 ▶ Becoming a Police Officer in San Jose

## CHAPTER SUMMARY

This chapter describes in detail the selection process for becoming a police officer in San Jose. It offers the applicant useful information in such key areas as training, requirements and procedures, salary and benefits, and initial assignment.

The city of San Jose Police Department, known as the SJPD, is the fourth-largest police department in the state of California with 1,342 sworn officers. San Jose sits in the heart of the computer-rich Silicon Valley, some 40 miles south of San Francisco. The city's population is a mix of highly educated and members of a high-tech business community, who share the sidewalks and streets with members of diverse economic and ethnic groups attracted by good wages and the promise of steady employment. To better serve this constituency, the SJPD is placing ever-greater emphasis on officer education and citizen involvement.

Drawing from the high-tech nature of its community, the San Jose Police Department offers a number of computer and law enforcement network training programs. The department is also taking part in a grant program to test a computer dispatch system in which officers carry a laptop computer into the field.

San Jose police officials work closely with citizens and business leaders to protect valuable commercial and home inventories from burglary. Police officers have assisted companies in their private security patrols and have advised companies on their termination procedures to offset possible security breaches from ex-employees.

A citizen volunteer program increases the scope of community served by the police department. One community group, for instance, helps enforce a curfew program that police officials credit with reducing gang activity.

The San Jose Police Department has developed the following statement to express its vision, values, and mission to the San Jose community:

*The San Jose Police Department is a dynamic, progressive, and professional organization dedicated to maintaining community partnerships that promote a high quality of life for the city's diverse population. The department is committed to treating all people with dignity, fairness, and respect, protecting their rights and providing equal protection under the law.*

In particular, the San Jose Police Department's mission is to:

1. promote public safety.
2. prevent, suppress and investigate crimes.
3. provide emergency and nonemergency services.
4. create and maintain strong community partnerships.
5. adapt a multidisciplinary approach to solving community problems.
6. develop and promote a diverse, professional workforce.

The values considered important by the Department are the following:

- Integrity
- Courage
- Service
- Innovation
- Respect
- Diversity
- Excellence

## ▶ Applying to Become a Police Officer in San Jose

### Minimum Requirements

To apply for the entry-level position of **police recruit** in San Jose, you must meet the following minimum requirements:

- You must be at least $20\frac{1}{2}$ years old at the time of the written examination.
- You must have completed a minimum of 40 college *semester* units, or 60 college *quarter* units at the time of application. (Note that three quarter units equal two semester units.)
- You must be a U.S. citizen or eligible to work in the United States. You must obtain citizenship within three years of filing an application with the SJPD.
- You must possess a valid driver's license.
- Your vision must be at least 20/40 uncorrected.

It is your responsibility to ensure that the employment office receives your application and verification of education. If you have credits or units from a nonaccredited college, credits from a foreign college or university, or military education or experience, you must submit this information to the Educational Records Evaluation Service in Sacramento for evaluation. This office will provide you with documentation of the equivalent college units, and you must in turn provide this documentation to the San Jose employment office.

## ▶ Selection Process

The selection process for San Jose police recruits involves a series of examinations and interviews, which determine your suitability for police work. The steps of the process are as follows:

## Important Addresses and Phone Numbers

San Jose Human Resources
Department/Employment Office
200 E. Santa Clara Street
San Jose, CA 95113
408-535-1285
(mail applications to this address)
employee.services@sanjoseca.gov

San Jose Police Department
201 West Mission Street
San Jose, CA 95110
General number 408-277-5300
For the deaf and hearing impaired:
408-293-3323

Recruiting Office
408-277-4951

Backgrounds Section
408-277-4131

South Bay Regional Safety Training Center
(Police Academy)
3095 Yerba Buena Road
San Jose, CA 95135
408-270-6458

Educational Records Evaluation Service
(College Credentialing Service)
601 University Avenue #127
Sacramento, CA 95825
916-921-0793
edu@eres.com

---

1. The Application
2. Written Examination
3. Physical Agility Test
4. Oral Board Interview
5. Background Investigation
6. Medical Exam

Questions about the application process should be directed to 800-989-4445 or 408-227-4951.

### Step One: The Application
The application for the position of police recruit is available from the San Jose Human Resources Department in City Hall. Applications are available only when there is a scheduled date for the written examination. To find out when and where the next written examination will be held, contact the San Jose Police Department recruiting office.

## Important

Applicants who are fluent in English as well as Chinese, Korean, Spanish, Vietnamese, Cambodian, or Filipino may be given special hiring considerations.

You must notify the human resources department if your address changes during any phase of the selection process.

### Step Two: Written Examination
The written test evaluates your ability to read and write clearly; to understand laws, ordinances, and procedures; to learn police academy subjects; and to analyze situations and judge effective courses of action. Your communication skills, such as your ability to interact well with others and to understand and follow written and oral instructions are tested. Your basic logic skills are also assessed, such as

- determining relevant details in a given situation.
- organizing and planning.
- recognizing potential danger.
- utilizing city street maps.

### Step Three: Physical Agility Test

This test evaluates your ability to perform the physical maneuvers necessary in police work. To pass the physical agility test, you must successfully complete the following events:

- run $1\frac{1}{2}$ miles in less than 14 minutes
- climb a six-foot wall in 17 seconds or less
- lift and drag an 85-pound dummy for a certain distance in 33 seconds or less
- perform a foot pursuit in 25 seconds or less

### Step Four: Oral Board Interview

This interview consists of job-related questions. You are interviewed by an analyst from the human resources department, a sergeant from the recruiting unit, and a member of the community of San Jose. Interviewers look for personality attributes common among effective police officers, such as

- compassion.
- the ability to use sound judgment based on given information.
- understanding.

Upon successful completion of the written exam, physical agility test, and oral board interview, you qualify for a place on an eligibility list. The police department selects recruits whose scores rank in the top ten score bands on the list; therefore, the higher you score, the better chance you may have of getting the job. (A "score band" is a compilation of identical, rounded, whole number scores.) However, you must pass all steps of the selection process before you are hired by the department.

### Step Five: Background Investigation

After you have passed the written and oral exams and the physical agility test, an extensive background investigation is conducted on your work, education, driving, financial, criminal, and related history. Information you supply about your past is verified in a polygraph test. Your fingerprints are also taken for the background investigation.

The city of San Jose recommends you consider the following questions to assess yourself on your suitability as a law enforcement officer. Answering yes to any of these questions, however, does not automatically disqualify you from the selection process.

1. Have you ever been convicted or had involvement with any felony or other crime, either as an adult or as a juvenile, that would reflect negatively on the city of San Jose or deny you the ability to perform necessary duties as a police officer?
2. Do you have a history of negligent driving, such as driving under the influence of alcohol or drugs, having your license suspended or restricted, driving with an invalid license, or with no license at all?
3. Have you ever been forced to resign from, been terminated from, or failed your probationary period with any law enforcement agency?
4. Have you previously applied but been taken off any police officer eligibility list in any city, county, or other law enforcement agency?
5. Are you currently on probation for any offense, however minor, including traffic violations?
6. Have you used marijuana or narcotics (including abuse of prescribed drugs and medicine) within the last three years? (Your past use is evaluated on an individual basis. Failure to *disclose* prior use is cause for disqualification.)
7. Have you falsified any information on the required police recruit application or forms?

You must also take a psychological evaluation as part of the background investigation.

If you have questions about whether certain aspects of your background are disqualifying, the SJPD recruiting office suggests you contact their backgrounds section for further assistance.

## Step Six: Medical Exam

Prior to appointment, you must pass a complete medical exam. This exam determines that you are free from physical conditions that may impair your ability to perform all the duties of the job on a regular basis.

Your vision is tested during the medical exam. Your vision must be corrected to 20/20 in each eye with glasses, soft contact lenses, or radial keratotomy (RK) surgery. (Radial keratotomy is a laser procedure that corrects near-sighted vision.) You must have normal depth perception and no color vision deficiencies. You must have a minimum peripheral vision field of 70. If you have any questions about the medical exam or the department's vision requirements, the city of San Jose suggests you contact the city's Medical Services Office at 408-277-4177.

## ▶ Training

If you successfully complete all the phases of the selection process and your name is chosen from the eligibility list by the police department, you attend the police academy. Once accepted by the police academy, you become a paid employee of the city of San Jose. Police academy training, which lasts from five to six months, covers all areas of police work, including the following:

- Criminal Law
- Vehicle Operations
- Search and Seizure
- Firearms
- Cultural Diversity
- Preliminary Investigation
- Traffic
- Physical Fitness and Stress Management
- Self-Defense

## Initial Assignment

Upon graduation from the academy, you receive a California basic POST certificate. Graduates immediately begin a field training program as a police officer. An officer's field training is not assigned a specific time limit; it may be abbreviated or extended, depending on how quickly training is completed.

After successfully completing field training, you are given a regular patrol assignment and serve for one year as a probationary officer.

## ▶ Salary and Benefits

The chart on page 100 lists monthly and annual salaries for different ranks within the police department.

## Foreign Language Incentive

You receive an additional foreign language incentive biweekly if you are fluent in both English and one of the following languages: Spanish, Vietnamese, Chinese, Korean, Cambodian, or Filipino.

## Educational Incentive

If you have a bachelor's degree and have served at least eight years on the force, you receive up to a percentage of your base pay in educational incentives. Officers who have at least 60 college credits receive the same incentive after ten years of service.

## Holidays

Officers are entitled to paid holidays per year and are compensated a percentage of their base pay for working on holidays.

## Uniform and Equipment Allowance

Officers receive an annual allowance for uniforms and equipment.

## Sick Leave

Officers are entitled to paid sick leave.

## Vacation

Paid vacation entitlements are as follows:

- One to five years of service = 80 hours vacation
- Six to ten years = 120 hours vacation
- 11 to 12 years = 140 hours vacation
- 13 to 14 years = 160 hours vacation
- 15 years and above = 180 hours vacation

## Health Insurance

You may choose from a variety of health plans, which include dental coverage.

## Retirement

The city contributes 22.24% of your base salary into your retirement fund and you contribute 9.3% of your base salary into your retirement fund.

If you have 25 years of service, you may retire at age 50; with 20 years of service, you may retire at age 55; after 30 years of service, you may retire at any age, up to the mandatory retirement age 70. You will receive a service retirement allowance of 3% of your 12 consecutive highest-paying months multiplied by years of service on the force. The maximum amount you can receive for retirement is 75% of your normal full pay. If you choose to retire early, at age 50 to 54 with 20 years of service, you will receive a discounted pension.

| SALARY: AT A GLANCE | | |
|---|---|---|
| **POSITION** | **MONTHLY SALARY** | **AVERAGE ANNUAL SALARY** |
| Police Recruit | $4,749 | NA |
| Police Officer | $4,4994 – $6,687 | $70,086 |
| Sergeant | $6,370 – $7,743 | $84,678 |
| Lieutenant | $7,375 – 8,967 | $98,052 |
| Captain | $8,537 – $10,376 | $113,478 |

Note: *Figures supplied by the San Jose Employee Office.*

# 13 ▶ California Police Officer Application Forms

I f you want to know what police departments will ask of you when you first apply for a job as a police officer, you've turned to the right place. Starting on the next page, you'll find reprints of actual application forms for California cities featured in the previous chapters.

These are not applications that you can submit to the various police departments represented; you'll need to get the real thing from the appropriate department when you're ready to apply. Most forms are available via the Internet. Meanwhile, you can read through these copies to find out what sort of personal data you'll be asked to provide—and to practice filling out the application.

This initial application form is often provided by a city's Civil Service Department or Human Relations Department and is usually a relatively brief questionnaire. Remember that this is followed later in the selection process by a lengthy and detailed personal history statement. Also, be sure to always check on the deadline for filing an application, which is often several weeks before the police exam.

Finally, it's important to fill out your application honestly and completely—not to mention neatly! After all, this is the way you'll introduce yourself to your potential employer. It's how you get your foot in the door—and how police departments decide whether you can come in a little farther. In other words, never underestimate the power of this piece of paper. It's a key part of the employment process.

City of **FRESNO**

# Application for Employment

Equal Opportunity Employer
Personnel Department
Human Resources Division

2600 Fresno Street, First Floor
Fresno, California 93721-3614
Phone (559) 621-6950

## Application Acceptance Policy

A complete application is required for each exam. Every applicable blank must be filled to insure proper evaluation. In item #5, do not refer to resumes or previously submitted applications. Resumes are viewed as additional information and will not be used to evaluate minimum requirements.

### DEPARTMENT USE ONLY

| | |
|---|---|
| Received by | Veterans Credit |
| Approved by | Rejected by |
| Reason: | |

**Notices mailed**

| Grade | List # |
|---|---|

## Application must be completed in ink or typewritten

**1. Name (print)**   Last   First   Middle

**2. Position applying for (Show exact title - Separate application required for each examination)**

**3. Mailing Address**   No. and Street or P.O. Box No.   Apt. No.

City and State   Zip Code

**4. *Social Security No.**   _____ — _____ — _____

Home Phone:

Alternate Phone:

E-mail:

*Use of your Social Security number is voluntary. Social Security numbers are used for identification purposes only. If you do not wish to use your Social Security number we will assign you an identification number.

## 5. Applicable Experience - List your current or most recent position first.

| | From / To | Job Info | Employer |
|---|---|---|---|
| **A** | Hours worked per week / From Month Day Yr. / To Month Day Yr. / Salary | Your Job Title: / Your Duties: | Employer's Name, Address and Telephone No. / Reason for Leaving: |
| **B** | Hours worked per week / From Month Day Yr. / To Month Day Yr. / Salary | Your Job Title: / Your Duties: | Employer's Name, Address and Telephone No. / Reason for Leaving: |
| **C** | Hours worked per week / From Month Day Yr. / To Month Day Yr. / Salary | Your Job Title: / Your Duties: | Employer's Name, Address and Telephone No. / Reason for Leaving: |
| **D** | Hours worked per week / From Month Day Yr. / To Month Day Yr. / Salary | Your Job Title: / Your Duties: | Employer's Name, Address and Telephone No. / Reason for Leaving: |
| **E** | Hours worked per week / From Month Day Yr. / To Month Day Yr. / Salary | Your Job Title: / Your Duties: | Employer's Name, Address and Telephone No. / Reason for Leaving: |

SEE REVERSE SIDE-USE ADDITIONAL SHEETS IF NECESSARY

**6. Have you ever been convicted or declared guilty of a misdemeanor or felony by any court?** YES ☐ NO ☐
If YES, give details in item 16. Conviction is not necessarily disqualifying. Each case will be evaluated on its own merits and its applicability to this position. FAILURE TO DISCLOSE THIS INFORMATION WILL BE CAUSE FOR DISQUALIFICATION, REMOVAL FROM LIST OR DISCHARGE FROM EMPLOYMENT.
You may omit:
**A.** Traffic violations for which the fine imposed was $100 or less. (Any Traffic violations over $100 must be shown.)
**B.** Any offense committed prior to your 18th birthday which was finally adjudicated in a juvenile court or under a youth offender law.
**C.** Any incident that has been sealed under Welfare and Institutions Code Section 781 or Penal Code Section 1203 45.
(If appointed, your fingerprints will be taken for a criminal history check. Certain positions may require a driving record check.)

**7. Have you ever been terminated from any employment or ever forced to resign?** YES ☐ NO ☐
If YES, give details in item 16.

**8. Are you now or have you ever been employed by the City of Fresno?** YES ☐ NO ☐
If YES, give details in item 16.

**9. Are you related by blood or marriage to any person presently employed by the City of Fresno?** YES ☐ NO ☐
If YES, give name, relationship, and department in which employed.

**10. Do you wish to apply for veterans credits?** YES ☐ NO ☐
If YES, acceptable documentary proof of U.S. military service Form DD214 must be submitted with this application during the filing period.

**11. Selective Service Registration.** Federal Law requires male U.S. citizens and aliens residing in the U.S. who are ages 18 through 25 to register with the Selective Service System.
**A.** I have registered with the Selective Service System. My Selective Service Number is _____ **(A copy of your Selective Service confirmation MUST be attached.)**
**B.** I am not required to register with the Selective Service System because I am exempt under the stated age/gender requirements.

**12. Did you graduate from High School, pass the State High School Equivalency Exam., or do you possess a G.E.D. High School level Certificate?** YES ☐ NO ☐
**A.** Name of High School _____
**B.** Location of School _____

**13. Colleges and Schools attended after high school.**

| Name and Location | Major | Total Units or Hours | Degrees Received |
|---|---|---|---|
| | | | |
| | | | |

**14. Driver's Lic. No.** _____ Expires _____
Completion of this question is required only if the position for which you are applying requires the possession of a valid California Driver's License.

**15. If you possess any license or certificate, give the following information:**
**A.** Title _____
**B.** License No. _____ Issuing State _____
Date Issued _____ Date Expires _____

**16. Additional Remarks: (Attach extra sheet if necessary)**

**17. We want to know how you heard about this position you are applying for:**
☐ Bulletin Board (Lobby)  ☐ Friend or Relative  ☐ Radio: which station? _____
☐ Job line  ☐ Newspaper: which one? _____  ☐ Other, please specify _____
☐ Job Announcement  ☐ Internet: which web site? _____

_____ Your Signature  _____ Date

R Code _____    CITY OF LONG BEACH    File# _____
CIVIL SERVICE
# POLICE RECRUIT APPLICATION

**This application will be held for future testing and information will be subject to verification.**

## PLEASE PRINT NEATLY OR TYPE

Social Security Number: _____ / _____ / _____

Name: _____
Last                          First                          Middle

Address: _____
Street and Number or P.O. Box (include apartment number if applicable)

_____
City and State                                                    Zip

Phone Number: ( ___ ) _____ Alternate Phone Number: ( ___ ) _____

NOTE: **In order to claim Veteran's Preference you must qualify under one of the following:**
1. **Served in the armed forces at least 181 days during the period of August 1, 1964 to May 7, 1975 and honorably discharged within the last 10 years.**
2. **Possess at least a 30% service connected disability certified by the VA.**
3. **Unremarried spouse of a deceased or disabled veteran.**

Are you claiming Veteran's Preference? [   ] YES    [   ] NO

Do you possess a valid driver's license? [   ] YES    [   ] NO

Are you 20 years of age or older? [   ] YES    [   ] NO

Are you a high school graduate? [   ] YES    [   ] NO    If you are not, have you passed the G.E.D. test? [   ] YES    [   ] NO

Have you ever worked for the City of Long Beach? _____ If yes, what department? _____ Dates: _____ to _____

Are you a U.S. citizen? [   ] YES    [   ] NO    If not, on what date did you apply for citizenship? _____ / _____ / _____

Have you ever been convicted of a crime? [   ] YES    [   ] NO    *If yes, give all facts on the reverse side.*

NOTE: *A conviction does not automatically mean you will not be hired. What you were convicted of and how long ago are important.*

*SIGNATURE:* _____    *DATE:* _____

IF YOU HAVE A DISABILITY WHICH MAY REQUIRE SPECIAL TESTING ARRANGEMENTS, YOU MUST CONTACT THE CIVIL SERVICE DEPARTMENT AT (310) 570-6202 PRIOR TO YOUR SCHEDULED EXAMINATION.

==================================For Civil Service Use Only==================================

Vet. YES [   ] NO [   ]    Documents Attached YES [   ]    Date rec'd: _____ / _____ / _____    Rec'd by: _____

Disqual. _____    DISPOSITION: _____

(PRAPPLTN.SPC)

# LONG BEACH CIVIL SERVICE EMPLOYMENT QUESTIONNAIRE

FILE #_____

TITLE OF POSITION APPLIED FOR: _____POLICE RECRUIT_____

SOCIAL SECURITY NUMBER: _____/___/_____

NAME: _____
(Print)   First        Middle Initial    Last

**ADDRESS: _____
         Number or P.O. Box   Street      Apt. #      City    State   Zip
**PLEASE FILL IN CORRECTLY AS THIS FORM WILL BE USED FOR MAILING INFORMATION PURPOSES.

HOME PHONE:(___)_____     ALTERNATE PHONE:(___)_____
=====================================================================

INSTRUCTIONS: The following information is voluntary and is requested for Federal statistical reports. This form will be separated from your application and maintained separately. It will NOT affect consideration of your application and will be kept confidential.

1. Ethnic Category (check ONE only)
   [ ] White
   [ ] African-American
   [ ] Hispanic/Latino: Mexican, Puerto Rican, Cuban, Central or South American or other
       Spanish origin or culture, regardless of race.
   [ ] Asian or Pacific Islander--Descendant of the people of the Far East, Southeast
       Asia, the Pacific Islands or the Indian sub-continent, including, for example,
       China, Japan, Korea, Samoa and the Philippine Islands.
   [ ] American Indian or Alaskan Native

2. Sex   [ ] Female      [ ] Male

3. While most positions are permanent, full-time, there are some which are part-time,
   temporary or require employees to work evening or night shifts. If you are willing and
   able to work these positions, please check below:
   [ ] Part-time    [ ] Temporary    [ ] Shifts (Evening/Night)

4. Recruitment Information: Check the box in front of the statement which best describes
   how you FIRST found out about this job opportunity.
   [ ] 1. Visit to Civil Service Dept.    [ ] 7. Journal/Newsletter:_____
   [ ] 2. Job Announcement                [ ] 8. Radio/TV:_____
   [ ] 3. Job Hotline                     [ ] 9. College/Trade School:_____
   [ ] 4. Long Beach City Employee        [ ] 10. Organization/Group:_____
   [ ] 5. Job/Career Fair:_____      [ ] 11. Other:_____
   [ ] 6. Newspaper:_____

5. If you are age 40 or more, please check this box. [ ] YES

6. If you have a disability, please check this box. [ ] YES

7. If you have a license to drive an automobile, please check this box. [ ] YES ____

8. If you are presently a City of Long Beach employee, please check this box. [ ] YES

9. If you claim Veterans Preference points, please check this box. [ ] YES ____
   (Submit a copy of your DD214 with your application.)

10. Please indicate below languages OTHER THAN ENGLISH which you speak.
    Conversational [ ]   Fluent [ ] Spanish
    Conversational [ ]   Fluent [ ] a Southeast Asian language
    Conversational [ ]   Fluent [ ] Other (please indicate)_____

(emplymtq.spc)

Downloadable Application

Form PDR--(Rev. 6/2004)

# APPLICATION FOR EMPLOYMENT

## CITY OF LOS ANGELES
### PERSONNEL DEPARTMENT
### AN EQUAL EMPLOYMENT OPPORTUNITY EMPLOYER

THIS PORTION OF THE APPLICATION IS NOT AVAILABLE TO AN INTERVIEW BOARD

| 1. CITY JOB (EXAMINATION) TITLE | 2. CLASS CODE NO. |
|---|---|

| 3. SOCIAL SECURITY NUMBER (See Instruction G) | 4. TYPE OF EXAMINATION (See Instruction B) ☐ OPEN ☐ PROMOTIONAL | (Mark only when specified on Examination Announcement) ☐ STATUS ☐ SPECIAL |
|---|---|---|

| 5. NAME: LAST | FIRST | MIDDLE |
|---|---|---|

| 6. PRESENT MAILING ADDRESS: NUMBER | STREET | APARTMENT | 6a. HOME PHONE — Area & Number |
|---|---|---|---|

| CITY | STATE | ZIP CODE | 7. WORK PHONE — Area & Number |
|---|---|---|---|

| 8. P.O. BOX NUMBER | CITY | 9. DRIVER'S LICENSE NUMBER | STATE | EXPIRATION DATE | 10. COMPLETE ONLY WHEN THE EXAMINATION ANNOUNCEMENT STATES AN AGE REQUIREMENT BIRTHDATE / MO. / DAY / YR. |
|---|---|---|---|---|---|

| 8a. STATE | ZIP CODE | 12. YOU WILL BE REQUIRED TO SUBMIT VERIFICATION OF THE LEGAL RIGHT TO WORK IN THE UNITED STATES WITHIN THREE (3) BUSINESS DAYS BEGINNING WITH YOUR FIRST DAY OF WORK. IN ACCORDANCE WITH THE IMMIGRATION REFORM AND CONTROL ACT OF 1986, WE ARE LEGALLY PROHIBITED FROM EMPLOYING ANYONE WHO CANNOT PROVIDE SUCH VERIFICATION. |
|---|---|---|

MARK ONLY WHEN REQUIRED BY THE EXAMINATION ANNOUNCEMENT
11. ARE YOU A UNITED STATES CITIZEN? ☐ YES ☐ NO

---

**RESEARCH AND SPECIAL DATA.** The City of Los Angeles is an Equal Employment Opportunity Employer. We request **voluntary** identification of your sex and ethnic/racial group and/or disability so that we can monitor the effectiveness of our Equal Employment Opportunity program. Completing sections 13, 14, 15 and 16 will not affect your employment.

**13. SEX**
☐ Male ☐ Female

**14. ETHNIC GROUP/RACE**
☐ Black (1)   ☐ Caucasian (4)
☐ Hispanic (2)   ☐ American Indian (5)
☐ Asian (3)   ☐ Filipino (7)

Reasonable Accommodations:
City examinations may include written tests, interviews, physical abilities tests or other processes. Reasonable accommodation will be provided to applicants who need assistance to participate in the selection process. Please review the Examination section of the Job Bulletin for the types of tests included in this examination.

15. Do you need a reasonable accommodation to participate in the selection process? YES ☐ NO ☐

16a. If Yes, please describe the desired accommodation:
_____

16.b Have you ever been granted an accommodation for a previous City examination? YES ☐ NO ☐

You will be contacted by telephone or by mail regarding your request for reasonable accommodation. If you have not previously done so, you will be required to provide written verification from an appropriate professional confirming your disability and appropriate accommodation. Verification forms may be obtained at the Personnel Dept. or by calling 213-847-9760.

17. RECRUITMENT RESEARCH: FOR OPEN CANDIDATES, PLEASE INDICATE WHERE YOU LEARNED ABOUT THIS JOB. CHECK ONE OR WRITE ANSWER:

☐ NOTIFICATION CARD (A)   ☐ FRIEND OR RELATIVE (B)   ☐ CITY BULLETIN BOARD (C)   ☐ CITY EMPLOYEE (D)
☐ NEWSPAPER AD (E)   ☐ CAREER DAY/JOB FAIR (F)   ☐ 24-HOUR JOBLINE (G)   ☐ CHANNEL 35 CITY VIEW (H)
☐ PERSONNEL DEPT. SATELLITE OFFICE (I)   ☐ INTERNET (J) - PLEASE LIST WEBSITE: _____   ☐ OTHER _____

---

**Applicants — Do not use the space below — For Personnel Department Use Only**

| STAFF | DATE |
|---|---|

**J K L M N O P Q R S T**

a
b
c
d
e
f
g
h
i
j
k

Dis. testing ☐ YES
Acc. Requested ☐ NO

| STAFF | DATE |
|---|---|

APPL. APPROVED

MIL. CREDIT

**Test Location A B C D E F**

U _____
V _____
W _____

continue on page 2          Page 1

**THIS PAGE OF THE APPLICATION IS NOT AVAILABLE TO AN INTERVIEW BOARD**

APPLICANTS – DO NOT DETACH THIS PAGE

18. May the Personnel Department contact **YOUR PAST EMPLOYERS** for references?
If YES, then read the following statements and sign your name on the line below. I authorize the City of Los Angeles Personnel Department to obtain employment information from any previous employer. A photostatic copy of this authorization will be considered to be as valid as the original.

☐ Yes
☐ No

Signature _____ Date: _____

May the Personnel Department contact **YOUR PRESENT EMPLOYER** for references?
If **YES**, then read the following statements and sign your name on the line below: I authorize the City of Los Angeles Personnel Department to obtain employment information from my current employer. A photostatic copy of this authorization will be considered to be as valid as the original.

☐ Yes
☐ No

Signature _____ Date: _____

19. Have you previously worked for the City of Los Angeles? If "yes", and you are not currently employed by the City, please complete the following:

☐ Yes
☐ No

FROM/TO: _____ Department/Class Title: _____

FROM/TO: _____ Department/Class Title: _____

20. Have you passed any examination given by the City of Los Angeles in the last two years?

☐ Yes
☐ No

If "yes", list examination titles and dates passed: _____

21. Have you ever been fired or asked to resign in order to avoid being fired from a job?

☐ Yes
☐ No

If "yes", please complete the following (List all cases except layoffs for lack of work. Attach additional sheet if necessary). (NOTE-**Promotional applicants** must list all **probationary terminations** while employed by the City but are not required to list terminations occurring prior to original City appointment if employed by the City for at least one year.):

Employer's Name and Address _____

Date and reason for discharge _____

22. Have you ever been CONVICTED of a MISDEMEANOR or FELONY other than minor traffic violations? A plea of "no lo contendere" has the same force and effect as a guilty plea, is considered a conviction, and must be disclosed. Have you ever been placed on probation, fined or given a suspended sentence in court? Include any convictions by military trial. List all cases other than minor traffic violations. (Driving under the influence, reckless or hit-and-run driving are **NOT** minor traffic violations.) Your fingerprints will, at some point, be sent to State and Federal agencies and all offers of employment or continued employment will be subject to satisfactory review of any criminal convictions. PLEASE NOTE: A full disclosure by you is to your advantage as (with the exception of a conviction or a plea of "no lo contendere" to either a felony or a misdemeanor for workers' compensation fraud) your record does not constitute an automatic bar to employment. Factors such as, but not limited to, age at time of offense(s) and recency of offense(s), as well as the relationship between the offense(s) and the job(s) for which you apply will be taken into account. HOWEVER, A CONVICTION FOR WORKERS' COMPENSATION FRAUD (either a felony or a misdemeanor) OR A PLEA OF "NO LO CONTENDERE" TO EITHER A FELONY OR A MISDEMEANOR FOR WORKERS' COMPENSATION FRAUD WILL RESULT IN YOUR DISQUALIFICATION FOR EMPLOYMENT WITH THE CITY OF LOS ANGELES. FAILURE TO ADMIT CONVICTIONS WILL ALSO RESULT IN DISQUALIFICATION. With the exception of a misdemeanor conviction for workers' compensation fraud, or a plea of "no lo contendere" to a misdemeanor for workers' compensation fraud, promotional applicants are not required to list misdemeanor convictions occurring prior to original appointment, if employed by the City for a least one year. However, you must still answer "yes", and list any felony conviction(s), regardless of when they occurred.

WRITE YES OR NO BELOW

22a. Have you ever been convicted of workers' compensation fraud as either a felony or as a misdemeanor? (A plea of "no lo contendere" is considered a conviction.) ☐ Yes ☐ No

23. List all convictions. **Attach additional sheet if necessary.** (Cite Penal Code if known.)

Offense: _____ Conviction Date: _____

Location: _____ Fine or Sentence: _____

Offense: _____ Conviction Date: _____

Location: _____ Fine or Sentence: _____

24. List names used in the past, including names used in other records:

25. <u>U.S. Military Service.</u> To receive military service credit of 5 points, allowed by City Charter Section 1006, veterans must have served on active duty in one of the periods authorized by the Personnel Department and have been released from active duty within the previous 5 years, or present evidence of a military service connected disability. **To receive such credit you must present proof of your honorable discharge and dates of active duty and/or proof of a military service connected disability along with your application to: Personnel Department, Employment Services Division, Room 100, 700 E. Temple Street, Los Angeles, CA 90012, at the time of filing.** This proof must be shown each time you file an application. <u>Military credit is allowed only in open examinations.</u>

continue on page 3

Page 2

| 26. CITY JOB (EXAMINATION) TITLE | 27. CLASS CODE NUMBER | 28. TYPE OF EXAMINATION (Same as Page 1, Space 4) |
|---|---|---|
| 29. PLEASE PRINT NAME — Last, First, Middle | 30. SOCIAL SECURITY NUMBER | ☐ OPEN  ☐ PROMOTIONAL ☐ STATUS  ☐ SPECIAL |

**HIGH SCHOOL EDUCATION:**

31a. DID YOU GRADUATE FROM HIGH SCHOOL OR PASS THE GED TEST?
☐ Yes  ☐ No (Answer 31b)

31b. IF UNDER 18 YEARS OF AGE, CAN YOU PROVIDE A WORK PERMIT OR A GED CERTIFICATE AFTER AN EMPLOYMENT OFFER IS MADE?
☐ Yes  ☐ No

32. SPECIAL TESTING INFORMATION IF REQUIRED IN THE EXAMINATION ANNOUNCEMENT INSTRUCTIONS:

33. ADDITIONAL EDUCATION: **ENTER REQUESTED INFORMATION IN ALL COLUMNS**

| NAME AND LOCATION OF UNIVERSITIES, COLLEGES OR TRADE SCHOOLS ATTENDED | COMPLETION DATES | UNITS COMPLETED SEMESTER QUARTER | MAJOR SUBJECT OR COURSE | UNITS COMPLETED IN MAJOR | TITLE OF DEGREE/ CERTIFICATE RECEIVED |
|---|---|---|---|---|---|
| | | | | | |
| | | | | | |
| | | | | | |
| | | | | | |

34. SPECIAL COURSES REQUIRED FOR THIS EXAMINATION:

Units Completed
Course Name:  Semester  Quarter  Name of School  Date Completed:

35. SPECIAL LICENSES REQUIRED FOR THIS EXAMINATION:
LICENSES:  DATE ISSUED:  ISSUING AGENCY:  EXPIRATION DATE:

36. LANGUAGE PROFICIENCY (OTHER THAN ENGLISH; INDICATE SPOKEN AND/OR WRITTEN) COMPLETE ONLY WHEN STATED ON EXAMINATION ANNOUNCEMENT

MARK ONLY WHEN REQUIRED BY THE EXAMINATION ANNOUNCEMENT.
37. SUPPLEMENTAL INFORMATION

(Attach additional sheet if necessary)

*APPLICANTS — DO NOT DETACH THIS PAGE*

**Read and complete below — Complete work experience on page 4**

The following statements are general conditions for employment. This application does not constitute an offer for employment, merely the opportunity to compete for the position. Your application is subject to review and may be rejected at any time if shown that you do not meet the qualifications specified in the bulletin for the position for which you are applying. Please read and initial the following three statements, and sign and date the application in Box 38. You **must** answer the work experience section on PAGE 4 for your application to be considered complete.

As a condition of employment for a safety-sensitive position, I may be required to undergo a drug and alcohol abuse screening test prior to appointment and I must meet background and medical standards as well.  _____ Initial Here

I also understand that this application, supplements and attachments become the property of the City of Los Angeles Personnel Department. No copies of these documents shall be made available to or provided to me until the entire examination is complete.  _____ Initial Here

I acknowledge my responsibility to comply with any court-ordered child support obligations and understand that as an employee of the City of Los Angeles, my name and any other pertinent information requested will be provided to the LA County District Attorney to assist in enforcement activities.  _____ Initial Here

I certify that all statements on this application form and attachments are true and complete to the best of my knowledge. I understand that false, misleading or incomplete information shall be sufficient cause for disqualification or dismissal and other penalties as may be prescribed by law.

| 38. SIGNATURE (Original in ink; pencil or photocopy not accepted. | DATE | PERFORMANCE (Do not use until instructed to do so) |
|---|---|---|
| COMPLETE THE WORK EXPERIENCE SECTION ON PAGE 4 | | INTERVIEW (Do not use until instructed to do so) |

continue on page 4

**39.** <u>WORK EXPERIENCE:</u> **BEGIN WITH YOUR MOST RECENT JOB - LIST EACH JOB SEPARATELY.** <u>List all jobs regardless of duration,</u> including part-time jobs, military service <u>and any periods of unemployment during the last ten years.</u> Also, list volunteer experience and jobs held more than ten years ago which relate to the job for which you are applying. **City employees must use the correct civil service class title.** If you have no work experience, indicate NONE. Please Note: **Incomplete information will delay the processing of your application.**

| DATES | | EMPLOYERS | DUTIES |
|---|---|---|---|
| MONTH AND YEAR: FROM | | NAME OF CURRENT OR LAST EMPLOYER | YOUR TITLE |
| TO | | ADDRESS (OR CITY DEPARTMENT) | DUTIES PERFORMED |
| TOTAL MOS. WORKED | HRS. PER WEEK | CITY, STATE AND ZIP CODE | |
| MONTHLY SALARY EARNED $ | | IMMEDIATE SUPERVISOR'S NAME | REASON FOR LEAVING |
| MONTH AND YEAR: FROM | | NAME OF FORMER EMPLOYER | YOUR TITLE |
| TO | | ADDRESS (OR CITY DEPARTMENT) | DUTIES PERFORMED |
| TOTAL MOS. WORKED | HRS. PER WEEK | CITY, STATE AND ZIP CODE | |
| MONTHLY SALARY EARNED $ | | IMMEDIATE SUPERVISOR'S NAME | REASON FOR LEAVING |
| MONTH AND YEAR: FROM | | NAME OF FORMER EMPLOYER | YOUR TITLE |
| TO | | ADDRESS (OR CITY DEPARTMENT) | DUTIES PERFORMED |
| TOTAL MOS. WORKED | HRS. PER WEEK | CITY, STATE AND ZIP CODE | |
| MONTHLY SALARY EARNED $ | | IMMEDIATE SUPERVISOR'S NAME | REASON FOR LEAVING |
| MONTH AND YEAR: FROM | | NAME OF FORMER EMPLOYER | YOUR TITLE |
| TO | | ADDRESS (OR CITY DEPARTMENT) | DUTIES PERFORMED |
| TOTAL MOS. WORKED | HRS. PER WEEK | CITY, STATE AND ZIP CODE | |
| MONTHLY SALARY EARNED $ | | IMMEDIATE SUPERVISOR'S NAME | REASON FOR LEAVING |
| MONTH AND YEAR: FROM | | NAME OF FORMER EMPLOYER | YOUR TITLE |
| TO | | ADDRESS (OR CITY DEPARTMENT) | DUTIES PERFORMED |
| TOTAL MOS. WORKED | HRS. PER WEEK | CITY, STATE AND ZIP CODE | |
| MONTHLY SALARY EARNED $ | | IMMEDIATE SUPERVISOR'S NAME | REASON FOR LEAVING |
| MONTH AND YEAR: FROM | | NAME OF FORMER EMPLOYER | YOUR TITLE |
| TO | | ADDRESS (OR CITY DEPARTMENT) | DUTIES PERFORMED |
| TOTAL MOS. WORKED | HRS. PER WEEK | CITY, STATE AND ZIP CODE | |
| MONTHLY SALARY EARNED $ | | IMMEDIATE SUPERVISOR'S NAME | REASON FOR LEAVING |
| MONTH AND YEAR: FROM | | NAME OF FORMER EMPLOYER | YOUR TITLE |
| TO | | ADDRESS (OR CITY DEPARTMENT) | DUTIES PERFORMED |
| TOTAL MOS. WORKED | HRS. PER WEEK | CITY, STATE AND ZIP CODE | |
| MONTHLY SALARY EARNED $ | | IMMEDIATE SUPERVISOR'S NAME | REASON FOR LEAVING |

APPLICANTS—DO NOT DETACH THIS PAGE

**IF MORE SPACE IS NEEDED ATTACH ADDITIONAL SHEETS**

Page 4

## Personnel Department, City of Los Angeles — APPLICATION INSTRUCTIONS

A.  Please fill out this application carefully on a typewriter or print in ink. No photostatic copy, fasimile (FAX) or resume in lieu of the original application form will be accepted. All questions must be answered completely and accurately, except items 13 – 16 (which are voluntary) or items 9 and 11 (which are completed only if specified in the examination announcement.) You may be disqualified for any false statement or for omitting information. We suggest you keep a copy of each application you file. You may not obtain a copy while the examination is in progress.

B.  You must file a separate application for each examination. Only Civil Service City employees who meet the definition of a **promotional** candidate may file for promotional examinations. All others must file as **open** candidates.

Employees who leave City service cannot be appointed from promotional eligible lists. Therefore, if an examination is being administered on both a Promotional and Open basis, Promotional candidates are encouraged to file separate applications on both an open and promotional basis. Do not file on a **status** or **special** basis, unless specified in the examination announcement.

C.  Your application MUST BE RECEIVED in Room 100, City Personnel Department, 700 East Temple Street, Los Angeles, CA 90012, by the last day to apply. If you change your address after applying, you must notify the Personnel Department in writing immediately.

D.  APPLYING BY MAIL - If you wish, you may file your application by mail unless otherwise specified by the examination bulletin. Be certain that you answer all questions on the application. Your application must be received, not post-marked, by the last day to apply. It is the applicant's responsibility to allow adequate mail or delivery time. Late applications will be disqualified.

E.  **ACCEPTANCE - Applicants who fail to submit all required information will not be considered for employment. All applications are accepted on a tentative basis subject to a later review of your employment history. If you do not meet the minimum bulletin requirements or your work record is not acceptable, you will not be considered for employment, even if you have taken and passed the examination.**

F.  BACKGROUND - Your application is subject to a complete background review, including a review of any criminal convictions. Applicants or new employees will be fingerprinted for the purpose of background review, and disqualification may result from factors considered in the review (i.e. work history and/or criminal history), after an employment offer is made.

G.  SOCIAL SECURITY NUMBER (items 3 & 30) - Federal law (P.L. 93-579, Section 7) requires that you be informed when asked for your Social Security Number that this number must be provided and that it will be used for identification purposes in the City's examination, employment and payroll processes. Our authority for requesting and requiring this information is based upon certain provisions of the Internal Revenue Code, the Social Security Act as amended, and payroll and Candidate Application Processing System (CAPS) procedures approved and implemented prior to June, 1984.

H.  RIGHT TO WORK (items 11, 12) - City jobs which require United States Citizenship are identified on the examination announcement. All applicants not currently employed by the City will be required to show proof of United States citizenship or the legal right to work in the United States within three business days of hire. Failure to comply with the requirements of the Immigration Reform and Control Act of 1986 within the time prescribed by the Act may result in termination.

I.  DISABILITY (items 15 and 16) - If you have a physical, mental or learning disability which may affect your ability to take the examination for which you are applying, please call our counselors at (213) 847-9780, (TDD) (213) 847-9267 who provide special assistance and job counseling for disabled applicants. Special testing accommodations may be arranged if verification of the disability is provided from a doctor, rehabilitation counselor or other authority. You will be contacted to make specific arrangements. Under provision of Title I of the Americans with Disabilities Act, this information is obtained only to arrange accommodations and/or special counseling.

J.  EDUCATION AND EXPERIENCE (items 31, 33, 34, 35 & 39) - You must list a complete record of your training and experience. If more space is needed, attach additional sheets. Read the requirements section of the examination bulletin carefully for any special application instructions for that job title. Claimed volunteer experience must also include verification on stationery from the organization served showing time periods volunteered and duties performed. City employees must list the specific Department for which they have worked and show their civil service class titles.

K.  SIGNATURE (item 38) - This application must be signed (not printed) in ink BY THE APPLICANT.

### DETACH INSTRUCTIONS FROM APPLICATION
### BEFORE MAILING OR PRESENTING IT TO THE PERSONNEL DEPARTMENT

### INSTRUCCIONES EN ESPAÑOL AL REVERSO

## DEPARTAMENTO DE PERSONAL

### CIUDAD DE LOS ANGELES

### INSTRUCCIONES PARA LLENAR LA SOLICITUD

A. Por favor llene esta solicitud cuidadosamente en tinta, en letra de molde o con maquina de escribir. No aceptamos copías fotostáticas, facsímile (FAX) o' resumen en lugar de una aplicacíon original. Conteste completamente y precisamente a todas las preguntas excepto preguntas 13 a 16 cuales son voluntarias, o preguntas 9 y 11 que deben completarse solamente si se pide en el anuncio del exámen. USTED PUEDE SER DESCALIFICADO POR INFORMACIÓN FALSA O SI DELIBERADAMENTE OMITE INFORMACIÓN. Sugerimos que se quede con una copía de cada solicitud que entregue. No se puede obtener una copía de la solicitud mientras que el examen esta en progreso.

B. Debe entregar una solicitud para cada examen. Solamente empleados del Servicio Civil de la Ciudad De Los Angeles seran aceptados para exámenes de promoción. Las demás personas deben someter solicitud declarando que no son empleados de la Ciudad de Los Angeles.

Empleados que dejan el servicio de la Ciudad, no podrán ser nombrados de los registros de Promoción. Por lo tanto, si un examen es anunciado promociónal y tambien para personas fuera de la Ciudad, se recomienda que candidatos de Promoción entregen solicitudes individuales para cada examen promociónal y abierto. No indique estado legal o base especial, a menos que este especificado en el anuncio de examen.

C. Su solicitud TIENE QUE SER RECIBIDA, no mas tarde de la fecha indicada en el anuncio, EN LA OFICINA NUMERO 100, Departamento de Personal, ubicado en el 700 East Temple Street, Los Angeles, CA 90012. Si cambia su dirección después de entregar su solicitud, necesita notificar, por escrito, al Departamento de Personal inmediatamente.

D. SOLICITUD POR CORREO - Si gusta, puede mandar su solicitud por correo al menos que indique lo contrario en el anuncio. Asegurese de que ha contestado todas las preguntas. Su solicitud tiene que ser **recibida,** en nuestra oficina numero 100, 700 East Temple Street, no en la oficina de correos, a más tardar por la fecha indicada en el anuncio. Es la responsabilidad del aplicante permitir tiempo adecuado para la entrega del correo. Solicitudes recibidas despues de la fecha indicada en el anuncio, seran descalificadas.

E. **ACEPTACION - Aplicantes que no logren someter toda información requerida no seran considerados para empleo. Todas las solicitudes son aceptadas tentativamente en espera de la evaluacion de su experiencia. Si no cumple con los requisitos mínimos del anuncio o si su experiencia de trabajo no es aceptable, su solicitud puede ser rechazada aunque haya tomado y pasado el examen.**

F. HISTORIAL - Su educacíon y experiencia serán evaluados, incluyendo revista de cualquier conviccíon criminal. Al ofrecer empleo al aplicante o empleado nuevo, se le tomaran sus huellas digitales con el proposito de revisar su historial de trabajo y/o criminal. Además, después de esta revista final, todavía puede ser descalificado y despedido.

G. NUMERO DE SEGURO SOCIAL (Espacio Nos. 3 y 30) - La ley Federal (P.L. 93-579, Sect.7) requiere que cuando se le pide su número de Seguro Social se le avise que tiene que darlo y que éste número se usará para identificacíon en el proceso de examen, empleo y nómina de pago de la Ciudad. Nuestra autoridad para pedir y requerir esta informacíon viene de ciertas provisiones del Código de Rentas Públicas (Internal Revenue), el Acto de Seguro Sócial y las reglas y procedimientos de nómina de pago y aplicacíon que fueron aprobados antes del primero de Junio de 1984.

H. DERECHO A TRABAJAR - (Espacio Nos. 11 y 12) Posiciones con la Ciudad de Los Angeles que requieren ciudadanía Americana son identificadas en el anuncio del examen. Aplicantes que no son empleados de la Ciudad tienen que someter prueba de ciudadanía Americana o el derecho legal de trabajar en los Estados Unidos, dentro de tres días después de ser apuntado en un puesto. Falta de cumplir con los requisitos del Acta y Control de Inmigración de 1986 dentro del tiempo indicado, puede resultar en descalificacíon.

I. IMPEDIMENTO (Espacio Nos. 15 y 16) - Si tiene algún impedimento físico o mental que podra afectar su habilidad para tomar el exámen que esta solicitando, por favor llame a nuestros consejeros al (213) 847-9780 o con TDD (213) 847-9267 para recibir asistencia. Al someter verificación de su médico, consejero u otra autoridad, sera notificado tocante arreglos especiales para que pueda tomar el exámen. En conformidad con el Titulo I del Acta de Americanos con Impedimentos, esta información es requisito solamente para hacer arreglos especiales y/o para aconsejar.

J. EDUCACION Y EXPERIENCIA (Espacios Nos. 31, 33, 34, 35, y 39) - Tiene que hacer una lista completa de su experiencia y educación. Si necesita más espacio, agrege más páginas. Lea cuidadosamente la sección sobre requisitos en el anuncio del exámen por si acaso hay instrucciones especiales para ese exámen. Experiencia voluntaria debe incluir verificación en papel de la organizacíon en membrete de la organización servida indicando el tiempo voluntario y tareas en esa posición. Los empleados de la Ciudad De Los Angeles deberán especificar los departamentos en los que han trabajado y deben indicar su título o categoría en el Servicio Civil.

K. FIRMA (Espacio 38) - El candidato debe firmar la aplicación (no con letra de molde) con tinta.

### SEPARE LAS INSTRUCCIONES DE LA
### SOLICITUD ANTES DE MANDARLA POR
### CORREO O AL PRESENTARLA EN
### PERSONA AL DEPARTAMENTO DE PERSONAL
#### ENGLISH INSTRUCTIONS ON REVERSE

# City of Oakland
## *Employment Application*

Exact title of position for which you are applying:

**Office of Personnel Resource Management**

150 Frank H. Ogawa Plaza, 2nd Floor, Oakland, CA 94612-2019 ☎ (510) 238-3112 ✧ (Job Hotline) (510) 238-3111 ✧ (Fax) (510) 238-6232 ✧ (TDD) (510) 238-6930
Web Site: www.oaklandnet.com

| 1. LAST NAME | FIRST NAME | MI | SOCIAL SECURITY NO. (TO BE USED AS YOUR CANDIDATE ID NO.) |
|---|---|---|---|

| 2. CURRENT ADDRESS | NUMBER & STREET | APT. NO. | CITY | STATE | ZIP CODE |
|---|---|---|---|---|---|

| 3. HOME PHONE | 4. BUS. PHONE | 5. OTHER NAMES USED WHILE EMPLOYED BY THE CITY OF OAKLAND: |
|---|---|---|

6. **Have you ever been convicted of a felony?** (Note: Conviction of a felony may not disqualify you. Qualifications and backgrounds are reviewed in relation to job requirements.)  ☐ Yes  ☐ No

7. ARE YOU NOW EMPLOYED BY THE CITY OF OAKLAND?  ☐ Yes  ☐ No
If "Yes," exact job title and department is:

8. ARE YOU RELATED BY BLOOD OR MARRIAGE TO ANY CITY OFFICIAL?  ☐ YES  ☐ NO
If "Yes," give name of person and relationship _____

(Article IX, Sec. 907 of the City of Oakland Charter prohibits employment of relatives of certain City officials.)

9. Type of employment that you will accept:  ☐ Full Time  ☐ Part-Time

10. **US MILITARY** (To claim veteran's preference points, you must present proof of honorable discharge (DD214) when you file your application. (This also applies to current City employees.) If you were separated from the service (Active Duty Status) within the last five (5) years from the date of examination, you may claim veteran's preference.)

DO YOU CLAIM VETERAN'S PREFERENCE?  YES ☐  NO ☐
DATE AND BRANCH OF DISCHARGE

FOR OFFICIAL USE ONLY

11. DO YOU HAVE ☐ HIGH SCHOOL DIPLOMA ☐ GED

| 12. NAME, CITY & STATE OF HIGH SCHOOL, COLLEGES/UNIVERSITIES ATTENDED | UNITS COMPLETED SEMESTER | QUARTER | COURSE OF STUDY/MAJOR | TYPE OF DEGREE: | COMPLETED: YES | NO |
|---|---|---|---|---|---|---|
|  |  |  |  |  | ☐ | ☐ |
|  |  |  |  |  | ☐ | ☐ |
|  |  |  |  |  | ☐ | ☐ |
|  |  |  |  |  | ☐ | ☐ |

| 13. OTHER RELEVANT COURSES AND TRAINING | NAME AND LOCATION OF INSTITUTION | LENGTH OF COURSE | ENDED |
|---|---|---|---|
|  |  |  |  |
|  |  |  |  |

| 14. PROFESSIONAL LICENSE OR CERTIFICATE, IF REQUIRED | CERTIFICATE NUMBER | DATE ISSUED | EXPIRATION DATE |
|---|---|---|---|
|  |  |  |  |
|  |  |  |  |

| 15. LIST ANY FOREIGN LANGUAGES YOU CAN SPEAK, READ OR WRITE FLUENTLY | 16. PLEASE INDICATE VALID DRIVER'S LICENSE OR ID NUMBER, STATE, EXPIRATION DATE |
|---|---|

17. DESIGNATE SKILLS, IF REQUIRED FOR THIS POSITION.
(Note: Testing of skills may be required prior to or following selection.)
Typing Speed _____ wpm
Data Entry Speed _____ wpm

18. NAME, ADDRESS AND PHONE NUMBER OF EMERGENCY CONTACT
NAME _____  PHONE _____
ADDRESS _____  CITY _____

FOR OFFICIAL USE ONLY
Examination Number _____
Approved ☐
Disapproved ☐

| Education | ☐ | Incomplete: | ☐ |
| Late | ☐ | License | ☐ |
| Not Elg. Prom | ☐ | Not Elg. Restr. | ☐ |
| Met MQs/Scrnd | ☐ | CSB Rule 4.12B | ☐ |
| Exp. | ☐ | CSB Rule 4.07 | ☐ |
| Other | _____ | | |

CERTIFICATE OF APPLICANT: I certify that all statements made in this application are true, and I agree and understand that misstatements or omissions of any material will subject me to disqualification or dismissal.

Signature: _____  Date: _____

Initials _____  Date _____

I received the Employment Information Pamphlet and understand its contents.

Initial here: _____

**CITY OF OAKLAND EQUAL EMPLOYMENT OPPORTUNITY QUESTIONNAIRE**

The City of Oakland asks all applicants to voluntarily complete this form in order to comply with the United States Government Equal Opportunity requirements. Data collected will be used for statistical purposes. The information will be immediately detached from your application and kept confidential.

The City of Oakland complies with all Federal, State and local laws guaranteeing Equal Employment Opportunities to all. If you feel you have been treated unfairly or discriminated against because of race, color, national origin, sex, age, disability, marital status, or sexual orientation, please contact the City's Equal Opportunity Programs Manager at (510) 238-3500.

**OAKLAND RESIDENTS:** OAKLAND residents may be given additional credit upon qualifying for selected positions.

**DISABLED APPLICANTS:** The Office of Personnel Resource Management will make reasonable accommodations in the exam process to accommodate disabled applicants. If you have a disability for which you need accommodation, please call (510) 238-6466/TDD (510) 238-6930.

Exact title of position for which you are applying: _____  Date: _____
Name _____  DOB _____  1. ☐ Male ☐ Female
2. Choose the one Ethnic Group with which you most closely identify:  3: Oakland Resident ☐ Yes ☐ No
☐ a. White - All persons having origins in any of the original people of Europe, North Africa or the Middle East.
☐ b. Black - All persons having origins in any of the Black racial groups.
☐ c. Hispanic - All persons of Mexican, Puerto Rican, Cuban, Central or South American, or other Spanish culture or origin, regardless of race.
☐ d. Asian or Pacific Islander - All persons except Filipinos, having origins in any of the original people of the Far East, Southeast Asia, the Indian subcontinent or the Pacific Islands. For example: China, India, Japan, Korea and Samoa. Filipino is listed below as F.
☐ e. American Indian or Alaskan native - All persons having origins in any of the original people of North America, and who maintain cultural identification through tribal affiliations or community recognition.
☐ f. Filipino Persons of Filipino Ancestry or ethnic origin.
4. Do you have a mental or physical disability* for which you may need special testing accommodations? _____
5. If the answer to #4 is yes, what testing accommodations do you need? _____
*As defined in the Rehabilitation Act of 1973 and the Americans with Disabilities Act of 1990.

OVER

This Section MUST be filled out or your application may not be considered. You may also attach a resume or other relevant documents to further describe your qualifications.

**19. EXPERIENCE:** Begin with your most recent experience. List all employment in the last SEVEN years that is related to the job for which you are applying. Indicate Self-employment, U.S. Military Service and Volunteer Experience. Indicate "Volunteer" in the space for salary. Include details that meet the entrance requirements of the position.

| FROM Mo/Yr | EMPLOYER (BUSINESS OR AGENCY NAME) | | TITLE OF YOUR POSITION | No. EMPLOYEES SUPERVISED BY YOU |
|---|---|---|---|---|
| TO Mo/Yr | ADDRESS CITY STATE ZIP | | NAME OF SUPERVISOR | SUPERVISOR'S PHONE No. |
| HRS. PER WK. | DUTIES:: | | | |
| SALARY: $ PER/ | | | | |
| REASON FOR LEAVING | | | | |

| FROM Mo/Yr | EMPLOYER (BUSINESS OR AGENCY NAME) | | TITLE OF YOUR POSITION | No. EMPLOYEES SUPERVISED BY YOU |
|---|---|---|---|---|
| TO Mo/Yr | ADDRESS CITY STATE ZIP | | NAME OF SUPERVISOR | SUPERVISOR'S PHONE No. |
| HRS. PER WK. | DUTIES: | | | |
| SALARY: $ PER/ | | | | |
| REASON FOR LEAVING | | | | |

| FROM Mo/Yr | EMPLOYER (BUSINESS OR AGENCY NAME) | | TITLE OF YOUR POSITION | No. EMPLOYEES SUPERVISED BY YOU |
|---|---|---|---|---|
| TO Mo/Yr | ADDRESS CITY STATE ZIP | | NAME OF SUPERVISOR | SUPERVISOR'S PHONE No. |
| HRS. PER WK. | DUTIES: | | | |
| SALARY: $ PER/ | | | | |
| REASON FOR LEAVING | | | | |

| FROM Mo/Yr | EMPLOYER (BUSINESS OR AGENCY NAME) | | TITLE OF YOUR POSITION | No. EMPLOYEES SUPERVISED BY YOU |
|---|---|---|---|---|
| TO Mo/Yr | ADDRESS CITY STATE ZIP | | NAME OF SUPERVISOR | SUPERVISOR'S PHONE No. |
| HRS. PER WK. | DUTIES: | | | |
| SALARY: $ PER/ | | | | |
| REASON FOR LEAVING | | | | |

| FROM Mo/Yr | EMPLOYER (BUSINESS OR AGENCY NAME) | | TITLE OF YOUR POSITION | No. EMPLOYEES SUPERVISED BY YOU |
|---|---|---|---|---|
| TO Mo/Yr | ADDRESS CITY STATE ZIP | | NAME OF SUPERVISOR | SUPERVISOR'S PHONE No. |
| HRS. PER WK. | DUTIES: | | | |
| SALARY: $ PER/ | | | | |
| REASON FOR LEAVING | | | | |

INQUIRY MAY BE MADE OF YOUR FORMER EMPLOYERS OR THE LAST SCHOOL YOU ATTENDED REGARDING YOUR PERFORMANCE RECORD.
MAY WE CONTACT YOUR PRESENT EMPLOYER? ☐ YES ☐ NO

DATE: _____

HOW DID YOU LEARN ABOUT THIS EXAMINATION?

☐ Bulletin - City of Oakland Bulletin Boards ☐ Radio Announcement ☐ City Job Hotline
☐ City Employee ☐ Television Announcement ☐ City Web Site

IF ONE OF THE FOLLOWING, PLEASE SPECIFY:

☐ Bulletin-Public Office other than City_____ ☐ Minority Organization/Group _____
☐ Women's Organization/Group _____ ☐ Newspaper/Name _____
☐ School/Name _____ ☐ Other Internet Site _____
☐ Other Community Organizations _____ ☐ Other _____

*Revised 8/99*

*City of Sacramento*
**EMPLOYMENT APPLICATION**
**CITY EMPLOYMENT OFFICE**
915 I STREET, HISTORIC CITY HALL, PLAZA LEVEL, SACRAMENTO, CA 95814
24 HOUR JOB LINE: (916) 808-8568 / TELEPHONE: (916) 808-5726
*An Equal Opportunity Employer*

**INSTRUCTIONS: This application is part of the examination process. It must be <u>completely filled out and signed</u> to be accepted. Late and/or incomplete applications will be rejected; omitted information cannot be considered or assumed.**

**PLEASE PRINT OR TYPE**

SOCIAL SECURITY NUMBER _____ - _____ - _____

JOB TITLE _____ Exam # _____

NAME _____
             Last                First             Middle Initial

MAILING ADDRESS _____
                 Street #      Street Name       Apartment #

_____
        City                State        Zip Code

HOME PHONE ( ) _____ OTHER PHONE ( ) _____

**FOR HR OFFICE USE ONLY**

☐ APPLICATION ACCEPTED
☑ APPLICATION REJECTED
   ☐ EDUCATION
   ☐ EXPERIENCE
   ☐ NMQ
   ☐ LATE
   ☐ OTHER

**ALL APPLICANTS, INCLUDING CITY EMPLOYEES, MUST IMMEDIATELY NOTIFY THE CITY EMPLOYMENT OFFICE AT THE ABOVE ADDRESS OF ANY ADDRESS OR PHONE CHANGES.**

**CONVICTIONS:** Conviction of a misdemeanor crime is not necessarily a bar to City employment. Each case is considered separately based on job requirements. Some classifications may require a fingerprinting check as verification. However, failure to list convictions, except as provided below may result in termination from the examination process or employment. You may omit a) traffic violations (Driving Under the Influence convictions must be reported); b) any conviction committed prior to your 18th birthday that was finally adjudicated in Juvenile Court or under a youth offender law; c) any incident sealed under Welfare and Institutions Code §781 or Penal Code §1203.45; d) any conviction more than two years old as specified in Labor Code §432.7 and e) any conviction that has been expunged or otherwise removed from the record. FAILURE TO LIST CONVICTIONS MAY RESULT IN TERMINATION FROM THE EXAMINATION PROCESS AND/OR EMPLOYMENT.

1. Have you ever been convicted by a court of a misdemeanor?   ☐ NO   ☐ YES

2. Have you ever been convicted by a court of a felony?   ☐ NO   ☐ YES

3. If "YES" to "1" or "2", state WHAT conviction, WHEN, WHERE, AND DISPOSITION OF CASE(S): _____

_____

**EDUCATION AND TRAINING:** Submit verification of your college education such as <u>copies</u> of transcripts or diplomas.

1. High School Graduate or Passed GED?  ☐ NO   ☐ YES   Where? _____

2.

| NAME AND LOCATION OF COLLEGE, UNIVERSITY, BUSINESS, CORRESPONDENCE, TRADE, OR SERVICE SCHOOL(S) | MAJOR COURSE OF STUDY | UNITS COMPLETED | | DIPLOMA, CERTIFICATE, OR DEGREE RECEIVED; # OF HOURS OF TRAINING PROGRAM OR COURSE(S) REQUIRED BY JOB ANNOUCEMENT |
|---|---|---|---|---|
| | | SEMESTER UNITS | QUARTER UNITS | |
| | | | | |
| | | | | |
| | | | | |

3. List current certificates of professional competence, licenses, membership in professional associations.

_____

_____

**QUALIFYING EMPLOYMENT HISTORY:** List your current job and other work experiences that relates to the qualifications of the position. Begin with your most recent experience. List all jobs separately. The experience you list will be used to determine if you meet the minimum qualifications as stated on the job announcement. Applications that do not list related job experience will be considered incomplete and will be rejected; omitted information cannot be considered or assumed! A resume will not substitute for the information required in this section. Your application will be rejected if you refer to attachments instead of completing the following boxes. If you wish to submit more detailed information, or if you have additional experience, you may attach additional sheet(s).

Note: Qualifying experience is based on 40 hours per week (pro-rated if less than 40 hours/week).

| | | |
|---|---|---|
| FROM: MO. DAY YR. | TITLE: | PRESENT OR MOST RECENT EMPLOYER: |
| TO: MO. DAY YR. | DUTIES: | |
| TOTAL TIME: _____ YRS. _____ MOS. | | ADDRESS: |
| HOURS PER WEEK: | | |
| # PEOPLE SUPERVISED: | | PHONE: |
| MONTHLY SALARY: | | SUPERVISOR: |
| REASON FOR LEAVING: | | If you are under serious consideration for appointment by the City, may we contact? Yes ☐ No ☐ |
| FROM: MO. DAY YR. | TITLE: | FORMER EMPLOYER: |
| TO: MO. DAY YR. | DUTIES: | |
| TOTAL TIME: _____ YRS. _____ MOS. | | ADDRESS: |
| HOURS PER WEEK: | | |
| # PEOPLE SUPERVISED: | | PHONE: |
| MONTHLY SALARY: | | SUPERVISOR: |
| REASON FOR LEAVING: | | |
| FROM: MO. DAY YR. | TITLE: | FORMER EMPLOYER: |
| TO: MO. DAY YR. | DUTIES: | |
| TOTAL TIME: _____ YRS. _____ MOS. | | ADDRESS: |
| HOURS PER WEEK: | | |
| # PEOPLE SUPERVISED: | | PHONE: |
| MONTHLY SALARY: | | SUPERVISOR: |
| REASON FOR LEAVING: | | |
| FROM: MO. DAY YR. | TITLE: | FORMER EMPLOYER: |
| TO: MO. DAY YR. | DUTIES: | |
| TOTAL TIME: _____ YRS. _____ MOS. | | ADDRESS: |
| HOURS PER WEEK: | | |
| # PEOPLE SUPERVISED: | | PHONE: |
| MONTHLY SALARY: | | SUPERVISOR: |
| REASON FOR LEAVING: | | |

**NAME:** _____ **SOCIAL SECURITY #** _____
           Last        First        Middle Initial

**JOB TITLE:** _____ **EXAMINATION #:** _____

**DRIVER LICENSE:**   ☐ CALIFORNIA  ☐ OTHER: _____ **DR. LICENSE #** _____

            CLASS _____      EXPIRES _____

**VETERAN'S PREFERENCE:** Are you requesting Veteran's Preference?    ☐ YES ☐ NO

To qualify for Veteran's Preference, a copy of your DD214 **must be** submitted with this application. There are several criteria you must meet before qualifying for this preference. Please ask for the **VETERAN'S PREFERENCE REGULATIONS** sheet.

Active Duty:   From _____ to _____

**OTHER INFORMATION:**

1. Will you require reasonable accommodation in the testing process?    ☐ YES ☐ NO

    If "Yes", what accommodations will you need? Attach documentation. _____

2. Are you currently employed by the City of Sacramento?    ☐ YES ☐ NO

    If "Yes", what department? _____

3. If "NO", have you ever been employed by the City of Sacramento?    ☐ YES ☐ NO

    If "Yes", state what department? Date you left? _____

4. Please list other name(s) used: _____

5. Please check the type(s) of work you will accept:  ☐ Part-Time  ☐ Full-Time  ☐ Temporary (12 months maximum)

## EMPLOYMENT QUESTIONNAIRE

**APPLICANT:** This completed section is confidential and will be detached from your application. This information is voluntary and is gathered in accordance with State and Federal laws for the purpose of evaluating the effectiveness of our equal opportunity and recruitment efforts.

**CHECK ONE:**    ☐ Male ☐ Female

PLEASE CHECK ONLY ONE BOX FOR THE RACIAL/ETHNIC CATEGORY WITH WHICH YOU MOST CLOSELY IDENTIFY WITH. (SEE BELOW FOR THE ETHNIC DEFINITIONS)

☐ WHITE          (Not Hispanic Origin) All persons having origins in any of the original peoples of Europe, North Africa, or the Middle East.

☐ BLACK          (Not Hispanic Origin) All persons having origins in any of the Black racial groups of Africa.

☐ HISPANIC      All persons of Mexican, Puerto Rican, Cuban, or any other Spanish Hispanic (does not include persons of Portuguese or Brazilian origin or persons who acquire a Spanish surname.)

☐ ASIAN or PACIFIC ISLANDER    All persons having origins in any of the original peoples of the Far East, Southeast Asia, the Indian Subcontinent, or the Pacific Islands (excluding the Philippine Islands). This area includes for example, China, Japan, Korea, and Samoa.

☐ AMERICAN INDIAN or ALASKAN NATIVE    All persons having origins in any of the original peoples of North America, and who maintain cultural identifications through tribal affiliation or community recognition.
PLEASE IDENTIFY YOUR TRIBAL AFFILIATION: _____

☐ FILIPINO      All persons having origins in the Philippine Islands.

**– CONTINUED ON THE NEXT PAGE –**

**I CERTIFY** that I am applying for _____ , Examination # _____
                                                        Job Title

I CERTIFY that all statements in this application are true and complete. I agree and understand that any misstatements or omissions of material facts herein will cause forfeiture on my part of all rights to employment by the City of Sacramento. I understand that if I do not meet the announced requirements, I will be eliminated from the examination process, and that applications must be received by the City of Sacramento Employment Office, Historic City Hall, 915 I Street, Plaza Level, Sacramento, CA 95814, by 5:00 p.m. on the final filing date specified on the job announcement. I hereby authorize the City to verify the accuracy of the information I have provided on this application.

**AUTHORIZATION TO RELEASE REMPLOYMENT RECORDS AND OTHER INFORMATION**

I authorize any duly accredited representative of the City of Sacramento to obtain any information relating to my activities from prior and current employers and others. This information may include, but not limited to, achievement, performance, attendance, personal history, and disciplinary information. I direct prior and current employers to release such information upon request to the duly accredited representative of the City of Sacramento regardless of any agreement I may have had with you previously to the contrary. I release any individual, including records custodians, from all liability for damages that may result to me on account of compliance or any attempts to comply with this authorization.

SIGNATURE: _____ DATE: _____
                    (Required for application to be complete)

**THIS APPLICATION AND ALL ATTACHMENTS ARE CONSIDERED PROPERTY OF THE CITY OF SACRAMENTO EMPLOYMENT OFFICE. PHOTOCOPIES WILL <u>NOT</u> BE FURNISHED. PLEASE ATTACH <u>COPIES</u> OF YOUR ORIGINAL DOCUMENTS.**

**EMPLOYMENT QUESTIONNAIRE:**

I first learned of this job opening through (check one only):

☐   A Friend or Relative

☐   The City's Employment Office/or Job Line

☐   Contact with a City Department/Employee: _____
                                                (Specify City Department/Employee)

☐   An Organization or Group: _____
                                (Specify Organization or Group)

☐   An Advertisement : _____
                        (Specify Newspaper, Publication, TV or Radio Station)

☐   Job Fair or Contact with a City Recruiter: _____
                                                (Specify Which Job Fair)

☐   Internet _____

☐   Other Means (Specify) _____

<u>**APPLICATIONS MUST BE RECEIVED BY 5:00 P.M. OF THE FINAL FILING DATE SPECIFIED ON THE JOB ANNOUNCEMENT**</u>

<u>**POSTMARKS ARE NOT ACCEPTED**</u>

REVISED June 1, 2005

# City of San José Employment Application

200 E. Santa Clara Street, San José, CA 95113
**Phone:** (408) 535-1285 **Job Hotline:** (408) 535-6800
http://jobs.cityofsj.org

*The City of San José is an Equal Opportunity Employer. Applicants for all job openings will be considered without regard to age, race, color, religion, sex, national origin, sexual orientation, marital status, pregnancy or childbirth, disability, medical condition, veteran status or any other consideration made unlawful under any federal, state or local laws.*

**Complete this application in its entirety. The City will only consider information contained on the application or supplemental materials specifically requested for this recruitment to determine your qualifications for the position in which you are applying. Incomplete or illegible applications may be disqualified. Documents submitted will not be returned. Resumes are not accepted in lieu of a completed application form.**

**POSITION APPLIED FOR:**

**JOB REQUISITION #:**

☐ Full-Time   ☐ Part-Time

**Current Employee:** ☐ Yes ☐ No
If yes, specify Employee ID #: _____

| Last Name | First Name | Middle Initial | Other names under which you have worked: |
|---|---|---|---|
| Address | | | Telephone Number (home) / Telephone Number (day) |
| City, State, Zip | | | Email |

## EDUCATION

Have you completed 8th grade? ☐ Yes ☐ No   Do you have a High School diploma or equivalent (GED or CA Proficiency)? ☐ Yes ☐ No

| Colleges, Universities (Name and Location) | Major | Total Units Earned | | Degree Received (AA, BA, BS, MA, etc.) |
|---|---|---|---|---|
| | | Semester | Quarter | |
| | | | | |
| | | | | |
| | | | | |

Languages spoken fluently, other than English which are related to the position for which you are applying for:
☐ Spanish ☐ Vietnamese ☐ Cantonese ☐ Mandarin ☐ Tagalog ☐ Ilocano ☐ Cambodian ☐ Sign
Other:

Licenses or Certificates which are related to the position for which you are applying for:

List professional, trade, business, or civic activities and offices held which are related to the position for which you are applying for:

If required by the job announcement, do you have a valid California Driver's License? ☐ Yes ☐ No  Class _____ License Number_____

Restrictions (other than eyeglasses):_____

If no California Driver's License, do you have one from another state in the US? ☐ Yes ☐ No
State_____ Class _____ License Number_____

## EMPLOYMENT HISTORY

Begin with your most recent experience. List experience gained in the last ten years, including periods of self-employment and military service. DO NOT omit any employers during the last 10 years. Include full details about experience that, in your opinion, makes you qualified for the job for which you are applying. **A resume will not, nor will reference to a resume, be accepted in lieu of providing complete information on a City application.**

| Dates of employment | Title of your position | Salary | ☐ Full-time |
|---|---|---|---|
| From: _____(month) _____(year) | | Beginning: | ☐ Part-time |
| To: _____(month) _____(year) | **Type of business or organization** | Ending: | Hours/Week_____ |
| Name **and** Address (include city, state, ZIP) of Current or Most Recent Employer | | Name/Title of your immediate supervisor Supervisor Phone:_____ May we contact her/him? ☐ Yes ☐ No | |
| Number of people and types of positions you supervised: | | | |
| Description of Duties, Responsibilities, and Accomplishments | | | |

Rev. 4/06 CSJ Appl.

## City of San José

| Dates of employment<br>From: _____(month) _____(year)<br>To: _____(month) _____(year) | Title of your position<br><br>**Type of business or organization** | Salary<br>Beginning:<br>Ending: | ☐ Full-time<br>☐ Part-time<br>Hours/Week_____ |
|---|---|---|---|
| **Name and** Address (include city, state, ZIP) of Current or Most Recent Employer | | Name/Title of your immediate supervisor<br><br>Supervisor Phone:_____<br>May we contact her/him? ☐ Yes ☐ No | |
| Number of people and types of positions you supervised: | | | |
| Description of Duties, Responsibilities, and Accomplishments | | | |

| Dates of employment<br>From: _____(month) _____(year)<br>To: _____(month) _____(year) | Title of your position<br><br>**Type of business or organization** | Salary<br>Beginning:<br>Ending: | ☐ Full-time<br>☐ Part-time<br>Hours/Week_____ |
|---|---|---|---|
| **Name and** Address (include city, state, ZIP) of Current or Most Recent Employer | | Name/Title of your immediate supervisor<br><br>Supervisor Phone:_____<br>May we contact her/him? ☐ Yes ☐ No | |
| Number of people and types of positions you supervised: | | | |
| Description of Duties, Responsibilities, and Accomplishments | | | |

| Dates of employment<br>From: _____(month) _____(year)<br>To: _____(month) _____(year) | Title of your position<br><br>**Type of business or organization** | Salary<br>Beginning:<br>Ending: | ☐ Full-time<br>☐ Part-time<br>Hours/Week_____ |
|---|---|---|---|
| **Name and** Address (include city, state, ZIP) of Current or Most Recent Employer | | Name/Title of your immediate supervisor<br><br>Supervisor Phone:_____<br>May we contact her/him? ☐ Yes ☐ No | |
| Number of people and types of positions you supervised: | | | |
| Description of Duties, Responsibilities, and Accomplishments | | | |

Have you ever been terminated or asked to resign from a position? ☐ Yes ☐ No
If yes, please give details.

Have you ever been convicted of a felony or misdemeanor in violation of any law, regulation, or ordinance? ☐ Yes ☐ No

If yes, provide court information and circumstances below. Conviction is not an automatic disqualification from employment. Each case is considered individually; however, failure to list a conviction is cause for automatic ineligibility for hire or dismissal. It is City policy to obtain and review conviction records. You may omit any traffic offense, which was an infraction and resulted in a fine of less than $400. You may also omit any conviction for marijuana-related offenses that are beyond two years in age.

Do you have any relatives employed by the City of San José? ☐ Yes ☐ No    If YES, please identify first and last name, department and title, and relationship.

| First Name | Last Name | Department | Title | Relationship |
|---|---|---|---|---|
|  |  |  |  |  |
|  |  |  |  |  |

CERTIFICATION OF APPLICANT (READ CAREFULLY BEFORE SIGNING)

I hereby certify that that the information provided in my resume, all statements made in this application, and all statements made during the interview process are true and correct to the best of my knowledge. I agree and understand that any misstatement, falsification, or omission of material facts will cause forfeiture of my eligibility for employment. I also understand that falsification or omission of information regarding convictions will result in my removal from eligible lists or dismissal from City of San Jose employment. I understand that I give the right to the City of San Jose to check any information regarding my employment application.

Signature of Applicant: _____    Date:_____

Rev. 4/06 CSJ Appl.

**City of San José**

---

Do you need an accommodation(s) to participate in the testing process? ☐ Yes ☐ No

Please explain:

---

### HOW DID YOU FIRST LEARN OF THIS JOB OPPORTUNITY?

☐ (1) City of San José website: www.jobs.cityofsj.org    ☐ (7) San José Mercury Newspaper

☐ (2) City of San José - Employee Services Department    ☐ (8) Other Newspaper _____

☐ (3) City of San José employee    ☐ (9) Job Fair _____

☐ (4) City of San José Job hotline: (408) 535-6800    ☐ (10) Internet job board _____

☐ (5) Mailed job announcement    ☐ (11) Radio/TV/Theater _____

☐ (6) Professional Journal _____    ☐ (12) Other _____

---

Section 1233 of the California Government Code gives each applicant the opportunity to voluntarily indicate his/her identification on an employment application. Each applicant also has the opportunity to voluntarily identify any disability(s). This information will be used by the City of San José in conducting research and in compiling statistical reports regarding the composition of its job applicants and work force. It is illegal to use this information to discriminate against, or give preference to, a person for hiring or promotion. After this information has been recorded by the Employee Services Department, it will be removed from the application prior to review by hiring departments.

**PLEASE INDICATE GENDER:**

☐ Male ☐ Female

**PLEASE CHECK ONE BOX WHICH APPLIES TO YOUR ETHNIC GROUP:**

☐ **African-American/Black (not of Hispanic Origins):** All persons having origins in any of the Black racial groups of Africa.

☐ **Asian or Pacific Islander:** All persons having origins in any of the original peoples of the Far East, Southeast Asia, the Indian Subcontinent, or the Pacific Islands.

☐ **Hispanic:** All persons of Mexican, Puerto Rican, Cuban, Central/South American, or other Spanish cultures, regardless of race.

☐ **Native American or Alaskan Native:** All persons having origins in any of the original peoples of North America, or who maintain cultural identification through tribal affiliation.

☐ **Filipino:** All persons having origins in the Philippine Islands

☐ **White (not of Hispanic Origin):** All persons having origins in any of the original peoples of Europe, North Africa, or the Middle East.

☐ **Other** _____

Rev. 4/06 CSJ Appl.

# 14 ▶ The California Police Exam Planner

## CHAPTER SUMMARY

This chapter helps you prepare for the written police exam in California by presenting a study plan designed specially for you. After gathering information and conducting a self-evaluation to see how much work you need to do in how much time, you can choose from four customized test preparation schedules.

**T**he customized schedules in this chapter are designed to give you a reasonable amount of time to study for the kinds of questions that appear on police officer exams, depending on how much time is left before exam day. You might be lucky—maybe the exam you're studying for doesn't include *all* of these kinds of questions. Once you've completed step one, "Get Information," you can customize one of the schedules offered here for *your* exam. If your exam doesn't include memory questions or math questions, for example, you don't have to study those chapters (although the techniques will be useful to you once you've become a police officer). Instead, you can spend more time honing those skills that *are* covered on the exam you have to take.

## ▶ Step One: Get Information

**When: Today**

**Time to complete:** $1\frac{1}{2}$ **hours**

The first thing you need is information. If you haven't already done so, read Chapter 2 to learn about the entire selection process. Then consult Chapter 4 for the phone number of the recruiting office in the police department you want to serve. If you're applying to one of the larger cities in your state, you'll find an outline of its exam in Chapters 5 through 12.

Next, contact the recruiting office. Request a position announcement or exam bulletin and ask when the next exam is scheduled. If no exam is scheduled, ask if you can be put on a mailing list for notification. Figure you have at least six months to prepare.

The exam bulletin usually gives a brief outline of what skills will be tested on the written exam. You can use this information to help you construct your plan in step three.

| IF THE EXAM IS SCHEDULED: | DO THE FOLLOWING SELF-EVALUATION AND THEN: |
|---|---|
| six months or more from now | go to Schedule A |
| three to six months from now | go to Schedule B |
| one to three months from now | go to Schedule C |
| three weeks or less from now | go to Schedule D |
| weekly or monthly | do the proceeding self-evaluation to help you decide when to take the exam and then go to the appropriate schedule |

▶ **Step Two: Self-Evaluation**

**When: This week**

**Time to complete: 4–5 hours**

Find out whether you're ready to take the written

exam. First, read Chapter 15, "The Secrets of Test Success." Then take the sample exam in Chapter 16. Score your exam using the answer key at the end. Then match your score with the following analysis.

| SCORE | ANALYSIS |
|-------|----------|
| under 50 | You need concentrated work in the skills tested. Consider taking classes at the local community college in the areas you're weakest in, or use some of the additional resources listed in Chapters 18–25. After you've spent at least four months working on your skills, retake the test in Chapter 16 and check your score. |
| 51–75 | You should spend some time working on your skills. Consider the LearningExpress Skill Builders listed at the back of this book or other books from the library or bookstore. Enlist friends or former teachers to give you some extra help. |
| 76–90 | You're in the ballpark. Work through all the exercises in Chapters 18–25 and then take the second practice test in Chapter 26. If your score hasn't improved much, try some of the tactics previously listed. |
| 90–100 | Congratulations! Your score is good enough to put you near the top of most eligibility lists as long as you can get through the rest of the selection process. For a few more points that can make the difference in whether you get hired, work through the exercises in Chapters 18–25, concentrating on the areas where a little practice will do the most good. Then take the second practice exam in Chapter 26. |

## ▶ Step Three: Make a Plan

**When: This week, after step two**
**Time to complete: 1 hour**

There are four sample schedules on the following pages, based on the amount of time you have before the exam. If you're the kind of person who needs deadlines and assignments to motivate you for a project, here they are. If you're the kind of person who doesn't like to follow other people's plans, you can use the suggested schedules here to construct your own.

In constructing your plan, you should take into account how much work you need to do. If your score on the sample test wasn't what you had hoped, consider taking some of the steps from Schedule A and getting them into Schedule D somehow, even if you do have only three weeks before the exam.

You can also customize your plan according to the information you gathered in step one. If the exam you have to take doesn't include memory questions, for instance, you can skip Chapter 25 and concentrate instead on some other area that *is* covered.

Even more important than making a plan is making a commitment. You can't improve your skills in reading, writing, and logical reasoning overnight. You have to set aside some time every day for study and practice. Try for at least 20 minutes a day. Twenty minutes daily will do you much more good than two hours on Saturday.

If you have months before the exam, you're lucky. Don't put off your study until the week before the exam! Start now. Even ten minutes a day, with half an hour or more on weekends, can make a big difference in your score—and in your chances of making the force!

# Schedule A: The Leisure Plan

You've already taken the sample test and know that you have at least six months in which to build on your strengths and improve in areas where you're weak. Make the most of your time.

| Time | Preparation |
|---|---|
| Exam minus 6 months | Study the explanations for the sample exam in Chapter 16 until you know you could answer all the questions right. Start going to the library once every two weeks to read books or magazines about law enforcement. Read through Chapter 17. |
| Exam minus 5 months | Read Chapters 18 and 19 and work through the exercises. Use at least one of the additional resources listed in each chapter. Find other people who are preparing for the test and form a study group. |
| Exam minus 4 months | Read Chapters 20 and 21 and work through the exercises. Use at least one of the additional resources for each chapter. Start making flash cards of vocabulary and spelling words. |
| Exam minus 3 months | Read Chapters 22 and 23 and work through the exercises. Use at least one of the additional resources from each chapter. Practice your math by making up problems out of everyday events. |
| Exam minus 2 months | Read Chapters 24 and 25 and work through the exercises. Exercise your memory by making note of people and places you see each day. You're still doing your reading and working with your flash cards, aren't you? |
| Exam minus 1 month | Take the sample test in Chapter 26. Use your score to help you decide where to concentrate your efforts this month. Go back to the relevant chapters and use the extra resources listed there, or get the help of a friend or teacher. |
| Exam minus 1 week | Review both sample tests. See how much you've learned in the past months. Concentrate on what you've done well and decide not to let any areas where you still feel uncertain bother you. |
| Exam minus 1 day | Relax. Do something unrelated to police exams. Eat a good meal and go to bed at your usual time. |

# Schedule B: The Just-Enough-Time Plan

If you have three to six months before the exam, that should be enough time to prepare for the written test, especially if you scored above 70 on the sample test in Chapter 16. This schedule assumes four months; stretch it out or compress it if you have more or less time.

| Time | Preparation |
|---|---|
| Exam minus 4 months | Read Chapters 17, 18, 19, and 20 and work through the exercises. Use at least one of the additional resources listed in each chapter. Find other people who are preparing for the test and form a study group. Start going to the library once every two weeks to read books about law enforcement. |
| Exam minus 3 months | Read Chapters 21 and 22 and work through the exercises. Use at least one of the additional resources for each chapter. Make flash cards of vocabulary and spelling words. |
| Exam minus 2 months | Read Chapters 23, 24, and 25 and work through the exercises. Exercise your memory by making note of people and places you see each day. You're still doing your reading and working with your flash cards, aren't you? |
| Exam minus 1 month | Take the sample test in Chapter 26. Use your score to help you decide where to concentrate your efforts this month. Go back to the relevant chapters and use the extra resources listed there, or get the help of a friend or teacher. |
| Exam minus 1 week | Review both sample tests. See how much you've learned in the past months. Concentrate on what you've done well, and decide not to let any areas where you still feel uncertain bother you. |
| Exam minus 1 day | Relax. Do something unrelated to police exams. Eat a good meal and go to bed at your usual time. |

# Schedule C: More Study in Less Time

If you have one to three months before the exam, you still have enough time for some concentrated study that will help you improve your score. This schedule is built around a two-month time frame. If you have only one month, spend an extra couple of hours a week to get all these steps in. If you have three months, take some of the steps from Schedule B and fit them in.

| Time | Preparation |
|------|-------------|
| Exam minus 8 weeks | Evaluate your performance on the sample test in Chapter 16 and the sample essays in Chapter 17 to find one or two of your weakest areas. Choose the appropriate chapter(s) from among Chapters 18–25 to read in these two weeks. Use some of the additional resources listed there. When you get to those chapters in this plan, review them. |
| Exam minus 6 weeks | Read Chapters 18–21 and work through the exercises. |
| Exam minus 4 weeks | Read Chapters 22–25 and work through the exercises. |
| Exam minus 2 weeks | Take the second sample test in Chapter 26. Then score it and read the answer explanations until you're sure you understand them. Review the areas where your score is lowest. |
| Exam minus 1 week | Review Chapters 18–25, concentrating on the areas where a little work can help the most. |
| Exam minus 1 day | Relax. Do something unrelated to police exams. Eat a good meal and go to bed at your usual time. |

## Schedule D: The Short-Term Plan

If you have three weeks or less before the exam, you really have your work cut out for you. Carve half an hour out of your day, *every day*, for study. This schedule assumes you have the whole three weeks to prepare in; if you have less time, you'll have to compress the schedule accordingly.

| Time | Preparation |
|---|---|
| Exam minus 3 weeks | Read the material in Chapters 18–21 and work through the exercises. |
| Exam minus 2 weeks | Read the material in Chapters 22–25 and work through the exercises. Take the sample test in Chapter 26. |
| Exam minus 1 week | Evaluate your performance on the second sample test. Review the parts of Chapters 18–25 that you had the most trouble with. Get a friend or teacher to help you with the section you had the most difficulty with. |
| Exam minus 2 days | Review both sample tests. Make sure you understand the answer explanations. |
| Exam minus 1 day | Relax. Do something unrelated to police exams. Eat a good meal and go to bed at your usual time. |

## ▶ Step Four: Score Your Best

**When: On Exam Day**
If you've followed the plan presented in this chapter, or invented your own based on these guidelines, you *will* score your best—because you'll be prepared.

# 15▶ The Secrets of Test Success

## CHAPTER SUMMARY

This chapter contains valuable advice for those planning to take a written law enforcement exam: how to prepare, how to beat test anxiety, how to pace yourself as you move through the test, and when to guess. Read this chapter before you take the first sample written exam in this book.

A little preparation goes a long way when it comes to taking a test. If you know about the test beforehand and come prepared physically and mentally, you're already a step ahead. Test preparation reduces your test anxiety, allows you to pace yourself properly on the test, and helps you to do as well as you possibly can. It's a good feeling to walk into a test knowing you've done your best to prepare for it.

## ▶ Finding Out about the Test

The first step is to learn as much as possible about the test you'll be taking. The information you need to know is summarized in the following list.

## Must-Know Information

- When and where will the test be given?
- Do I have more than one opportunity to take the test?
- How long will the test take?
- Do most people who take the test finish on time?
- What do I need to bring to the test?

Make sure you know the answers to these questions before you take the test.

## Structure and Format of the Test

Find out as much as you can about how the test is organized. Every test is different, but chances are the test you take will be timed and contain mostly multiple-choice questions. Learn as much as you can ahead of time.

- What skills are tested?
- How many sections does the test have?
- How many questions does each section have?
- Are the questions ordered from easy to hard, or is the sequence random?
- How much time is allotted for each section? Are there breaks between sections?
- What is the passing score? How many questions do I have to get right to get that score?
- Will a higher score give me any advantages, such as a higher salary or a better rank on the eligibility list? If so, what score would be ideal yet within reason for me?
- How is the test scored? Is there a penalty for wrong answers? If so, what is it?
- If I finish a section early, can I return to a previous section or move ahead to the next section?
- Can I write in the test booklet, or will I be given scratch paper for my work?
- What should I bring to the test with me? Pencils? Calculator? Ticket of admission? Photo identification? Proof of citizenship?

Some standardized tests are scored in such a way that you are penalized for wrong answers. You *need* this information before you take the test because it will affect how you approach the test. More on that later.

If you complete the "Test Information Sheet" on the next page, you'll be sure to have all the information you need.

## ▶ Combating Test Anxiety

Knowing what to expect and being prepared for it is the best defense against test anxiety—that worrisome feeling that keeps you from doing your best. Practice and preparation keep you from succumbing to that feeling.

Nevertheless, even the brightest, best prepared test takers may suffer from occasional bouts of test anxiety. But don't worry—you can overcome it.

## Take the Test One Question at a Time

Focus all of your attention on the one question you're answering. Block out any thoughts about questions you've already read or concerns about what's coming next. Concentrate your thinking where it will do the most good—on the question you're answering.

## Develop a Positive Attitude

Keep reminding yourself that you're prepared. The fact that you're reading this book means that you're better prepared than most of the others who are taking the test. Remember, it's only a test, and you're going to do your *best*. That's all anyone can ask of you. If that nagging drill sergeant voice inside your head starts sending negative messages, combat them with positive ones of your own.

- "I'm doing just fine."
- "I've prepared for this test."
- "I know exactly what to do."
- "I know I can get the score I'm aiming for."

# Test Information Sheet

## Must-Know Data

When is the test? _____

Where will it be given? _____

Do you know how to get to the testing site?

❒ Yes   Make a trial run to see how long it takes to get there at the time of day you'll be making the real trip.

❒ No   Find out how to get to the testing site and make your trial run.

| | |
|---|---|
| How long does it take to get to the testing site? _____ | What time do you need to leave to get there on time? _____ |

How long is the test? _____

List the items you need to bring to the test:

_____

_____

## Structure and Format of the Test

Format:   ❒ Multiple choice   ❒ Fill in the blanks
          ❒ True/false   ❒ Essay
          ❒ Other

Total # questions: _____

Total # sections: _____

|  | # Questions | Skills Tested |
|---|---|---|
| Section 1 | | _____ |
| Section 2 | | _____ |
| Section 3 | | _____ |
| Section 4 | | _____ |

Passing score: _____   Ideal score: _____

Knowing this information helps you prepare mentally for the test. You'll be able to walk into the test relaxed and confident, knowing you'll do your best.

---

You get the idea. Remember to drown out negative messages with positive ones of your own.

### If You Lose Your Concentration

Don't worry about it! It's normal. During a long test, it happens to everyone. When your mind is stressed or overexerted, it takes a break whether or not you want it to. It's easy to get your concentration back if you simply acknowledge the fact that you've lost it and take a quick break. Your brain needs very little time (seconds really) to rest.

Put your pencil down and close your eyes. Take a few deep breaths and listen to the sound of your breathing. Picture yourself doing something you really enjoy, like playing sports or listening to music. The ten seconds or so that this takes is really all the time your brain needs to relax and get ready to focus again.

Try this technique several times in the days before the test when you feel stressed. The more you practice, the better it will work for you on test day.

### If You Freeze

Don't worry about a question that stumps you even though you're sure you know the answer. Mark it and go on to the next question. You can come back to the "stumper" later. Try to put it out of your mind completely until you come back to it. Just let your subconscious mind chew on the question while your conscious mind focuses on the other questions (one at a time, of course). Chances are, the memory block will be gone by the time you return to the question.

If you freeze before you ever begin the test, here's what to do:

1. Take a little time to look over the test.
2. Read a few of the questions.
3. Decide which ones are the easiest and start there.

Before long, you'll be "in the groove."

## ▶ During the Test

As you are taking your test, you want to use your time wisely and avoid making errors. Here are a few suggestions for making the most of your time.

### Time Management Strategies
### Pace Yourself

The most important time management strategy is pacing yourself. Pacing yourself doesn't just mean how quickly or slowly you can progress through the test. It means knowing how the test is organized, knowing the number of questions you have to get right, and making sure you have enough time to do them. Before you begin a section, take just a few seconds to survey it, noting the number of questions, their organization, and the type of questions that look easier than the rest. Rough out a time schedule based on the time allotted for the section. Mark the halfway point in the section and make a note beside that mark of what time it will be when the testing period is half over.

### Keep Moving

Once you begin the test, keep moving! Don't stop to ponder a difficult question. Skip it and move on. Mark the question so you can quickly find it later, if you have time to come back to it. If all questions count the same,

then a question that takes you five seconds to answer counts as much as one that takes you several minutes, so pick up the easy points first. Besides, answering the easier questions first helps to build your confidence and gets you in the testing groove. Who knows? As you go through the test, you may even stumble across some relevant information to help you answer those tough questions.

### Don't Rush

Keep moving, but don't rush. Think of your mind as a teeter-totter. On one side is your emotional energy. On the other side is your intellectual energy. When your emotional energy is high, your intellectual capacity is low. Remember how difficult it is to reason with someone when you're angry? On the other hand, when your intellectual energy is high, your emotional energy is low. Rushing raises your emotional energy. Remember the last time you were late for work? All that rushing around causes you to forget important things—like your lunch. Move quickly to keep your mind from wandering, but don't rush and get yourself flustered.

### Check Yourself

Check yourself at the halfway mark. If you're a little ahead, you know you're on track and may even have time left to go back and check your work. If you're behind, you have several choices. You can pick up the pace a little, but do this only if you can do it comfortably. Remember—DON'T RUSH! You can also skip around in the remaining portion of the test to pick up as many easy points as possible. This strategy has one drawback, however. If you are marking a score sheet with circles (or "bubbles") and you put the right answers in the wrong bubbles—they're wrong. So pay close attention to the question numbers if you decide to do this.

### Set a Target Score

Earlier, you were asked to find out what constituted a passing score and if there was any advantage in earning a higher score. Here's how to use this information to your advantage.

First, let's assume that your only objective is to pass the test because there is no advantage to be gained from a higher score. Figure out how many questions you must answer correctly to pass. *That's how long your test is.* For example, if the test has 100 questions and you need only 70 correct to pass, once you're quite sure you've answered 70 questions correctly, you can just breeze through the rest of the test. You'll probably do even better than you did before you hit the passing mark.

Now, let's assume that you need to pass the test, but scoring higher than others who take the test gives you some advantage, a higher placement for example. In this case, you still want to calculate a passing score. Then set a goal, an ideal score you'd like to earn. Try to make your target score realistic, yet challenging. As you take the test, work first to pass it, and then concentrate on earning your target score. This strategy focuses you on the questions you answered correctly, rather than the ones you think are wrong. That way you can build confidence as you go and keep emotional energy to a minimum.

**Caution:** Don't waste too much time scoring as you go. Just make rough estimates along the way.

## Avoiding Errors

When you take the test, you want to make as few errors as possible in the questions you answer. Here are a few tactics to keep in mind.

## Control Yourself

Remember the comparison between your mind and a teeter-totter that you read about a few paragraphs ago? Keeping your emotional energy low and your intellectual energy high is the best way to avoid mistakes. If you feel stressed or worried, stop for a few seconds. Acknowledge the feeling (*Hmmm! I'm feeling a little pressure here!*), take two or three deep breaths, and send yourself a few positive messages. This relieves your emotional anxiety and boosts your intellectual capacity.

## Directions

In most testing situations, a proctor reads the instructions aloud before the test begins. Make certain you understand what is expected. If you don't, *ask!* Listen carefully for instructions about how to answer the questions and whether there's a penalty for wrong answers. Make certain you know how much time you have. You may even want to write the amount of time on your test. If you miss this vital information, *ask for it.* You need it to do well on your test.

## Answers

This may seem like a silly warning, but it is important. Place your answers in the right blanks or the corresponding bubbles. Correct answers in the wrong place earn no points. It's a good idea to check every five to ten questions, and every time you skip a question, to make sure you're in the right spot. That way you won't need much time to correct your answer sheet if you have made an error.

## Choosing the Right Answer by Process of Elimination

As you read a question, you may find it helpful to underline important information or make some notes about what you're reading. When you get to the heart of the question, circle it and make sure you understand what it is asking. If you're not sure of what's being asked, you'll never know whether you've chosen the right answer. What you do next depends on the type of question you're answering.

- If it's math, take a quick look at the answer choices for some clues. Sometimes this helps to put the question in a new perspective and makes it easier to answer. Then make a plan of attack to solve the problem.
- Otherwise, follow this simple *process of elimination* plan to manage your testing time as efficiently as possible: Read each answer choice and

make a *quick* decision about what to do with it, marking your test book accordingly:

The answer seems reasonable; keep it. Put a ✔ next to the answer.

The answer is awful. Get rid of it. Put an ✘ next to the answer.

You can't make up your mind about the answer, or you don't understand it. Keep it for now. Put a **?** next to it.

Whatever you do, don't waste time dilly-dallying over each answer choice. If you can't figure out what an answer choice means, don't worry about it. If it's the correct answer, you'll probably be able to eliminate all the others, and, if it's the wrong answer, another answer will probably strike you more obviously as the correct answer.

If you haven't eliminated any answers at all, skip the question temporarily, but don't forget to mark the question so you can come back to it later if you have time. If the test has no penalty for wrong answers, and you're certain that you could never answer this question in a million years, pick an answer and move on!

If you've eliminated all but one answer, just reread the circled part of the question to make sure you're answering exactly what's asked. Mark your answer sheet and move on to the next question.

Here's what to do when you've eliminated some, but not all of the answer choices. Compare the remaining answers looking for similarities and differences, reasoning your way through these choices. Try to eliminate those choices that don't seem as strong to you. But *don't* eliminate an answer just because you don't understand it. You may even be able to use relevant information from other parts of the test. If you've narrowed it down to a single answer, check it against the circled question to be sure you've answered it. Then mark your answer sheet and move on. If you're down to only two or three answer choices, you've improved your odds of getting the question right. Make an *educated* guess and move on. However, if you think you can do better with more time, mark the question as one to return to later.

## If You're Penalized for Wrong Answers

You *must know* whether you'll be penalized for wrong answers before you begin the test. If you don't, ask the proctor before the test begins. Whether or not you make a guess depends upon the penalty. Some standardized tests are scored in such a way that every wrong answer reduces your score by a fraction of a point, and these can really add up against you! Whatever the penalty, if you can eliminate enough choices to make the odds of answering the question better than the penalty for getting it wrong, make a guess. This is called *educated guessing*.

Let's imagine you are taking a test in which each answer has five choices and you are penalized one-fourth of a point for each wrong answer. If you cannot eliminate any of the answer choices, you're better off leaving the answer blank because the odds of guessing correctly are one in five. However, if you can eliminate two of the choices as definitely wrong, the odds are now in your favor. You have a one in three chance of answering the question correctly. Fortunately, few tests are scored using such elaborate means, but if your test is one of them, know the penalties and calculate your odds before you take a guess on a question.

## If You Finish Early

Use any time you have left to do the following:

- Go back to questions you skipped and try them again.
- Check your work on all the other questions. If you have a good reason for thinking a response is wrong, change it.
- Review your answer sheet. Make sure that you've put the answers in the right places and that you've marked only one answer for each question. (Most tests are scored in such a way that questions with more than one answer are marked wrong.)
- If you've erased an answer, make sure you've done a good job of it.
- Check for stray marks on your answer sheet that could distort your score.

Whatever you do, don't just take a nap when you've finished a test section. Make every second count by checking your work over and over again until time is called.

## ▶ The Days before the Test

### Physical Activity
Get some exercise in the days preceding the test. You'll send some extra oxygen to your brain and allow your thinking performance to peak on test day. Moderation is the key here. Don't exercise so much that you feel exhausted, but a little physical activity will invigorate your body and brain.

### Balanced Diet
Like your body, your brain needs the proper nutrients to function well. Eat plenty of fruits and vegetables in the days before the test. Foods that are high in lecithin, such as fish and beans, are especially good choices. Lecithin is a mineral your brain needs for peak performance. You may even consider a visit to your local pharmacy to buy a bottle of lecithin tablets several weeks before your test.

### Rest
Get plenty of sleep for a few nights before you take the test. Don't overdo it, though, or you'll make yourself as groggy as if you were overtired. Go to bed at a reasonable time, early enough to get the number of hours you need to function effectively. You'll feel relaxed and rested if you've gotten plenty of sleep in the days before you take the test.

### Trial Run
At some point before you take the test, make a trial run to the testing center to see how long it takes to get there. Rushing raises your emotional energy and lowers your intellectual capacity, so you want to allow plenty of time on test day to get to the testing center. Arriving ten to 15 minutes early gives you time to relax and get situated.

### The Night Before
Get ready all those things you need to bring with you to the test, such as pencils, identification, admission ticket, etc. Make sure you have at least three pencils, including one with a dull point for faster gridding of a bubble answer sheet. You don't want to waste time the morning of the test hunting around for these things.

## ▶ Test Day

It's finally here, the day of the big test. Set your alarm early enough to allow plenty of time. Eat a good breakfast. Avoid anything that's really high in sugar, such as doughnuts. A sugar high turns into a sugar low after an hour or so. Cereal and toast or anything with complex carbohydrates is a good choice. Eat only moderate amounts. You don't want to take a test feeling stuffed!

Dress in layers. You can never tell what the conditions will be in the testing room. Your proctor just might be a member of the polar bear club.

Pack a high energy snack to take with you. You might get a break sometime during the test when you can grab a quick snack. Bananas are great. They have a moderate amount of sugar and plenty of brain nutrients, such as potassium. Most proctors won't allow you to eat a snack while you're testing, but a peppermint shouldn't pose a problem. Peppermints are like smelling salts for your brain. If you lose your concentration or suffer from a momentary mental block, a peppermint can get you back on track.

Leave early enough so you have plenty of time to get to the test center. Allow a few minutes for unexpected traffic. When you arrive, locate the restroom and use it. Few things interfere with concentration as much as a full bladder. Then check in, find your seat, and make sure it's comfortable. If it isn't, tell the proctor and ask to change to a location you find more suitable.

Now relax and think positively! Before you know it the test will be over, and you'll walk away knowing you've done the best you can.

## ▶ After the Test

Two things:

1. Plan a little celebration.
2. Go to it.

If you have something to look forward to after the test is over, you may find it easier to prepare well for the test and to keep moving during the test. Good luck!

# 16 ▶ California Police Practice Exam 1

## CHAPTER SUMMARY

This is the first of two police exams in this book based on the entry-level law enforcement tests of the California Peace Officer Standards and Training (POST) Commission. Many police departments in California use the POST test as their written exam for police officer candidates. You can use this test to see how you would do if you had to take the test today.

The test that follows is modeled on the California POST Commission's reading and writing exam for entry-level law enforcement personnel. This test is used by many jurisdictions in California to assess police applicants. Even if the jurisdiction you are applying to doesn't use the POST test, this test will still provide good, relevant practice.

There are 105 questions on this test, 65 in Book One and 40 in Book Two. Book One covers clarity of expression (grammar), vocabulary, spelling, and reading comprehension. Book Two is a different kind of reading test in which you have to fill in the missing words in a passage. The directions for each kind of question are included in the test. The answer sheet you should use to mark your answers comes before the test, and the answer key and an explanation of how to score your test results come after.

The other test you need to prepare for is the essay examination. This is covered in more detail in Chapter 17. One of the keys to doing well on any exam is simply knowing what to expect. While there's no substitute for having the skills the exam is testing for, the experience of taking similar exams goes a long way toward enhancing your self-confidence—and self-confidence is key to doing well.

Use this test to get a benchmark: Where are you starting as you begin your preparation for the police exam? On the real test, you'll have two-and-a-half hours to answer all the questions, but, for now, don't worry about timing. Just take the test in as relaxed a manner as you can. Make sure you have enough time, however, to do the whole test in one sitting. Find a quiet spot where you won't be interrupted, and turn off the radio and TV. When you've finished, turn to the answer key to see how you did.

# BOOK ONE

| 1. | (a) | (b) | (c) | (d) |
| 2. | (a) | (b) | (c) | (d) |
| 3. | (a) | (b) | (c) | (d) |
| 4. | (a) | (b) | (c) | (d) |
| 5. | (a) | (b) | (c) | (d) |
| 6. | (a) | (b) | (c) | (d) |
| 7. | (a) | (b) | (c) | (d) |
| 8. | (a) | (b) | (c) | (d) |
| 9. | (a) | (b) | (c) | (d) |
| 10. | (a) | (b) | (c) | (d) |
| 11. | (a) | (b) | (c) | (d) |
| 12. | (a) | (b) | (c) | (d) |
| 13. | (a) | (b) | (c) | (d) |
| 14. | (a) | (b) | (c) | (d) |
| 15. | (a) | (b) | (c) | (d) |
| 16. | (a) | (b) | (c) | (d) |
| 17. | (a) | (b) | (c) | (d) |
| 18. | (a) | (b) | (c) | (d) |
| 19. | (a) | (b) | (c) | (d) |
| 20. | (a) | (b) | (c) | (d) |
| 21. | (a) | (b) | (c) | (d) |
| 22. | (a) | (b) | (c) | (d) |
| 23. | (a) | (b) | (c) | (d) |
| 24. | (a) | (b) | (c) | (d) |
| 25. | (a) | (b) | (c) | (d) |

| 26. | (a) | (b) | (c) | (d) |
| 27. | (a) | (b) | (c) | (d) |
| 28. | (a) | (b) | (c) | (d) |
| 29. | (a) | (b) | (c) | (d) |
| 30. | (a) | (b) | (c) | (d) |
| 31. | (a) | (b) | (c) | (d) |
| 32. | (a) | (b) | (c) | (d) |
| 33. | (a) | (b) | (c) | (d) |
| 34. | (a) | (b) | (c) | (d) |
| 35. | (a) | (b) | (c) | (d) |
| 36. | (a) | (b) | (c) | (d) |
| 37. | (a) | (b) | (c) | (d) |
| 38. | (a) | (b) | (c) | (d) |
| 39. | (a) | (b) | (c) | (d) |
| 40. | (a) | (b) | (c) | (d) |
| 41. | (a) | (b) | (c) | (d) |
| 42. | (a) | (b) | (c) | (d) |
| 43. | (a) | (b) | (c) | (d) |
| 44. | (a) | (b) | (c) | (d) |
| 45. | (a) | (b) | (c) | (d) |
| 46. | (a) | (b) | (c) | (d) |
| 47. | (a) | (b) | (c) | (d) |
| 48. | (a) | (b) | (c) | (d) |
| 49. | (a) | (b) | (c) | (d) |
| 50. | (a) | (b) | (c) | (d) |

| 51. | (a) | (b) | (c) | (d) |
| 52. | (a) | (b) | (c) | (d) |
| 53. | (a) | (b) | (c) | (d) |
| 54. | (a) | (b) | (c) | (d) |
| 55. | (a) | (b) | (c) | (d) |
| 56. | (a) | (b) | (c) | (d) |
| 57. | (a) | (b) | (c) | (d) |
| 58. | (a) | (b) | (c) | (d) |
| 59. | (a) | (b) | (c) | (d) |
| 60 | (a) | (b) | (c) | (d) |
| 61. | (a) | (b) | (c) | (d) |
| 62. | (a) | (b) | (c) | (d) |
| 63. | (a) | (b) | (c) | (d) |
| 64 | (a) | (b) | (c) | (d) |
| 65. | (a) | (b) | (c) | (d) |

# BOOK TWO

WRITE 1ST LETTER OF WORD HERE

CODE LETTERS HERE

| 1 | 2 | 3 | 4 | 5 | 6 | 7 | 8 | 9 | 10 |
|---|---|---|---|---|---|---|---|---|---|

Ⓐ Ⓐ Ⓐ Ⓐ Ⓐ Ⓐ Ⓐ Ⓐ Ⓐ Ⓐ
Ⓑ Ⓑ Ⓑ Ⓑ Ⓑ Ⓑ Ⓑ Ⓑ Ⓑ Ⓑ
Ⓒ Ⓒ Ⓒ Ⓒ Ⓒ Ⓒ Ⓒ Ⓒ Ⓒ Ⓒ
Ⓓ Ⓓ Ⓓ Ⓓ Ⓓ Ⓓ Ⓓ Ⓓ Ⓓ Ⓓ
Ⓔ Ⓔ Ⓔ Ⓔ Ⓔ Ⓔ Ⓔ Ⓔ Ⓔ Ⓔ
Ⓕ Ⓕ Ⓕ Ⓕ Ⓕ Ⓕ Ⓕ Ⓕ Ⓕ Ⓕ
Ⓖ Ⓖ Ⓖ Ⓖ Ⓖ Ⓖ Ⓖ Ⓖ Ⓖ Ⓖ
Ⓗ Ⓗ Ⓗ Ⓗ Ⓗ Ⓗ Ⓗ Ⓗ Ⓗ Ⓗ
Ⓘ Ⓘ Ⓘ Ⓘ Ⓘ Ⓘ Ⓘ Ⓘ Ⓘ Ⓘ
Ⓙ Ⓙ Ⓙ Ⓙ Ⓙ Ⓙ Ⓙ Ⓙ Ⓙ Ⓙ
Ⓚ Ⓚ Ⓚ Ⓚ Ⓚ Ⓚ Ⓚ Ⓚ Ⓚ Ⓚ
Ⓛ Ⓛ Ⓛ Ⓛ Ⓛ Ⓛ Ⓛ Ⓛ Ⓛ Ⓛ
Ⓜ Ⓜ Ⓜ Ⓜ Ⓜ Ⓜ Ⓜ Ⓜ Ⓜ Ⓜ
Ⓝ Ⓝ Ⓝ Ⓝ Ⓝ Ⓝ Ⓝ Ⓝ Ⓝ Ⓝ
Ⓞ Ⓞ Ⓞ Ⓞ Ⓞ Ⓞ Ⓞ Ⓞ Ⓞ Ⓞ
Ⓟ Ⓟ Ⓟ Ⓟ Ⓟ Ⓟ Ⓟ Ⓟ Ⓟ Ⓟ
Ⓠ Ⓠ Ⓠ Ⓠ Ⓠ Ⓠ Ⓠ Ⓠ Ⓠ Ⓠ
Ⓡ Ⓡ Ⓡ Ⓡ Ⓡ Ⓡ Ⓡ Ⓡ Ⓡ Ⓡ
Ⓢ Ⓢ Ⓢ Ⓢ Ⓢ Ⓢ Ⓢ Ⓢ Ⓢ Ⓢ
Ⓣ Ⓣ Ⓣ Ⓣ Ⓣ Ⓣ Ⓣ Ⓣ Ⓣ Ⓣ
Ⓤ Ⓤ Ⓤ Ⓤ Ⓤ Ⓤ Ⓤ Ⓤ Ⓤ Ⓤ
Ⓥ Ⓥ Ⓥ Ⓥ Ⓥ Ⓥ Ⓥ Ⓥ Ⓥ Ⓥ
Ⓦ Ⓦ Ⓦ Ⓦ Ⓦ Ⓦ Ⓦ Ⓦ Ⓦ Ⓦ
Ⓧ Ⓧ Ⓧ Ⓧ Ⓧ Ⓧ Ⓧ Ⓧ Ⓧ Ⓧ
Ⓨ Ⓨ Ⓨ Ⓨ Ⓨ Ⓨ Ⓨ Ⓨ Ⓨ Ⓨ
Ⓩ Ⓩ Ⓩ Ⓩ Ⓩ Ⓩ Ⓩ Ⓩ Ⓩ Ⓩ

| 11 | 12 | 13 | 14 | 15 | 16 | 17 | 18 | 19 | 20 |
|---|---|---|---|---|---|---|---|---|---|

Ⓐ Ⓐ Ⓐ Ⓐ Ⓐ Ⓐ Ⓐ Ⓐ Ⓐ Ⓐ
Ⓑ Ⓑ Ⓑ Ⓑ Ⓑ Ⓑ Ⓑ Ⓑ Ⓑ Ⓑ
Ⓒ Ⓒ Ⓒ Ⓒ Ⓒ Ⓒ Ⓒ Ⓒ Ⓒ Ⓒ
Ⓓ Ⓓ Ⓓ Ⓓ Ⓓ Ⓓ Ⓓ Ⓓ Ⓓ Ⓓ
Ⓔ Ⓔ Ⓔ Ⓔ Ⓔ Ⓔ Ⓔ Ⓔ Ⓔ Ⓔ
Ⓕ Ⓕ Ⓕ Ⓕ Ⓕ Ⓕ Ⓕ Ⓕ Ⓕ Ⓕ
Ⓖ Ⓖ Ⓖ Ⓖ Ⓖ Ⓖ Ⓖ Ⓖ Ⓖ Ⓖ
Ⓗ Ⓗ Ⓗ Ⓗ Ⓗ Ⓗ Ⓗ Ⓗ Ⓗ Ⓗ
Ⓘ Ⓘ Ⓘ Ⓘ Ⓘ Ⓘ Ⓘ Ⓘ Ⓘ Ⓘ
Ⓙ Ⓙ Ⓙ Ⓙ Ⓙ Ⓙ Ⓙ Ⓙ Ⓙ Ⓙ
Ⓚ Ⓚ Ⓚ Ⓚ Ⓚ Ⓚ Ⓚ Ⓚ Ⓚ Ⓚ
Ⓛ Ⓛ Ⓛ Ⓛ Ⓛ Ⓛ Ⓛ Ⓛ Ⓛ Ⓛ
Ⓜ Ⓜ Ⓜ Ⓜ Ⓜ Ⓜ Ⓜ Ⓜ Ⓜ Ⓜ
Ⓝ Ⓝ Ⓝ Ⓝ Ⓝ Ⓝ Ⓝ Ⓝ Ⓝ Ⓝ
Ⓞ Ⓞ Ⓞ Ⓞ Ⓞ Ⓞ Ⓞ Ⓞ Ⓞ Ⓞ
Ⓟ Ⓟ Ⓟ Ⓟ Ⓟ Ⓟ Ⓟ Ⓟ Ⓟ Ⓟ
Ⓠ Ⓠ Ⓠ Ⓠ Ⓠ Ⓠ Ⓠ Ⓠ Ⓠ Ⓠ
Ⓡ Ⓡ Ⓡ Ⓡ Ⓡ Ⓡ Ⓡ Ⓡ Ⓡ Ⓡ
Ⓢ Ⓢ Ⓢ Ⓢ Ⓢ Ⓢ Ⓢ Ⓢ Ⓢ Ⓢ
Ⓣ Ⓣ Ⓣ Ⓣ Ⓣ Ⓣ Ⓣ Ⓣ Ⓣ Ⓣ
Ⓤ Ⓤ Ⓤ Ⓤ Ⓤ Ⓤ Ⓤ Ⓤ Ⓤ Ⓤ
Ⓥ Ⓥ Ⓥ Ⓥ Ⓥ Ⓥ Ⓥ Ⓥ Ⓥ Ⓥ
Ⓦ Ⓦ Ⓦ Ⓦ Ⓦ Ⓦ Ⓦ Ⓦ Ⓦ Ⓦ
Ⓧ Ⓧ Ⓧ Ⓧ Ⓧ Ⓧ Ⓧ Ⓧ Ⓧ Ⓧ
Ⓨ Ⓨ Ⓨ Ⓨ Ⓨ Ⓨ Ⓨ Ⓨ Ⓨ Ⓨ
Ⓩ Ⓩ Ⓩ Ⓩ Ⓩ Ⓩ Ⓩ Ⓩ Ⓩ Ⓩ

| 21 | 22 | 23 | 24 | 25 | 26 | 27 | 28 | 29 | 30 |
|---|---|---|---|---|---|---|---|---|---|

Ⓐ Ⓐ Ⓐ Ⓐ Ⓐ Ⓐ Ⓐ Ⓐ Ⓐ Ⓐ
Ⓑ Ⓑ Ⓑ Ⓑ Ⓑ Ⓑ Ⓑ Ⓑ Ⓑ Ⓑ
Ⓒ Ⓒ Ⓒ Ⓒ Ⓒ Ⓒ Ⓒ Ⓒ Ⓒ Ⓒ
Ⓓ Ⓓ Ⓓ Ⓓ Ⓓ Ⓓ Ⓓ Ⓓ Ⓓ Ⓓ
Ⓔ Ⓔ Ⓔ Ⓔ Ⓔ Ⓔ Ⓔ Ⓔ Ⓔ Ⓔ
Ⓕ Ⓕ Ⓕ Ⓕ Ⓕ Ⓕ Ⓕ Ⓕ Ⓕ Ⓕ
Ⓖ Ⓖ Ⓖ Ⓖ Ⓖ Ⓖ Ⓖ Ⓖ Ⓖ Ⓖ
Ⓗ Ⓗ Ⓗ Ⓗ Ⓗ Ⓗ Ⓗ Ⓗ Ⓗ Ⓗ
Ⓘ Ⓘ Ⓘ Ⓘ Ⓘ Ⓘ Ⓘ Ⓘ Ⓘ Ⓘ
Ⓙ Ⓙ Ⓙ Ⓙ Ⓙ Ⓙ Ⓙ Ⓙ Ⓙ Ⓙ
Ⓚ Ⓚ Ⓚ Ⓚ Ⓚ Ⓚ Ⓚ Ⓚ Ⓚ Ⓚ
Ⓛ Ⓛ Ⓛ Ⓛ Ⓛ Ⓛ Ⓛ Ⓛ Ⓛ Ⓛ
Ⓜ Ⓜ Ⓜ Ⓜ Ⓜ Ⓜ Ⓜ Ⓜ Ⓜ Ⓜ
Ⓝ Ⓝ Ⓝ Ⓝ Ⓝ Ⓝ Ⓝ Ⓝ Ⓝ Ⓝ
Ⓞ Ⓞ Ⓞ Ⓞ Ⓞ Ⓞ Ⓞ Ⓞ Ⓞ Ⓞ
Ⓟ Ⓟ Ⓟ Ⓟ Ⓟ Ⓟ Ⓟ Ⓟ Ⓟ Ⓟ
Ⓠ Ⓠ Ⓠ Ⓠ Ⓠ Ⓠ Ⓠ Ⓠ Ⓠ Ⓠ
Ⓡ Ⓡ Ⓡ Ⓡ Ⓡ Ⓡ Ⓡ Ⓡ Ⓡ Ⓡ
Ⓢ Ⓢ Ⓢ Ⓢ Ⓢ Ⓢ Ⓢ Ⓢ Ⓢ Ⓢ
Ⓣ Ⓣ Ⓣ Ⓣ Ⓣ Ⓣ Ⓣ Ⓣ Ⓣ Ⓣ
Ⓤ Ⓤ Ⓤ Ⓤ Ⓤ Ⓤ Ⓤ Ⓤ Ⓤ Ⓤ
Ⓥ Ⓥ Ⓥ Ⓥ Ⓥ Ⓥ Ⓥ Ⓥ Ⓥ Ⓥ
Ⓦ Ⓦ Ⓦ Ⓦ Ⓦ Ⓦ Ⓦ Ⓦ Ⓦ Ⓦ
Ⓧ Ⓧ Ⓧ Ⓧ Ⓧ Ⓧ Ⓧ Ⓧ Ⓧ Ⓧ
Ⓨ Ⓨ Ⓨ Ⓨ Ⓨ Ⓨ Ⓨ Ⓨ Ⓨ Ⓨ
Ⓩ Ⓩ Ⓩ Ⓩ Ⓩ Ⓩ Ⓩ Ⓩ Ⓩ Ⓩ

| 31 | 32 | 33 | 34 | 35 | 36 | 37 | 38 | 39 | 40 |
|---|---|---|---|---|---|---|---|---|---|

Ⓐ Ⓐ Ⓐ Ⓐ Ⓐ Ⓐ Ⓐ Ⓐ Ⓐ Ⓐ
Ⓑ Ⓑ Ⓑ Ⓑ Ⓑ Ⓑ Ⓑ Ⓑ Ⓑ Ⓑ
Ⓒ Ⓒ Ⓒ Ⓒ Ⓒ Ⓒ Ⓒ Ⓒ Ⓒ Ⓒ
Ⓓ Ⓓ Ⓓ Ⓓ Ⓓ Ⓓ Ⓓ Ⓓ Ⓓ Ⓓ
Ⓔ Ⓔ Ⓔ Ⓔ Ⓔ Ⓔ Ⓔ Ⓔ Ⓔ Ⓔ
Ⓕ Ⓕ Ⓕ Ⓕ Ⓕ Ⓕ Ⓕ Ⓕ Ⓕ Ⓕ
Ⓖ Ⓖ Ⓖ Ⓖ Ⓖ Ⓖ Ⓖ Ⓖ Ⓖ Ⓖ
Ⓗ Ⓗ Ⓗ Ⓗ Ⓗ Ⓗ Ⓗ Ⓗ Ⓗ Ⓗ
Ⓘ Ⓘ Ⓘ Ⓘ Ⓘ Ⓘ Ⓘ Ⓘ Ⓘ Ⓘ
Ⓙ Ⓙ Ⓙ Ⓙ Ⓙ Ⓙ Ⓙ Ⓙ Ⓙ Ⓙ
Ⓚ Ⓚ Ⓚ Ⓚ Ⓚ Ⓚ Ⓚ Ⓚ Ⓚ Ⓚ
Ⓛ Ⓛ Ⓛ Ⓛ Ⓛ Ⓛ Ⓛ Ⓛ Ⓛ Ⓛ
Ⓜ Ⓜ Ⓜ Ⓜ Ⓜ Ⓜ Ⓜ Ⓜ Ⓜ Ⓜ
Ⓝ Ⓝ Ⓝ Ⓝ Ⓝ Ⓝ Ⓝ Ⓝ Ⓝ Ⓝ
Ⓞ Ⓞ Ⓞ Ⓞ Ⓞ Ⓞ Ⓞ Ⓞ Ⓞ Ⓞ
Ⓟ Ⓟ Ⓟ Ⓟ Ⓟ Ⓟ Ⓟ Ⓟ Ⓟ Ⓟ
Ⓠ Ⓠ Ⓠ Ⓠ Ⓠ Ⓠ Ⓠ Ⓠ Ⓠ Ⓠ
Ⓡ Ⓡ Ⓡ Ⓡ Ⓡ Ⓡ Ⓡ Ⓡ Ⓡ Ⓡ
Ⓢ Ⓢ Ⓢ Ⓢ Ⓢ Ⓢ Ⓢ Ⓢ Ⓢ Ⓢ
Ⓣ Ⓣ Ⓣ Ⓣ Ⓣ Ⓣ Ⓣ Ⓣ Ⓣ Ⓣ
Ⓤ Ⓤ Ⓤ Ⓤ Ⓤ Ⓤ Ⓤ Ⓤ Ⓤ Ⓤ
Ⓥ Ⓥ Ⓥ Ⓥ Ⓥ Ⓥ Ⓥ Ⓥ Ⓥ Ⓥ
Ⓦ Ⓦ Ⓦ Ⓦ Ⓦ Ⓦ Ⓦ Ⓦ Ⓦ Ⓦ
Ⓧ Ⓧ Ⓧ Ⓧ Ⓧ Ⓧ Ⓧ Ⓧ Ⓧ Ⓧ
Ⓨ Ⓨ Ⓨ Ⓨ Ⓨ Ⓨ Ⓨ Ⓨ Ⓨ Ⓨ
Ⓩ Ⓩ Ⓩ Ⓩ Ⓩ Ⓩ Ⓩ Ⓩ Ⓩ Ⓩ

## ► California Police Exam 1 Book One

### Part One: Clarity

In the following sets of sentences, choose the sentence that is most clearly written.

**1.**

a. Because Officer Alvarez had a warrant, she was able to search the suspect's car, where she found $200,000 worth of cocaine.

b. Officer Alvarez was able to search the suspect's car, where she found $200,000 worth of cocaine. Because she had a warrant.

c. $200,000 worth of cocaine was found. The result of a search by Office Alvarez of the suspect's car, because she had a warrant.

d. Because of a warrant and a search of the suspect's car. $200,000 worth of cocaine was found by Officer Alvarez.

**2.**

a. The guard, like the prisoners, were sick of the food in the prison mess hall, and yesterday he went to the warden and complained.

b. The guard, like the prisoners, was sick of the food in the prison mess hall, and yesterday he goes to the warden and complains.

c. The guard, like the prisoners, was sick of the food in the prison mess hall, and yesterday he went to the warden and complained.

d. The guard, like the prisoners, were sick of the food in the prison mess hall, and yesterday he goes to the warden and complained.

**3.**

a. Lieutenant Wells did not think the prisoner could be capable to escape.

b. Lieutenant Wells did not think that the prisoner capable of escaping.

c. Lieutenant Wells did not think the prisoner capable of escape.

d. Lieutenant Wells did not think that the prisoner capable to escape.

**4.**

a. The masked gunman ordered the bank customers to remove their jewelry and lie down on the floor, with a growl.

b. The masked gunman ordered the bank customers to remove their jewelry, with a growl, and lie down on the floor.

c. The masked gunman ordered the bank customers with a growl. To remove their jewelry and lie down on the floor.

d. With a growl, the masked gunman ordered the bank customers to remove their jewelry and lie down on the floor.

**5.**

a. Officers Antwerp and Simpson, while searching their police vehicle for contraband, finds secreted drugs under the seat.

b. Officers Antwerp and Simpson, while searching their police vehicle for contraband, find secreted drugs under the seat.

c. Officers Antwerp and Simpson, while he searched their police vehicle for contraband, finds secreted drugs under the seat.

d. Officers Antwerp and Simpson, while searching his police vehicle for contraband, have finds secreted drugs under the seat.

**6.**
a. The animal control officers, but not the other officers at the crime scene, were upset at the news media on scene.
b. The animal control officers, but not the other officers at the crime scene, was upset at the news media on scene.
c. The animal control officer, but not the other officers at the crime scene, was upseted at the news media on scene.
d. The animal control officers, but not the other officers at the crime scene, were upseted at the news media on scene.

**7.**
a. Over the crackle of the radio, a voice could be heard asking "Where are you at?"
b. Over the crackle of the radio, voices was heard asking, "Where are you at?"
c. Over the crackle of the radio, a voice could be heard asking, "Where is you?"
d. Over the crackle of the radio, a voice could be heard asking, "Where are you?"

**8.**
a. The police service worker, and her husband of five months, was the best dressed at the party, and each of them received a nice prize.
b. The police service worker, and her husband of five months, were the best dressed at the party, and each of them received a nice prizes.
c. The police service worker and her husband of five months was the best dressed at the party, and each of them receives a nice prize.
d. The police service worker and her husband of five months were the best dressed at the party, and each of them received a nice prize.

**9.**
a. The impoverished childrens' clothes were old and dirty.
b. The impoverished children's clothes were old and dirty.
c. The impoverished children clotheses were old and dirty.
d. The impoverished children's clothes was old and dirty.

**10.**
a. For three weeks the Merryville fire chief received taunting calls from an arsonist, who would not say where he intended to set the next fire.
b. The Merryville fire chief received taunting calls from an arsonist, but he would not say where he intended to set the next fire, for three weeks.
c. He would not say where he intended to set the next fire, but for three weeks the Merryville fire chief received taunting calls from an arsonist.
d. The Merryville fire chief received taunting calls from an arsonist for three weeks, not saying where he intended to set the next fire.

**11.**
a. Some people say jury duty is a nuisance that just takes up their precious time and that we don't get paid enough.
b. Some people say jury duty is a nuisance that just takes up your precious time and that one doesn't get paid enough.
c. Some people say jury duty is a nuisance that just takes up one's precious time and that one doesn't get paid enough.
d. Some people say jury duty is a nuisance that just takes up our precious time and that they don't get paid enough.

**12.**
   a. Kate Meyers and several other officers has recently received a well-deserved promotion.
   b. Several officers, including Kate Meyers, has recently received a well-deserved promotion.
   c. Kate Meyers, along with several other officers, have recently received well-deserved promotions.
   d. Several officers, including Kate Meyers, have recently received well-deserved promotions.

**13.**
   a. Doctor Falkenrath believes that neither immorality nor amorality is a spiritual defect.
   b. Doctor Falkenrath believes that neither immorality nor amorality are a spiritual defect.
   c. Doctor Falkenrath believes that immorality and amorality are not a spiritual defect.
   d. Doctor Falkenrath believes that both immorality and amorality is not spiritual defects.

**14.**
   a. An abused woman's cries for help were sometimes ignored, and she is advised to go back to her abuser.
   b. An abused woman's cries for help were sometimes ignored, and she will be advised to go back to her abuser.
   c. An abused woman's cries for help are sometimes ignored, and she is advised to go back to her abuser.
   d. An abused woman's cries for help are sometimes ignored, and she was advised to go back to her abuser.

**15.**
   a. Sergeant Ahlamady often bought pizza for herself and I.
   b. Sergeant Ahlamady often bought pizza for herself and me.
   c. Sergeant Ahlamady often bought pizza for her and me.
   d. Sergeant Ahlamady often bought pizza for herself and myself.

**Part Two: Vocabulary**
In each of the following sentences, choose the word or phrase that most nearly expresses the same meaning as the underlined word.

**16.** The <u>median</u> age of police officers entering the workforce in California is 23.4 years old.
   a. average
   b. lowest
   c. highest
   d. best

**17.** Officer Best's report on the Earthenware Company burglary was <u>exemplary</u>.
   a. exhibited
   b. excellent
   c. extreme
   d. examination

**18.** This new procedure will improve the accuracy of the process and enhance <u>compliance</u> with state law.
   a. complaining
   b. reliance
   c. protocol
   d. conformity

**19.** The police department is recommending that the new integrity policy be <u>integrated</u> into the practices of the Professional Standards Bureau.
   **a.** intimidated
   **b.** excluded
   **c.** incorporated
   **d.** practiced

**20.** In the small suburb in California, local police have <u>implemented</u> a neighborhood watch program that has yielded extraordinary results.
   **a.** implant
   **b.** ceased
   **c.** started
   **d.** prolonged

**21.** The county coroner's examination of the body was <u>meticulous</u>.
   **a.** delicate
   **b.** painstaking
   **c.** responsible
   **d.** objective

**22.** The police spokesperson must <u>articulate</u> the philosophy of an entire department.
   **a.** trust
   **b.** refine
   **c.** verify
   **d.** express

**23.** Different methods to <u>alleviate</u> the situation were debated.
   **a.** ease
   **b.** tolerate
   **c.** clarify
   **d.** intensify

**24.** The matter reached its conclusion only after <u>diplomatic</u> efforts by both sides.
   **a.** tactful
   **b.** delaying
   **c.** elaborate
   **d.** combative

**25.** Although the neighborhood was said to be safe, they heard <u>intermittent</u> gunfire all night long.
   **a.** protracted
   **b.** periodic
   **c.** disquieting
   **d.** vehement

**26.** As soon as the details of the robbery were released to the media, the police department was <u>inundated</u> with calls from people who said they had seen the mysterious blue van.
   **a.** provided
   **b.** bothered
   **c.** rewarded
   **d.** flooded

**27.** Regarding the need for more police protection in city park, the group's opinion was <u>unanimous</u>.
   **a.** divided
   **b.** uniform
   **c.** adamant
   **d.** clear-cut

**28.** The city council has given <u>tentative</u> approval to the idea of banning smoking from all public buildings.
   **a.** provisional
   **b.** ambiguous
   **c.** wholehearted
   **d.** unnecessary

**29.** Most members of the community thought the neighborhood guards' red hats were <u>ostentatious</u>.
a. hilarious
b. pretentious
c. outrageous
d. obnoxious

**30.** The <u>prerequisite</u> training for this exercise is an advanced firearms course.
a. required
b. optional
c. preferred
d. advisable

## Part Three: Spelling

In each of the following sentences, choose the correct spelling of the missing word.

**31.** The patrol officers were severely _____ by the trauma of the event.
a. effected
b. affected
c. iffected
d. afficted

**32.** New _____ are constantly being implemented in this police department.
a. procedures
b. proceedures
c. precedures
d. proseedures

**33.** We should be able to _____ the installation of the new laptop computers in the patrol vehicles.
a. acommodate
b. accomodate
c. accommodate
d. accomedate

**34.** Officer Jimenez _____ an award for the highest number of felony arrests in the month of August.
a. receved
b. recieved
c. receeved
d. received

**35.** Shelly said she wanted to go, _____ .
a. to
b. two
c. too
d. towe

**36.** Officer Alvarez would have fired her weapon, but she did not want to place the hostage in _____.
a. jeoperdy
b. jepardy
c. jeapardy
d. jeopardy

**37.** Because of the danger they were in, the soldiers were unable to enjoy the _____ scenery.
a. magniffisent
b. magnifisent
c. magnificent
d. magnifficent

**38.** From inside the box came a strange _____ whirring sound.
a. mechinical
b. mechanical
c. mechenical
d. machanical

**39.** The community was shocked when Cindy Pierce, the president of the senior class, was arrested for selling _____ drugs.
a. elicitt
b. ellicit
c. illicet
d. illicit

**40.** There will be an immediate _____ into the mayor's death.
   **a.** inquiry
   **b.** inquirry
   **c.** enquirry
   **d.** enquery

**41.** Al Guggins was thrown into the East River after he attempted to _____ his contract with the mob.
   **a.** termanate
   **b.** termenate
   **c.** terrminate
   **d.** terminate

**42.** Ben Alshieka feels that he is being _____ for his religious beliefs.
   **a.** persecuted
   **b.** pursecuted
   **c.** presecuted
   **d.** perrsecuted

**43.** What on earth is that _____ odor?
   **a.** peculior
   **b.** peculiar
   **c.** peculliar
   **d.** puculior

**44.** Some people say that _____ is not a true science.
   **a.** psycology
   **b.** pyschology
   **c.** psychollogy
   **d.** psychology

**45.** Ronald Pinkington was 27 years old before he got his driver's _____.
   **a.** lisense
   **b.** lisence
   **c.** lycence
   **d.** license

## Part Four: Reading Comprehension

Following are several reading passages, each accompanied by three or more questions. Answer each question based on what is stated or implied in the passage.

Most criminals do not suffer from antisocial personality disorder; however, nearly all persons with this disorder have been in trouble with the law. Sometimes labeled "sociopaths," they are a grim problem for society. Their crimes range from con games to murder, and they are set apart by what appears to be a complete lack of conscience. Often attractive and charming, and always inordinately self-confident, they nevertheless demonstrate a disturbing emotional shallowness, as if they had been born without a faculty as vital as sight or hearing. These individuals are not legally insane, nor do they suffer from the distortions of thought associated with mental illness; however, some experts believe they are mentally ill. If so, it is an illness that is exceptionally resistant to treatment, particularly because these individuals have a marked inability to learn from the past. It is this latter trait that makes them a special problem for law enforcement officials. Their ability to mimic true emotion enables them to convince prison officials, judges, and psychiatrists that they feel remorse. When released from incarceration, however, they go back to their old tricks, to their con games, their impulsive destructiveness, and their sometimes lethal deceptions.

**46.** Based on the passage, which of the following is likely NOT a characteristic of the person with antisocial personality disorder?
   **a.** delusions of persecution
   **b.** feelings of superiority
   **c.** inability to suffer deeply
   **d.** inability to feel joy

**47.** Which of the following careers would probably best suit the person with an antisocial personality?
 a. soldier with ambition to make officer
 b. warden of a large penitentiary
 c. loan officer in a bank
 d. salesperson dealing in nonexistent real estate

**48.** Based on the passage, which of the following words best sums up the inner emotional life of the person with an antisocial personality?
 a. angry
 b. empty
 c. anxious
 d. repressed

**49.** According to the passage, which of the following characteristics is most helpful to the person with an antisocial personality in getting out of trouble with the law?
 a. inability to learn from the past
 b. ability to mimic the emotions of others
 c. attractiveness and charm
 d. indifference to the suffering of others

Conducting a traffic stop is perhaps the most dangerous event in a police officer's day. The officer does not know who is driving the vehicle and, therefore, does not know if that person is a criminal bent on taking the life of the officer or a person with no criminal record who may have simply committed a traffic violation. Officers must be patient, calm, observant, and professional, yet be on guard for the immediate threat of violence that can escalate the situation to an unimaginable level of danger. Once the decision is made to conduct a traffic stop, it is important to radio to communications the exact location of the traffic stop, the license plate of the vehicle, and how many occupants are in the vehicle. The officer should enter the license plate into the computer database and inquire about its history or if it is wanted for any particular crime. The sixth sense that officers develop comes into play here, as there may

be danger signs that are not immediately recognizable to the ordinary citizen, but the officer may "feel" that there is danger ahead. This sense has saved the lives of many police officers who heed its warnings. Patience and diligence are on the side of the officer, and he or she should not do anything until the time is right and the threat is absent.

**50.** Based upon the passage, which of the following traits should the officer NOT display when conducting traffic stops?
 a. patience
 b. professionalism
 c. vigilance
 d. intensity

**51.** What is the first thing an officer must do when conducting a traffic stop?
 a. Tell his partner how many people he sees inside the vehicle.
 b. Turn his overhead lights on to stop the vehicle.
 c. Inform communications where he stopping the vehicle.
 d. Act upon his "sixth sense."

**52.** Based upon the passage, which of the following statements is NOT true?
 a. When conducting a traffic stop, an officer should radio to communications the race of a vehicle's occupants.
 b. When conducting a traffic stop, an officer should radio to communications the number of vehicle occupants.
 c. Entering a vehicle's license plate into the computer database may reveal that a vehicle's owner is wanted for a crime.
 d. The officer should always enter a vehicle's license plate into the computer database during a traffic stop.

Police officers are held to a higher standard of conduct than most citizens. Should an officer behave in a disruptive manner, make an offensive joke, or behave in an otherwise uncivil manner, even while off duty, community leaders, public officials, and the media react not only with disapprobation and censure, but with surprise. Police officers are expected to be idealists. One often hears the expression "jaded cop," but when is a corporate executive ever disparaged as a "jaded executive"? An executive whose moral sense has been fatigued or one who lacks compassion is not considered notable, yet a police officer is expected to have high ideals even though he or she confronts human nature at its most disillusioning every day.

This is as it should be. As police officers are the keepers of civil order, they must exemplify civil behavior. Civil order depends less upon legal coercion than upon mutual respect and common ideals. Committed to the ideals of justice and truth, police officers must practice fairness and accuracy, even in their speech. Sworn to uphold individual rights, they must treat every individual with respect. A high standard of civil conduct is not merely a matter of community relations, but speaks to the essence of a police officer's role. By the same token, the public should treat police officers with the respect due to those who must adhere to a higher standard of tolerance, understanding, moderation, and civility, even while working under extraordinarily trying conditions.

**53.** Which of the following best expresses the main idea of the passage?
   **a.** High standards should apply to executives as well as to police officers.
   **b.** Police officers are held to unrealistic standards of behavior.
   **c.** Police officers must remain idealistic, despite the disillusioning nature of their work.
   **d.** A police officer should uphold common ideals, both as expressed in law and as required to keep the peace.

**54.** The passage suggests that police officers should refrain from racial slurs for all of the following reasons EXCEPT that
   **a.** as generalizations, such slurs are unfair and inaccurate.
   **b.** such slurs are disrespectful to individuals.
   **c.** such slurs harm the relationship between the community and the police.
   **d.** such slurs are hurtful to the morale of a multiracial police force.

**55.** According to the passage, a police officer should be held to a different standard from an executive because
   **a.** a police officer's very job is concerned with civil behavior.
   **b.** police officers are more jaded.
   **c.** police officers are expected to be honest.
   **d.** a police officer is a figure of civil authority.

**56.** Why does civil conduct "speak to the very essence of a police officer's role"?
   **a.** because a police officer is a public servant
   **b.** because a police officer who behaves in an uncivil manner meets with public censure
   **c.** because civil conduct is necessary in order to keep the civil peace
   **d.** because a police officer upholds the law

**57.** Which of the following is NOT mentioned in the passage as a quality a police officer must exemplify?
   **a.** politeness
   **b.** courage
   **c.** justice
   **d.** moderation

At 9:30 P.M., while parked at 916 Woodward Avenue, Police Officers Whitebear and Morgan were asked to respond to an anonymous complaint of a disturbance at 826 Rosemary Lane. When they arrived, they found the back door open and the jamb splintered. They drew their weapons, identified themselves, and entered the dwelling, where they found Mr. Darrell Hensley, of 1917 Roosevelt Avenue, sitting on the couch. Mr. Hensley calmly stated he was waiting for his wife. At that point, two children emerged from a hallway: Dustin Hensley, age seven, who lives in the dwelling, and Kirstin Jackson, age 14, Dustin's babysitter, who lives at 916 Ambrose Street. Kirstin stated she and Dustin had been sitting at the kitchen table when the back door was kicked in and Mr. Hensley entered, shouting obscenities and calling for Karen Hensley, Dustin's mother. Kirstin then hid with Dustin in a hallway storage closet. The officers contacted Mrs. Hensley at her place of employment at O'Reilley's Restaurant at 415 Ralston. At 9:55, she returned home and showed an Order of Protection stating Mr. Hensley was not to have contact with his wife or child. Mr. Hensley was placed under arrest and taken in handcuffs to the station house.

**58.** Based on Darrell Hensley's behavior when he first arrived at his wife's house, what was his most likely motivation for being there?
  **a.** to see his child, whom he loved
  **b.** to force his wife to deal with him
  **c.** to have a place to stay that night
  **d.** to reconcile peacefully with his family

**59.** Who called the police to investigate the disturbance described in the passage?
  **a.** the babysitter
  **b.** the arrestee's wife
  **c.** a neighbor
  **d.** an unknown person

**60.** Based on the information in the passage, what is the most likely reason the officers drew their weapons before entering the Hensley home?
  **a.** There were signs of forced entry into the house.
  **b.** There was an Order of Protection against Mr. Hensley.
  **c.** Children were in danger inside the premises.
  **d.** They knew Mr. Hensley to be a violent man.

**61.** Based on the information in the passage, what was Mr. Hensley's demeanor when the police first spoke to him?
  **a.** He was enraged.
  **b.** He was remorseful.
  **c.** He was matter-of-fact.
  **d.** He was confused.

At 12:45 A.M. on October 15, while parked at 1910 Fairlane, Police Officers Flores and Steinbrenner were asked to respond to a disturbance at 1809 Clarkson. When they arrived at the one-story dwelling, the complainant, Alan Weber, who resides next door at 1807 Clarkson, told them that he had been kept awake for two hours by the sound of yelling and breaking glass. He said the occupant of 1809 Clarkson, Mr. Everett Hayes, lived alone. When the officers knocked on the door, Mr. Hayes answered promptly and said, "It's about time you got here." Inside, broken furniture was strewn about. Mr. Hayes stated he had been protecting himself from persons who lived inside the woodwork of his home. He went willingly with the officers to Fairfield County Hospital at 1010 Market, where he was admitted to the psychiatric unit for observation. No arrests were made.

**62.** The call to the police was most likely made from which of the following addresses?
  **a.** 1910 Fairlane
  **b.** 1809 Clarkson
  **c.** 1807 Clarkson
  **d.** 1010 Market

**63.** Based on the passage, what was the most likely reason the police were called?
   **a.** A neighbor was bothered by the noise coming from Mr. Hayes's home.
   **b.** A neighbor was worried for Mr. Hayes's safety.
   **c.** A neighbor was worried for the safety of Mr. Hayes's family.
   **d.** A neighbor was curious about Mr. Hayes's personal life.

**64.** What was Mr. Hayes's demeanor when the police arrived at his door?
   **a.** He seemed surprised.
   **b.** He seemed to have been expecting them.
   **c.** He seemed frightened and distrustful.
   **d.** He seemed angered by their presence.

**65.** Based on the passage, what reason would Mr. Hayes himself most likely give for the commotion at his house?
   **a.** He was acting in self-defense.
   **b.** He was mentally ill.
   **c.** He was cleaning the woodwork.
   **d.** He was annoyed at his neighbors.

## ▶ Book Two

This is a test of your reading ability. In the following passages, words have been omitted. Each numbered set of dashed blank lines indicates where a word has been left out; each dash represents one letter of the missing word. The correct word should not only make sense in the sentence, but also have the number of letters indicated by the dashes.

Read through the whole passage, and then begin filling in the missing words. Fill in as many missing words as possible. If you aren't sure of the answer, take a guess.

Then mark your answers on the answer sheet as follows: Write the **first letter** of the word you have chosen in the square under the number of the word. Then blacken the circle of that letter of the alphabet under the square.

**Only the blackened alphabet circles will be scored.** The words you write on this page and the letters you write at the top of the column on the answer sheet **will not be scored**. Make sure that you blacken the appropriate circle in each column.

Many people become angry when they hear that prison inmates have the opportunity to study for their **1)** _ _ _ _ school equivalency diplomas, take college courses, and even earn **2)** _ _ _ _ _ _ _ degrees while they are serving **3)** _ _ _ _. Such educational services are often provided at **4)** _ _ charge to the inmates, which means that the **5)** _ _ _ _ _ are shouldered by taxpayers. Many people see these **6)** _ _ _ _ educational services as coddling criminals and providing "rewards" for lawbreakers. Higher education is **7)** _ _ _ _ _ _ _ _ _, and it is frustrating to many people to see convicted criminals **8)** _ _ _ for free what working people have to struggle so hard to **9)** _ _ _ _ _ _ _ for their children. On the other hand, those **10)** _ _ _ support educational services for inmates argue that it is in society's **11)** _ _ _ _ interest to provide such services. Rather **12)** _ _ _ _ being seen as a reward for **13)** _ _ _ _ _ _ _ _ _ _ _, education should be viewed as an investment in social order. A decent **14)** _ _ _ _ _ _ _ _ will make the ex-offender **15)** _ _ _ _ employable, and that, in turn, should remove one **16)** _ _ _ _ _ _ for repeat offenses—the inability to earn a living in a socially acceptable **17)** _ _ _. We should not **18)** _ _ _ _ educational opportunities to those in **19)** _ _ _ _ _ _ if we expect them to become useful citizens when **20)** _ _ _ _ leave.

(*continued on page 152*)

Members for high-risk occupations such as law enforcement and firefighting form tightly knit groups. The dangers they share naturally **21)** _ _ _ _ _ them close, as does the knowledge that their **22)** _ _ _ _ _ are sometimes in one another's hands. The bonds of loyalty and trust help police **23)** _ _ _ _ _ _ _ _ work more effectively. However, the sense **24)** _ _ loyalty can be taken to **25)** _ _ _ _ _ _ _ _. Sometimes officers believe that they always must defend their comrades' actions. What happens, though, **26)** _ _ _ _ those actions are wrong? Frank Serpico found a disturbing **27)** _ _ _ _ _ _ to that question. Serpico **28)** _ _ _ _ _ _ the New York City Police Department assuming **29)** _ _ _ _ high moral standards were typical of his fellow officers. When he **30)** _ _ _ _ _ out otherwise, he was faced with a dilemma: **31)** _ _ _ _ _ _ he violate the trust of his fellow officers by exposing the corruption, **32)** _ _ should he close his **33)** _ _ _ _ because loyalty to his **34)** _ _ _ _ _ _ officers outweighed all other moral (and legal) considerations? Serpico made his **35)** _ _ _ _ _ _. Public attention was focused on police **36)** _ _ _ _ _ _ _ _ _ _, and the NYPD was improved as a **37)** _ _ _ _ _ _, but those improvements came at a tremendous personal **38)** _ _ _ _ to Serpico. Ostracized and reviled by other officers, who felt **39)** _ _ _ _ _ _ _ _, Serpico eventually left the **40)** _ _ _ _ _.

# ▶ Answer Key

## Book One
### Part One: Clarity

1. **a.** Each of the other choices includes a sentence fragment.

2. **c.** The verb should be *was*, not *were*, to agree with *the guard*. The verbs in the second half of the sentence should be in the past tense, as in the first half of the sentence.

3. **c.** The correct preposition is *of*. *Think that* in choices **b** and **d** would require a complete clause with a verb, rather than the phrase that actually completes the sentence.

4. **d.** The modifier *with a growl* should be placed next to *the masked gunman*.

5. **b.** The subject *Officers Antwerp and Simpson* agrees in number with its verb *find*. In addition, there is no unnecessary shift in person, from *Officers Antwerp and Simpson* to *he* in choice **c**.

6. **a.** The subject *animal control officers* agrees in number with its verb *were*. In choice **d**, *upseted* should simply be *upset*.

7. **d.** This choice uses the correct verb form for the corresponding subjects. In addition, all necessary punctuation is present.

8. **d.** This choice does not include incorrect commas and uses the proper verb (*were*) for the plural subject.

9. **b.** Choice **a** mistakenly places the apostrophe after the *s* in *childrens*, not before it. Choice **c** includes an unnecessary *es* after the word *clothes*. In choice **d**, the verb *was* does not agree with the plural subject *clothes*.

10. **a.** The other choices are unclear because they are awkwardly constructed, obscuring who intends to set the fire.

11. **c.** The other choices contain unnecessary shifts in person, from *people* to *their* and *we* in choice **a**, to *your* and *one* in choice **b**, and to *our* and *they* in choice **d**.

12. **d.** This is the only choice in which subject and verb agree.

13. **a.** The verb *is* agrees with its noun *neither*.

14. **c.** There is no unnecessary shift in tense between *are* in the first half of the sentence and *is* in the second half; in the other choices, there are unnecessary shifts in tense.

15. **b.** *Herself* is the proper pronoun because it refers to something Sgt. Ahlamady does *for herself*, but there is no reason for the speaker to refer to *myself*. Incorrect pronouns are used in the other choices.

### Part Two: Vocabulary

Consult a dictionary if you're not sure why the answers for vocabulary and spelling questions are correct.

16. a.
17. b.
18. d.
19. c.
20. c.
21. b.
22. d.
23. a.
24. a.
25. b.
26. d.
27. b.
28. a.
29. b.
30. a.

### Part Three: Spelling

31. b.
32. a.
33. c.
34. d.
35. c.
36. d.
37. c.

**38.** b.
**39.** d.
**40.** a.
**41.** d.
**42.** a.
**43.** b.
**44.** d.
**45.** d.

## Part Four: Reading Comprehension

**46.** **a.** The discussion of the traits of a person with antisocial personality disorder in the middle of the passage specifies that such a person does not have distortions of thought. The passage speaks of the antisocial person as being "inordinately self-confident" (choice **b**) and of the person's "emotional shallowness" (choices **c** and **d**).

**47.** **d.** The third sentence of the passage speaks of "con games." None of the other professions would suit an impulsive, shallow person who has been in trouble with the law.

**48.** **b.** The passage mentions "emotional shallowness." The other choices hint at the capability to feel meaningful emotion.

**49.** **b.** The passage says that a person with antisocial personality disorder can mimic real emotion, thereby conning prison officials, judges, and psychiatrists. The other choices are mentioned in the passage, but not in connection with getting out of trouble with the law.

**50.** **d.** The passage specifically states that an officer should be patient, vigilant, and professional. Being intense is never alluded to.

**51.** **c.** The passage states that it is important to "radio to communications the exact location of the traffic stop."

**52.** **a.** Carefully reread the passage. Race is not mentioned in this section.

**53.** **d.** The passage deals not only with the sphere of law, but more centrally with the sphere of values and civil conduct. Nowhere does the passage say that police officers should be idealistic (choice **c**).

**54.** **d.** Fairness and accuracy, respect for individuals, and the importance of maintaining community relations are all mentioned in the second paragraph. Maintaining morale on a multiracial force is also important, but it is not mentioned in the passage.

**55.** **a.** See the first sentence of the second paragraph. Choice **d** is close, but the passage suggests a police officer must be not only an authority but also an exemplar.

**56.** **c.** See the second sentence of the second paragraph.

**57.** **b.** *Moderation* is explicitly referred to near the end of the second paragraph. *Justice* and *politeness* are synonymous with *fairness* and *civil conduct* in the passage. *Courage* is never mentioned.

**58.** **b.** Mr. Hensley has forced open the door and has told police he is waiting for his wife. Choice **a** is incorrect; Mr. Hensley's child hid from him in a closet, and he evidently didn't try to get the child to come out. Choice **c** is incorrect, because Mr. Hensley has a residence of his own at 1917 Roosevelt. Mr. Hensley evidently didn't intend peaceful reconciliation (choice **d**), because he kicked the door in.

**59.** **d.** The first sentence of the passage states that the complaint was anonymous.

**60.** **a.** The door had been kicked in. The officers didn't know any of the other facts until after they were inside the house.

**61.** **c.** Mr. Hensley spoke to the police "calmly," and he made a seemingly matter-of-fact statement. There is no indication in the passage that Mr. Hensley was enraged at police or that he was remorseful or confused.

**62.** **c.** The complainant, Alan Weber, lives at 1807 Clarkson.

**63.** **a.** The neighbor, Mr. Weber, said the noise kept him awake for two hours. There is no men-

tion in the passage of Mr. Weber being worried (choices **b** and **c**) or curious (choice **d**).
If he had been worried, he probably wouldn't
have waited two hours to call the police.

**64. b.** Mr. Hayes's first words to the police were "It's
about time you got here." There is no indication that Mr. Hayes was surprised—his statement shows the opposite—nor that he was
frightened, distrustful, or angry at the police.
He went with them "willingly."

**65. a.** Mr. Hayes stated that he was protecting himself. There is no indication in the passage that
he knows he is mentally ill (choice **b**) or that
he was annoyed by neighbors (choice **d**). He
would be unlikely to clean the woodwork
(choice **c**) because he believes it houses his
enemies.

## ▶ Book Two

1. high
2. college
3. time
4. no
5. costs
6. free
7. expensive
8. get
9. provide
10. who
11. best
12. than
13. lawbreakers
14. education

15. more
16. reason
17. way
18. deny
19. prison
20. they
21. bring
22. lives
23. officers
24. of
25. extremes
26. when
27. answer
28. joined

29. that
30. found
31. should
32. or
33. eyes
34. fellow
35. choice
36. corruption
37. result
38. cost
39. betrayed
40. force

## ► Scoring

To pass the California POST test, you need a *score* of 70%. But that doesn't necessarily mean that you must answer 70 questions right. The number of correct answers you need for a score of 70% changes each time the test is given. It depends on how many questions the test contains. A good estimate of a passing score is 70%, or 74 questions right.

Take your score from this first practice exam and apply it to the self-evaluation section of the Police Exam Planner in Chapter 15. A table there suggests what kind of preparation you should undertake based on your score on this exam.

But your total score isn't the main point right now. Analyzing your performance on the exam is much more important. Take a subscore of each of the categories of questions. Did you do better on reading questions than on clarity questions, or vice versa? Then you should spend more of your preparation time on the area in which you scored lower and less time on the area in which you scored well. If you did not do as well as you expected on the whole test, your overall reading skills are probably one reason. Lots of challenging reading between now and the time of the exam can make a difference in your score.

On the other hand, if you scored pretty well, you can feel confident as you undertake your preparation. (No, having a good score does *not* mean you shouldn't prepare. It means you don't have to prepare *a lot*.) You probably just need to brush up on a few things and continue to familiarize yourself with what's likely to be on the exam.

The chapters that follow this test focus on the areas tested in the California POST exams and on other areas that often appear on police exams. These chapters offer helpful hints and advice for doing well on the various kinds of questions. Depending on your score on the test you just took, you might choose to breeze quickly through those chapters or really knuckle down and study hard. Either way, those chapters will give you what you need to score your best.

# 17▶ Essay Examination

## CHAPTER SUMMARY

It is an absolute fact that the best way to prepare for an essay test is to write. And to write, and to write, and to write. There is no substitute for experience and practice.

The following information provides the scoring guide used in the California police exam, a group of example essays, and four sample essay prompts. The sample prompts should be a guide for you to see what you need to do to score well on the test. The essay exam is a 40-minute exam, so you should practice by giving yourself 40-minute intervals to practice writing.

If you have not written anything for some time, or if you are insecure about your writing abilities, you may want to enroll in a writing class at a community college or look up some commercially available writing or grammar handbooks on the Internet or at your local bookstore.

## ▶Scoring Guide

In the essay portion of the California police exam, candidates are first asked to describe an event or situation, using information from their personal experience. In the second part of the question, candidates are asked to provide some sort of analysis of that experience. Here is an example of an essay question:

All of us have had situation in our past in which we were confronted with a difficult choice. Describe a situation you have encountered in the past and the difficult choice you made. Explain how you learned from this experience.

When you complete your essay, it is given to two raters who give your essay individual scores. The range of scores is from 1 to 6, with 6 being best. Following is the essay-grading scale used by raters, along with a description associated with each score.

## The "6" essay

- responds effectively to the writing task
- explores the issues thoughtfully and in depth
- is coherently and logically organized and fully developed
- has a fluent style marked by sentence variety and language control
- is generally free from errors in mechanics, usage, and sentence structure

## The "5" essay

- responds clearly to the writing task
- explores the issues in some depth
- is clearly organized and well developed
- displays some sentence variety and facility in language
- may have a few errors in mechanics, usage, and sentence structure

## The "4" essay

- responds adequately to the writing task
- may not explore the issues in depth
- is adequately organized and has sufficient development
- basic competence in mechanics, usage, and sentence structure

## The "3" essay

- does not clearly respond to the writing task
- may not provide adequate development or may lack specificity
- may be poorly organized
- may have an accumulation of errors in mechanics, usage, and sentence structure

## The "2" essay

- may indicate confusion about the topic
- may have weak organization or be seriously underdeveloped
- may lack focus or demonstrate confusion about the writing task
- may be marred by frequent errors in mechanics, usage, and sentence structure

## The "1" essay

- suggests an inability to comprehend the question
- may be off topic
- is unfocused or disorganized
- is undeveloped
- may have serious and persistent errors in mechanics, usage, and sentence structure

Each essay is read by two raters, and the raters' scores are added together. A total score of 6 or below is failing. That is, an essay that receives two scores of "3" does not pass the written exam.

There are several reasons that essays do not score high on the exam. For example:

1. Some essays are difficult to follow. The writer may know what he or she trying to say, but the reader has difficulty following. These essays usually contain a number of errors and seem to leave out details and reasons that would make the essay more clear.

2. Some essays are filled with grammatical errors, especially those types of errors that make the meaning of the essay hard to comprehend. One

common problem that can be avoided by practice is the shifting from one tense to another (e.g., "She got out of her house, and then she starts to walk down the street."). Usually, writers who take time to proofread their work can find these errors and correct them.

3. Some essays do not provide sufficient, specific detail, or they fail to expand on the main idea appropriately. The general instructions for the essay exam call for a fully developed essay. Exams that are only a few sentences long are probably not sufficiently developed.

4. Some candidates fail to follow specific directions. When the prompts ask the candidates to write about a specific incident, some candidates write about a general incident, which misses the point of the topic. Usually, a "2" essay is indicative of this approach. Police reports in general follow this type of writing style—that of a chronological set of events and a conclusion.

## ▶ Practice Essays

Following are four practice writing prompts. They are typical of the kinds of questions you will face on the exam. These prompts ask you to write about a specific incident and then to reflect upon the experience. These prompts are intended to test the candidates' ability to write a clear, coherent narrative, much like what one expects in good police report writing—the ability to provide ample and appropriate detail and to draw well-reasoned conclusions.

The following prompts will provide you with a good deal of practice. You should try each prompt as a timed writing experience. You should be able to use each prompt more than once if you discuss a different incident with each attempt. Write your responses to the prompts on a blank sheet of paper.

1. All of us have had experiences in our lives when the odds seemed stacked against us, but we persevered and ultimately succeeded. Describe a difficult task that you carried out successfully or a difficult goal that you achieved. Explain the steps you used in achieving this success, and what you learned from it.

2. Despite our best efforts, often situations or events do not go according to plan. Write about a situation in your past in which things did not go according to plan and something unexpected resulted. Describe how you dealt with the event and what you learned from it.

3. Describe a time when you were confronted with two choices, neither of which was ideal. How did this make you feel? What steps did you take to arrive at one of the decisions? Describe what you learned from this experience.

4. Write about a situation in which you had to interject yourself in a volatile situation. What choices did you have? What did you do? Describe the outcome and what you took away from this.

# 18 ▶ Reading Comprehension

## CHAPTER SUMMARY

Reading is a vital skill for any potential law enforcement officer, so most civil service tests include reading comprehension questions. The tips and exercises in this chapter will help you improve your reading comprehension so that you can increase your score in this area.

**M**ost civil service tests attempt to measure how well applicants understand what they read. Understanding written materials is part of almost any job, including law enforcement. The tests are usually in a multiple-choice format and have questions based on brief passages, much like the standardized tests that are offered in schools. For that matter, almost all standardized test questions test your reading skills. After all, you can't answer the question if you can't read it! Similarly, you can't study your course material at the academy or learn new procedures once you're on the job if you can't read well. So reading comprehension is vital not only on the test, but also for the rest of your career.

## ▶ Types of Reading Comprehension Questions

You have probably encountered reading comprehension questions before—you are given a passage to read and then have to answer multiple-choice questions about it. The advantages of these questions for you, the test taker, are that you don't have to know anything about the topic in the passage and that the answers are usually right there—if you know where to find them. This leads to one of the disadvantages: You have to search quickly for answers in an unfamiliar text. It's easy to fall for one of the wrong answer choices, which may be designed to mislead you.

The best way to do well on this passage/question format is to be very familiar with the kinds of questions that are typically asked on the test. Questions most frequently ask you to

1. identify a specific **fact or detail** in the passage.
2. note the **main idea** of the passage.
3. define a **vocabulary** word from the passage.
4. make an **inference** based on the passage.

## Practice Passage 1:
## Using the Four Question Types

The following is a sample test passage, followed by four questions. Read the passage, and then answer the questions, based on your reading of the text, by circling your choice. Then note under your answer the type of question you believe each to be, based on the preceding list. Correct answers appear immediately after the questions.

Community policing has been frequently touted as the best way to reform urban law enforcement. The idea of putting more officers on foot patrol in high crime areas, where relations with police have frequently been strained, was initiated in Houston in 1983 under the leadership of then-Commissioner Lee Brown. He believed that officers should be accessible to the community on the street. If officers were assigned to the same area over a period of time, those officers would eventually build a network of trust with neighborhood residents. That trust would mean that merchants and residents in the community would let officers know about criminal activities in the area and would support police intervention. Since then, many large cities have experimented with community-oriented policing (COP) with mixed results. Some have found that police and citizens are grateful for the opportunity to work together. Others have found that unrealistic expectations by citizens and resistance from officers have combined to hinder the effectiveness of COP. It seems possible, therefore, that a good idea may need improvement before it can truly be considered a reform.

1. Community policing has been used in law enforcement since
   a. the late 1970s.
   b. the early 1980s.
   c. the Carter administration.
   d. Lee Brown was New York City police commissioner.

   Question type: _____

2. The phrase *a network of trust* in this passage suggests that
   a. police officers can rely only on one another for support.
   b. community members rely on the police to protect them.
   c. police and community members rely on each other.
   d. community members trust only one another.

   Question type: _____

3. The best title for this passage would be
   a. "Community Policing: The Solution to the Drug Problem"
   b. "Houston Sets the Pace in Community Policing"
   c. "Communities and Cops: Partners for Peace"
   d. "Community Policing: An Uncertain Future?"

   Question type: _2_____

**4.** The word *touted* in the first sentence of the passage most nearly means
a. praised.
b. denied.
c. exposed.
d. criticized.

Question type: _____ 3

## Answers and Explanations for Practice Passage 1

Don't just look at the right answers and move on. The explanations are the most important part. Use these explanations to help you understand how to tackle each kind of question the next time you come across it.

**1. b.** Question type: 1, fact or detail. The passage identifies 1983 as the first large-scale use of community policing in Houston. Don't be misled by trying to figure out when Carter was president. Also, if you happen to know that Lee Brown was also once New York City's police commissioner, don't let that information lead you away from the information contained in the passage alone. Brown was commissioner in Houston when he initiated community policing.

**2. c.** Question type: 4, inference. The "network of trust" referred to in this passage is between the community and the police, as you can see from the sentence where the phrase appears. The key phrase in the question is *in this passage*. You may think that police can rely only on one another, or one of the other answer choices may appear equally plausible to you. But your choice of answers must be limited to the one suggested *in this passage*. Another tip for questions like this: Beware of absolutes! Be suspicious of any answer containing words like *only, always,* or *never.*

**3. d.** Question type: 2, main idea. The title always expresses the main idea. In this passage, the main idea comes at the end. The sum of all the details in the passage suggests that community policing is not without its critics and that, therefore, its future is uncertain. Another key phrase is *mixed results,* which means that some communities haven't had full success with community policing.

**4. a.** Question type: 3, vocabulary. The word *touted* is linked in this passage with the phrase *the best way to reform.* Most people would think that a good way to reform something is praiseworthy. In addition, the next few sentences in the passage describe the benefits of community policing. Criticism or a negative response to the subject doesn't come until later in the passage.

## ▶ Detail and Main Idea Questions

Main idea questions and fact or detail questions are both asking you for information that's right there in the passage. All you have to do is find it.

### Detail or Fact Questions

In detail or fact questions, you have to identify a specific item of information from the test. This is usually the simplest kind of question. You just have to be able to separate important information from less important information. However, the choices may often be very similar, so you must be careful not to get confused.

### Main Idea Questions

The main idea of a passage, such as that of a paragraph or a book, is what it is *mostly* about. The main idea is the summary of all the details. Sometimes, the main idea is stated, often in the first or last sentence. Sometimes, it is implied in the overall text. The key word in the definition is *mostly*. There may be much information in the passage. The trick is to understand what all that information adds up to—the gist of what the author wants us to know. Often some of the wrong answers on main idea questions are specific facts or details from the passage.

## Practice Passage 2:
## Detail and Main Idea Questions

Practice answering main idea and detail questions by working on the questions that follow this passage. Circle the answers to the questions, and then check your answers against the key that appears immediately after the questions.

There is some evidence that crime rates are linked to social trends such as demographic and socioeconomic changes. Crime statistics showed a decline in the post–World War II era of the 1940s and 50s. Following the Vietnam War in the 1970s, however, reported crimes were on the rise again, only to be followed by lower numbers of such reports in the 1980s. One of the reasons for these fluctuations appears to be age. When the population is younger, as in the 1960s when the baby boomers came of age, there was a greater incidence of crime nationwide. A second cause for the rise and fall of crime rates appears to be economic. Rising crime rates appear to follow falling economies. A third cause cited for the cyclical nature of crime statistics appears to be the ebb and flow of public policy decisions, which sometimes protect personal freedoms at the expense of government control. A youthful, economically disadvantaged population that is not secured by social controls of family and community or by government authority is likely to see an upswing in reported crimes.

**1.** Crime statistics seem to rise when populations are
   **a.** younger.
   **b.** older.
   **c.** veteran.
   **d.** richer.

   Question type: _____

**2.** The main idea of the passage is that
   **a.** times of prosperity show lower crime statistics.
   **b.** when the economy slows, crime statistics rise.
   **c.** incidence of reported crime is related to several social and economic variables.
   **d.** secure families are less likely to be involved in crime.

   Question type: _____

**3.** The best title for this passage would be
   **a.** "Wars and Crime Statistics"
   **b.** "Why Crime Statistics Rise and Fall"
   **c.** "Youth and Crime Statistics"
   **d.** "Poverty and Crime Statistics"

   Question type: _____

**4.** Crime statistics show that crime is
   **a.** random.
   **b.** cyclical.
   **c.** demographic.
   **d.** social.

   Question type: _____

## Answers and Explanations for
## Practice Passage 2

   **1. a.** Question type: 1, detail. This is a fairly clear example of how you can look quickly through a passage and locate a clearly stated detail. The word *young* appears in relation to the baby boomers; the idea is also suggested in the last sentence by the word *youthful*.

2. **c.** Question type: 2, main idea. The other answer choices are details—they're all in the passage, but they're not what the passage is *mostly* about. Choice **c** is the only one that combines several details into a statement that reflects the first sentence, which is also the topic sentence, of the paragraph.

3. **b.** Question type: 2, main idea. Each of the other choices expresses a detail, one of the reasons listed in the passage for fluctuation in crime rates. Choice **b** is the only one that expresses the sum of those details.

4. **b.** Question type: 1, detail. The passage mentions "the cyclical nature of crime statistics." Other phrases that suggest this answer include *fluctuations, rise and fall,* and *ebb and flow.*

## ▶ Vocabulary and Inference Questions

Questions that ask you about the meaning of vocabulary words in the passage and those that ask what the passage *suggests* or *implies* (inference questions) are different from detail or main idea questions. In vocabulary and inference questions, you usually have to pull ideas from the passage, sometimes from more than one place in the passage.

### Vocabulary Questions

Questions designed to test vocabulary are really trying to measure how well you can figure out the meaning of an unfamiliar word simply by making a good association based on context. Theoretically you should be able to substitute a nonsense word for the one being sought, and you would still make the right choice because you could determine meaning strictly from the

sense of the sentence. Try to determine the meaning of this nonsense word from the rest of the sentence:

> The chief noted that it gave him great *terivinix* to announce the award for Officer of the Year.

In this sentence, *terivinix* most likely means

  **a.** pain.
  **b.** sympathy.
  **c.** pleasure.
  **d.** anxiety.

Clearly, the context of an award makes choice **c**, *pleasure,* the best answer. Awards don't usually bring pain, sympathy, or anxiety. When confronted with an unfamiliar word, try substituting a nonsense word and see if the context gives you the clue.

### Inference Questions

Inference questions can be the most difficult to answer because they require you to take meaning from the text even when that meaning is not directly stated. Inferences are hints that we take based on the clues the writer has given us. You have to read between the lines in order to make a judgment about what an author was implying in the passage.

### Practice Passage 3: Vocabulary and Inference Questions

The questions that follow this passage are strictly vocabulary and inference questions. Circle the answers to the questions, and then check your answers against the key that appears immediately after the questions.

> In recent years, issues of public and personal safety have become a major concern to many Americans. Violent incidents in fast-food restaurants, libraries, hospitals, schools, and offices have led many to seek greater security inside and outside of their homes. Sales of burglar alarms and high-tech security

devices such as motion detectors and video moni-tors have skyrocketed in the last decade. Conve-nience stores and post offices have joined banks and jewelry stores in barricading staff behind iron bars and safety glass enclosures. Communities employ private security forces and encourage homeowners to keep trained attack dogs on their premises. While some people have sympathy for the impetus behind these efforts, there is also some concern that these measures will create a "siege mentality" leading to general distrust among people that could foster a dangerous isolationism within neighborhoods and among neighbors.

**1.** The passage suggests which of the following about community security?
   **a.** Communities are more dangerous today than they were ten years ago.
   **b.** Too much concern for security can destroy trust among neighbors.
   **c.** Poor security has led to an increase in public violence.
   **d.** Isolated neighborhoods are safe neighborhoods.

   Question type: _____

**2.** The word *foster* in the last sentence of the pas-sage most nearly means
   **a.** adopt.
   **b.** encourage.
   **c.** prevent.
   **d.** secure.

   Question type: _____

**3.** The author believes that
   **a.** more security is needed to make neighborhoods safer.
   **b.** people should spend more money on home security.
   **c.** people should not ignore the problems created by excessive safety concerns.
   **d.** attack dogs and high-tech devices are the best protection against violent crime.

   Question type: _____

**4.** In the last sentence, the phrase *siege mentality* means
   **a.** hostility.
   **b.** defensiveness.
   **c.** fear.
   **d.** corruption.

   Question type: _____

## Answers and Explanations for Practice Passage 3

   **1. b.** Question type: 4, inference. The key word here is *distrust,* which implies that neighbors become suspicious of one another if they are worried about safety.
   **2. b.** Question type: 3, vocabulary. The first answer choice is meant to confuse you if you associate the word *foster* with foster care and, by exten-sion, with adoption. *Foster* means *nurture* or *help to grow.* Look again at the sentence. What could *a general distrust*—the thing that fos-ters—do to *a dangerous isolationism*—the thing being fostered? A general distrust could *encourage* a dangerous isolationism.
   **3. c.** Question type: 4, inference. By using a phrase such as *dangerous isolationism,* the author suggests that he or she doesn't approve of the move toward more use of security devices. The other answer choices all indicate the

One of the difficulties of taking reading tests for nonnative English speakers is the lack of a frame of reference that allows for quick comprehension of the text. People who have not lived in or been educated in the United States often don't have the background information that comes from reading American newspapers, magazines, and textbooks.

A second problem for nonnative English speakers is the difficulty in recognizing vocabulary and idioms that assist comprehension. In order to read with good understanding, the test taker must have an immediate grasp of as many words as possible in the text.

### The Long View

Read newspapers, magazines, and other periodicals that deal with current events and matters of local, state, and national importance. Pay special attention to articles related to law enforcement issues.

Be alert to new or unfamiliar vocabulary or terms that occur frequently in the popular press. Get a highlighter pen and use it to pick out new or unfamiliar words as you read. Keep a list of those words and their definitions. Review them for 15 minutes each day.

### During the Test

When you are taking the test, make a picture in your mind of the situation being described in the passage. Ask yourself, "What did the writer mostly want me to think about this subject?"

Locate and underline the topic sentence that carries the main idea of the passage. Remember that the topic sentence may not always be the first sentence.

---

author's approval of the trend being discussed.

**4. b.** Question type: 3, vocabulary. The key word here is *siege.* People who perceive themselves to be under attack tend to stick together in the face of a common enemy. They become quick to defend themselves against that enemy.

### Review: Putting It All Together

A good way to solidify what you've learned about reading comprehension questions is for you to write the questions. Here's a passage, followed by space for you to write your own questions. Write one question of each of the four types: fact or detail, main idea, vocabulary, and inference.

In recent years, law enforcement officers have welcomed the advent of a number of new technologies that have aided them greatly in their work. These include long-range eavesdropping devices and computer scanners that allow police to identify possible suspects by merely typing a license number into a computer in the patrol car. The scanner allows instant access to motor vehicle and criminal records and gives officers the opportunity to snare wrongdoers, even when they are not involved in criminal activity at the time. Police departments have praised the use of the computers, which they say help them get criminals off the streets and out of the way of honest citizens. Not all of those citizens agree with this attitude, however; some believe that arrests made solely on the basis of scanner identification constitute an invasion of privacy. They regard the accessing of records as illegal search and seizure. In

New Jersey, Florida, and Arizona, lawsuits have been filed by citizens who believe that their constitutional rights have been violated. They believe that much computer-generated information is inaccurate and vulnerable to computer hackers who invade computer databases. Some believe that such information from scanners could be used to charge innocent citizens with crimes or to target particular neighborhoods for harassment.

**1.** Main idea question: _____

_____

   **a.**

   **b.**

   **c.**

   **d.**

**2.** Detail question: _____

_____

   **a.**

   **b.**

   **c.**

   **d.**

**3.** Vocabulary question: _____

_____

   **a.**

   **b.**

   **c.**

   **d.**

**4.** Inference question: _____

_____

   **a.**

   **b.**

   **c.**

   **d.**

## Possible Questions

Here is one question of each type based on the preceding passage. Your questions may be very different, but these will give you an idea of the kinds of questions that could be asked.

**1.** Main idea question: Which of the following best expresses the main idea of the passage?
   **a.** New technologies are available to police officers.
   **b.** Police are skeptical of new policing technologies.
   **c.** New technologies raise questions of privacy.
   **d.** New technologies may be discriminatory.

**2.** Detail question: Computer scanners allow police to
   **a.** identify suspects.
   **b.** access computer databases.
   **c.** locate wrongdoers.
   **d.** all of the above

**3.** Vocabulary question: In this passage the word *snare* means
   **a.** question.
   **b.** interrupt.
   **c.** capture.
   **d.** free.

**4.** Inference question: The writer implies, but does not directly state, that
   **a.** computer technologies must be used with care.
   **b.** high-tech policing is the wave of the future.
   **c.** most citizens believe that high-tech policing is beneficial.
   **d.** most police officers prefer using the new technologies.

## ▶ How to Answer Fill-in-the-Blank Reading Questions

Some exams test your reading skills by having you fill in the missing words in a reading passage. To do well, you need both good reading skills and good test-taking skills. Following are some tips to help you sharpen your test-taking techniques.

### Finding the Missing Word

You will be given reading passages with words omitted. Each missing word is indicated by a series of dashes. There is one dash for each letter in the missing word. You will have to determine the missing words and mark them correctly on your answer sheet. Here's how:

- Read the paragraph through quickly to get the general idea of it.
- Now go back to fill in the blanks by putting one letter on each line. Do the easy words first, and then work on the harder ones. Choose only one word for each blank space. Make sure that word has exactly as many letters as there are dashes *and* makes sense in the sentence.
- Try to fill in every blank. Guess if you have to.
- Don't be alarmed if you're not sure of some of your answers. You can miss several words and still do well.

Look at the following sample sentence:

Fortunately, no one was hurt when the _ _ _ _ _ was derailed.

There are five dashes so the word you need must have five letters. The correct answer is **train** because it makes sense and has five letters. The word *engine* makes sense in the sentence, but it is incorrect because it is not a five-letter word. *Plane* is a five-letter word but is incorrect because planes cannot be derailed. Write the word *train* in the blank spaces.

### Marking the Answer Sheet

Once you have completed the passage, you will have to mark your answers on the answer sheet. On the answer sheet, you will find numbered columns. Each column contains the letters A–Z, and the number at the top of the column corresponds to the number of a missing word in the passage. To mark your answer on the answer sheet, print the **first letter** of the word you wrote in the blank space in the passage in the box directly under the appropriate item number. Then, completely blacken the circle in that column containing the letter you wrote in the box.

---

### Important

The words you wrote in the blank spaces in the passage will not be scored. Neither will the letters you write at the top of the columns on the answer sheet. Only the darkened circles of the letters you have chosen will be scored. Make sure you mark your answers correctly.

---

As you mark your answer sheet, check to make sure that

1. the item number on the answer sheet is the same as the item number in the passage.
2. you have written the correct first letter in the box.
3. you have completely blackened the correct circle below the box.

For example, if you chose *train* as the first missing word in a passage, you would find column 1, print T in the box, and blacken the circle with T in it.

## Practice Fill-in-the-Blank Passage

Now read the following sample paragraph.

Fortunately, no one was hurt when the **1)** _Train_ was derailed. The derailment occurred **2)** _because_ lumber and other debris were piled on the tracks. Investigators believe a **3)** _number_ of people were involved. They are looking into the possibility **4)** _that_ a local gang caused the accident for **5)** _fun_. It would not be the first **6)** _time_ that members of this **7)** _gang_ caused serious damage.

First, write the answers in the blank spaces (one letter per line), and then mark them on the answer sheet. Work as quickly as you can without sacrificing accuracy. Double-check often to be sure you are marking your answers correctly. See the end of the chapter for answers.

| 1 | 2 | 3 | 4 | 5 | 6 | 7 |
|---|---|---|---|---|---|---|
|   |   |   |   |   |   |   |

WRITE 1ST LETTER OF WORD HERE

CODE LETTERS HERE

Ⓐ Ⓐ Ⓐ Ⓐ Ⓐ Ⓐ Ⓐ
Ⓑ Ⓑ Ⓑ Ⓑ Ⓑ Ⓑ Ⓑ
Ⓒ Ⓒ Ⓒ Ⓒ Ⓒ Ⓒ Ⓒ
Ⓓ Ⓓ Ⓓ Ⓓ Ⓓ Ⓓ Ⓓ
Ⓔ Ⓔ Ⓔ Ⓔ Ⓔ Ⓔ Ⓔ
Ⓕ Ⓕ Ⓕ Ⓕ Ⓕ Ⓕ Ⓕ
Ⓖ Ⓖ Ⓖ Ⓖ Ⓖ Ⓖ Ⓖ
Ⓗ Ⓗ Ⓗ Ⓗ Ⓗ Ⓗ Ⓗ
Ⓘ Ⓘ Ⓘ Ⓘ Ⓘ Ⓘ Ⓘ
Ⓙ Ⓙ Ⓙ Ⓙ Ⓙ Ⓙ Ⓙ
Ⓚ Ⓚ Ⓚ Ⓚ Ⓚ Ⓚ Ⓚ
Ⓛ Ⓛ Ⓛ Ⓛ Ⓛ Ⓛ Ⓛ
Ⓜ Ⓜ Ⓜ Ⓜ Ⓜ Ⓜ Ⓜ
Ⓝ Ⓝ Ⓝ Ⓝ Ⓝ Ⓝ Ⓝ
Ⓞ Ⓞ Ⓞ Ⓞ Ⓞ Ⓞ Ⓞ
Ⓟ Ⓟ Ⓟ Ⓟ Ⓟ Ⓟ Ⓟ
Ⓠ Ⓠ Ⓠ Ⓠ Ⓠ Ⓠ Ⓠ
Ⓡ Ⓡ Ⓡ Ⓡ Ⓡ Ⓡ Ⓡ
Ⓢ Ⓢ Ⓢ Ⓢ Ⓢ Ⓢ Ⓢ
Ⓣ Ⓣ Ⓣ Ⓣ Ⓣ Ⓣ Ⓣ
Ⓤ Ⓤ Ⓤ Ⓤ Ⓤ Ⓤ Ⓤ
Ⓥ Ⓥ Ⓥ Ⓥ Ⓥ Ⓥ Ⓥ
Ⓦ Ⓦ Ⓦ Ⓦ Ⓦ Ⓦ Ⓦ
Ⓧ Ⓧ Ⓧ Ⓧ Ⓧ Ⓧ Ⓧ
Ⓨ Ⓨ Ⓨ Ⓨ Ⓨ Ⓨ Ⓨ
Ⓩ Ⓩ Ⓩ Ⓩ Ⓩ Ⓩ Ⓩ

# ► Additional Resources

Here are some other ways you can build the vocabulary and knowledge that will help you do well on reading comprehension questions.

- Practice asking the four sample question types about passages you read for information or pleasure.
- Search the Internet for articles related to law enforcement. Exchange views with others on the Internet. All of these exchanges will contribute to the knowledge needed to relate to the passage material on the tests.
- Use your library. Many public libraries have sections, sometimes called "Lifelong Learning Centers," that contain materials for adult learners. In these sections, you can find books with exercises in reading and study skills. It's also a good idea to enlarge your base of information about the criminal justice field by reading books and articles on subjects related to criminology. Many libraries have computer systems that allow you to access information quickly and easily. Library personnel will show you how to use the computers and microfilm and microfiche machines.
- Begin now to build a broad knowledge of the law enforcement profession. Get in the habit of reading articles in newspapers and magazines on law enforcement issues. Keep a clipping file of those articles. This will help keep you informed of trends in the profession and aware of pertinent vocabulary related to policing issues.
- Consider reading or subscribing to professional journals. The following journals are written for a general readership among law enforcement personnel and are available for a reasonable annual fee. They may also be available in your public library or via the Internet.

Corrections Today
American Correctional Association
206 N. Washington Street #200
Alexandria, VA 22314
800-ACA-JOIN
www.aca.org

FBI Law Enforcement Bulletin
935 Pennsylvania Ave NW
Washington, D.C. 20535-0001
www.fbi.gov/publications/leb/leb.htm

Law and Order
Hendon, Inc.
130 N. Waukegan Road # 202
Deerfield, IL 60015-5652
www.hendonpub.com/publications/lawandorder

Police Chief
International Association of Chiefs of Police, Inc.
515 North Washington Street
Alexandria, VA 22314
800-THE-IACP
www.policechiefmagazine.org

Police: The Law Enforcement Magazine
3520 Challenge Street
Torrance, CA 90503
310-533-2400
www.policemag.com

If you need more help building your reading skills and taking reading comprehension tests, consider *LearningExpress's Reading Comprehension Success* or *501 Reading Comprehension Questions*.

## Answers to Fill-in-the-Blank Reading Questions

| | |
|---|---|
| **1.** train | **5.** fun |
| **2.** because | **6.** time |
| **3.** number | **7.** gang |
| **4.** that | |

# 19 ▶ Grammar

## CHAPTER SUMMARY

This chapter reviews the sentence-level writing skills often tested on multiple-choice exams, including complete sentences, capitalization, punctuation, subject-verb agreement, verb tenses, pronouns, and confusing word pairs.

An effective law enforcement professional needs to know how to use a variety of tools well to do a good job. Probably few of the tools are as important or will be used as often as written language. Knowing how to use written language is vital, not just for the exam, but for your career. This chapter covers the smaller, sentence-level grammatical and mechanical aspects of writing well.

## ▶ Complete Sentences

Sentences are the basic unit of written language. Most writing is done using complete sentences, so it's important to distinguish sentences from fragments. A sentence expresses a complete thought, while a fragment requires something more to express a complete thought.

Look at the following pairs of word groups. The first in each pair is a sentence fragment; the second is a complete sentence.

| COMPLETE SENTENCES | |
|---|---|
| **Fragment** | **Complete Sentence** |
| The dog walking down the street. | The dog was walking down the street. |
| Exploding from the bat for a home run. | The ball exploded from the bat for a home run. |

These examples show that a sentence must have a subject and a verb to complete its meaning. The first fragment has a subject, but not a verb. *Walking* looks like a verb, but it is actually an adjective describing *dog*. The second fragment has neither a subject nor a verb. *Exploding* looks like a verb, but it too is an adjective describing something not identified in the word group.

Now look at the next set of word groups. Mark those that are complete sentences.

**1.**
   **a.** We saw the tornado approaching.
   **b.** When we saw the tornado approaching.

**2.**
   **a.** Before the house was built in 1972.
   **b.** The house was built in 1972.

**3.**
   **a.** Because we are leaving in the morning.
   **b.** We are leaving in the morning.

If you chose **1. a., 2. b.,** and **3. b.,** you are correct. You may have noticed that the groups of words are the same, but the fragments have an extra word at the beginning. These words are called subordinating conjunctions. If a group of words that would normally be a complete sentence is preceded by a subordinating conjunction, something more is needed to complete the thought.

- When we saw the tornado approaching, we headed for cover.

- Before the house was built in 1972, the old house was demolished.
- Because we were leaving in the morning, we went to bed early.

Here is a list of words that can be used as subordinating conjunctions.

| | |
|---|---|
| after | that |
| although | though |
| as | unless |
| because | until |
| before | when |
| if | whenever |
| once | where |
| since | wherever |
| than | while |

If you can tell when a group of words isn't a sentence, then you can tell when one or more sentences have been run together, sometimes with a comma in between. Some tests will ask you to find run-on sentences. Each of the following sentences is a run-on sentence. Can you find where to put a period and begin a new sentence?

**1.** We went to the beach, we had a good time.
**2.** Without exception, the prisoners conformed to the new ruling they kept their cells clean.
**3.** The defense needed time to examine the new evidence, the lawyer asked for an extension.

If you noticed that a new sentence begins after *beach* in the first sentence, after *ruling* in the second, and after *evidence* in the third, you are right. Generally, you can tell whether you're looking at a run-on by covering the second half of the sentence and asking yourself whether the first half by itself is a sentence. Then cover the first half. Is the second half a sentence by itself? If your answer to the first and/or second question is *no*, then the sentence is fine. If you answered both questions *yes*—both halves of the sentence could be sentences by themselves—then you've got a run-on, unless there happens to be a semicolon (;) between the two halves.

You may be asked to distinguish a sentence from a fragment or a run-on. Check for a subject and a verb, as well as for subordinating conjunctions. Check yourself with the following sample questions. The answers are at the end of this chapter.

1. Which of the following groups of words is a complete sentence?
   a. The treasure buried beneath the floorboards beside the furnace.
   b. After we spent considerable time examining all of the possibilities before making a decision.
   c. In addition to the methods the doctor used to diagnose the problem.
   d. The historical account of the incident bore the most resemblance to fact.

2. Which of the following groups of words is a complete sentence?
   a. This was fun to do.
   b. We looking.
   c. Before the door opened.
   d. If we ever see you again.

3. Which of the following groups of words is a run-on?
   a. Whenever I see the moon rise, I am awed by the deep orange color.
   b. The special services unit completed its work and made its report to the chief.
   c. Unless we hear from the directors of the board before the next meeting, we will not act on the new proposal.
   d. We slept soundly we never heard the alarm.

## ▶ Capitalization

You may encounter questions that test your ability to capitalize correctly. Here is a quick review of the most common capitalization rules.

- Capitalize the first word of a sentence. If the first word is a number, write it as a word.
- Capitalize the pronoun *I*.
- Capitalize the first word of a quotation: I said, "What's the name of your dog?" Do not capitalize the first word of a partial quotation: He called me "the worst excuse for a student" he had ever seen.
- Capitalize proper nouns and proper adjectives.

See the table on the next page.

The following passage contains no capitalized words. Circle those letters that should be capitalized.

when I first saw the black hills on january 2, 1995, i was shocked by their beauty. we had just spent new year's day in sioux falls, south dakota, and had headed west toward our home in denver, colorado. as we traveled along interstate 90, i could see the black hills rising slightly in the distance. president calvin coolidge had called them "a wondrous sight to behold." i understood why. after driving through the badlands and stopping at wall drug in wall, south dakota, we liked the way the evergreen-covered hills broke the barren monotony of the landscape. my oldest daughter said, "dad, look! there's something that's not all white." we could see why the lakota sioux regarded them as a native american holy ground. we saw mount rushmore and custer state park, the home of the largest herd of buffalo in north america. we also drove the treacherous spearfish canyon road. fortunately, our jeep cherokee had no trouble with the ice and snow on the winding road.

| CAPITALIZATION | |
| --- | --- |
| **CATEGORY** | **EXAMPLE (PROPER NOUNS)** |
| days of the week, months of the year | Friday, Saturday; January, February |
| holidays, special events | Christmas, Halloween; Two Rivers Festival, Dilly Days |
| names of individuals | John Henry, George Billeck |
| names of structures, buildings | Lincoln Memorial, Principal Building |
| names of trains, ships, aircraft | Queen Elizabeth, Chicago El |
| product names | Corn King hams, Dodge Intrepid |
| cities and states | Des Moines, Iowa; Juneau, Alaska |
| streets, highways, roads | Grand Avenue, Interstate 29, Deadwood Road |
| landmarks, public areas | Continental Divide, Grand Canyon, Glacier National Park |
| bodies of water | Atlantic Ocean, Mississippi River |
| ethnic groups, languages, nationalities | Asian American, English, Arab |
| official titles | Mayor Daley, President Johnson |
| institutions, organizations, businesses | Dartmouth College, Lions Club, Chrysler Corporation |
| proper adjectives | English muffin, Polish sausage |

Check your circled version against the following corrected version of the passage.

When I first saw the Black Hills on January 2, 1995, I was shocked by their beauty. We had just spent New Year's Day in Sioux Falls, South Dakota, and had headed west toward our home in Denver, Colorado. As we traveled along Interstate 90, I could see the Black Hills rising slightly in the distance. President Calvin Coolidge had called them "a wondrous sight to behold." I understood why. After driving through the Badlands and stopping at Wall Drug in Wall, South Dakota, we liked the way the evergreen-covered hills broke the barren monotony of the landscape. My oldest daughter said, "Dad, look! There's something that's not all white." We could see why the Lakota Sioux regarded them as a Native American holy ground. We saw Mount Rushmore and Custer State Park, the home of the largest herd of buffalo in North America. We also drove the treacherous Spearfish Canyon Road. Fortunately, our Jeep Cherokee had no trouble with the ice and snow on the winding road.

Now try these sample questions. Choose the option that is capitalized correctly. Answers are at the end of the chapter.

**4.**
a. This year we will celebrate christmas on Tuesday, December 25, in Manchester, Ohio.
b. This year we will celebrate Christmas on Tuesday, December 25, in manchester, Ohio.
c. This year we will celebrate Christmas on Tuesday, December 25, in Manchester, Ohio.
d. This year we will celebrate christmas on Tuesday, December 25, in manchester, Ohio.

**5.**
a. Steven Arcane was able to free himself from the Police Officer's grip and run away.
b. Steven Arcane was able to free himself from the police Officer's grip and run away.
c. Steven Arcane was able to free himself from the police officer's grip and run away.
d. Steven Arcane was able to free himself from the Police officer's grip and run away.

**6.**
a. Ms. Abigal Dornburg, MD, was named head of the review board for Physicians Mutual.
b. Ms. Abigal Dornburg, MD, was named Head of the Review Board for Physicians Mutual.
c. Ms. Abigal Dornburg, md Was named head of the review board for Physicians mutual.
d. Ms. Abigal dornburg, MD, was named head of the review board for Physicians Mutual.

## ▶ Punctuation

### Periods

Here is a quick review of the rules regarding the use of a period.

- Use a period at the end of a sentence that is not a question or an exclamation.
- Use a period after an initial in a name: Millard K. Furham.
- Use a period after an abbreviation, unless the abbreviation is an acronym.
  Abbreviations: Mr., Ms., Dr., A.M., General Motors Corp., Allied Inc.
  Acronyms: NASA, AIDS
- If a sentence ends with an abbreviation, use only one period. (We brought food, tents, sleeping bags, etc.)

### Commas

Using commas correctly can make the difference between presenting information clearly and distorting the facts. The following chart demonstrates the necessity of commas in written language. How many people are listed in the sentence?

| COMMAS AND MEANING | |
|---|---|
| Number undetermined | My sister Diane John Carey Melissa and I went to the fair. |
| Four people | My sister Diane, John Carey, Melissa, and I went to the fair. |
| Five people | My sister, Diane, John Carey, Melissa, and I went to the fair. |
| Six people | My sister, Diane, John, Carey, Melissa, and I went to the fair. |

Here is a quick review of the most basic rules regarding the use of commas.

- Use a comma before *and, but, or, for, nor,* and *yet* when they separate two groups of words that could be complete sentences.
  **Example:** The coaches laid out the game plan, and the team executed it to perfection.
- Use a comma to separate items in a series.
  **Example:** The student driver stopped, looked, and listened when she got to the railroad tracks.
- Use a comma to separate two or more adjectives modifying the same noun.
  **Example:** The hot, black, rich coffee tasted great after an hour in below-zero weather. [Notice that there is no comma between *rich* (an adjective) and *coffee* (the noun *rich* describes)].
- Use a comma after introductory words, phrases, or clauses in a sentence.
  **Examples:** Usually, the class begins with a short writing assignment. [Word]
  Racing down the street, the yellow car ran a stoplight. [Phrase]
  After we found the source of the noise, we relaxed and enjoyed the rest of the evening. [Clause]
- Use a comma after a name followed by Jr., Sr., or some other abbreviation.
  **Example:** The class was inspired by the speeches of Martin Luther King, Jr.
- Use a comma to separate items in an address.
  **Example:** The car stopped at 1433 West G Avenue, Orlando, Florida 36890.
- Use a comma to separate a day and a year, as well as after the year.
  **Example:** I was born on July 21, 1954, during a thunderstorm.
- Use a comma after the greeting of a friendly letter and after the closing of any letter.
  **Example:** Dear Uncle Jon,
  Sincerely yours,
- Use a comma to separate contrasting elements in a sentence.

**Example:** Your essay needs strong arguments, not strong opinions, to convince me.
- Use commas to set off appositives (words or phrases that explain or identify a noun).
  **Example:** My cat, a Siamese, is named Ron.

The following passage contains no commas or periods. Add commas and periods as needed.

Dr Newton Brown Jr a renowned chemist has held research positions for OPEC Phillips Petroleum Inc Edward L Smith Chemical Designs and RJ Reynolds Co His thorough exhaustive research is recognized in academic circles as well as in the business community as the most well-designed reliable data available Unfortunately on July 6 1988 he retired after a brief but serious illness He lives in a secluded retirement community at 2401 Beach Sarasota Springs Florida

Check your version against the following corrected version.

Dr. Newton Brown, Jr., a renowned chemist, has held research positions for OPEC, Phillips Petroleum Inc., Edward L. Smith Chemical Designs, and R.J. Reynolds Co. His thorough, exhaustive research is recognized in academic circles, as well as in the business community, as the most well-designed, reliable data available. Unfortunately, on July 6, 1988, he retired after a brief, but serious illness. He lives in a secluded retirement community at 2401 Beach, Sarasota Springs, Florida.

## Apostrophes

Apostrophes communicate important information in written language. Here is a quick review of the two most important rules regarding the use of apostrophes.

- Use an apostrophe to show that letters have been omitted from a word to form a contraction.
  **Examples:** do not = don't; I will = I'll; it is = it's
- Use an apostrophe to show possession.

Check yourself with these sample test questions. Choose which of the four options is punctuated correctly. Answers are at the end of the chapter.

**7.**

**a.** Although it may seem strange, my partners purpose in interviewing Dr. E.S. Sanders Jr. was to eliminate him as a suspect in the crime.

**b.** Although it may seem strange my partner's purpose in interviewing Dr. E. . Sanders, Jr. was to eliminate him, as a suspect in the crime.

**c.** Although it may seem strange, my partner's purpose in interviewing Dr. E.S. Sanders, Jr., was to eliminate him as a suspect in the crime.

**d.** Although it may seem strange, my partner's purpose in interviewing Dr. E.S. Sanders, Jr. was to eliminate him, as a suspect in the crime.

**8.**

**a.** After colliding with a vehicle at the intersection of Grand, and Forest Ms. Anderson saw a dark hooded figure crawl through the window, reach back and grab a small parcel, and run north on Forest.

**b.** After colliding with a vehicle at the intersection of Grand, and Forest, Ms. Anderson saw a dark hooded figure crawl through the window, reach back and grab a small parcel, and run north on Forest.

**c.** After colliding with a vehicle at the intersection of Grand and Forest Ms. Anderson saw a dark, hooded figure crawl through the window, reach back and grab a small parcel, and run north on Forest.

**d.** After colliding with a vehicle at the intersection of Grand and Forest, Ms. Anderson saw a dark, hooded figure crawl through the window, reach back and grab a small parcel, and run north on Forest.

**9.**

**a.** In todays world, childrens clothing has to be made of nonflammable material and with nontoxic fibers.

**b.** In today's world, childrens clothing has to be made of nonflammable material and with nontoxic fibers.

**c.** In todays world, children's clothing has to be made of nonflammable material and with nontoxic fibers.

**d.** In today's world, children's clothing has to be made of nonflammable material and with nontoxic fibers.

## ▶ Verbs

### Subject-Verb Agreement

In written language, a subject must agree with its verb in number. In other words, if a subject is singular, the verb must be singular. If the subject is plural, the verb must be plural. If you are unsure whether a verb is singular or plural, apply this simple test. Fill in the blanks in the two sentences below with the matching form of the verb. The verb form that best completes the first

| APOSTROPHES TO SHOW POSSESSION | | |
| --- | --- | --- |
| SINGULAR NOUNS (ADD 'S) | PLURAL NOUNS ENDING IN S (ADD ') | PLURAL NOUNS NOT ENDING IN S |
| boy's | boys' | men's |
| child's | kids' | children's |
| lady's | ladies' | women's |

sentence is singular. The verb form that best completes the second sentence is plural.

One person _____. [Singular]
Two people _____. [Plural]

Look at these examples using the verbs *speak* and *do.* Try it yourself with any verb that confuses you.

One person *speaks.*    One person *does.*
Two people *speak.*    Two people *do.*

## Pronoun Subjects

Few people have trouble matching noun subjects and verbs, but pronouns are sometimes difficult for even the most sophisticated speakers of English. Some pronouns are always singular, others are always plural, and still others can be both singular and plural.

These pronouns are always singular:

| | |
|---|---|
| each | everyone |
| either | no one |
| neither | nobody |
| anybody | one |
| anyone | somebody |
| everybody | someone |

The indefinite pronouns *each, either,* and *neither* are the ones most often misused. You can avoid a mismatch by mentally adding the word *one* after the pronoun and removing the other words between the pronoun and the verb. Look at the following examples.

Each **of the men** wants his own car.
Each **one** wants his own car.

Either **of the salesclerks** knows where the sale merchandise is located.
Either **one** knows where the sale merchandise is located.

These sentences may sound awkward because many speakers misuse these pronouns, and you are probably used to hearing them used incorrectly. Despite that, the substitution trick (*one* for the words following the pronoun) will help you avoid this mistake.

Some pronouns are always plural and require a plural verb:

| | |
|---|---|
| both | many |
| few | several |

Other pronouns can be either singular or plural:

| | |
|---|---|
| all | none |
| any | some |
| most | |

The words or prepositional phrases following them determine whether they are singular or plural. If what follows the pronouns is plural, the verb must be plural. If what follows is singular, the verb must be singular.

**All** of the **work is** finished.
**All** of the **jobs are** finished.
**Is any** of the **pizza** left?
**Are any** of the **pieces** of pizza left?

**None** of the **time was** wasted.
**None** of the **minutes were** wasted.

## Subjects Joined by *and*

If two nouns or pronouns are joined by *and,* they require a plural verb.

He and she want to buy a new house.
Jack and Jill want to buy a new house.

## Subjects Joined by *or* or *nor*

If two nouns or pronouns are joined by *or* or *nor,* they require a singular verb. Think of them as two separate sentences and you'll never make a mistake in agreement.

He or she wants to buy a new house.
He wants to buy a new house.
She wants to buy a new house.

Neither Jack nor Jill wants to buy a new house.
Jack wants not to buy a new house.
Jill wants not to buy a new house.

Circle the correct verb in each of the following sentences. Answers are at the end of the chapter.

**10.** Every other day either Bert or Ernie (takes, take) out the trash.

**11.** A woman in one of my classes (works, work) at the Civic Center box office.

**12.** A good knowledge of the rules (helps, help) you understand the game.

**13.** Each of these prescriptions (causes, cause) bloating and irritability.

**14.** (Have, Has) either of them ever arrived on time?

## Verb Tense

The tense of a verb tells a reader when the action occurs. Present tense verbs tell the reader to imagine that action happening as it is being read, while past tense verbs tell the reader the action has already happened. Read the following two paragraphs. The first one is written in the present tense, the second in the past tense. Notice the difference in the verbs. They are highlighted to make them easier to locate.

As Horace **opens** the door, he **glances** around cautiously. He **sees** signs of danger everywhere. The centerpiece and placemats from the dining room table **are scattered** on the floor next to the table. An end table in the living room **is lying** on its side. He **sees** the curtains flapping and **notices** glass on the carpet in front of the window.

As Horace **opened** the door, he **glanced** around cautiously. He **saw** signs of danger everywhere. The centerpiece and placemats from the dining room table **were scattered** on the floor next to the table. An end table in the living room **was lying** on its side. He **saw** the curtains flapping and **noticed** glass on the carpet in front of the window.

It's easy to distinguish present tense from past tense by simply fitting the verb into a sentence.

| VERB TENSE | |
|---|---|
| **PRESENT TENSE (TODAY, I ___ . . .)** | **PAST TENSE (YESTERDAY, I ___ . . .)** |
| drive | drove |
| think | thought |
| rise | rose |
| catch | caught |

The important thing to remember about verb tense is to keep it consistent. If a passage begins in the present tense, keep it in the present tense unless there is a specific reason to change—to indicate that some action occurred in the past, for instance. If a passage begins in the past tense, it should remain in the past tense. Verb tense should never be mixed as it is in the following sentence.

**Wrong:** Terry **opens** the door and **saw** the crowd.
**Correct:** Terry **opens** the door and **sees** the crowd.
Terry **opened** the door and **saw** the crowd.

However, sometimes it is necessary to use a different verb tense in order to clarify when an action occurred. Read the following sentences and the explanations following them.

The game warden **sees** the fish that you **caught**. [The verb **sees** is in the present tense, indicating that the action is occurring in the present. However, the verb **caught** is in the past tense, indicating that the fish were caught at some earlier time.]

The house that **was built** over a century ago **sits** on top of the hill. [The verb phrase **was built** is in the past tense, indicating that the house was built in the past. However, the verb **sits** is in the present tense, indicating that the action is still occurring.]

Check yourself with these sample questions. Choose the option that uses verb tense correctly. Answers are at the end of the chapter.

**15.**
a. When I cry, I always get what I want.
b. When I cry, I always got what I want.
c. When I cried, I always got what I want.
d. When I cried, I always get what I wanted.

**16.**
a. It all started after I came home and am in my room studying for a big test.
b. It all started after I came home and was in my room studying for a big test.
c. It all starts after I come home and was in my room studying for a big test.
d. It all starts after I came home and am in my room studying for a big test.

**17.**
a. The child became excited and dashes into the house and slams the door.

b. The child becomes excited and dashed into the house and slammed the door.
c. The child becomes excited and dashes into the house and slammed the door.
d. The child became excited and dashed into the house and slammed the door.

## ▶ Pronouns

### Pronoun Case

Most of the time, a single pronoun in a sentence is easy to use correctly. In fact, most English speakers would readily identify the mistakes in the following sentences.

**Me** went to the movie with **he**.
My teacher gave **she** a ride to school.

Most people know that **Me** in the first sentence should be **I** and that **he** should be **him**. They would also know that **she** in the second sentence should be **her**. Such errors are easy to spot when the pronouns are used alone in a sentence. The problem occurs when a pronoun is used with a noun or another pronoun. See if you can spot the errors in the following sentences.

The director rode with Jerry and **I**.
Belle and **him** are going to the ice arena.

The errors in these sentences are not as easy to spot as those in the sentences with a single pronoun. The easiest way to attack this problem is to turn the sentence with two pronouns into two separate sentences. Then the error once again becomes very obvious.

The director rode with Jerry.
The director rode with **me** (not I).

Belle is going to the ice arena. [Notice the singular verb *is* in place of *are*.]
**He** (not him) is going to the ice arena.

## Pronoun Agreement

Another common error in using pronouns involves singular and plural pronouns. Like subjects and verbs, pronouns must match the number of the nouns they represent. If the noun a pronoun represents is singular, the pronoun must be singular. On the other hand, if the noun a pronoun represents is plural, the pronoun must be plural. Sometimes a pronoun represents another pronoun. If so, either both pronouns must be singular or both pronouns must be plural. Consult the list of singular and plural pronouns you saw earlier in this chapter.

> The **doctor** must take a break when **she** (or **he**) is tired. [singular]
> **Doctors** must take breaks when **they** are tired. [plural]

> **One** of the girls misplaced **her** purse. [singular]
> **All** of the girls misplaced **their** purses. [Plural]

If two or more singular nouns or pronouns are joined by *and,* use a plural pronoun to represent them.

> **Buddha and Muhammad** built religions around **their** philosophies.
> If **he and she** want to know where I was, **they** should ask me.

If two or more singular nouns or pronouns are joined by *or,* use a singular pronoun. If a singular and a plural noun or pronoun are joined by *or,* the pronoun agrees with the closest noun or pronoun it represents.

> **Matthew or Jacob** will loan you **his** calculator.
> **The elephant or the moose** will furiously protect **its** young.

> Neither **the soldiers** nor **the sergeant** was sure of **his** location.

> Neither **the sergeant** nor **the soldiers** were sure of **their** location.

Circle the correct pronoun in the following sentences. Answers are at the end of the chapter.

**18.** Andy or Arvin will bring (his, their) camera so (he, they) can take pictures of the party.

**19.** One of the file folders isn't in (its, their) drawer.

**20.** The NAPA store sent Bob and Ray the parts (he, they) had ordered.

**21.** Sally and Sara should bring (their, her) camera to the crime scene.

**22.** George or Bill should take (their, his) information to the detective.

## ▶ Easily Confused Word Pairs

The following words pairs are often misused in written language. By reading the explanations and looking at the examples, you can learn to use them correctly every time.

### Its/it's

*Its* is a possessive pronoun that means "belonging to it." *It's* is a contraction for *it is* or *it has.* The only time you will ever use *it's* is when you can also substitute the words *it is* or *it has.*

### Who/that

*Who* refers to people. *That* refers to things.

> There is the man **who** helped me find a new pet.
> The woman **who** invented the copper-bottomed kettle died in 1995.
> This is the house **that** Harold bought.
> The magazine **that** I needed was no longer in print.

## There/their/they're

*Their* is a possessive pronoun that indicates ownership. *There* is an adverb that tells where an action or item is located. *They're* is a contraction for the words *they are*. Here is an easy way to remember these words.

- *Their* means "belonging to them." Of the three words, *their* can be most easily transformed into the word *them*. Extend the *r* on the right side and connect the *i* and the *r* to turn *their* into *them*. This clue will help you remember that *their* means "belonging to them."
- If you examine the word *there*, you can see from the way it's written that it contains the word *here*. Whenever you use *there*, you should be able to substitute *here*. The sentence should still make sense.
- Imagine that the apostrophe in *they're* is actually a very small letter *a*. Use *they're* in a sentence only when you can substitute *they are*.

## Your/you're

*Your* is a possessive pronoun that means "belonging to you." *You're* is a contraction for the words *you are*. The only time you will ever use *you're* is when you can also substitute the words *you are*.

## To/too/two

*To* is a preposition or indicates the infinitive form of a verb.

- As a preposition: to the mall, to the bottom, to my church, to our garage, to his school, to his hideout, to our disadvantage, to an open room, to a ballad, to the gymnasium
- As an infinitive (*to* followed by a verb, sometimes followed by adverbs): to walk, to leap, to see badly, to find, to advance, to read, to build, to want sorely, to misinterpret badly, to peruse carefully

*Too* means "also." Whenever you use the word *too*, substitute the word *also*. The sentence should still make sense.

*Two* is a number, as in one, two. If you give it any thought at all, you'll never misuse this form.

The key is to think consciously about these words when you see them in written language. Circle the correct form of these easily confused words in the following sentences. Answers are at the end of the chapter.

**23.** (Its, It's) (to, too, two) late (to, too, two) remedy the problem now.

**24.** This is the man (who, that) helped me find the book I needed.

**25.** (There, Their, They're) going (to, too, two) begin construction as soon as the plans are finished.

**26.** We left (there, their, they're) house after the storm subsided.

**27.** It is (to, two, too) soon (to, two, too) pick the (to, two, too) apples from the tree.

**28.** Sara, Paul, and Steve do not know if (their, they're, there) selected for promotion.

# Answering Multiple-Choice Questions on Grammar in Sentences

As you take the portion of the test that assesses your writing skills, apply what you know about the rules of grammar:

- Look for complete sentences.
- Check for endmarks, commas, and apostrophes.
- Look for subject-verb agreement and consistency in verb tense.
- Check the punctuation to make sure the correct form is used and that the number (singular or plural) is correct.
- Check those easily confused pairs of words.

## ▶ Additional Resources

This has been a very fast review of only a few aspects of written English. For more help with these aspects and more, here are some LearningExpress books you can consult.

- *Grammar Essentials*
- *501 Grammar and Writing Questions*
- *Writing Skills Success in 20 Minutes a Day*

## ▶ Answers

| | | |
|---|---|---|
| **1.** d. | **11.** works | **21.** their |
| **2.** a. | **12.** helps | **22.** his |
| **3.** d. | **13.** causes | **23.** It's, too, to |
| **4.** c. | **14.** Has | **24.** who |
| **5.** c. | **15.** a. | **25.** They're, to |
| **6.** a. | **16.** b. | **26.** their |
| **7.** c. | **17.** d. | **27.** too, to, two |
| **8.** d. | **18.** his, he | **28.** they're |
| **9.** d. | **19.** its | |
| **10.** takes | **20.** they | |

# 20 ▶ Writing

## CHAPTER SUMMARY

This chapter gives vital help on writing an essay or a report for the police exam, as well as on multiple-choice tests in which you have to choose the most clearly written paragraph. Even if the exam you have to take doesn't test writing skills in these ways, your career as a law enforcement officer will require these skills.

**M**ost people would be stunned to learn that law enforcement officers spend up to a third of their duty time writing reports. Other professionals, such as lawyers and judges, base their actions and decisions on the data in these reports. Because of this, law enforcement candidates need solid writing skills.

## ▶ Kinds of Writing Questions on Civil Service Exams

A civil service exam might test your writing skills in one of three ways:

- by asking you to write an essay from scratch
- by asking you to view a video (perhaps a dramatization of officers responding to a call) or listen to an interview, take notes, and write an incident report
- by asking you to choose from several sentences the one that most clearly and accurately presents the facts

No matter which of the three methods is used, learning and applying a few basic principles will help you do well on this section of your test.

## ▶ Writing an Essay

Your exam may actually have you write an essay not that different from the kinds of essays you might have written in school. This is the best way to tell whether you can use written language to express your ideas clearly. The most important thing to remember is to keep your writing simple and straightforward. You're writing to express yourself so that others can read and understand what you write. You're *not* writing to impress your high school English teacher. Use words most people will understand, and avoid long, drawn-out sentences that may confuse a reader.

### Choosing a Topic

It's impossible to predict the questions, but chances are you'll be allowed to choose a general interest question most people could answer, such as:

- What events in your life caused you to choose law enforcement as a profession?
- Describe a person or event that has influenced your life.
- Describe a significant accomplishment in your life.
- Describe yourself.

Whatever the question, answer it by writing about something you know well. If you would enjoy having a conversation about the topic you're considering, it's probably a good choice.

Your time to write this essay will undoubtedly be limited. Start quickly and don't get too fancy. Starting is sometimes the hardest part, but if you begin with a thesis, you'll find writing much easier. A thesis is simply a sentence that *tells what the essay is about* and *forecasts how you will present your information*. The easiest way to write a thesis is to turn the question into a statement and add the main ideas. Take a look at these examples.

**Question**

How did you develop self-discipline?

**Thesis**

I learned self-discipline from taking music lessons and by caring for my younger siblings.

This thesis answers the question by suggesting the two ways the writer will present the information: writing about music lessons and writing about caring for siblings.

**Question**

Describe an event that taught you an important lesson.

**Thesis**

The car accident I was in when I was 22 taught me that I am not immortal and that life is a precious gift.

This thesis tells specifically what the essay is going to be about—a car accident at age 22. It also forecasts how the writer will present the information: as a lesson about being mortal and as a lesson about the value of life. You may have noticed that the "question" isn't in the form of a question. That's common on tests.

Now try writing your own thesis statements for these two questions.

**Question**

How did you develop self-discipline?

**Your Thesis**

**Question**

Describe an event that taught you an important lesson.

**Your Thesis**

Do your thesis statements answer the question and forecast what your essay will cover? If so, you have written a thesis statement that will make the actual essay easier to write.

## Organizing Your Ideas

The thesis establishes the destination and the direction for your essay; the essay will be easier to write when you know where you're going and how you're going to get there. Before you actually write the essay, take a few minutes to organize your thoughts and to make a quick outline. Choose two or three main ideas to write about in support of your thesis. Make a list of what you will write concerning each main idea. Once you've jotted down the ideas so you can see how they look, it's easier to consider the order. When you have to write an essay under timed testing conditions, it's best to begin with the strongest point first. Try to arrange the ideas in such a way that they can be easily hooked together, so your essay will flow smoothly from one idea to another. This brief outline will make your essay easier to write.

Organize your ideas in paragraphs—units of thought that fully develop a single idea. Each paragraph should begin with a topic sentence that states the subject of the paragraph. The rest of the sentences in the paragraph should support, illustrate, or prove the topic sentence. These sentences can offer examples, narrate a sequence of events, explain an idea, or describe something.

## Writing the Essay

You have a thesis, you have an outline, now all you need to do is write. Start with the topic sentence for your first paragraph, and then follow it with several sentences that prove or develop the idea presented in the topic sentence.

Remember the purpose behind the essay. You're trying to show that you can **express** your ideas clearly. You're *not* out to impress anyone with your huge vocabulary or your ability to write long, involved, "intellectual-sounding" sentences. Just keep it simple. Write using complete sentences. Each sentence should present just one point in support of the topic sentence. If you keep your sentences short and specific, you're less likely to muddle your facts or make other mistakes that might distort the meaning or confuse the reader.

The topics you're given will most likely ask you to write about yourself. Use the first person ("I, me") point of view as you write the essay to give it a natural, informal tone. The tone or attitude of your essay is important. You don't want your writing to be filled with slang or street language, but you don't want it to sound formal and stuffy either. It should sound like an educated person speaking in an informal situation, like a conversation. Think through each sentence before you write it. If it would sound awkward in a conversation, think of a way to rephrase the sentence before you write it.

Write using active verbs to make your essay more interesting. In a sentence with an active verb, the person or thing that performs the action is named before the verb, or the action word(s), in a sentence. The following examples illustrate the difference between active and passive verbs. The underlined words show who is performing the action. The italicized words are verbs.

**Passive Verbs**

I *was taken* to my first horse show by my <u>grandfather</u>. I *was taught* to fish by my <u>mother</u> almost before I *was taught* to walk.

## Active Verbs

My <u>grandfather</u> *took me* to my first horse show.

My <u>mother</u> *taught me* to fish almost before <u>I</u> *learned* to walk.

In each of the active verb sentences, the person performing the action is named first. If you look more closely at these examples, you'll notice that the active verb versions are shorter and clearer. They sound more like natural conversation. Strive for these qualities in your essay.

Finally, be concise and specific when you write. The best writing clearly says the most using the fewest words. Avoid *general* statements that don't really say anything. Instead, write *specific* statements that give the reader a clear picture of what you have in mind. Detailed, *specific* language keeps readers interested and makes your ideas easier to remember. The following examples illustrate the difference.

## General

My sister and I enjoyed each other's company as we were growing up. We had a lot of fun, and I will always remember her. We did interesting things and played fun games.

## Specific

As children, my sister and I built rafts out of old barrels and tires, and then tried to float them on the pond behind our house. I'll never forget playing war or hide-and-seek in the grove beside the pond.

The idea behind both of these versions is similar, but the specific example is more interesting and memorable. Be specific when you write.

### Tips for Writing an Essay

- Keep it simple. Express, not impress.
- Start with a thesis. State the idea and forecast the direction.
- Organize first!
- Present ideas in paragraphs
- Use the first-person (*I, me*) point of view.
- Use active verbs.
- Be concise and specific.

Examine the following sample question, thesis, and outline to see this plan in action.

## Question

Describe a well-known personality whom you admire.

## Thesis

I admire Larry King because he is interesting to watch, because he handles controversial subjects well, and because he has staying power in a high-profile occupation.

I. Interesting to watch

   A. timely topics

   B. interesting guests

   C. humor

II. Handles controversial topics well

   A. straightforward and informative:

      doesn't gloss over tough issues

      doesn't "beat around the bush"

      probes for ideas behind opinions

B. fair:

tries to represent both sides of an issue equally

steers callers and guests away from prejudicial assumptions

III. Staying power

A. hasn't become sensational or extreme

B. more impressed with his guests than with himself

C. manages to stay fresh and enthusiastic night after night

Following the thesis in this essay, the writer would develop the essay in three paragraphs: one about how interesting Larry King is, one about how well he handles controversial issues, and one about the reasons behind his staying power as a media personality. The first sentence of each paragraph would be a complete sentence stating the main idea. Each subheading could be turned into a sentence supporting the topic sentence. The writer would give examples for each point.

You may want to write the essay outlined here for practice. Better yet, write your own thesis, outline, and essay about a personality you admire.

## ▶ Writing from Video or Interview Notes

This kind of written exam most nearly represents the kind of writing law enforcement officers do in their jobs. You may see a video of officers responding to a call, or you may listen to a dramatization of an interview an officer might conduct. You'll be asked to take notes from which you'll write an incident report. This

exercise tests your ability to record facts and events accurately and write about them clearly.

### Taking Notes

Taking good notes is a vital first step. First, make sure you accurately record the most important information (who, what, when, where). Clearly identify the people involved and record all of the data the officers request: name, date of birth, address, age, etc. List every event, no matter how small or insignificant it may seem, in chronological order. If a time is mentioned, record the time next to the event.

When you write your report, you'll include "just the facts"—no conclusions, assumptions, or predictions— so be sure to record specific data rather than the judgments you might make. For example, rather than writing "violent suspect," record the specific behavior from which you drew that conclusion: "threw a bottle, knocked over a lamp and end table, said, 'I'm gonna strangle you.'" Include as much specific detail as you can. Write clearly so you can decipher your notes later when it's time to write.

### Writing the Incident Report

The purpose of an incident report is to create a permanent record that clearly and accurately represents the facts. The same advice you read earlier about writing an essay applies to an incident report. Use plain English. Rather than trying to make your report sound "official" by writing jargon, use the ordinary language you would use in a conversation. Here, too, write short sentences with active verbs. Write in past tense (*asked, drove, went, escaped*) reporting action that has already happened. Keep your writing clear and crisp.

Begin with the most important information (who, what, when, where). Following are two versions of a beginning sentence. Which one is a better beginning for an incident report?

■ On or approximately at 0335 hours on the date of February 5, 2006, I was dispatched to go to 628 Elm to investigate a noise disturbance complaint allegedly called in by one Andrea Jones, a resident at the above-stated address (date of birth January 18, 1971).

- At 3:35 A.M. on February 5, 2006, I arrived at 628 Elm and interviewed Andrea Jones (date of birth January 18, 1971), the resident who had called with a noise complaint.

If you chose the second option, you were correct. Although both sentences include identical information, the second one is shorter and easier to read. All of the important data appears in the first line. The writer uses active verbs and avoids unnecessary words. On the other hand, the first option is long and difficult to read. It contains unnecessary words (*On or approximately at, the date of, go to*). The writer uses passive verbs (*was dispatched*) and jargon (*allegedly, above-stated address*) probably in an attempt to sound "official." The effect is to make the writing cumbersome and unclear. The report should begin with the most important information stated clearly and concisely.

After you've recorded the vital information, write about what happened in chronological order. Remember to keep your sentences and paragraphs clear and concise. Record only the facts, not your interpretations or assumptions, and write in such a way that others who read what you have written will draw the same conclusions you did. Don't state the conclusions for them; let the facts speak for themselves. Facts take longer to record than conclusions, but they are infinitely more valuable in an incident report. The examples below illustrate the difference.

### Conclusion

Strader was drunk.

### Facts

Strader smelled strongly of alcohol, slurred his words when he spoke, and stumbled often as he walked.

## Tips for Writing from Notes

- Take thorough, accurate notes.
- Begin with the most important information first.
- Use plain English.
- Use active verbs in past tense.
- Report events in chronological order.
- Include just the facts, not conclusions or assumptions.
- Write in the first person.

## ▶ Choosing the Best Option

Your writing skills may be tested in yet another way. You may be asked to read two or more written versions of the same information and to choose the one that most clearly presents accurate information. Check for accuracy first. If the facts are wrong, the answer is wrong, no matter how well written the answer choice is. If the facts are accurately represented in several of the answer choices, then you must evaluate the writing itself. Here are a few tips for choosing the **best** answer.

1. The **best** answer will be written in plain English in such a way that most readers can understand it the first time through. If you read through an answer choice and find you need to reread it to understand what it says, look for a better option.
2. The **best** option will present the information in logical order, usually chronological order. If the order seems questionable or is hard to follow, look for a better option.
3. The **best** option will be written with active rather than passive verbs. Answer choices written with passive verbs sound formal and stuffy. Look for an option that sounds like normal conversation. Here's an example.

## Passive Voice

At 8:25 P.M., I, Officer Sanchez, was dispatched to 18 Grand, an apartment complex, where a burglary had been reported by Milo Andrews, the manager.

## Active Voice

At 8:25 P.M., I, Officer Sanchez, responded to a burglary reported by Milo Andrews, the manager of an apartment complex at 18 Grand.

The first version uses the passive verbs *was dispatched* and *had been reported* rather than active verbs. Example 2 uses the active verb "responded."

4. The **best** answer contains clearly identified pronouns (he, she, him, her, them, etc.) that match the number of nouns they represent. First, the pronouns should be clearly identified.

## Unclear

Ann Dorr and the officer went to the precinct house, where she made her report.
Bob reminded his father that he had an appointment.

## Clear

Ann Dorr and the officer went to the precinct house, where the officer made her report.
Bob reminded his father that Bob had an appointment.

An answer choice with clearly identified pronouns is a better choice than one with uncertain pronoun references. Sometimes the noun must be repeated to make the meaning clear.

In addition, the pronoun must match the noun it represents. If the noun is singular, the pronoun must be singular. Similarly, if the noun is plural, the pronoun must match.

## Mismatch

I stopped the driver to tell them a headlight was burned out.

## Match

I stopped the driver to tell him a headlight was burned out.

In the first example, *driver* is singular but the pronoun *them* is plural. In the second, the singular pronoun *him* matches the word it refers to.

5. The **best** option is one in which the verb tense is consistent. Look for answer choices that describe the action as though it has already happened, using past tense verbs (mostly *-ed* forms). The verb tense must remain consistent throughout the passage.

## Inconsistent

I opened the trunk and find nothing unusual.

## Consistent

I opened the trunk and found nothing unusual.

The verbs *opened* and *found* are both in the past tense in the second version. In the first, *find*, in the present tense, is inconsistent with *opened*.

6. The **best** option will use words clearly. Watch for unclear modifying words or phrases such as the ones in the following sentences. Misplaced and dangling modifiers can be hard to spot because your brain tries to make sense of things as it reads. In the case of misplaced or dangling modifiers, you may make a logical connection that is not present in the words.

### Dangling Modifiers

Nailed to the tree, Cedric saw a "No Hunting" sign.
Waddling down the road, we saw a skunk.

### Clear Modifiers

Cedric saw a "No Hunting" sign nailed to a tree.
We saw a skunk waddling down the road.

In the first version of the sentences, it sounds as if *Cedric* was nailed to a tree and *we* were waddling down the road. The second version probably represents the writer's intentions: the *sign* was nailed to a tree and the *skunk* was waddling.

### Misplaced Modifier

A dog followed the boy who was growling and barking.
George told us about safe sex in the kitchen.

### Clear Modifiers

A dog who was growling and barking followed the boy.
In the kitchen, George told us about safe sex.

Do you think the boy was growling and barking? Did George discuss avoiding sharp knives and household poisons? The second version of each sentence represents the real situation.

> 7. Finally, the **best** option will use words efficiently. Avoid answer choices that are redundant (repeat unnecessarily) or wordy. Extra words take up valuable time and increase the chances that facts will be misunderstood. In the following examples, the italicized words are redundant or unnecessary. Try reading the sentences without the italicized words.

### Redundant

They refunded our money *back to us*.
We can proceed *ahead* with the plan we made *ahead of time*.
The car was red *in color*.

### Wordy

*The reason* he pursued the car was that it ran a stoplight.
We didn't know what *it was* we were doing.
There are many citizens *who* obey the law.

In each case, the sentence is simpler and easier to read without the italicized words. When you find an answer choice that uses unnecessary words, look for a better option.

## The Best Option

- Is ACCURATE
- Is written in plain English
- Presents information in a logical order
- Uses active verbs
- Has clearly identified pronouns that match he number of the nouns they represent
- Has a consistent verb tense
- Uses words clearly
- Uses words efficiently

Here are four sample multiple-choice questions. By applying the principles explained in this section, choose the best version of each of the four sets of sentences. The answers and a short explanation for each question are at the end of the chapter.

**1.**

**a.** Vanover caught the ball. This was after it had been thrown by the shortstop. Vanover was the first baseman who caught the double-play ball. The shortstop was Hennings. He caught a line drive.

**b.** After the shortstop Hennings caught the line drive, he threw it to the first baseman Vanover for the double play.

c. After the line drive was caught by Hennings, the shortstop, it was thrown to Vanover at first base for a double play.

d. Vanover the first baseman caught the flip from shortstop Hennings.

**2.**

a. This writer attended the movie *Casino* starring Robert DeNiro.

b. The movie *Casino* starring Robert DeNiro was attended by me.

c. The movie *Casino* starring Robert DeNiro was attended by this writer.

d. I attended the movie *Casino* starring Robert DeNiro.

**3.**

a. They gave cereal boxes with prizes inside to the children.

b. They gave cereal boxes to children with prizes inside.

c. Children were given boxes of cereal by them with prizes inside.

d. Children were given boxes of cereal with prizes inside by them.

**4.**

a. After playing an exciting drum solo, the crowd rose to its feet and then claps and yells until the band plays another cut from their new album.

b. After playing an exciting drum solo, the crowd rose to its feet and then clapped and yelled until the band played another cut from their new album.

c. After the drummer's exciting solo, the crowd rose to its feet and then claps and yells until the band plays another cut from their new album.

d. After the drummer's exciting solo, the crowd rose to its feet and then clapped and yelled until the band played another cut from their new album.

Whether you write an essay yourself or choose the **best** option written by someone else, remember the basic principles of good writing. Use them in your writing and look for them in the writing you read.

## ▶ Answers

**1. b.** Choice **a** is unnecessarily wordy and the order is not logical. Choice **c** is written using passive voice verbs. Choice **d** omits a piece of important information.

**2. d.** Both choices **a** and **c** use the stuffy-sounding *this writer*. Choice **d** is best because it uses an active verb.

**3. a.** In both choices **b** and **c**, the modifying phrase *with prizes inside* is misplaced. Both choices **c** and **d** are written in passive rather than active voice.

**4. d.** Both choices **a** and **b** contain a dangling modifier, stating that the crowd played an exciting drum solo. Both choices **b** and **c** mix past and present verb tense. Only choice **d** has clearly written modifiers and a consistent verb tense.

## ▶ Additional Resources

This chapter has touched on only a few aspects of learning to write clearly. If you need more assistance to prepare for the exam, or if you want to improve your writing skills for your career, you might want additional help. Many high schools and community colleges offer inexpensive writing courses for adults in their continuing education departments, or you may be able to find a teacher who is willing to tutor you for a modest fee. In addition, you might consult one of the following LearningExpress books.

- *Write Better Essays in Just 20 Minutes a Day*
- *Better Writing Right Now!*
- *How to Write Great Essays*

# 21 ▶ Vocabulary and Spelling

## CHAPTER SUMMARY

Vocabulary and spelling are tested, at least indirectly, on most law enforcement exams. This chapter provides tips and exercises to help you improve your score in both areas.

**A** person's vocabulary is seen as a measure of an ability to express ideas clearly and precisely. Law enforcement officers must know the working vocabulary of the profession or have the tools for acquiring that vocabulary quickly. Spelling is regarded as a measure of a person's accuracy in presenting information. Law enforcement officers must be able to write correctly in order to communicate clearly. In addition, accurate spelling and a wide and flexible vocabulary are seen as the marks of thoughtful and well-educated people.

Although all word processing programs like Microsoft Word® and Corel WordPerfect® include a spelling verifier, you should not rely on these alone. It is imperative that you know how to spell, particularly in the testing process. You will not have access to a computer or a word processor during any test, but you may have access to a dictionary. The ability to spell correctly will improve your grade substantially during the testing process.

# ▶ Vocabulary

Many civil service exams test vocabulary. There are three basic kinds of questions.

- Synonyms and antonyms: identifying words that mean the same or the opposite of given words
- Context: determining the meaning of a word or phrase by noting how it is used in a sentence or paragraph
- Word parts: choosing the meaning suggested by a part of the word, such as a prefix or suffix

## Synonym and Antonym Questions

A word is a *synonym* of another word if it has the same or nearly the same meaning as the other word. *Antonyms* are words with opposite meanings. Test questions often ask you to find the synonym or antonym of a word. If you're lucky, the word will be surrounded by a sentence that helps you guess what the word means. If you're less lucky, you'll just get the word, and then you have to figure out what the word means without any help.

Questions that ask for synonyms and antonyms can be tricky because they require you to recognize the meaning of several words that may be unfamiliar—not only in the questions but also the answer choices. Usually the best strategy is to *look* at the structure of the word and to *listen* for its sound. See if a part of a word looks familiar. Think of other words you know that have similar key elements. How could those words be related?

## Synonym Practice

Try your hand at identifying the word parts and related words in these sample synonym questions. Circle the word that means the same or about the same as the underlined word. Answers and explanations appear right after the questions.

1. a set of *partial* prints
   a. identifiable
   b. incomplete
   c. visible
   d. enhanced

2. *substantial* evidence
   a. inconclusive
   b. weighty
   c. proven
   d. alleged

3. lifted *latent* fingerprints
   a. labeled
   b. hidden
   c. late
   d. obvious

4. *extracurricular* activities
   a. supplementary
   b. circular
   c. free
   d. obscure

## Answers to Synonym Questions

The explanations are just as important as the answers, because they show you how to go about choosing a synonym if you don't know the word.

1. **b.** *Partial* means *incomplete.* The key part of the word here is *part.* A partial print is only part of the whole.
2. **b.** *Substantial* evidence is *weighty.* The key part of the word here is *substance.* Substance has weight.
3. **b.** *Latent* is *hidden.* *Latent* means present though not now visible.
4. **a.** *Extracurricular* questions are supplementary or additional.

## Antonym Practice

The main danger in answering questions with antonyms is forgetting that you are looking for *opposites* rather than synonyms. Most questions will include one or more synonyms as answer choices. The trick is to keep your mind on the fact that you are looking for the opposite of the word. If you're allowed to mark in the books or on the test paper, circle the word *antonym* or *opposite* in the directions to help you remember.

Otherwise, the same tactics that work for synonym questions work for antonyms as well: Try to determine the meaning of part of the word or to remember a context in which you've seen the word before.

Circle the word that means the *opposite* of the underlined word in the following sentences. Answers are immediately after the questions.

**5.** *zealous* pursuit
   **a.** envious
   **b.** eager
   **c.** idle
   **d.** comical

**6.** *inadvertently* left
   **a.** mistakenly
   **b.** purposely
   **c.** cautiously
   **d.** carefully

**7.** *exorbitant* prices
   **a.** expensive
   **b.** unexpected
   **c.** reasonable
   **d.** outrageous

**8.** *compatible* workers
   **a.** comfortable
   **b.** competitive
   **c.** harmonious
   **d.** experienced

**9.** *rampant* drug activity
   **a.** rampart
   **b.** ramped up
   **c.** contained
   **d.** random

## Answers to Antonym Questions

Be sure to read the explanations as well as the correct answers.

**5.** **c.** *Zealous* means *eager*, so *idle* is most nearly opposite. Maybe you've heard the word *zeal* before. One trick in this question is not to be misled by the similar sounds of *zealous* and *jealous*. The other trick is not to choose the synonym, *eager*.

**6.** **b.** *Inadvertently* means *by mistake*, so *purposely* is the antonym. The key element in this word is the prefix *in-*, which usually means *not, the opposite of*. As usual, one of the answers (choice a) is a synonym.

**7.** **c.** The key element here is *ex-*, which means *out of* or *away from*. *Exorbitant* literally means "out of orbit." The opposite of an *exorbitant* or *outrageous* price would be a *reasonable* one.

**8.** **b.** The opposite of *compatible* is *competitive*. Here you have to distinguish among three words that contain the same prefix, *com-*, and to let the process of elimination work for you. The other choices are too much like synonyms.

**9.** **c.** *Rampant* means profusely widespread; the antonym is *contained*.

## Context Questions

Context is the meaning of the text surrounding a word. Most people use context to help them determine the definition of an unknown word. A vocabulary question that gives you a sentence around the vocabulary word is usually easier to answer than one with little or no context. The surrounding text can help you as you look for synonyms for the specified words in the sentences.

The best way to take meaning from context is to look for key words in sentences or paragraphs that convey the meaning of the text. If nothing else, the context will give you a means to eliminate wrong answer choices that clearly don't fit. The process of elimination will often leave you with the correct answer.

## Context Practice

Try these sample questions. Circle the word that best describes the meaning of the italicized word in the sentence.

**10.** The members of the jury were *appalled* by the wild and uncontrolled behavior of the witness in the case.
   **a.** horrified
   **b.** amused
   **c.** surprised
   **d.** dismayed

**11.** Despite the fact that he appeared to have financial resources, the defendant claimed to be *destitute.*
   **a.** wealthy
   **b.** ambitious
   **c.** solvent
   **d.** impoverished

**12.** Although she was *distraught* over the disappearance of her child, the woman was calm enough to give the officer her description.
   **a.** punished
   **b.** distracted
   **c.** composed
   **d.** anguished

**13.** The unrepentant criminal expressed no *remorse* for his actions.
   **a.** sympathy
   **b.** regret
   **c.** reward
   **d.** complacency

Some tests may ask you to fill in the blank by choosing a word that fits the context. In the following questions, circle the word that best completes the sentence.

**14.** Professor Washington was a very _____ man known for his reputation as a scholar.
   **a.** stubborn
   **b.** erudite
   **c.** illiterate
   **d.** disciplined

**15.** His _____ was demonstrated by his willingness to donate large amounts of money to worthy causes.
   **a.** honesty
   **b.** loyalty
   **c.** selfishness
   **d.** altruism

## Answers

Check to see whether you were able to pick out the key words that help you define the target word, as well as whether you got the right answer.

**10. a.** The key words *wild* and *uncontrolled* signify *horror* rather than the milder emotions described by the other choices.

**11. d.** The key words here are *financial resources,* but this is a clue by contrast. The introductory *Despite the fact* signals that you should look for the opposite of the idea of having financial resources.

**12. d.** The key words here are *although* and *disappearance of her child,* signaling that you are looking for an opposite of *calm* in describing how the mother spoke to the officer. The only word strong enough to match the situation is *anguish*.

**13. b.** *Remorse* means *regret* for one's actions. The part of the word here to beware of is the prefix *re-*. It doesn't signify anything in this word, although it often means *again* or *back*. Don't be confused by the two choices which also contain the prefix *re-*. The strategy here is to see which word sounds better in the sentence. The key words are *unrepentant* and *no*, indicating that you're looking for something that shows no repentance.

**14. b.** The key words here are *professor* and *scholarly*. Even if you don't know the word *erudite*, the other choices don't fit the description of the professor.

**15. d.** The key words here are *large amounts of money to worthy causes*. They give you a definition of the word you're looking for. Again, even if you don't know the word *altruism*, the other choices seem inappropriate to describe someone so generous.

## For Nonnative Speakers of English

Be very careful not to be confused by the *sounds* of words that may mislead you. Be sure you look at the word carefully, and pay attention to the structure and appearance of the word as well as its sound. You may be used to hearing English words spoken with an accent. The sounds of those words may be misleading in choosing a correct answer.

## Questions about Word Parts

Some tests may ask you to find the meaning of a part of a word: roots, which are the main part of the word; prefixes, which go before the root word; or suffixes, which go after. Any of these elements can carry meaning or change the use of a word in a sentence. For instance, the suffix *-s* or *-es* can change the meaning of a noun from singular to plural: *boy, boys*. The prefix *un-* can change the meaning of a root word to its opposite: *necessary, unnecessary*.

To identify most parts of words, the best strategy is to think of words you already know that carry the same root, suffix, or prefix. Let what you know about those words help you to see the meaning in words that are less familiar.

## Word Part Practice

Circle the word or phrase that best describes the meaning of the underlined portion of the word. Answers appear after the questions.

**16.** <u>dis</u>allow
   **a.** negative
   **b.** positive
   **c.** to do
   **d.** not to do

**17.** <u>omni</u>present
   **a.** not present
   **b.** over present
   **c.** all present
   **d.** under present

**18.** <u>contem</u>porary
   **a.** with
   **b.** over
   **c.** apart
   **d.** time

**19.** etymo<u>logy</u>
  **a.** state of
  **b.** prior to
  **c.** study of
  **d.** quality of

**20.** vandal<u>ize</u>
  **a.** to make happen
  **b.** to stop
  **c.** to fill
  **d.** to continue

## Answers

Even if the word in the question was unfamiliar, you might have been able to guess the meaning of the prefix or suffix by thinking of some other word that has the same prefix or suffix.

**16. d.** Remember, *dis-* is to do the opposite of something.
**17. c.** *Omni-* means universally, or all.
**18. a.** Think of *congregation*: a group of people gather *with* each other in a house of worship.
**19. c.** Think of *biology*, the *study of* life.
**20. a.** Think of *scandalize*: to *make* something shocking *happen*.

## Words That Are Easily Confused

Vocabulary tests of any kind often contain words that are easily confused with each other. A smart test taker will be aware of these easily mixed up words or phrases:

| | | |
|---|---|---|
| **accept:** to receive willingly | **except:** exclude or leave out | |
| **complement:** to complete | **compliment:** to say something flattering | |
| **council:** a group that makes decisions | **counsel:** to give advice | |
| **contemptuous:** having an attitude of contempt | **contemptible:** worthy of contempt | |
| **continuous:** without interruption | **continual:** from time to time | |
| **emigrate:** to move from | **immigrate:** to move to | |
| **ingenious:** something clever | **ingenuous:** guileless or naive | |
| **oral:** pertaining to the mouth | **verbal:** pertaining to language | |
| **persecute:** to oppress someone | **prosecute:** to bring a legal action against someone | |
| **lie:** to put oneself horizontal (I'm going to lie down) | **lay:** to put or place something (lay the book on the table) | |
| **affect:** to influence or act upon | **effect:** to bring about | |
| **overt:** obvious | **avert:** to turn away | |
| **no:** not so; negative | **know:** to understand | **now:** currently |
| **to:** toward | **two:** twice one | **too:** also |

## How to Answer Vocabulary Questions

- The key to answering vocabulary questions is to **notice and connect** what you do know to what you may not recognize.
- **Know your word parts.** You can recognize or make a good guess at the meanings of words when you see some suggested meaning in a root word, prefix, or suffix.
- **Note directions very carefully.** Remember when you are looking for opposites rather than synonyms.
- **Use the process of elimination.** Think of how the word makes sense in the sentence.
- **Don't be confused by words that sound like other words**, but may have no relation to the word you need.

### A List of Word Parts

On the next page are some of the word elements seen most often in vocabulary tests. Simply reading them and their examples five to ten minutes a day will give you the quick recognition you need to make a good association with the meaning of an unfamiliar word.

## ► Spelling

Generally, spelling tests are in a multiple-choice format. You will be given several possible spellings for a word and be asked to identify the one that is correct. Thus, you must be able to see fine differences between word spellings. The best way to prepare for a spelling test is to have a good grasp of the spelling fundamentals and be able to recognize when those rules don't apply. Remember that English is full of exceptions in spelling. You have to develop a keen eye to spot the errors.

Even though there are so many variant spellings for words in English, civil service tests generally are looking to make sure that you know and can apply the basic rules. Here are some of those rules for review:

- *i* before *e*, except after *c*, or when *ei* sounds like *a*
  **Examples:** piece, receive, neighbor
- *gh* can replace *f* or be silent
  **Examples:** enough, night
- Double the consonant when you add an ending
  **Examples:** forget/forgettable, shop/shopping
- Drop the *e* when you add *ing*
  **Example:** hope/hoping
- The spelling of prefixes and suffixes generally doesn't change
  **Examples:** project, propel, proactive

### Spelling Practice

Here are some examples of how spelling would appear on a civil service test. Choose the word that is spelled correctly in the following sentences. This time there's no answer key. Instead, use your dictionary to find the correct answers.

**21.** We went to an _____ of early Greek art.
   a. exibition
   b. exhibition
   c. excibition
   d. exebition

**22.** We will _____ go to the movies tonight.
   a. probly
   b. probbaly
   c. probely
   d. probably

| WORD ELEMENT | MEANING | EXAMPLE |
| --- | --- | --- |
| ama | love | amateur |
| ambi | both | ambivalent, ambidextrous |
| aud | hear | audition |
| bell | war | belligerent, bellicose |
| bene | good | benefactor |
| cid/cis | cut | homicide, scissor |
| cogn | know | recognize |
| curr | run | current |
| flu/flux | flow | fluid, fluctuate |
| gress | to go | congress, progress |
| in | not | ingenious |
| ject | throw | inject, reject |
| luc/lux | light | lucid, translucent |
| neo | new | neophyte |
| omni | all | omnivorous |
| pel/puls | push | propeller, impulse |
| pro | forward | project |
| pseudo | false | pseudonym |
| rog | ask | interrogate |
| sub | under | subjugate |
| spec | look, see | spectator |
| super | over | superfluous |
| temp | time | contemporary, temporal |
| un | not, opposite | uncoordinated |
| viv | live | vivid |

**23.** We took _____ of pictures on our vacation.
- **a.** allot
- **b.** alot
- **c.** a lot
- **d.** alott

**24.** The high scorer had the greatest number of _____ answers.
- **a.** accurate
- **b.** acurate
- **c.** accuret
- **d.** acccurit

**25.** He was warned not to use

_____ force.

- **a.** exessive
- **b.** excesive
- **c.** excessive
- **d.** excesive

## Using Spelling Lists

Some test makers will give you a list to study before you take the test. If you have a list to work with, here are some suggestions.

- Divide the list into groups of three, five, or seven to study. Consider making flash cards of the words you don't know.
- Highlight or circle the tricky elements in each word.
- Cross out or discard any words that you already know for certain. Don't let them get in the way of the ones you need to study.
- Say the words as you read them. Spell them out in your mind so you can "hear" the spelling.

Here's a sample spelling list. These words are typical of the words that appear on exams. If you aren't given a list by the agency that's testing you, study this one.

| | | |
|---|---|---|
| achievement | doubtful | ninety |
| allege | eligible | noticeable |
| anxiety | enough | occasionally |
| appreciate | enthusiasm | occurred |
| asthma | equipped | offense |
| arraignment | exception | official |
| autonomous | fascinate | pamphlet |
| auxiliary | fatigue | parallel |
| brief | forfeit | personnel |
| ballistics | gauge | physician |
| barricade | grieve | politics |
| beauty | guilt | possess |
| beige | guarantee | privilege |
| business | harass | psychology |
| bureau | hazard | recommend |
| calm | height | referral |

| | | |
|---|---|---|
| cashier | incident | recidivism |
| capacity | indict | salary |
| cancel | initial | schedule |
| circuit | innocent | seize |
| colonel | irreverent | separate |
| comparatively | jeopardy | specific |
| courteous | knowledge | statute |
| criticism | leisure | surveillance |
| custody | license | suspicious |
| cyclical | lieutenant | tentative |
| debt | maintenance | thorough |
| definitely | mathematics | transferred |
| descend | mortgage | warrant |

## How to Answer Spelling Questions

- **Sound out the word in your mind.** Remember that long vowels inside words usually are followed by single consonants: *sofa*, *total*. Short vowels inside words usually are followed by double consonants: *dribble*, *scissors*.
- **Give yourself auditory (listening) clues when you learn words.** Say "*Wed-nes-day*" or "*lis-ten*" or "*bus-i-ness*" to yourself so that you remember to add letters you do not hear.
- **Look at each part of a word.** See if there is a root, prefix, or suffix that will always be spelled the same way. For example, in *uninhabitable*, *un-*, *in-*, and *-able* are always spelled the same. What's left is *habit*, a self-contained root word that's pretty easy to spell.

## More Practice in Vocabulary and Spelling

Here is a second set of practice exercises with samples of each kind of question covered in this chapter. Answers to all questions except spelling questions are at the end of the chapter. For spelling questions, use a dictionary.

Circle the word that means the same or nearly the same as the underlined word.

**26.** <u>convivial</u> company
   a. lively
   b. dull
   c. tiresome
   d. dreary

**27.** <u>conspicuous</u> behavior
   a. secret
   b. notable
   c. visible
   d. boorish

**28.** <u>meticulous</u> record keeping
   a. dishonest
   b. casual
   c. painstaking
   d. careless

**29.** <u>superficial</u> wounds
   a. life-threatening
   b. bloody
   c. severe
   d. shallow

**30.** <u>impulsive</u> actions
   a. cautious
   b. imprudent
   c. courageous
   d. cowardly

Circle the word that is most nearly opposite in meaning to the underlined word.

**31.** <u>amateur</u> athlete
   a. professional
   b. successful
   c. unrivaled
   d. former

**32.** <u>lucid</u> opinions
   a. clear
   b. strong
   c. hazy
   d. heartfelt

**33.** traveling <u>incognito</u>
   a. unrecognized
   b. alone
   c. by night
   d. publicly

**34.** <u>incisive</u> reporting
   a. mild
   b. sharp
   c. dangerous
   d. insightful

**35.** <u>tactful</u> comments
   a. rude
   b. pleasant
   c. complimentary
   d. sociable

Using the context, choose the word that means the same or nearly the same as the underlined word.

**36.** Although he had little time, the student took <u>copious</u> notes in preparation for the test.
   **a.** limited
   **b.** plentiful
   **c.** illegible
   **d.** careless

**37.** Although flexible about homework, the teacher was <u>adamant</u> that papers be in on time.
   **a.** liberal
   **b.** casual
   **c.** strict
   **d.** pliable

**38.** The condition of the room after the party was <u>deplorable</u>.
   **a.** regrettable
   **b.** pristine
   **c.** festive
   **d.** tidy

Choose the word that best completes the following sentences.

**39.** Her position as a(n) _____ teacher took her all over the city.
   **a.** primary
   **b.** secondary
   **c.** itinerant
   **d.** permanent

**40.** Despite her promise to stay in touch, she remained _____ and difficult to locate.
   **a.** steadfast
   **b.** stubborn
   **c.** dishonest
   **d.** elusive

Choose the word or phrase closest in meaning to the underlined part of the word.

**41.** <u>uni</u>verse
   **a.** one
   **b.** three
   **c.** under
   **d.** opposite

**42.** <u>re</u>entry
   **a.** back
   **b.** push
   **c.** against
   **d.** forward

**43.** <u>bene</u>fit
   **a.** bad
   **b.** suitable
   **c.** beauty
   **d.** good

**44.** educa<u>tion</u>
   **a.** something like
   **b.** state of
   **c.** to increase
   **d.** unlike

**45.** urban<u>ite</u>
   **a.** resident of
   **b.** relating to
   **c.** that which is
   **d.** possessing

Circle the correct spelling of the word that belongs in the blank.

**46.** The information was _____ to the action.
   **a.** irelevent
   **b.** irrevelent
   **c.** irrelevant
   **d.** irrevelent

**47.** He made no _____ to take the job.
   **a.** comittment
   **b.** commitment
   **c.** comitment
   **d.** comittmint

**48.** He made an income _____ to meet his needs.
   **a.** adaquate
   **b.** adequate
   **c.** adiquate
   **d.** adequet

**49.** We went to eat at a fancy new _____.
   **a.** restarant
   **b.** restaraunt
   **c.** restaurant
   **d.** resteraunt

**50.** The vote was _____ to elect the chairman.
   **a.** unannimous
   **b.** unanimous
   **c.** unanimus
   **d.** unaminous

*unanimous*

## ▶ Additional Resources

One of the best resources for any adult student is the public library. Many libraries have sections for adult learners or for those preparing to enter or change careers. Those sections contain skill books and review books on a number of subjects, including spelling and vocabulary. Here are some LearningExpress books you might consult:

- *Vocabulary & Spelling Success in 20 Minutes a Day*
- *Practical Vocabulary*
- *Practical Spelling*
- *1001 Vocabulary & Spelling Questions*
- *Just in Time Vocabulary*

## ▶ Answers

| | | |
|---|---|---|
| **21.** b. | **30.** b. | **39.** c. |
| **22.** d. | **31.** a. | **40.** d. |
| **23.** c. | **32.** c. | **41.** a. |
| **24.** a. | **33.** d. | **42.** a. |
| **25.** c. | **34.** a. | **43.** d. |
| **26.** a. | **35.** a. | **44.** b. |
| **27.** c. | **36.** b. | **45.** a. |
| **28.** c. | **37.** c. | |
| **29.** d. | **38.** a. | |

# 22 ▶ Math

## CHAPTER SUMMARY

This chapter gives you some important tips for dealing with math questions on a civil service exam and reviews some of the most commonly tested concepts. If you've forgotten most of your high school math or have math anxiety, this chapter is for you.

**N**ot all civil service exams test your math knowledge, but many do. Knowledge of basic arithmetic, as well as the more complex kinds of reasoning necessary for algebra and geometry problems, are important qualifications for law enforcement officers. You have to be able to add up the value of stolen property, compute the street price of drugs, evaluate percentages, and other such tasks to be an effective officer. Even if your exam doesn't include math, you'll find that the material in this chapter will be useful on the job.

The math portion of the test covers the subjects you probably studied in grade school and high school. Although every test is different, most emphasize arithmetic skills and word problems.

## ► Math Strategies

- **Don't work in your head! Use your test book or scratch paper to take notes, draw pictures, and calculate.** Although you might think that you can solve math questions more quickly in your head, that's a good way to make mistakes. Write out each step.

- **Read a math question in *chunks* rather than straight through from beginning to end.** As you read each *chunk*, stop to think about what it means and make notes or draw a picture to represent that *chunk*.

- **When you get to the actual question, circle it.** This will keep you more focused as you solve the problem.

- **Glance at the answer choices for clues.** For example, if they're fractions, you probably should do your work in fractions; if they're decimals, you should probably work in decimals.

- **Make a plan of attack** to help you solve the problem.

- **If a question stumps you, try one of the *backdoor* approaches** explained in the next section. These are particularly useful for solving word problems.

- **When you get your answer, reread the circled question to make sure you've answered it.** This helps avoid the careless mistake of answering the wrong question.

- **Check your work after you get an answer.** Test takers get a false sense of security when they get an answer that matches one of the multiple-choice answers. Here are some good ways to check your work *if you have time*:
  - Ask yourself if your answer is reasonable, if it makes sense.
  - Plug your answer back into the problem to make sure the problem holds together.
  - Do the question a second time, but use a different method.

- **Approximate when appropriate.** For example:
  - $5.98 + $8.97 is a little less than $15. (Add: $6 + $9)
  - $0.9876 \times 5.0342$ is close to 5. (Multiply: $1 \times 5$)

- **Skip hard questions and come back to them later.** Mark them in your test book so you can find them quickly.

### Backdoor Approaches for Answering Questions That Puzzle You

Remember those word problems you dreaded in high school? Many of them are actually easier to solve by backdoor approaches. The two techniques that follow are terrific ways to solve multiple-choice word problems that you don't know how to solve with a straightforward approach. The first technique, *nice numbers*, is useful when there are unknowns (like $x$) in the text of the word problem, making the problem too abstract for you. The second technique, *working backward*, presents a quick way to substitute numeric answer choices back into the problem to see which one works.

### Nice Numbers

1. When a question contains unknowns, like $x$, plug nice numbers in for the unknowns. A nice number is easy to calculate with and makes sense in the problem.
2. Read the question with the nice numbers in place. Then solve it.
3. If the answer choices are all numbers, the choice that matches your answer is the right one.

4. If the answer choices contain unknowns, substitute the same nice numbers into **all** the answer choices. The choice that matches your answer is the right one. If more than one answer matches, do the problem again with different nice numbers. You'll have to check only the answer choices that have already matched.

>    **Example:** Judi went shopping with $p$ dollars in her pocket. If the price of shirts was $s$ shirts for $d$ dollars, what is the maximum number of shirts Judi could buy with the money in her pocket?
>
>    **a.** $psd$          **b.** $\frac{ps}{d}$          **c.** $\frac{pd}{s}$          **d.** $\frac{ds}{p}$

To solve this problem, let's try these nice numbers: $p = \$100$, $s = 2$; $d = \$25$. Now reread it with the numbers in place:

>    Judi went shopping with **$100** in her pocket. If the price of shirts was **2** shirts for **$25**, what is the maximum number of shirts Judi could buy with the money in her pocket?

Because 2 shirts cost $25, that means that 4 shirts cost $50, and 8 shirts cost $100. So our answer is **8**. Let's substitute the nice numbers into all 4 answers:

>    **a.** $100 \times 2 \times 25 = 5{,}000$     **b.** $\frac{100 \times 2}{25} = 8$     **c.** $\frac{100 \times 25}{2} = 1{,}250$     **d.** $\frac{25 \times 2}{100} = \frac{1}{2}$

>    The answer is **b** because it is the only one that matches our answer of **8**.

## Working Backward

You can frequently solve a word problem by plugging the answer choices back into the text of the problem to see which one fits all the facts stated in the problem. The process is faster than you think because you'll probably only have to substitute one or two answers to find the right one.

>    This approach works only when

- all of the answer choices are numbers.
- you're asked to find a simple number, not a sum, product, difference, or ratio.

Here's what to do:

1. Look at all the answer choices and begin with the one in the middle of the range. For example, if the answers are 14, 8, 2, 20, and 25, begin by plugging 14 into the problem.
2. If your choice doesn't work, eliminate it. Determine if you need a bigger or smaller answer.
3. Plug in one of the remaining choices.
4. If none of the answers work, you may have made a careless error. Begin again or look for your mistake.

>    **Example:** Juan ate $\frac{1}{3}$ of the jelly beans. Maria then ate $\frac{3}{4}$ of the remaining jelly beans, which left 10 jelly beans. How many jelly beans were there to begin with?
>
>    **a.** 60          **b.** 80          **c.** 90          **d.** 120          **e.** 140

Starting with the middle answer, let's assume there were **90** jelly beans to begin with:

Because Juan ate $\frac{1}{3}$ of them, that means he ate 30 ($\frac{1}{3} \times 90 = 30$), leaving 60 of them ($90 - 30 = 60$). Maria then ate $\frac{3}{4}$ of the 60 jelly beans, or 45 of them ($\frac{3}{4} \times 60 = 45$). That leaves 15 jelly beans ($60 - 45 = 15$).

The problem states that there were **10** jelly beans left, and we wound up with **15** of them. That indicates that we started with too big a number. Thus, 90, 120, and 140 are all wrong! With only two choices left, let's use common sense to decide which one to try. The next lower answer is only a little smaller than 90 and may not be small enough. So, let's try **60**:

Because Juan ate $\frac{1}{3}$ of them, that means he ate 20 ($\frac{1}{3} \times 60 = 20$), leaving 40 of them ($60 - 20 = 40$). Maria then ate $\frac{3}{4}$ of the 40 jelly beans, or 30 of them ($\frac{3}{4} \times 40 = 30$). That leaves 10 jelly beans ($40 - 30 = 10$).

Because this result of **10** jelly beans left agrees with the problem, the right answer is **a.**

## ▶ Word Problems

Many of the math problems on tests are word problems. A word problem can include any kind of math, including simple arithmetic, fractions, decimals, percentages, even algebra and geometry.

The hardest part of any word problem is translating English into math. When you read a problem, you can frequently translate it *word for word* from English statements into mathematical statements. At other times, however, a key word in the word problem hints at the mathematical operation to be performed. Here are the translation rules:

**EQUALS   key words: is, are, has**

| *English* | *Math* |
| --- | --- |
| Bob **is** 18 years old. | $B = 18$ |
| There **are** 7 hats. | $H = 7$ |
| Judi **has** 5 books. | $J = 5$ |

**ADDITION   key words: sum; more, greater, or older than; total; altogether**

| *English* | *Math* |
| --- | --- |
| The **sum** of two numbers is 10. | $X + Y = 10$ |
| Karen has $5 **more than** Sam. | $K = 5 + S$ |
| The base is 3″ **greater than** the height. | $B = 3 + H$ |
| Judi is 2 years **older than** Tony. | $J = 2 + T$ |
| The **total** of three numbers is 25. | $A + B + C = 25$ |
| How much do Joan and Tom have **altogether**? | $J + T = ?$ |

**SUBTRACTION   key words: difference, less, fewer, or younger than, remain, left over**

| *English* | *Math* |
| --- | --- |
| The **difference** between two numbers is 17. | $X + Y = 17$ |
| Mike has 5 **fewer** cats **than** twice the number Jan has. | $M = 2J - 5$ |
| Jay is 2 years **younger than** Brett. | $J = B - 2$ |
| After Carol ate 3 apples, $R$ apples **remained**. | $R = A - 3$ |

**MULTIPLICATION    key words: of, product, times**

| English | Math |
| --- | --- |
| 20% **of** Matthew's baseball caps | $.20 \times M$ |
| Half **of** the boys | $\frac{1}{2} \times B$ |
| The **product** of two numbers is 12 | $A \times B = 12$ |

**DIVISION    key word: per**

| English | Math |
| --- | --- |
| 15 drops **per** teaspoon | $\frac{15 \text{ drops}}{\text{teaspoon}}$ |
| 22 miles **per** gallon | $\frac{22 \text{ miles}}{\text{gallon}}$ |

## ▶ Key to Remember

You can often solve a math problem by looking at the types of things you are trying to solve. To do this, however, you must have similar terms. For example, for a distance problem, you usually are given how fast you are going (miles per hour) and a length of time (hour). By arranging the units so that they cancel each other out to arrive at your answer in miles per hour, you can solve the problem. Let's try one:

If a train is going 80 miles per hour, how far will it travel in 90 minutes?

First, change minutes into hours (90 minutes = 1.5 hours). Then arrange the units so that they cancel each other out and you are left with what you are looking for—hours:

80 *miles/hour* × 1.5 *hours* = 120 miles

Let's try another one. How far did the goat travel in 10 hours if it averaged 2 miles per hour?

10 hours × 2 *miles/hour* = 20 miles

### Distance Formula: Distance = Rate × Time

The key words are movement words such as **plane**, **train**, **boat**, **car**, **walk**, **run**, **climb**, and **swim**.

- How far did the **plane** travel in 4 hours if it averaged 300 miles per hour?
    $D = 300 \times 4$
    $D = 1{,}200$ miles
- Ben **walked** 20 miles in 4 hours. What was his average speed?
    $20 = r \times 4$
    5 miles per hour $= r$

## Solving a Word Problem Using the Translation Table

Remember the problem at the beginning of this chapter about the jelly beans?

Juan ate $\frac{1}{3}$ of the jelly beans. Maria then ate $\frac{3}{4}$ of the remaining jelly beans, which left 10 jelly beans. How many jelly beans were there to begin with?

  **a.** 60      **b.** 80      **c.** 90      **d.** 120      **e.** 140

We solved it by *working backward.* Now let's solve it using our translation rules.

Assume Juan started with $J$ jelly beans. Eating $\frac{1}{3}$ **of** them means eating $\frac{1}{3} \times J$ jelly beans. Maria ate a fraction of the **remaining** jelly beans, which means we must **subtract** to find out how many are left: $J - \frac{1}{3} \times J = \frac{2}{3} \times J$. Maria then ate $\frac{3}{4}$ **of** the $\frac{2}{3} \times J$ jelly beans, or $\frac{3}{4} \times \frac{2}{3} \times J$ jelly beans. Multiplying out $\frac{3}{4} \times \frac{2}{3} \times J$ gives $\frac{1}{2} J$ as the number of jelly beans left. The problem states that there were 10 jelly beans left, meaning that we set 1–2 × J **equal** to 10:

$$\frac{1}{2} \times J = 10$$

Solving this equation for $J$ gives $J = 20$. Thus, the correct answer is **a** (the same answer we got when we *worked backward*). As you can see, both methods—working backward and translating from English to math—work. You should use whichever method is more comfortable for you.

## Practice Word Problems

You will find word problems using fractions, decimals, and percentages in those sections of this chapter. For now, practice using the translation table on problems that just require you to work with basic arithmetic. Answers are at the end of the chapter.

_____ **1.** Joan went shopping with $100 and returned home with only $18.42. How much money did she spend?
 **a.** $81.58    **b.** $72.68    **c.** $72.58    **d.** $71.68    **e.** $71.58

_____ **2.** Mark invited 10 friends to a party. Each friend brought 3 guests. How many people came to the party, excluding Mark?
 **a.** 3     **b.** 10     **c.** 30     **d.** 40     **e.** 41

_____ **3.** The office secretary can type 80 words per minute on his word processor. How many minutes will it take him to type a report containing 760 words?
 **a.** 8    **b.** $8\frac{1}{2}$    **c.** 9    **d.** $9\frac{1}{2}$    **e.** 10

_____ **4.** Officer Wallace has to write a report on a woman's handbag given to him while he was on foot patrol by a man who found it in the gutter. He estimates the value of the handbag at $100. Inside, he finds two rings, which he values at $350 each; a makeup kit, which he values at $25; and $249 in cash. What should Officer Wallace write as the total value of the found cash and property?
 **a.** $724    **b.** $974    **c.** $1,049    **d.** $1,064    **e.** $1,074

# ▶ Fraction Review

Problems involving fractions may be straightforward calculation questions, or they may be word problems. Typically, they ask you to add, subtract, multiply, divide, or compare fractions.

## Working with Fractions

A fraction is a part of something.

> **Example:** Let's say that a pizza was cut into 8 equal slices and you ate 3 of them. The fraction $\frac{3}{8}$ tells you what part of the pizza you ate. The pizza below shows this: 3 of the 8 pieces (the ones you ate) are shaded.

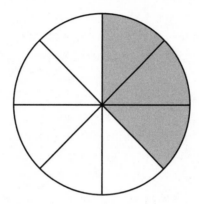

## Three Kinds of Fractions

| | |
|---|---|
| Proper fraction: | The top number is less than the bottom number: |
| | $\frac{1}{2}; \frac{2}{3}; \frac{4}{9}; \frac{8}{13}$ |
| | The value of a proper fraction is less than 1. |
| Improper fraction: | The top number is greater than or equal to the bottom number: |
| | $\frac{3}{2}; \frac{5}{3}; \frac{14}{9}; \frac{12}{12}$ |
| | The value of an improper fraction is 1 or more. |
| Mixed number: | A fraction written to the right of a whole number: |
| | $3\frac{1}{2}; 4\frac{2}{3}; 12\frac{3}{4}; 24\frac{3}{4}$ |
| | The value of a mixed number is more than 1: it is the sum of the whole number plus the fraction. |

## Changing Improper Fractions into Mixed or Whole Numbers

It's easier to add and subtract fractions that are mixed numbers rather than improper fractions. To change an improper fraction, say $\frac{13}{2}$, into a mixed number, follow these steps:

1. Divide the bottom number (2) into the top number (13) to get the whole number portion (6) of the mixed number:

$$2\overline{\smash)13} \; \begin{array}{r} 6 \\ \hline 13 \\ 12 \\ \hline 1 \end{array}$$

2. Write the remainder of the division (1) over the old bottom number (2): $6\frac{1}{2}$
3. Check: Change the mixed number back into an improper fraction (see following steps).

## Changing Mixed Numbers into Improper Fractions

It's easier multiply and divide fractions when you're working with improper fractions rather than mixed numbers. To change a mixed number, say $2\frac{3}{4}$, into an improper fraction, follow these steps:

1. Multiply the whole number (2) by the bottom number (4).          $2 \times 4 = 8$
2. Add the result (8) to the top number (3).                        $8 + 3 = 11$
3. Put the total (11) over the bottom number (4).                   $\frac{11}{4}$
4. Check: Reverse the process by changing the improper fraction into a mixed number. If you get back the number you started with, your answer is correct.

## Reducing Fractions

Reducing a fraction means writing it in *lowest terms*, that is, with smaller numbers. For instance, 50¢ is $\frac{50}{100}$ of a dollar, or $\frac{1}{2}$ of a dollar. In fact, if you have 50¢ in your pocket, you say that you have half a dollar. Reducing a fraction does not change its value.

Follow these steps to reduce a fraction:

1. Find a whole number that divides *evenly* into both numbers that make up the fraction.
2. Divide that number into the top of the fraction, and replace the top of the fraction with the quotient (the answer you got when you divided).
3. Do the same thing to the bottom number.
4. Repeat the first three steps until you can't find a number that divides evenly into both numbers of the fraction.

For example, let's reduce $\frac{8}{24}$. We could do it in 2 steps: $\frac{8 \div 4}{24 \div 4} = \frac{2}{6}$ then $\frac{2 \div 2}{6 \div 2} = \frac{1}{3}$. Or we could do it in a single step: $\frac{8 \div 8}{24 \div 8} = \frac{1}{3}$.

**Shortcut:** When the top and bottom numbers both end in zero, cross out the same number of zeros in both numbers to begin the reducing process. For example $\frac{300}{4,000}$ reduces to $\frac{3}{40}$ when you cross out two zeros in both numbers.

Whenever you do arithmetic with fractions, reduce your answer. On a multiple-choice test, don't panic if your answer isn't listed. Try to reduce it and then compare it to the choices.

Reduce these fractions to lowest terms:

_____  **5.**  $\frac{3}{12}$

_____  **6.**  $\frac{17}{51}$

_____  **7.**  $\frac{21}{33}$

## Raising Fractions to Higher Terms

Before you can add and subtract fractions, you have to know how to raise a fraction to higher terms. This is actually the opposite of reducing a fraction.

Follow these steps to raise $\frac{2}{3}$ to 24ths:

1. Divide the old bottom number (3) into the new one (24):        $3\overline{\smash{)}24} = 8$
2. Multiply the answer (8) by the old top number (2):        $2 \times 8 = 16$
3. Put the answer (16) over the new bottom number (24):        $\frac{16}{24}$
4. Check: Reduce the new fraction to see if you get back the original one:        $\frac{16 \div 8}{24 \div 8} = \frac{2}{3}$

Raise these fractions to higher terms:

_____ **8.** $\frac{5}{12} = \frac{}{24}$

_____ **9.** $\frac{2}{9} = \frac{}{27}$

_____ **10.** $\frac{2}{5} = \frac{}{500}$

## Adding Fractions

If the fractions have the same bottom numbers, just add the top numbers together and write the total over the bottom number.

**Examples:**    $\frac{2}{9} + \frac{4}{9} = \frac{2+4}{9} = \frac{6}{9}$    Reduce the sum: $\frac{2}{3}$

                 $\frac{5}{8} + \frac{7}{8} = \frac{12}{8}$    Change the sum to a mixed number: $1\frac{4}{8}$; then reduce: $1\frac{1}{2}$

There are a few extra steps to add mixed numbers with the same bottom numbers, say $2\frac{3}{5} + 1\frac{4}{5}$:

1. Add the fractions:        $\frac{3}{5} + \frac{4}{5} = \frac{7}{5}$
2. Change the improper fraction into a mixed number:        $\frac{7}{5} = 1\frac{2}{5}$
3. Add the whole numbers:        $2 + 1 = 3$
4. Add the results of steps 2 and 3:        $1\frac{2}{5} + 3 = 4\frac{2}{5}$

## Finding the Least Common Denominator

If the fractions you want to add don't have the same bottom number, you'll have to raise some or all of the fractions to higher terms so that they all have the same bottom number, called the **common denominator**. All of the original bottom numbers divide evenly into the common denominator. If it is the smallest number that they all divide evenly into, it is called the **least common denominator (LCD)**.

Here are a few tips for finding the LCD, the smallest number that all the bottom numbers evenly divide into:

- See if all the bottom numbers divide evenly into the biggest bottom number.
- Check out the multiplication table of the largest bottom number until you find a number that all the other bottom numbers evenly divide into.

■ When all else fails, multiply all the bottom numbers together.

**Example:** $\frac{2}{3} + \frac{4}{5}$

1. Find the LCD. Multiply the bottom numbers:
2. Raise each fraction to 15ths:

$$3 \times 5 = 15$$
$$\frac{2}{3} = \frac{10}{15}$$
$$+\frac{4}{5} = \frac{12}{15}$$
$$\frac{22}{15}$$

3. Add as usual:

Try these addition problems:

_____ **11.** $\frac{1}{6} + \frac{3}{8}$

_____ **12.** $\frac{1}{8} + \frac{3}{32}$

_____ **13.** $4\frac{1}{3} + 2\frac{3}{4} + \frac{1}{6}$

## Subtracting Fractions

If the fractions have the same bottom numbers, just subtract the top numbers and write the difference over the bottom number.

**Example:** $\frac{4}{9} - \frac{3}{9} = \frac{4-3}{9} = \frac{1}{9}$

If the fractions you want to subtract don't have the same bottom number, you'll have to raise some or all of the fractions to higher terms so that they all have the same bottom number, or LCD. If you forgot how to find the LCD, just read the section on adding fractions with different bottom numbers.

**Example:** $\frac{5}{6} - \frac{3}{4}$

1. Raise each fraction to 12ths because 12 is the LCD, the smallest number that 6 and 4 both divide into evenly:
2. Subtract as usual:

$$\frac{5}{6} = \frac{10}{12}$$
$$-\frac{3}{4} = \frac{9}{12}$$
$$\frac{1}{12}$$

Subtracting mixed numbers with the same bottom number is similar to adding mixed numbers.

**Example:** $4\frac{3}{5} - 1\frac{2}{5}$

1. Subtract the fractions:
2. Subtract the whole numbers:
3. Add the results of steps 1 and 2:

$$\frac{3}{5} - \frac{2}{5} = \frac{1}{5}$$
$$4 - 1 = 3$$
$$\frac{1}{5} + 3 = 3\frac{1}{5}$$

Sometimes there is an extra "borrowing" step when you subtract mixed numbers with the same bottom numbers, say $7\frac{3}{5} - 2\frac{4}{5}$:

1. You can't subtract the fractions the way they are because $\frac{4}{5}$ is bigger than $\frac{3}{5}$.
   So you borrow 1 from the 7, making it 6, and change that 1 to $\frac{5}{5}$ because
   5 is the bottom number:                             $7\frac{3}{5} = 6\frac{5}{5} + \frac{3}{5}$
2. Add the numbers from step 1:             $6\frac{5}{5} + \frac{3}{5} = 6\frac{8}{5}$
3. Now you have a different version of the original problem:     $6\frac{8}{5} - 2\frac{4}{5}$
4. Subtract the fractional parts of the two mixed numbers:     $\frac{8}{5} - \frac{4}{5} = \frac{4}{5}$
5. Subtract the whole number parts of the two mixed numbers:     $6 - 2 = 4$
6. Add the results of the last two steps together:     $4 + \frac{4}{5} = 4\frac{4}{5}$

Try these subtraction problems:

_____ **14.** $\frac{5}{8} - \frac{9}{16}$

_____ **15.** $\frac{1}{3} - \frac{1}{4}$

_____ **16.** $4\frac{1}{3} - 2\frac{3}{4}$

Now let's put what you've learned about adding and subtracting fractions to work in some real-life problems.

_____ **17.** Officer Peterson drove $3\frac{1}{2}$ miles to the police station. Then he drove $4\frac{3}{4}$ miles to his first assignment. When he left there, he drove 2 miles to his next assignment. Then he drove $3\frac{2}{3}$ miles back to the police station for a meeting. Finally, he drove $3\frac{1}{2}$ miles home. How many miles did he travel in total?

     **a.** $17\frac{5}{12}$      **b.** $16\frac{5}{12}$      **c.** $15\frac{7}{12}$      **d.** $15\frac{5}{12}$      **e.** $13\frac{11}{12}$

_____ **18.** Before leaving the police station, Officer Sorensen noted that the mileage gauge registered $4,357\frac{4}{10}$ miles. When he arrived at the crime scene, the mileage gauge then registered $4,400\frac{1}{10}$ miles. How many miles did he drive from the police station to the crime scene?

     **a.** $42\frac{3}{10}$      **b.** $42\frac{7}{10}$      **c.** $43\frac{7}{10}$      **d.** $47\frac{2}{10}$      **e.** $57\frac{3}{10}$

## Multiplying Fractions

Multiplying fractions is actually easier than adding them. All you do is multiply the top numbers and then multiply the bottom numbers.

    **Examples:**   $\frac{2}{3} \times \frac{5}{7} = \frac{2 \times 5}{3 \times 7} = \frac{10}{21}$        $\frac{1}{2} \times \frac{3}{5} \times \frac{7}{4} = \frac{1 \times 3 \times 7}{2 \times 5 \times 4} = \frac{21}{40}$

Sometimes you can *cancel* before multiplying. Canceling is a shortcut that makes the multiplication go faster because you're multiplying with smaller numbers. It's very similar to reducing: If there is a number that divides evenly into a top number and bottom number, do that division before multiplying. If you forget to cancel, you'll still get the right answer, but you'll have to reduce it.

**Example:** $\frac{5}{6} \times \frac{9}{20}$

1. Cancel the 6 and the 9 by dividing 3 into both of them: $6 \div 3 = 2$ and $9 \div 3 = 3$. Cross out the 6 and the 9.

$$\frac{5}{\cancel{6}_2} \times \frac{\cancel{9}^3}{20}$$

2. Cancel the 5 and the 20 by dividing 5 into both of them: $5 \div 5 = 1$ and $20 \div 5 = 4$. Cross out the 5 and the 20.

$$\frac{\cancel{5}^1}{\cancel{6}_2} \times \frac{\cancel{9}^3}{\cancel{20}_4}$$

3. Multiply across the new top numbers and the new bottom numbers:

$$\frac{1 \times 3}{2 \times 4} = \frac{3}{8}$$

Try these multiplication problems:

_____ **19.** $\frac{1}{3} \times \frac{10}{25}$

_____ **20.** $\frac{2}{3} \times \frac{4}{7} \times \frac{3}{5}$

_____ **21.** $\frac{1}{3} \times \frac{3}{16}$

To multiply a fraction by a whole number, first rewrite the whole number as a fraction with a bottom number of 1.

**Example:** $5 \times \frac{2}{3} = \frac{5}{1} \times \frac{2}{3} = \frac{10}{3}$   (Optional: Convert $\frac{10}{3}$ to a mixed number: $3\frac{1}{3}$)

To multiply with mixed numbers, it's easier to change them to improper fractions before multiplying.

**Example:** $4\frac{2}{3} \times 5\frac{1}{2}$

1. Convert $4\frac{2}{3}$ to an improper fraction:

$$4\frac{2}{3} = \frac{4 \times 3 + 2}{3} = \frac{14}{3}$$

2. Convert $5\frac{1}{2}$ to an improper fraction:

$$5\frac{1}{2} = \frac{5 \times 2 + 1}{2} = \frac{11}{2}$$

3. Cancel and multiply the fractions:

$$\frac{\cancel{14}^7}{3} \times \frac{11}{\cancel{2}_1} = \frac{77}{3}$$

4. Optional: Convert the improper fraction to a mixed number:

$$\frac{77}{3} = 25\frac{2}{3}$$

Now try these multiplication problems with mixed numbers and whole numbers:

_____ **22.** $4\frac{1}{3} \times \frac{2}{5}$

_____ **23.** $2\frac{1}{2} \times 6$

_____ **24.** $3\frac{3}{4} \times 4\frac{2}{5}$

Here are a few more real-life problems to test your skills:

_____ **25.** After driving $\frac{2}{3}$ of the 15 miles to work, Sergeant Stone stopped to make a phone call. How many miles had he driven when he made his call?

    **a.** 5       **b.** $7\frac{1}{2}$       **c.** 10       **d.** 12       **e.** $15\frac{2}{3}$

_____ **26.** If Detective Block worked $\frac{3}{4}$ of a 40-hour week, how many hours did he work?

    **a.** $7\frac{1}{2}$       **b.** 10       **c.** 20       **d.** 25       **e.** 30

_____ **27.** Officer Jones makes $14.00 an hour. When she works more than 8 hours a day, she gets over-time pay of $1\frac{1}{2}$ times her regular hourly wage for the extra hours. How much did she earn for working 11 hours in one day?

    **a.** $77       **b.** $154       **c.** $175       **d.** $210       **e.** $231

## Dividing Fractions

To divide one fraction by a second fraction, invert the second fraction (that is, flip the top and bottom numbers) and then multiply. That's all there is to it!

    **Example:** $\frac{1}{2} \div \frac{3}{5}$

**1.** Invert the second fraction ($\frac{3}{5}$):                                                     $\frac{5}{3}$

**2.** Change the division sign ($\div$) to a multiplication sign ($\times$).

**3.** Multiply the first fraction by the new second fraction:           $\frac{1}{2} \times \frac{5}{3} = \frac{1 \times 5}{2 \times 3} = \frac{5}{6}$

To divide a fraction by a whole number, first change the whole number to a fraction by putting it over 1. Then follow the division steps above.

    **Example:** $\frac{3}{5} \div 2 = \frac{3}{5} \div \frac{2}{1} = \frac{3}{5} \times \frac{1}{2} = \frac{3 \times 1}{5 \times 2} = \frac{3}{10}$

When the division problem has a mixed number, convert it to an improper fraction and then divide as usual.

**Example:** $2\frac{3}{4} \div \frac{1}{6}$

1. Convert $2\frac{3}{4}$ to an improper fraction:

2. Divide $\frac{11}{4}$ by $\frac{1}{6}$:

3. Flip $\frac{1}{6}$ to $\frac{6}{1}$, change $\div$ to $\times$, cancel and multiply:

$$2\frac{3}{4} = \frac{2 \times 4 + 3}{4} = \frac{11}{4}$$

$$\frac{11}{4} \div \frac{1}{6} = \frac{11}{4} \times \frac{6}{1}$$

$$\frac{11}{\underset{2}{4}} \times \frac{\overset{3}{6}}{1} = \frac{11 \times 3}{2 \times 1} = \frac{33}{2}$$

Here are a few division problems to try:

_____ **28.** $\frac{1}{5} \div \frac{10}{25}$

_____ **29.** $\frac{1}{4} \div \frac{1}{5}$

_____ **30.** $\frac{3}{5} \div 3$

_____ **31.** $3\frac{3}{4} \div 2\frac{1}{3}$

Let's wrap this up with some real-life problems.

_____ **32.** If four detectives evenly split $6\frac{1}{2}$ pounds of candy, how many pounds of candy does each detective get?

    **a.** $\frac{8}{13}$      **b.** $1\frac{5}{8}$      **c.** $1\frac{1}{2}$      **d.** $1\frac{5}{13}$      **e.** 4

_____ **33.** How many $2\frac{1}{2}$-pound chunks of cheese can be cut from a single 20-pound piece of cheese?

    **a.** 2      **b.** 4      **c.** 6      **d.** 8      **e.** 10

_____ **34.** Lieutenant Goldbaum earned $36.75 for working $3\frac{1}{2}$ hours. What was her hourly wage?

    **a.** $10.00      **b.** $10.50      **c.** $10.75      **d.** $12.00      **e.** $12.25

# ▶ Decimals

## What Is a Decimal?

A decimal is a special kind of fraction. You use decimals every day when you deal with money—$10.35 is a decimal that represents 10 dollars and 35 cents. The decimal point separates the dollars from the cents. Because there are 100 cents in one dollar, 1¢ is $\frac{1}{100}$ of a dollar, or $0.01.

Each decimal digit to the right of the decimal point has a name:

**Example:** $0.1 = 1$ tenth $= \frac{1}{10}$

$0.02 = 2$ hundredths $= \frac{2}{100}$

$0.003 = 3$ thousandths $= \frac{3}{1000}$

$0.0004 = 4$ ten thousandths $= \frac{4}{10,000}$

When you add zeros after the rightmost decimal place, you don't change the value of the decimal. For example, 6.17 is the same as all of these:

6.170

6.1700

6.17000000000000000

If there are digits on both sides of the decimal point (like 10.35), the number is called a mixed decimal. If there are digits to the right of the decimal point only (like 0.53), the number is called a decimal. A whole number (like 15) is understood to have a decimal point at its right (15.). Thus, 15 is the same as 15.0, 15.00, 15.000, and so on.

## Changing Fractions to Decimals

To change a fraction to a decimal, divide the bottom number into the top number after you put a decimal point and a few zeros on the right of the top number. When you divide, bring the decimal point up into your answer.

**Example:** Change $\frac{3}{4}$ to a decimal.

1. Add a decimal point and two zeros to the top number (3):     3.00
2. Divide the bottom number (4) into 3.00:
   Bring the decimal point up into the answer:

3. The quotient (result of the division) is the answer:     0.75

Some fractions may require you to add many decimal zeros in order for the division to come out evenly. In fact, when you convert a fraction like $\frac{2}{3}$ to a decimal, you can keep adding decimal zeros to the top number forever because the division will never come out evenly! As you divide 3 into 2, you'll keep getting 6s:

$$2 \div 3 = 0.6666666666, \text{ etc.}$$

This is called a *repeating decimal,* and it can be written as $0.66\overline{6}$ or as $0.66\frac{2}{3}$. You can approximate it as $0.67, 0.667,$ $0.6667,$ and so on.

## Changing Decimals to Fractions

To change a decimal to a fraction, write the digits of the decimal as the top number of a fraction and write the decimal's name as the bottom number of the fraction. Then reduce the fraction, if possible.

> **Example:** 0.018

1. Write 18 as the top of the fraction: $\quad\quad\quad\quad\quad\quad\quad\quad\quad\quad\quad\quad\quad$ $\frac{18}{\phantom{18}}$
2. Three places to the right of the decimal means *thousandths,* so write 1,000 as the bottom number: $\quad\quad\quad\quad\quad\quad\quad\quad\quad\quad\quad$ $\frac{18}{1,000}$
3. Reduce by dividing 2 into the top and bottom numbers: $\quad\quad\quad\quad$ $\frac{18 \div 2}{1,000 \div 2} = \frac{9}{500}$

> Change these decimals or mixed decimals to fractions:

_____ **35.** 3.55

_____ **36.** 21.4

_____ **37.** 123.456

## Comparing Decimals

Because decimals are easier to compare when they have the same number of digits after the decimal point, tack zeros onto the end of the shorter decimals. Then all you have to do is compare the numbers as if the decimal points weren't there:

> **Example:** Compare .08 and .1

1. Tack one zero at the end of .1: $\quad\quad\quad\quad\quad\quad\quad\quad\quad\quad\quad\quad\quad\quad\quad\quad$ .10
2. To compare .10 to .08, just compare 10 to 8.
3. Since 10 is larger than 8, .1 is larger than .08.

## Adding and Subtracting Decimals

To add or subtract decimals, line them up so their decimal points are even. You may want to tack on zeros at the end of shorter decimals so you can keep all your digits lined up evenly. Remember, if a number doesn't have a decimal point, then put one at the right end of the number.

> **Example:** 1.23 + 57 + 0.038

**1.** Line up the numbers like this:

$$\begin{array}{r} 1.230 \\ 57.000 \\ +\ 0.038 \\ \hline \end{array}$$

**2.** Add:

$$58.268$$

    **Example:** $1.23 - 0.038$

**1.** Line up the numbers like this:

$$\begin{array}{r} 1.230 \\ -\ 0.038 \\ \hline \end{array}$$

**2.** Subtract:

$$1.192$$

Try these addition and subtraction problems:

_____ **38.** $0.905 + 0.02 + 3.075$

_____ **39.** $0.005 + 8 + 0.3$

_____ **40.** $3.48 - 2.573$

_____ **41.** $123.456 - 122$

_____ **42.** Officer Peterson drove 3.7 miles to the state park. He then walked 1.6 miles around the park to make sure everything was all right. He got back into the car, drove 2.75 miles to check on a broken traffic light, and then drove 2 miles back to the police station. How many miles did he drive in total?

    **a.** 8.05       **b.** 8.45       **c.** 8.8       **d.** 10       **e.** 10.05

_____ **43.** The average number of thefts in the third precinct fell from 486.4 per month to 402.5 per month. By how many thefts per month did the average fall?

    **a.** 73.9       **b.** 83       **c.** 83.1       **d.** 83.9       **e.** 84.9

## Multiplying Decimals

To multiply decimals, ignore the decimal points and just multiply the numbers. Then count the total number of decimal digits (the digits to the *right* of the decimal point) in the numbers you're multiplying. Count off that number of digits in your answer beginning at the right side and put the decimal point to the *left* of those digits.

    **Example:** $215.7 \times 2.4$

**1.** Multiply 2157 times 24:

$$
\begin{array}{r}
2157 \\
\times\ 24 \\
\hline
8628 \\
4314\phantom{0} \\
\hline
51768
\end{array}
$$

**2.** Because there are a total of two decimal digits in 215.7 and 2.4, count off

two places from the right in 51768, placing the decimal point to the *left*

of the last two digits: 517.68

If your answer doesn't have enough digits, tack zeros on to the left of the answer.

**Example:** $.03 \times .006$

**1.** Multiply 3 times 6: $3 \times 6 = 18$
**2.** You need 5 decimal digits in your answer, so tack on 3 zeroes: 00018
**3.** Put the decimal point at the front of the number (which is 5 digits in from the right): 0.00018

You can practice multiplying decimals with these:

_____ **44.** $0.27 \times 0.3$

_____ **45.** $0.44 \times 0.1$

_____ **46.** $38.1 \times 0.0184$

_____ **47.** Joe earns $14.50 per hour. Last week he worked 37.5 hours. How much money did he earn that week?
  **a.** $518.00  **b.** $518.50  **c.** $525.00  **d.** $536.50  **e.** $543.75

_____ **48.** Nuts cost $3.50 per pound. Approximately how much will 4.25 pounds of nuts cost?
  **a.** $12.25  **b.** $12.50  **c.** $12.88  **d.** $14.50  **e.** $14.88

## Dividing Decimals

To divide a decimal by a whole number, set up the division ($8\overline{)0.256}$) and immediately bring the decimal point straight up into the answer ($8\overline{)0.256}$). Then divide as you would normally divide whole numbers:

**Example:**

$$
\begin{array}{r}
0.032 \\
8\overline{)0.256} \\
\underline{0}\phantom{..} \\
25 \\
\underline{24} \\
16 \\
\underline{16} \\
0
\end{array}
$$

To divide any number by a decimal, there is an extra step to perform before you can divide. Move the decimal point to the very right of the number you're dividing by, counting the number of places you're moving it. Then move the decimal point the same number of places to the right in the number you're dividing into. In other words, first change the problem to one in which you're dividing by a whole number.

**Example:** $0.06\overline{)1.218}$

1. Because there are two decimal digits in 0.06, move the decimal point two places to the right in both numbers and move the decimal point straight up into the answer: $\qquad\qquad$ $0.06\overline{)1.218}$

2. Divide using the new numbers:

$$
\begin{array}{r}
20.3 \\
6\overline{)121.8} \\
\underline{12}\phantom{...} \\
01 \\
\underline{00} \\
18 \\
\underline{18} \\
0
\end{array}
$$

Under certain conditions, you have to tack on zeros to the right of the last decimal digit in number you're dividing into:

- If there aren't enough digits for you to move the decimal point to the right, or
- If the answer doesn't come out evenly when you do the division, or
- If you're dividing a whole number by a decimal, then you'll have to tack on the decimal point as well as some zeros.

Try your skills on these division problems:

_____ **49.** $7\overline{)9.8}$

_____ **50.** $0.0004\overline{)0.0512}$

_____ **51.** $0.05\overline{)28.6}$

_____ **52.** $0.14\overline{)196}$

_____ **53.** If Officer Worthington drove 92.4 miles in 2.1 hours, what was his average speed in miles per hour?
<br>

      **a.** 41        **b.** 44        **c.** 90.3        **d.** 94.5        **e.** 194.04

_____ **54.** Sergeant Sanders walked a total of 18.6 miles in 4 days. On average, how many miles did she walk each day?

      **a.** 4.15        **b.** 4.60        **c.** 4.65        **d.** 22.60        **e.** 74.40

# ▶ Percents

## What Is a Percent?

A percent is a special kind of fraction or part of something. The bottom number (the *denominator*) is always 100. For example, 17% is the same as $\frac{17}{100}$. Literally, the word *percent* means *per 100*. The root *cent* means 100: A *century* is 100 years, there are 100 *cents* in a dollar, etc. Thus, 17% means 17 parts out of 100. Because fractions can also be expressed as decimals, 17% is also equivalent to 0.17, which is 17 hundredths.

You come into contact with percents every day. Sales tax, interest, and discounts are just a few common examples.

If you're shaky on fractions, you may want to review the fraction section before reading further.

## Changing a Decimal to a Percent and Vice Versa

To change a decimal to a percent, move the decimal point two places to the **right** and tack on a percent sign (%) at the end. If the decimal point moves to the very right of the number, you don't have to write the decimal point. If there aren't enough places to move the decimal point, add zeros on the **right** before moving the decimal point.

To change a percent to a decimal, drop off the percent sign and move the decimal point two places to the **left**. If there aren't enough places to move the decimal point, add zeros on the **left** before moving the decimal point.

Try changing these decimals to percents:

_____ **55.** 0.45

_____ **56.** 0.008

_____ **57.** $0.16\frac{2}{3}$

Now change these percents to decimals:

_____ **58.** 12%

_____ **59.** $87\frac{1}{2}$%

_____ **60.** 250%

## Changing a Fraction to a Percent and Vice Versa

To change a fraction to a percent, there are two techniques. Each is illustrated by changing the fraction $\frac{1}{4}$ to a percent:

Technique 1:      Multiply the fraction by 100%.

                        Multiply $\frac{1}{4}$ by 100%:

$$\frac{1}{{}_1 4} \times \frac{\overset{25}{\cancel{100\%}}}{1} = 25\%$$

Technique 2:      Divide the fraction's bottom number into the top number; then move the decimal point two places to the **right** and tack on a percent sign (%).

                        Divide 4 into 1 and move the decimal point two places to the right:

$$4\overline{)1.00}\phantom{xx}^{\displaystyle 0.25}\qquad\qquad 0.25 = 25\%$$

To change a percent to a fraction, remove the percent sign and write the number over 100. Then reduce if possible.

**Example:** Change 4% to a fraction.

1.  Remove the % and write the fraction 4 over 100:                  $\frac{4}{100}$

2.  Reduce:                                                 $\frac{4 \div 4}{100 \div 4} = \frac{1}{25}$

Here's a more complicated example: Change $16\frac{2}{3}\%$ to a fraction.

1. Remove the % and write the fraction $16\frac{2}{3}$ over 100:

$$\frac{16\frac{2}{3}}{100}$$

2. Because a fraction means "top number divided by bottom number," rewrite the fraction as a division problem:

$$16\frac{2}{3} \div 100$$

3. Change the mixed number ($16\frac{2}{3}$) to an improper fraction ($\frac{50}{3}$):

$$\frac{50}{3} \div \frac{100}{1}$$

4. Flip the second fraction ($\frac{100}{1}$) and multiply:

$$\frac{\overset{1}{50}}{3} \times \frac{1}{\underset{2}{100}} = \frac{1}{6}$$

Try changing these fractions to percents:

_____ **61.** $\frac{1}{8}$

_____ **62.** $\frac{13}{25}$

_____ **63.** $\frac{7}{12}$

Now change these percents to fractions:

_____ **64.** 95%

_____ **65.** $37\frac{1}{2}\%$

_____ **66.** 125%

Sometimes it is more convenient to work with a percentage as a fraction or a decimal. Rather than have to *calculate* the equivalent fraction or decimal, consider memorizing the following equivalence table. Not only will this increase your efficiency on the math test, but it will also be practical for real-life situations.

| CONVERSION TABLE | | |
|---|---|---|
| **DECIMAL** | **%** | **FRACTION** |
| 0.25 | 25% | $\frac{1}{4}$ |
| 0.50 | 50% | $\frac{1}{2}$ |
| 0.75 | 75% | $\frac{3}{4}$ |
| 0.10 | 10% | $\frac{1}{10}$ |
| 0.20 | 20% | $\frac{1}{5}$ |
| 0.40 | 40% | $\frac{2}{5}$ |
| 0.60 | 60% | $\frac{3}{5}$ |
| 0.80 | 80% | $\frac{4}{5}$ |
| $0.33\bar{3}$ | $33\frac{1}{3}\%$ | $\frac{1}{3}$ |
| $0.66\bar{6}$ | $66\frac{2}{3}\%$ | $\frac{2}{3}$ |

## Percent Word Problems

Word problems involving percents come in three main varieties:

- Find a percent of a whole.

   **Example:** What is 30% of 40?

- Find what percent one number is of another number.

   **Example:** 12 is what percent of 40?

- Find the whole when the percent of it is given.

   **Example:** 12 is 30% of what number?

While each variety has its own approach, there is a single shortcut formula you can use to solve each of these:

$$\frac{is}{of} = \frac{\%}{100}$$

The **is** is the number that usually follows or is just before the word **is** in the question.

The **of** is the number that usually follows the word **of** in the question.

The **%** is the number that in front of the **%** or **percent** in the question.

Or you may think of the shortcut formula as:

$$\frac{part}{whole} = \frac{\%}{100}$$

To solve each of the three varieties, we're going to use the fact that the **cross-products** are equal. The cross-products are the products of the numbers diagonally across from each other. Remembering that *product* means *multiply*, here's how to create the cross-products for the percent shortcut:

$$\frac{part}{whole} = \frac{\%}{100}$$

$$part \times 100 = whole \times \%$$

Here's how to use the shortcut with cross-products:

- Find a percent of a whole.

   What is 30% of 40?

   30 is the % and 40 is the *of* number:

   Cross-multiply and solve for *is*:

$$\frac{is}{40} = \frac{30}{100}$$
$$is \times 100 = 40 \times 30$$
$$is \times 100 = 1{,}200$$
$$\mathbf{12} \times 100 = 1{,}200$$

Thus, **12 *is*** 30% of 40.

- Find what percent one number is of another number.

   12 is what percent of 40?

   12 is the *is* number and 40 is the *of* number:

   Cross-multiply and solve for %:

$$\frac{12}{40} = \frac{\%}{100}$$
$$12 \times 100 = 40 \times \%$$
$$1{,}200 = 40 \times \%$$
$$1{,}200 = 40 \times \mathbf{30}$$

Thus, 12 is **30%** of 40.

- Find the whole when the percent of it is given.

    12 is 30% of what number?

    12 is the *is* number and 30 is the %:

    Cross-multiply and solve for the *of* number:

$$\frac{12}{of} = \frac{30}{100}$$
$$12 \times 100 = of \times 30$$
$$1{,}200 = of \times 30$$
$$1{,}200 = \mathbf{40} \times 30$$

Thus 12 is 30% **of 40**.

You can use the same technique to find the percent increase or decrease. The *is* number is the actual increase or decrease, and the *of* number is the original amount.

**Example:** If a merchant puts his $20 hats on sale for $15, by what percent does he decrease the selling price?

1. Calculate the decrease, the *is* number:

    $20 − $15 = $5

2. The *of* number is the original amount, $20.

3. Set up the equation and solve for *of* by cross-multiplying:

$$\frac{5}{20} = \frac{\%}{100}$$
$$5 \times 100 = 20 \times \%$$
$$500 = 20 \times \%$$
$$500 = 20 \times \mathbf{25}$$

4. Thus, the selling price is decreased by **25%**.

If the merchant later raises the price of the hats from $15 back to $20, don't be fooled into thinking that the percent increase is also 25%! It's actually more, because the increase amount of $5 is now based on a lower original price of only $15:

Thus, the selling price is increased by **33%**.

$$\frac{5}{15} = \frac{\%}{100}$$
$$5 \times 100 = 15 \times \%$$
$$500 = 15 \times \%$$
$$500 = 15 \times \mathbf{33\tfrac{1}{3}}$$

Find a percent of a whole.

_____ **67.** 1% of 25

_____ **68.** 18.2% of 50

_____ **69.** $37\tfrac{1}{2}$% of 100

_____ **70.** 125% of 60

Find what percent one number is of another number.

_____ **71.** 10 is what % of 20?

_____ **72.** 4 is what % of 12?

_____ **73.** 12 is what % of 4?

Find the whole when the percent of it is given.

_____ **74.** 15% of what number is 15?

_____ **75.** $37\frac{1}{2}$% of what number is 3?

_____ **76.** 200% of what number is 20?

Now try your percent skills on some real-life problems.

_____ **77.** Last Monday, 20% of the 140-member police department was absent. How many police officers were absent that day?
  **a.** 14      **b.** 20      **c.** 28      **d.** 112      **e.** 126

_____ **78.** 40% of Vero's police department are women. If there are 80 women in Vero's police department, how many men are in the department?
  **a.** 32      **b.** 112      **c.** 120      **d.** 160      **e.** 200

_____ **79.** Of the 840 crimes committed last month, 42 involved petty theft. What percent of the crimes involved petty theft?
  **a.** 0.5%      **b.** 2%      **c.** 5%      **d.** 20%      **e.** 50%

_____ **80.** Sam's Shoe Store put all of its merchandise on sale for 20% off. If Jason saved $10 by purchasing one pair of shoes during the sale, what was the original price of the shoes before the sale?
  **a.** $12      **b.** $20      **c.** $40      **d.** $50      **e.** $70

## Additional Resources

If you need more assistance to prepare for the math section of the exam, consult the following LearningExpress titles:

- *Math Essentials*
- *501 Math Word Problems*
- *Math for Civil Service Tests*
- *Math Builder*

## ▶ Answers to Math Problems

### Word Problems

1. a.
2. d.
3. d.
4. e.

### Fractions

5. $\frac{1}{4}$
6. $\frac{1}{3}$
7. $\frac{7}{11}$
8. 10
9. 6
10. 200
11. $\frac{13}{24}$
12. $\frac{7}{32}$
13. $7\frac{1}{4}$
14. $\frac{1}{16}$
15. $\frac{1}{12}$
16. $\frac{19}{12}$ or $1\frac{7}{12}$
17. a.
18. b.
19. $\frac{2}{25}$
20. $\frac{8}{35}$
21. $\frac{1}{16}$
22. $\frac{26}{15}$ or $1\frac{11}{15}$
23. 15
24. $\frac{33}{2}$ or $16\frac{1}{2}$
25. c.
26. e.
27. c.
28. $\frac{5}{10}$ or $\frac{1}{2}$

29. $\frac{5}{4}$ or $1\frac{1}{4}$
30. $\frac{1}{5}$
31. $\frac{45}{28}$ or $1\frac{17}{28}$
32. b.
33. d.
34. b.

### Decimals

35. $3\frac{55}{100}$ or $3\frac{11}{20}$
36. $21\frac{4}{10}$ or $21\frac{2}{5}$
37. $123\frac{456}{1,000}$ or $123\frac{57}{125}$
38. 4
39. 8.305
40. 0.907
41. 1.456
42. b.
43. d.
44. 0.072
45. 0.044
46. 0.70104
47. e.
48. e.
49. 1.4
50. 128
51. 572
52. 1,400
53. b.
54. c.

### Percents

55. 45%
56. 0.8%
57. 16.67% or $16\frac{2}{3}$%
58. 0.12
59. 0.875
60. 2.5
61. 12.5% or $12\frac{1}{2}$%
62. 52%
63. 58.33% or $58\frac{1}{3}$%
64. $\frac{19}{20}$
65. $\frac{3}{8}$
66. $\frac{5}{4}$ or $1\frac{1}{4}$
67. $\frac{1}{4}$ or 0.25
68. 9.1
69. $37\frac{1}{2}$ or 37.5
70. 75
71. 50%
72. $33\frac{1}{3}$%
73. 300%
74. 100
75. 8
76. 10
77. c.
78. c.
79. c.
80. d.

# 23 ▶ Judgment

## CHAPTER SUMMARY

This chapter shows you how to deal with exam questions that test your judgment and common sense. Reading carefully and learning to think like a police officer are the keys to doing well on these types of questions.

**W**alk into any police academy around the country and you are likely to see the following words emblazoned across a wall: "Common Sense and Good Judgment." While it might seem obvious that a police officer needs common sense and good judgment, not everyone has these traits, and some people who *do* have them need to be reminded to use them. Police agencies have to have some way of determining who has these traits and who is clueless. Multiple-choice civil service exams are the quickest, most cost-effective method of finding out.

Judgment questions are designed to see if you can make a sound decision—pick the right multiple-choice answer—based on the information given to you. To come to the right conclusion, you will need your common sense, good judgment, and good reading skills. (A little good luck never hurts either, so feel free to stick that four-leaf clover in your pocket.)

Judgment questions fall into three categories: situational judgment, application of rules and procedures, and judgment based on eyewitness accounts. This chapter will look at each category, take apart an example of each type of judgment question, and then identify the best approach to answering the question. There are also tips on what is most likely to trip up the unwary test taker.

## ▶ Situational Judgment Questions

Situational judgment questions ask you to climb inside the mind of a police officer and make decisions from this viewpoint. It isn't necessary for you to know the laws of any state or the policies and procedures of any law enforcement agency. The test itself will give you the information you need to answer the question.

Some exams load you right into the hot seat with language such as "You are on patrol in a high-crime area . . . ," while other exams use a more subtle approach: "Officer Jones is on patrol when she sees a man breaking into a car." Although the approach is different, both test makers are asking you to look at their questions from the same viewpoint—a police officer's view.

The structure of the questions is pretty simple. You'll be given a situation, and then you'll be asked to choose how you would handle the situation if you were the police officer handling this call. The nice part is that you don't have to come up with your own plan. You get to choose the best answer from four multiple-choice options listed below the question. Eye-bulging panic, of course, will make all of the options appear to be the right one, but keep in mind that there is only *one* best answer.

Here's an example:

1. Officer Johnson is directing traffic at a busy intersection after the end of a football game near the stadium. A small car stalls, and the driver can't restart the engine. He is blocking the one lane of traffic leading out of the stadium area. There is a shoulder next to each lane of traffic on this flat roadway. What should Officer Johnson do?
   a. Call for a tow truck to move the vehicle.
   b. Push the car onto the shoulder of the road so that the other traffic may proceed.
   c. Tell the driver to keep trying to start the engine in hope that the car will start after a brief wait.
   d. Direct traffic around the stalled vehicle by having the cars drive on the shoulder of the road.

In this situation, all of the options could conceivably happen, but only one answer is the best answer. The best way to approach this type of question is to start by eliminating the options that you know aren't going to work. Choice **a** is not as appealing as some of the other options because traffic would be snarled until the tow truck arrived to clear the lane. Choice **c** is not much of an option for the same reason. The idea here is to keep traffic moving safely. Now we've narrowed the choices down to two, which makes the odds of getting this question right much better. If you compare the two, choice **d** is not as good as choice **b** because it is not as practical or as safe as simply pushing the small car several feet until it is on the shoulder of the road. The shoulder of the road is intended for this sort of emergency. Also, this option should appeal to your good judgment and common sense: You want to remove the problem (the stalled vehicle) in the safest, most effective manner.

The temptation with situational judgment questions is to project your thoughts and feelings into the scenario. You may catch yourself chewing on your pencil, thinking, "Well, I'd have the driver behind the stalled vehicle get out and help the other driver push the car to the side of the road. That's what I would do."

That may be how this situation would play out in real life if the other driver were amenable, but that's not one of your options, so this kind of thinking merely complicates the question.

Another temptation is to read more into the situation than is there. You may think, "Maybe the car is too heavy to push, or it won't roll right, or maybe this department doesn't allow its officers to push cars . . ." The list goes on. Use the information you *see on the page*, not the information that *could* be there, to make your decision.

In some testing situations, you may be shown situations on a video and then asked to respond. These tests are a bit more nerve-racking because you might have to come up with your own options to the situations you see. Here, you'll just have to think as much like a police officer as possible, watch the situation on the video monitor as closely as you can, and *listen* to what the actors are saying if the video has dialogue.

Whether the test is written or audiovisual, you will be required to exercise your good judgment and common sense. And it certainly helps to know what it means to "think like a cop."

## Through Their Eyes

It's easy to say "think like a cop" if you know how cops think. The ideal way to learn is to ride with officers in your area and ask tons of questions. See what officers handle in real, day-to-day settings, find out how they feel about the calls they make, and *ask* them—in calmer moments, of course—what they were looking for when they handled specific calls. Do what you can to look at the world through their eyes.

If you've run out of time for ride-alongs to be a viable option, then arm yourself with the next few paragraphs.

## Safety First

If you got tired of hearing your momma say, "Safety first!" when you were growing up, get ready for an exhausting experience. In every action an officer takes, the safety and well-being of everyone involved is

Priority Number One. Even the bad guy's safety is an issue. Protecting life is an officer's first responsibility.

When you look at a test question, remember that officers have the importance of safety drilled into them from day one at the academy. Is it safer to let the man stand in the street while he tells you how the accident happened, or is it better to have him move onto the sidewalk? Is it safer for the accident victims if the patrol car is blocking this lane of traffic or that lane of traffic? Is it safer for you to stand in front of a door or to the side of a door before knocking? Is it safer for bystanders if you pursue the speeder through downtown traffic or let him go?

The safety issue may not surface in every question, but when it does, be aware that safety is a police officer's highest priority.

## Use of Force

Use of force situations are the most critically examined and heavily litigated situations a police officer must face. Some officers working in tough neighborhoods find themselves using some type of force upon someone a few times a week. Other officers in less dangerous areas may not use force upon someone in a year's time. However, expect to see a few test questions on the subject of uses of force. Here are some general guidelines.

California law and most police agencies teach their officers to use a variety of force techniques in field situations. The exact type of force to be used is based upon the type of situation the officer is confronted with. The first question to be asked by the prospective officer in a force situation is whether to use force at all.

By law, officers may use force to overcome the resistance of another in three types of situations: to effect an arrest; to prevent escape; and to prevent injury to themselves, their partners, or the public. Once a force option is decided, the next question is what type of force to use.

Current case law in California tells us that the force employed by police officers must be *reasonable* under the circumstances of the event. What is reasonable is the question. The courts will look at each specific situation when deciding whether the force used was reasonable, and compare that to what a reasonable police officer with the same amount of training and experience would do. Officers do not have to use the "least amount of force" or a "reasonable and necessary" amount of force. They must only be able to articulate in their reports and in court testimony under oath that the force they chose to use was reasonable under the circumstances to effect the arrest, to prevent escape, or to protect themselves or others from violence.

So, when you are confronted with a question on force, examine the situation carefully and choose your force option wisely.

Obviously, we must use a force option that seems reasonable under the circumstances. For example, if a suspect is ranting and raving only, perhaps some command presence or the use of a firm grip upon the suspect will be enough to overcome his resistance. It would be unreasonable for the officer to use deadly force in this situation. If the suspect escalates his force (that is, using his fists to try to inflict injury or escape), you can then use your baton, OC spray, or a number of take-down grappling techniques to overcome his resistance. All the while, you must continue to verbalize to the suspect to stop resisting.

Finally, there is no provision in any law that prohibits a police officer from using equal or lesser force than the suspect. If this were the case, officers would be injured or killed every time they had a use of force situation in the field. Officers are trained to use appropriate force to stop the situation from escalating and to do so safely and effectively. Police officers must (and do) have the support of the legal system to quickly and efficiently use force in certain circumstances to stop the perpetrator immediately.

### The Choices: Lecture, Cite, or Arrest

Do you write a ticket, or are the law and the public better served with a warning and a brief lecture on good driving? Is every breach of the peace a signal to break out the handcuffs? Situational judgment questions will demand that you know the answers. For example, you might see a question like this:

2. You are on foot patrol downtown when you see one man punch another man in the stomach. You separate the two men and find out that it was a minor disturbance. The two men are embarrassed that you witnessed the altercation because they are good friends. They assure you that no one is hurt. The victim laughs and says no when you ask if he wants to file assault charges. What should you do about this obvious breach of the peace that has occurred in your presence?
   a. Arrest the suspect anyway because the assault occurred in front of you.
   b. Arrest the suspect because the victim may change his mind later.
   c. Let the suspect go free because the victim does not want to file charges.
   d. Arrest the suspect because bystanders are watching to see what kind of action you will take.

Once again, the process of elimination will come in handy to answer this question. After reading all of the options, you should reason immediately that choice **d** is not a good option. Police work, especially in a city, is rarely conducted in total privacy. The opinions of bystanders should not affect how you enforce the law. Choice **a** is not the best option either. It is not in the best interest of the public or the overcrowded justice system to take a person into custody physically each and every time a violation of the law occurs in your presence. Choice **b** is a bad option for the same reason. The victim obviously knows the suspect. In the unlikely event that he changes his mind later and wants to file charges, he knows the identity of his attacker and can contact the police department with that information. A warrant can always be issued for the suspect.

That leaves us with choice **c**, the best option. Maybe you've heard the expression "no victim, no crime." If the man who was assaulted did not consider himself a victim of a crime, then you have no need to arrest the "suspect" for assault. Arresting the suspect for any other violation in this situation would not be in the best interest of the law, the public, or the police department. Common sense should tell you that arrest is not warranted because the two men resolved the situation themselves, no one was hurt, no damage to property occurred, and no one else was affected by the altercation. And by not arresting this man you remain available for more serious calls.

## Tips for Answering Situational Judgment Questions

- Read carefully, but don't read anything into the situation that isn't there.
- Think like a cop:
  Safety first.
  Use a reasonable amount of force.
- Use your common sense.

## ▶ Application of Laws and Procedures

Another kind of test question asks you to read rules, laws, policies, or procedures and then apply those guidelines to a hypothetical situation. You may still be able to use your good judgment and common sense in these questions, but even more important is your ability to read carefully and accurately.

These kinds of questions ask you to do something police officers do every day: take their knowledge of the laws of their city and state or of their department's procedures and use that knowledge to decide what to do in a given situation. The questions don't expect you to know the laws or procedures; they're right there as part of the test question. And that's why your reading skills really come into play.

Questions that ask you to apply rules and laws are a little different from ones that ask you to apply procedures, so each kind of question is treated separately in this chapter.

## Application of Laws

Some questions will give you a definition of a crime and then ask you to apply that definition to hypothetical situations to see which situation matches the definition. Here's an example:

**Shoplifting** is a theft of goods from a store, shop, or place of business during business hours where the suspect takes the good(s) past the threshold of the business to the outside without attempting to offer payment.

3. Which situation below is the best example of shoplifting?
   a. Terry walks into the Bag 'n' Save grocery store and gets a piece of candy. He takes it to the counter and discovers he has no money. The clerk tells him to go ahead and keep the candy this time. Terry leaves the store eating the candy.
   b. Gloria walks into an electronics store to get a pack of triple-A batteries. She sticks the small package in her coat pocket while she looks at the computer display. After a few minutes, she turns to walk out. Before she reaches the door, she remembers the batteries and turns back to the counter to pay for them.
   c. Gail enters Philo's Pharmacy on Twelfth Street to pick up a prescription. After paying for the medicine, she walks over to the perfume counter where she finds a small bottle of cologne she likes. She puts the cologne in her purse and walks out of the front door of the pharmacy.
   d. Pete and his mother, Abby, are grocery shopping. Pete picks up a candy bar, peels off the wrapper, and hands Abby the wrapper. When they reach the checkout counter, Pete walks out of the store while Abby puts the groceries, along with the candy wrapper, on the stand for checkout. The clerk rings up the price of the candy along with the groceries.

The best approach to application of definition questions is to read each option carefully and decide whether or not it fits the definition. You have to rely on your good judgment, your careful reading skills, and your ability to put two and two together to reach a conclusion. The questions do not assume that you have any knowledge of the law or of police procedures; you are given all the information you need to reason out the best possible answer.

Let's look at the options in our example. Choice **a** is not an example of shoplifting because the clerk told Terry he did not have to pay for the candy. Terry did not hide the candy or try to leave the business without an attempt to pay. The clerk had the option of having Terry put back the candy, but he instead chose to give it away.

Choice **b** is not an example of shoplifting because Gloria did not pass the threshold of the store without making an attempt to pay for the batteries. In businesses where the checkout stands are located in the middle or toward the rear of the store, the benefit of the doubt goes to the shopper until he or she walks out the door.

Choice **c** *is* an example of shoplifting because Gail made no attempt to pay for the cologne before leaving the business.

Choice **d** is not an example of shoplifting because Abby paid for her son's candy, even though he ate the candy in the store and eventually walked out of the store.

Again, careful reading is the key to getting the application of definition questions correct. You have to read exactly what is there while not reading anything more into the situation than is actually written on the page. For example, if while reading choice **b** you focus on Gloria putting the batteries in her pocket instead of whether or not she attempted to pay for the item, you may end up with an incorrect answer. Reread the definition and note that *where* someone carries goods while they are shopping has no bearing on the crime as defined. Do not complicate the situation.

## Application of Procedures

Application of procedures questions are a lot like the previous type. You'll be given information about police procedures and then asked to apply these procedures to a hypothetical situation. You might have to decide which step in a set of procedures is the next step to be taken in the situation, or you might have to decide whether a hypothetical officer followed the procedures properly in the situation given. In either case, you're being tested on your ability to follow directions, including your reading comprehension skills.

The question is usually preceded by a brief passage telling you about the procedure; for example:

When an officer handles "found" property—property that has been discovered by someone, but is not necessarily evidence from a crime scene—the officer should follow these procedures:

1. Write a report detailing who found the property, what the property is, where it was found, and where it is now located, and turn in the report before the end of his or her shift.
2. Attach a tag to the property.
3. Write the report number on the tag, along with the officer's name, badge number, and the date and time the property was turned in.
4. Turn the property into the property room before the end of his or her shift.

**4.** Officer Smith is on patrol when he is flagged down by a pedestrian on the northeast corner of Elm and St. John. The pedestrian, Carl Randal, tells Officer Smith that he found a gold watch on the sidewalk in the 200 block of Elm. The clasp is broken on the watch, and Randal tells the officer he believes the watch must have fallen off of someone without that person's knowledge. He gives the watch to the officer and provides his name and other information to the officer for the report. Officer Smith writes a found property report using all the details provided by Randal, places a tag on the property, and writes the report number, his name, his badge number, and the date and time the watch came into his possession. He then puts the watch in the glove box of the patrol car. He turns in his report an hour after writing it, and at the beginning of his next shift he takes the watch to the property room. In this situation, Officer Smith acted

a. improperly, because he should have let Carl Randal keep the watch until someone reported it as missing.

b. properly, because he turned in his report before the end of his shift.

c. improperly, because he failed to take the property to the property room before the end of his shift.

d. properly, because he wrote all of the pertinent information in his report.

What the test maker wants you to do is study how Officer Smith handled the found property case and see if he followed his department's rules on handling found property.

Each choice actually has two parts that require you to make two decisions. You have to decide if the officer acted properly or improperly, and then you have to decide if the reason stated in the option is correct or incorrect. In this case, choice **c** is correct on both counts because the officer did not act properly, according to the procedures for turning in found property. He should have turned the watch in before the end of his shift (step four).

One way to approach picking the right choice is to see if you can assign a step to the information in the option. For example, choice **a** states that Officer Smith should have let Randal, the man who found the watch, keep it until someone reported it stolen. If you look at the steps in the list of procedures, you will not see that action in any of the steps.

These questions can be tricky if you read too fast or read only part of the answer choices. Take your time and make sure both parts of the answer are correct. For example, in choice **b**, the second part of the answer is correct. That action, turning in the report in a timely manner, is what Officer Smith is supposed to do according to step one. However, if you look at the first part of the answer it says Smith acted correctly in this situation because he turned in his report on time. This is not the *best* answer—Smith did *not* act properly because he failed to turn in the found property before the end of his shift. Remember, there's only one *best* answer.

## Tips for Answering Application Questions

- Read what's there, not what might have been there.
- Read through all the options before you choose an answer.
- Find the spot in the law or procedure that supports your answer.

## ▶ Judgment Questions Based on Eyewitness Accounts

You'll need a careful eye for detail for the kinds of judgment questions that ask you to choose among eyewitness accounts. The test maker is looking to see if you can pick out the common elements in the list of answers you have to choose from in order to arrive at the right answer. The question usually will contain a description of suspects, vehicles, or license plates. Here's an example:

**5.** You are called to the scene of a gasoline theft at a neighborhood gas station. The station manager tells you that a woman in a green Chevy Cavalier pumped $20 of unleaded gasoline into her car and took off northbound on Elm St. He and three other witnesses tell you they saw the license plate on the vehicle. Which of the plates listed below is most likely to be the correct plate?
   **a.** PG-2889
   **b.** PG-2089
   **c.** PG-2880
   **d.** PC-2889

In eyewitness account questions, the actual situation in the question has little bearing on what the test maker wants you to do. You are being asked to pick out which license plate is most likely to be the license plate for the suspect vehicle. The answer to this question lies in the answers themselves. The end result isn't focusing on the crime that took place so much as on your ability to take information, average it all up, and arrive at a conclusion.

Your best approach to this question is to start comparing the similarities in each answer. You'll notice that all of the answers start with the letter "P." The second letter is the letter "G" in all of the answers except for choice **d.** The first number is the number 2 for all of the answers. Then you see that all of the answers except for choice **b** agree that the number 8 is the second number on the license plate. The third number of the plate is 8 in all of the answers. The final number of the plate is 9 in all of the answers except for choice **d.** You should have picked choice **a** as the correct answer because the license plate that has the most common elements is PG-2889.

You'll be asked to use the same kind of reasoning when you see a test question asking you to pick out a suspect description. Once again, the scenario described in the question is not going to carry as much weight as the answers themselves. Your task will be to find the common threads in each answer until you come up with the most likely description of the suspect.

## Tips for Answering Eyewitness Account Questions

- Stay calm and work methodically.
- Compare each element of each answer choice until you find the ones that have the common elements.

## ▶ Improving Your Judgment Skills

You have more options than you may realize when it comes to honing your judgment skills—not only for the police exam, but also for your career as a police officer. There are some surprisingly simple exercises you can do in your everyday life that will get you ready.

### What If . . .

There's a game most police officers play in their minds called "What if." You play, too, but you may not be aware of it. "What if I won the lottery tomorrow? If I did, I'd empty my desk drawers on top of my supervisor's desk and run screaming out of the building." Sound familiar?

Some professional baseball players watch slow-motion videos of a batter with perfect form in the hope that by memorizing and studying his moves, they will be able to improve their own performance. And research shows that this works: In times of stress, people are more likely to carry out a task if they've practiced it—mentally or physically.

"What if" uses the same logic. If you've thought about a situation and you've arrived at a conclusion about what you would do under the given circumstances, then you've given your brain a plan for the situation if it actually comes up. Maybe you've heard someone say, "I didn't have any idea what to do. I just froze." That brain didn't have a plan to follow. Playing "What if" can give it a plan.

Train yourself to play "What if." Do it in the grocery store. You're standing in line behind a man in a heavy coat. Ask yourself "If I were a police officer, *what* would I do *if* I saw this man slip a package of batteries into his coat pocket and go through the checkout line and then out of the store without paying for them?" This could turn out to be one of the situational judgment questions you find on a civil service exam. Practice. At the very least it might add a new dimension to your grocery shopping.

## Self-Confidence Checks

Practice your self-confidence. Odd advice? Not really. Self-confidence is what makes most police officers able to make decisions with a minimum of confusion and self-doubt. Although you aren't a police officer yet, you need the same self-confidence to make the right decisions as a test taker. If you aren't confident about your judgment skills and your ability to decide what to do in a situation, then you are likely to torture yourself with every judgment question.

Believe it or not, it is possible to practice self-confidence. Many people practice the opposite of self-confidence by thinking and saying things like "I don't know if I can do that" or "What if I can't do that?"

Start listening to yourself to see if you talk like that. And then turn it around. Tell yourself and others, "The civil service test is coming up and I intend to ace it." And "I know I will make a good police officer. I know that when I read the test questions, I can rely on my own good judgment to help me. My common sense will point me in the right direction."

This isn't bragging. It's how you set yourself up for success. You'll start thinking of what you need to do to ace the test. You're practicing self-confidence right now by reading this book. You are getting the tools you need to do the job. Your self-confidence has no option but to shoot straight up—and your score along with it.

## Read, Read, Read

Reading is as vital on judgment questions as it is on questions that call themselves reading questions. This isn't the kind of reading you do when you are skimming a novel or skipping through articles in a newspaper. It's the kind where you not only have to pay attention to what the writer is telling you, but also must make decisions based on the information you've received. There's a whole chapter in this book on reading. Check out the suggestions there, under "Additional Resources," on ways to improve your reading skills.

# 24 ▶ Map Reading

## CHAPTER SUMMARY

This chapter shows you how to do well on civil service examinations that ask you to read a map and then answer questions about it.

**I**f you don't have a "sense of direction," the time is ripe to develop one. Police officers are expected to arrive at calls as quickly and safely as possible while obeying the traffic laws (depending on the nature of the situation). The catch here, at least for rookie officers, is that calls for service rarely occur in the two locations you are most familiar with—the station house and your residence. And, unfortunately, you won't have the opportunity to say "Excuse me, I don't know where that is. Assign the call to someone who does and I'll take the next one." Once you get the call you have to know where to go, and often that means relying on a street map. That's why many police exams test your map reading ability.

Reading a map sounds simple enough, but in practice, it can be quite a frustrating experience. And practice is the only way to get good at map reading.

Civil service exams have a method for testing your map reading skills. Typically, you'll see a simple map with the north-south-east-west directions clearly marked and a key explaining symbols. You'll find instructions on which questions should be answered based on the map. Don't be surprised to find several different maps in one test.

A sentence or two is usually devoted to telling you that you can't make up your own traffic laws in order to get from Point A to Point B. You can't go up one-way streets the wrong way or choose paths that will have you driving through office buildings to get to the call. After that, you'll find one or more questions about the map you're looking at. The questions may ask you which is the shortest route from Point A to Point B, or they may tell you to make a series of right and left turns and then ask you in which direction you're heading.

## ▶ Finding the Shortest Route

Questions that ask you to find the shortest legal route are based on a map like the one on the next page. A scenario follows the instructions, followed by a question asking for the shortest route and the answer choices.

The best approach to solving these puzzles is to study the map for a minute first to get your bearings. Read the question, and then turn to the map and figure out what looks like the best route to you. (Do not look at the answers before figuring out the route you would take.) Start with the first answer choice and study each route turn-by-turn. If none of the options looks like the route you came up with after first reading the question, then you may need to reconsider your route. If this is the case, then you'll also need to start over and consider all of the options with a fresh eye. Try this strategy on the sample question that follows.

### Sample Shortest-Route Question

Here's a question that asks you to find the shortest route on the map on the next page.

Answer questions 1 through 3 based solely on the following map. You are required to follow traffic laws and the flow of traffic. A single arrow depicts one-way streets and two arrows pointing in opposite directions represent two-way streets.

1. Officer Harolds is sitting at a red light at the intersection of Fourth Street and Washington Road facing south. The dispatcher sends him on a one-vehicle collision call. A motorist has run into the northwest corner of the City Hall building. What is the quickest route for Officer Harolds to take to City Hall?
   a. Turn west onto Washington Road, then south on Third Street, and then west on Main Street to Parker Road.
   b. Turn west onto Washington Road, then south onto Parker Road, and then east to Lincoln Avenue.
   c. Turn west onto Washington Road, south on Second Street, and then east onto Main Street to Parker Road.
   d. Turn west onto Washington Road, then south onto Parker Road, and then east onto Main Street.

### Strategy for Shortest-Route Questions

Here's how to apply the strategy outlined for this question.

The situation tells you that Officer Harolds needs to answer a collision call. You have an idea of an even more specific location when you read that a motorist has run into the northwest corner of City Hall. As you can see by the map, the City Hall building can be approached on four sides by four different streets. Because you'd like to be close to the northwest corner of the building, you should be considering a route that will put you on that side of City Hall.

Your first step will be to study the map and pick out the quickest legal route to the collision. The arrows show you that Washington Road is a one-way street. Because Officer Harolds is facing south on Fourth Street at Washington Road, his only option available is to turn west onto Washington Road. Notice that Washington Road runs parallel to Lincoln Avenue, the street on which City Hall is located. Also notice that Lincoln

**HINT:** Draw your vehicle right on the map. Then place an X on the map at the location you need to get to. This makes it easier to keep track of where you need to drive to get to the X. It is easy to get confused during the pressure of taking an exam, so draw right on the map to aid your memory.

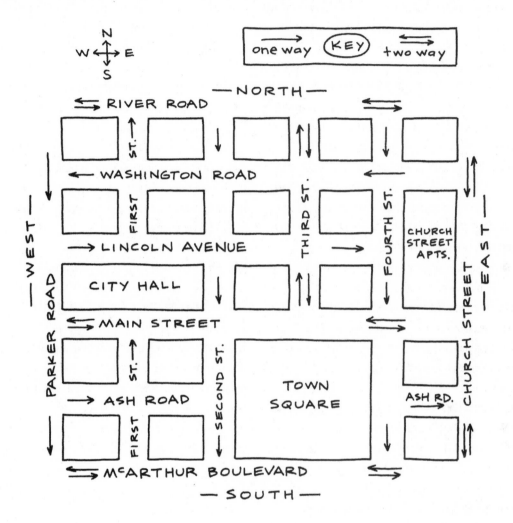

Avenue runs east and you want to end up on the northwest corner of the building. Now look at City Hall. The northwest corner of this building is at the intersection of Parker Road and Lincoln Avenue. (To determine the northwest corner of the building, you may want to imagine that the north-south-east-west indicator is written in the middle of the word "City Hall." That makes it easy to see where the northwest corner would be for the building.) The quickest, easiest route appears to be west on Washington Road, south on Parker Road, and east on Lincoln Avenue. You have your route, so now it's time to see if one of the multiple-choice options matches the route you determined.

When you first glance at the four options, it's fairly obvious that they all start with a west turn onto Washington Road. Starting with choice **a**, we see that this option lists turning south onto Third Street and then west on Main Street. Main Street is one block south of the street you'd like to be on, so this option is not as efficient as the route you arrived at. Eliminate this option and go on to choice **b**.

In choice **b**, you see that the first turn after heading west on Washington Road is to turn south onto Parker Road, then east to Lincoln Avenue, which will put the officer at the scene of the collision. This option matches the route you figured out before reading the answers, so choice **b** is more than likely the right option.

However, it's always best to continue reading the answers to make sure you don't pass up an option that turns out to be better than the one you figured out. Choice **c** makes Officer Harolds turn east on Main Street, which is heading away from the call and does not end up at Parker Road. Choice **d** is not the best answer because the corner of Parker Road and Main Street is one block too far to the south. You'd choose either of these options only if you didn't know which was the northwest corner of City Hall.

Remember, even when you feel like you already have the right answer, it is best to examine *all* the answer choices to be on the safe side.

## ▶ Finding the Direction

Question 2 is based on the same map you used to answer question 1 but is different because the test maker wants to know if you can figure out which direction you are facing.

### Sample Direction Question

**2.** Officer Watson is driving eastbound on Main Street at Fourth Street. If he makes a U-turn on Main Street, turns onto Third Street, and then makes another U-turn, which direction will he be facing?
   **a.** east
   **b.** west
   **c.** north
   **d.** south

### Strategy for Direction Questions

The best strategy for solving this type of question is the same as you used on question 1. Trace out your path after reading the question, and then look through the answers until you find the one that matches your decision. Obviously, you don't have much reading to do to pick out the right answer. You'll mainly be looking to see which letter is in front of the answer you want.

In the case of question 2, the answer you want is choice **d**. When you traced out your path on the map, you should have seen that if Officer Watson is heading east on Main Street and he makes a U-turn, he will be heading west. If he turns onto Third Street, the only way he can turn will have him heading north on Third Street. If he makes a second U-turn, he will now be facing south.

## ▶ More Map Reading Practice

The key to answering map reading questions is to *take your time*. If you hurry through a question, you may misread the question or the answer choices, which will naturally cause you to choose the wrong answer.

Let's try a third question using the same sample map.

- Read carefully and follow all directions.
- Feel free to move the map around during the test to face the direction you find comfortable.
- Trace your path lightly on the map with your pencil. Make sure you erase all marks as you complete each question so that you do not confuse yourself for the next question.
- Place your vehicle mark right on the map. Place an X at the location you need to get to.

**3.** On a rainy, windy night, Officers Epps and Burton are dispatched to a burglar alarm at a business on Ash Road and Church Street. They are driving north on First Street and have just passed Washington Road. What is the quickest route they can take?

a. North on First Street, west on River Road, then south on Parker Road, then east on McArthur Boulevard, and then north on Church Street to Ash Road.

b. North on First Street, then east on River Road, then south on Third Street, then east on Main Street, and then north on Church Street to Ash Road.

c. North on First Street, then east on River Road, and then south on Church Street to Ash Road.

d. North on First Street, then west on River Road, then south on Parker Road, then east on Lincoln Avenue, then south on Second Street, then east on McArthur Boulevard, and then north on Church Street to Ash Road.

After reading the question, you are ready to trace your route. Keep in mind that you want to get to Ash Road and Church Street in the quickest, easiest manner without going the wrong way on any one-way streets. First Street is a one-way street going toward a two-way street, River Road. You have the option of heading east or west on River Road. East makes more sense because it is in the direction of Church Street. The most direct route appears to be east on River Road to Church Street, and then south on Church Street to Ash Road.

Now it's time to check your answer against the options. Choice **a** has you turning west on First Street, and you've already determined that west is not the most efficient direction to turn. Choice **b** suggests that you turn east on River Road, then south on Third Street, then east on Main Street, and then north on Church Street. You should turn South on Church Street to get to Ash Road, not north. You already have too many turns for this to be an efficient route in any event. Time to look at choice **c**. Choice **c** directs you east on River Road, then south on Church Street—and there you are at Ash Road. This route matches the route we had in mind. Choice **d** has too many turns (like choice **b**), in addition to involving a west turn onto River Road, which we already decided was inefficient.

Now that you're becoming an expert in map reading—be sure to make up your own questions to test your growing skills.

# 25 ▶ Memory and Observation

## CHAPTER SUMMARY

This chapter contains hints and tips to help you answer questions that test your memory skills. Memory questions can be based on pictures or on written materials; you may get the materials ahead of time or on test day. However the memory questions are structured, this chapter will help you deal with them.

**I**t's amazing what your mind will file away in that cabinet we call *memory*. You remember every snippet of dialogue uttered by Clint Eastwood in his first Dirty Harry movie from years ago, but you can't remember which bus route you used yesterday to get to the dentist. Some people remember names well but can't put them with the right faces. Others forget names quickly but know exactly when, where, and why they met the person whose name they've forgotten. There are a few lucky individuals with what is commonly referred to as a photographic memory or total recall. And then there are those of us who wake up every morning to a radio alarm so we can find out what day of the week it is. Fortunately for most of us, a good memory is actually a skill that can be developed—with the right incentive.

A high score on the civil service exam is plenty of incentive.

Civil service exams may test your short-term memory or long-term memory skills. In tests of short-term memory, you're often required to look at a sketch of a street scene; drawings of men and women with differing facial features, weapons, and other property; or photographs. Usually, you'll be given a set amount of time (five minutes is common) to look at the scene, and then you'll be asked to answer test questions about what you saw. Your goal is to memorize as much of that drawing or photograph as you can in the allotted time.

Some departments are more interested in long-term memory skills. They may send you a study booklet a few weeks in advance of the test and ask you to memorize several items in the booklet. In that case, you'll answer questions based on what you've been memorizing from the study booklet.

This chapter covers both kinds of memory questions, so you'll be prepared for either one.

## ▶ Short-Term Memory Questions

### Questions Based on Written Passages

A common method of testing short-term memory is to have you read a lengthy, detailed block of text and then have you answer several multiple-choice questions based on that material. Here is an example:

Answer questions 1, 2, and 3 based on the following passage.

Police dispatchers sent Officer Becky Mann to 2400 Ulit Avenue. Officer Mann received the call at 10:49 P.M. and arrived on the scene at 10:55 P.M. She met Lisa Garret, who told her that she had just moved into the garage apartment behind 2400 Ulit Avenue, which carries the address of $2400\frac{1}{2}$ Ulit Avenue, three days ago on Monday, November 26. Larry Goddard, who lives at 2400 Ulit Avenue, let Garret use his phone to call 911. Her other neighbor, Karen Ellen, was not at home. Officer Mann asked Garret to tell her what happened. Garret said she got home late tonight from an overtime assignment at her job at the tropical fish food plant. She said she pulled into the driveway at around 10:45 P.M., got out of her Jeep, and walked up the wooden stairs to the landing next to her front door. While she was digging in her purse for the keys to the front door, a man stepped from the shadows of the landing and grabbed her from behind. He held a knife to her throat and told her to give him her purse or he would slit her throat. She said she handed him the purse which had two $20 bills inside, along with one credit card and her driver's license. He pushed her down on the floor and told her to stay down, hide her face, and count out loud to 100, or he'd kill her. She said she hid her face in both of her hands and started counting aloud. She heard him run down the stairs. Garret said she counted to 20 before she sat up, ran down the stairs to 2400 Ulit Avenue, and begged her neighbor, Larry Goddard, to let her inside to call police.

**1.** What is the victim's address?
   **a.** 2400 Ulit Avenue
   **b.** 2400.5 Ulit Avenue
   **c.** 240 Ulit Avenue
   **d.** $2400\frac{1}{2}$ Ulit Avenue

**2.** Who called 911?
   **a.** the victim's landlord
   **b.** Larry Goddard
   **c.** Lisa Garret
   **d.** Karen Ellen

**3.** When did the victim move into this garage apartment?
   **a.** two days ago
   **b.** three days ago
   **c.** three months ago
   **d.** the day of the robbery

### What to Do

Short-term memory questions based on what you have read are fairly straightforward. Your best approach to these questions is to

1. read the instructions to find out what questions you will have to answer based on the passage you are about to read.

2. read the questions before the passage so that your mind will be primed for the kind of information that should catch your eye as you read the passage.

3. after reading the passage, read the answers and try to eliminate the wrong ones first.

4. when you have the right answer, glance back at the passage to check your accuracy.

Using the previous example, let's try these techniques. The instructions in the example tell you to answer questions 1 through 3 after reading the passage. That's simple enough. Let your eyes drop down to the first question: "What is the victim's address?" As you read the passage, your eyes will be on the lookout for the victim's address. The next question asks, "Who called 911?" Once again, your brain is primed to wave red flags when you read the passage. The final question is, "When did the victim move into this garage apartment?" Because you are primed with the questions, you are ready to read the passage. You'll find that the answers are **1. d., 2. c.,** and **3. b.**

## What Not to Do

- **Do not** read through the passage looking for only the right answers. Read the entire story before you make your decisions. A lazy reader who skims this passage and stops reading as each question is apparently answered might get an unpleasant surprise when the "obvious" answer is wrong. For example, it's not exactly clear at first that the victim lives at $2400\frac{1}{2}$ Ulit Avenue. The first address you see is 2400 Ulit Avenue. If you didn't read past that point, you could choose the wrong answer for question 2.

- **Do not** make this task harder than it is by trying to draw conclusions. Your memory skills are being tested here, not your crime-solving abilities or your knowledge of the law. Don't add elements to the story that aren't really there.

## Questions Based on Pictures

Looking at a picture for a set length of time—usually five minutes—and then answering a series of questions about details in the scene is a very common way for civil service exams to test your short-term memory. This is a simple test of your ability to recall details. You aren't being asked to solve crimes, use judgment skills, or draw conclusions about what you see.

The picture will usually be a scene of a busy city street with plenty of details for you to pick up on: store names, buses, taxis, people, clothing, action scenes (an assault or maybe someone changing a flat tire on a car), and street signs. You'll be asked to study this drawing or photograph until a specific time limit is up, then you will turn to a set of questions in the test booklet. Let's assume that the picture you studied for five minutes showed a man holding a knife in his left hand while stealing a woman's purse. You might see a test question like this:

4. What is the man who is stealing the woman's purse holding in his left hand?
   a. a gun
   b. a stick
   c. a bottle
   d. a knife

The questions are simple and the answers are simple. If you don't remember what the robber had in his hand or didn't notice the scene in the picture, then you will have to give this question your best guess.

At the end of this chapter you'll find a street scene and several questions about it that you can use to practice.

## What to Do

Use a methodical approach to studying what you see. When you read sentences on a page, you read from left to right. This skill is as unconscious as breathing for most English-language readers. Approach memorizing a picture the same way you read, taking in the information from left to right. Instead of staring at the street scene with the whole picture in focus, make yourself start at the left and work your way across the page until you get to the right.

### What Not to Do

- **Do not** go into brain-lock when you first see the busy street scene. Take a deep breath and decide to be methodical.
- **Do not** try to start memorizing with a shotgun approach, letting your eyes roam all over the page without really taking in the details.

### Questions Based on a Videotape

Some departments will show you a video and then have you answer questions about what you have observed. This test is not widely used because it's difficult to have large numbers of people watch a video, but this is a method you may encounter. Your best bet is to relax, study the situation on the screen carefully and with *confidence* that you will remember what you see, and then tackle the questions.

## ▶ Long-Term Memory Questions

For questions that test long-term memory, you will be sent a study booklet a few weeks in advance of the test. The booklet contains detailed instructions on what you will be expected to know for the test. The expectation is that you will have plenty of time to memorize the information and that you will be able to answer questions based on what you have memorized.

For example, you may see several pictures of items stolen in a burglary—maybe a wristwatch or a crown inlaid with six rubies. On test day, you may see a question like this:

5. In the study booklet provided to you, there are several drawings of items taken in a burglary. One of the items was a crown. How many jewels did you see on the crown?
   a. three
   b. four
   c. none
   d. six

The questions are simple. No tricks here. You just have to be able to recall details.

### What to Do

If you get material to study in advance, study it *in advance.* Don't start the day before the test. Spend a little time on your study booklet every day from the day you get it until the day before the test.

### What Not to Do

- **Do not** read the questions too quickly. If you're having trouble remembering the details, going with what initially feels like the correct answer is usually a good idea—but *you must make sure you're answering the right question.* If you were reading quickly and didn't look at the last sentence in the previous example, you may anticipate that the question asks you how many crowns you saw in the drawing, not how many jewels were on the crown. Haste can produce easily avoidable errors.

## ▶ Memorization Tips

Memorization is much easier if you approach the task with the expectation that you *will* remember what you see. Call it positive thinking, self-hypnosis, or concentration—it doesn't really matter as long as you get results. When you run through the practice questions in this book, prepare your mind before you start. Tell yourself over and over that you will remember

## Tips for Memory and Observation Questions

- Use a methodical approach to memorization.
- For questions based on passages, read the questions first so you'll know what to look for.
- For questions based on pictures, "read" the picture from left to right.
- For questions based on materials you receive in advance, study the materials for a few minutes every day before the test.
- Read the questions carefully; make sure you're answering the question that's being asked.
- Practice your memory and observation skills in your daily routine.

what you see as you study the images. Your performance level will rise to meet your expectations.

Yes, it's easy for your brain to seize up when you see a drawing filled with details, a test section full of questions, and a test proctor standing above you with a stopwatch in one hand intoning, "You have five minutes to study this drawing. You may begin." But if you've programmed yourself to stay calm, stay alert, and execute your plan, you'll remember the details when you need them.

Plan? Yes, you need a plan. If you have a method for memorizing, say, a busy urban street scene—such as the left-to-right scheme previously outlined—then you will be more likely to relax and allow yourself to retain what you've seen long enough to answer the test questions. Keep in mind that you aren't trying to memorize the scene to learn it for life, you are doing it to retain the information long enough to answer the test questions. What will it matter if you remember the scene three months from now? Your goal is to retain the information long enough to get through this test.

## ▶ Observation Tips

It's almost impossible to talk about memorization without bringing up observation. Some people are naturally observant. Some drift off into never-never land frequently and have no awareness of the world around them. Whatever category you think you are in, it's

never too late to sharpen, or acquire, strong observation skills. How? Practice, of course.

Newspaper photos make great practice tools. News photos are action-oriented and usually have more than one person in the scenes. Sit down in a quiet place, clear your mind, remind yourself for several minutes that you will retain all the details you need when you study the picture, and then turn to a picture and study it for about five minutes. At the end of the time, turn the picture over, get a piece of paper and a pencil and then write down all the details you can think of in the picture. Make yourself do this as often as possible before the test.

You can tone up your observation skills on the way to work or school, too. Instead of sitting in your car waiting for the light to change with a blank stare on your face, look around you and say out loud what you see. "I'm at the corner of Twelfth and Walnut. I see a man in a black, full-length raincoat standing on the northeast corner looking in the display window of Hank's Motorcycle Shop. There's a black Subaru station wagon parked at a meter near the motorcycle shop. The license plate is . . ." (If you ride to work on a bus or train, you can say these things silently to yourself.) Not only are you practicing a basic skill you will need to become an excellent police officer, you are training your mind to succeed at whatever memory questions the test maker throws your way.

# ▶ Memory and Observation Practice

On the previous pages is a street scene like those found on some police exams. Following are several questions asking about details of the scene. Use this scene to practice your memory skills. Take five minutes (no more!) to study the picture and then answer the questions that follow, without looking back at the picture.

Then check your answers by looking back at the scene. If you get all the questions right, you know you're well prepared for memory questions. If you miss a few, you know you need to spend more time practicing, using the tips previously outlined. Remember, you *can* improve your memory with practice.

**6.** The scene is taking place on which street corner?
   **a.** Grand Dr. at 8 St.
   **b.** Green Blvd. at 6 Ave.
   **c.** Grant Sq. at 7 Ave.
   **d.** Georges Blvd. at 5 St.

**7.** The street number of the drug store is
   **a.** 311.
   **b.** 312.
   **c.** 411.
   **d.** 412.

**8.** The man with the gun is standing next to
   **a.** the hot dog stand.
   **b.** Johnny's Bar.
   **c.** the woman carrying the shopping bag.
   **d.** the trash can.

**9.** What is the name printed on the newsstand?
   **a.** Al's News
   **b.** Ace News
   **c.** Abe's News
   **d.** A + G News

**10.** Who is getting off the bus?
   **a.** a group of senior citizens
   **b.** a group of middle-aged tourists
   **c.** a group of school children
   **d.** a group of teenagers

**11.** The name printed on the truck in the street is
   **a.** Adam's Market.
   **b.** Alfonse's Fine Merchandising.
   **c.** Alvin's Fresh Produce.
   **d.** Al's Fruit Market.

**12.** What name is printed on the hot dog stand?
   **a.** Tony
   **b.** Frank
   **c.** Henry
   **d.** Toby

**13.** What is written above the bus's open door?
   **a.** Al's Tour Bus
   **b.** Ajax Tours
   **c.** All Around Tours
   **d.** A-1 Bus Tours

**14.** What is the phone number for the dentist office?
   **a.** 555-3030
   **b.** 555-2020
   **c.** 555-2200
   **d.** 555-3300

**15.** The elderly man about to be mugged is carrying
   **a.** a shopping bag.
   **b.** an umbrella.
   **c.** a briefcase.
   **d.** an overcoat.

# California Police Practice Exam 2

## CHAPTER SUMMARY

This chapter presents a second police exam based on the widely used test written by the California Peace Officer Standards and Training (POST) Commission. After working through the material in the preceding chapters on various kinds of exam questions, take this exam to see how much you've improved since you took the first test.

**T**he test that follows, like the first practice test, is modeled on the California POST Commission's reading and writing exam for entry-level law enforcement personnel. Many cities in California use this test to screen police recruits. The city you're applying to might use a different test but, because cities try to meet POST standards, the skills tested here are most likely the same ones your exam assesses. The test in this chapter is good practice for police exams anywhere in California.

Book One of this test covers clarity of expression (grammar), vocabulary, spelling, and reading comprehension. Book Two is a different kind of reading test in which you have to fill in the missing words in a passage. **If you haven't read the section in Chapter 18 on answering fill-in-the-blank reading questions, do it now, before you take the test.**

You have two-and-a-half hours to answer 105 questions on this test. Book One has 65 multiple-choice questions, and Book Two has 20 answer blanks in each of two reading passages for a total of 40 questions. Allow yourself only those two-and-a-half hours to take this test. Remember what you learned about timing and pacing in Chapter 15 of this book, so you'll be able to get through the test in that amount of time.

The answer sheet for the test is on the next page, and the test comes right after. At the end of the test is an answer key, including explanations for clarity and reading questions. If you need to know why a vocabulary or spelling answer is correct, use a dictionary. After the key is a scoring guide. But remember, this is a learning experience, not the real exam. You should use this test to help you understand how the test works—which means that the explanations of the answers are as important as the test itself.

# BOOK ONE

| | | | | | | | | | | | | | | |
|---|---|---|---|---|---|---|---|---|---|---|---|---|---|---|
| 1. | (a) | (b) | (c) | (d) | 26. | (a) | (b) | (c) | (d) | 51. | (a) | (b) | (c) | (d) |
| 2. | (a) | (b) | (c) | (d) | 27. | (a) | (b) | (c) | (d) | 52. | (a) | (b) | (c) | (d) |
| 3. | (a) | (b) | (c) | (d) | 28. | (a) | (b) | (c) | (d) | 53. | (a) | (b) | (c) | (d) |
| 4. | (a) | (b) | (c) | (d) | 29. | (a) | (b) | (c) | (d) | 54. | (a) | (b) | (c) | (d) |
| 5. | (a) | (b) | (c) | (d) | 30. | (a) | (b) | (c) | (d) | 55. | (a) | (b) | (c) | (d) |
| 6. | (a) | (b) | (c) | (d) | 31. | (a) | (b) | (c) | (d) | 56. | (a) | (b) | (c) | (d) |
| 7. | (a) | (b) | (c) | (d) | 32. | (a) | (b) | (c) | (d) | 57. | (a) | (b) | (c) | (d) |
| 8. | (a) | (b) | (c) | (d) | 33. | (a) | (b) | (c) | (d) | 58. | (a) | (b) | (c) | (d) |
| 9. | (a) | (b) | (c) | (d) | 34. | (a) | (b) | (c) | (d) | 59. | (a) | (b) | (c) | (d) |
| 10. | (a) | (b) | (c) | (d) | 35. | (a) | (b) | (c) | (d) | 60 | (a) | (b) | (c) | (d) |
| 11. | (a) | (b) | (c) | (d) | 36. | (a) | (b) | (c) | (d) | 61. | (a) | (b) | (c) | (d) |
| 12. | (a) | (b) | (c) | (d) | 37. | (a) | (b) | (c) | (d) | 62. | (a) | (b) | (c) | (d) |
| 13. | (a) | (b) | (c) | (d) | 38. | (a) | (b) | (c) | (d) | 63. | (a) | (b) | (c) | (d) |
| 14. | (a) | (b) | (c) | (d) | 39. | (a) | (b) | (c) | (d) | 64 | (a) | (b) | (c) | (d) |
| 15. | (a) | (b) | (c) | (d) | 40. | (a) | (b) | (c) | (d) | 65. | (a) | (b) | (c) | (d) |
| 16. | (a) | (b) | (c) | (d) | 41. | (a) | (b) | (c) | (d) | | | | | |
| 17. | (a) | (b) | (c) | (d) | 42. | (a) | (b) | (c) | (d) | | | | | |
| 18. | (a) | (b) | (c) | (d) | 43. | (a) | (b) | (c) | (d) | | | | | |
| 19. | (a) | (b) | (c) | (d) | 44. | (a) | (b) | (c) | (d) | | | | | |
| 20. | (a) | (b) | (c) | (d) | 45. | (a) | (b) | (c) | (d) | | | | | |
| 21. | (a) | (b) | (c) | (d) | 46. | (a) | (b) | (c) | (d) | | | | | |
| 22. | (a) | (b) | (c) | (d) | 47. | (a) | (b) | (c) | (d) | | | | | |
| 23. | (a) | (b) | (c) | (d) | 48. | (a) | (b) | (c) | (d) | | | | | |
| 24. | (a) | (b) | (c) | (d) | 49. | (a) | (b) | (c) | (d) | | | | | |
| 25. | (a) | (b) | (c) | (d) | 50. | (a) | (b) | (c) | (d) | | | | | |

# BOOK TWO

WRITE 1ST LETTER OF WORD HERE

CODE LETTERS HERE

| 1 | 2 | 3 | 4 | 5 | 6 | 7 | 8 | 9 | 10 |
|---|---|---|---|---|---|---|---|---|---|

| 11 | 12 | 13 | 14 | 15 | 16 | 17 | 18 | 19 | 20 |
|---|---|---|---|---|---|---|---|---|---|

| 21 | 22 | 23 | 24 | 25 | 26 | 27 | 28 | 29 | 30 |
|---|---|---|---|---|---|---|---|---|---|

| 31 | 32 | 33 | 34 | 35 | 36 | 37 | 38 | 39 | 40 |
|---|---|---|---|---|---|---|---|---|---|

## ► California Police Exam 2 Book One

### Part One: Clarity

In the following sets of sentences, choose the sentence that is most clearly written.

**1.**
a. There was a time when a woman were frowned upon for expressing their desire to become police officers.
b. There was a time when a woman was frowned upon for expressing her desire to become a police officer.
c. There was a time when women were frowned upon for expressing her desire to become a police officer.
d. There was a time when women was frowned upon for expressing a desire to become police officers.

**2.**
a. Malinda and Ilsa wanted to become troopers because they wanted to be a part of a well-respected organization.
b. Malinda and Ilsa wanted to become a trooper because they wanted to be a part of a well-respected organization.
c. Malinda and Ilsa wanted to become troopers because they wanted to be apart of a well-respected organization.
d. Malinda and Ilsa wanted to become troopers because she wanted to be part of a well-respected organization.

**3.**
a. In many cities in the United States, the tenure of a mayor is four years before they must run for reelection.
b. In many city's in the United States, the tenure of a mayor is four years before he or she must run for reelection.
c. In many cities in the United States, the tenure of a mayor is four years before he or she must run for reelection.
d. In many citys in the united states, the tenure of a mayor is four years before he or she must run for reelection.

**4.**
a. Sergeant Hamm asked Trooper Annunziata whether he wanted to run an extra mile on Friday mornings.
b. Sergeant Hamm asked Trooper Annunziata did he want to run a extra mile on Friday mornings.
c. Sergeant Hamm ask Trooper Annunziata if he want to run an extra mile on Friday mornings.
d. Sergeant Hamm asked Trooper Annunziata why he don't want to run an extra mile on Friday mornings.

**5.**
a. The amount of summons that Trooper Wolny wrote in March was 42.
b. The amount of summonses that Trooper Wolny wrote in March were 42.
c. The number of summons that Trooper Wolny wrote in March was 42
d. The number of summonses that Trooper Wolny wrote in March was 42.

**6.**

a. The severity of Trooper Gana's injury was not known.

b. The severeness of Trooper Ganas injury was not known.

c. The severity of Trooper Ganas' injury was not known.

d. The severeness of Trooper Gana's injury was not known.

**7.**

a. Trooper Detweiler and Trooper Berg likes his or her job.

b. Trooper Detweiler and Trooper Berg like their job.

c. Trooper Detweiler and Trooper Berg like his and her jobs.

d. Trooper Detweiler and Trooper Berg like their jobs.

**8.**

a. Once the investigation begins, and there will be no turning back.

b. Once the investigation begins, there will be no turning back.

c. Once the investigation begins, so there will be no turning back.

d. Once the investigation begins, thus there will be no turning back.

**9.**

a. Officer DeAngelo phoned his partner every day when he was in the hospital.

b. When his partner was in the hospital, Officer DeAngelo phoned him every day.

c. When in the hospital, a phone call was made every day by Officer DeAngelo to his partner.

d. His partner received a phone call from Officer DeAngelo every day while he was in the hospital.

**10.**

a. Some of the case transcripts I have to type are very long, but that doesn't bother one if the cases are interesting.

b. Some of the case transcripts I have to type are very long, but that doesn't bother you if the cases are interesting.

c. Some of the case transcripts I have to type are very long, but it doesn't bother a person if the cases are interesting.

d. Some of the case transcripts I have to type are very long, but that doesn't bother me if the cases are interesting.

**11.**

a. Lieutenant Jenny Crabtree, along with one of her coworkers, has written a pamphlet about public safety.

b. Lieutenant Jenny Crabtree, along with one of her coworkers, have written a pamphlet about public safety.

c. Lieutenant Jenny Crabtree and one of her coworkers has written a pamphlet about public safety.

d. Lieutenant Jenny Crabtree have written a pamphlet about public safety with one of her coworkers.

**12.**

a. When not on duty, Officer Mike O'Rourke enjoys attending cooking class. Where he recently learned how to make an excellent soufflé.

b. When not on duty, Officer Mike O'Rourke enjoys attending cooking class, where he recently learned how to make an excellent soufflé.

c. Officer Mike O'Rourke enjoys attending cooking class. Where, when not on duty, he recently learned how to make an excellent soufflé.

d. When not on duty. Mike O'Rourke enjoys attending cooking class, where he recently learned how to make an excellent soufflé.

**13.**
- **a.** Some people believe that "you can't legislate morality"; moreover, it's done every day.
- **b.** Some people believe that "you can't legislate morality"; secondly, it's done every day.
- **c.** Some people believe that "you can't legislate morality"; in addition, it's done every day.
- **d.** Some people believe that "you can't legislate morality"; however, it's done every day.

**14.**
- **a.** There is no true relationship between ethics and the law.
- **b.** Ethics and the law having no true relationship.
- **c.** Between ethics and the law, no true relationship.
- **d.** Ethics and the law is no true relationship.

**15.**
- **a.** Before he realized it, he had drunken the entire bottle of schnapps.
- **b.** Before he realized it, he had drank the entire bottle of schnapps.
- **c.** Before he realized it, he had drinked the entire bottle of schnapps.
- **d.** Before he realized it, he had drunk the entire bottle of schnapps.

**Part Two: Vocabulary**

In each of the following sentences, choose the word or phrase that most nearly expresses the same meaning as the underlined word.

**16.** The general public was <u>apathetic</u> about the verdict.
- **a.** enraged
- **b.** indifferent
- **c.** suspicious
- **d.** saddened

**17.** The theories of some criminal psychologists were <u>fortified</u> by the new research.
- **a.** reinforced
- **b.** altered
- **c.** disputed
- **d.** developed

**18.** One of the duties of a captain is to <u>delegate</u> responsibility.
- **a.** analyze
- **b.** respect
- **c.** criticize
- **d.** assign

**19.** The lecture about prison overcrowding <u>aroused</u> many audience members.
- **a.** informed
- **b.** disappointed
- **c.** provoked
- **d.** deceived

**20.** The police department building was an <u>expansive</u> facility.
- **a.** obsolete
- **b.** meager
- **c.** spacious
- **d.** costly

**21.** Two inmates were involved in an <u>animated</u> conversation.
- **a.** abbreviated
- **b.** civil
- **c.** secret
- **d.** lively

**22.** The residents of that area were considered to be <u>compliant</u> in regard to the seat belt law.
- **a.** skeptical
- **b.** obedient
- **c.** forgetful
- **d.** appreciative

**23.** Following the disturbance, town officials felt the need to <u>augment</u> the laws pertaining to mass demonstrations.
  **a.** repeal
  **b.** evaluate
  **c.** expand
  **d.** criticize

**24.** Although Marty Albertson's after-hours security job was regarded by many as <u>menial</u>, he liked the peace and solitude it offered.
  **a.** lowly
  **b.** boring
  **c.** unpleasant
  **d.** unrewarding

**25.** Although the police might be able to help Mr. Chen recover his stolen property, he <u>obstinately</u> refuses to file a complaint.
  **a.** repeatedly
  **b.** reluctantly
  **c.** foolishly
  **d.** stubbornly

**26.** For all the problems faced by his district, Congressman Owly regarded budget cuts as a <u>panacea</u>.
  **a.** cure
  **b.** result
  **c.** cause
  **d.** necessity

**27.** The attorney's <u>glib</u> remarks irritated the judge.
  **a.** angry
  **b.** superficial
  **c.** insulting
  **d.** dishonest

**28.** On the witness stand, the suspect, who was accused of several murders, appeared <u>nondescript</u>.
  **a.** lethargic
  **b.** undistinguished
  **c.** respectable
  **d.** impeccable

**29.** When the Bakaras heard that a drug dealer had moved in next door, they were <u>incredulous</u>.
  **a.** fearful
  **b.** outraged
  **c.** disbelieving
  **d.** inconsolable

**30.** The police department recruited Officer Long because she was <u>proficient</u> in the use of computers to track down deadbeats.
  **a.** experienced
  **b.** unequaled
  **c.** efficient
  **d.** skilled

## Part Three: Spelling

In each of the following sentences, choose the correct spelling of the missing word.

**31.** The tip came from an _____ source.
  **a.** anynonimous
  **b.** anonimous
  **c.** anounymous
  **d.** anonymous

**32.** The officers brought back an _____ amount of evidence.
  **a.** extraordinary
  **b.** extraordinery
  **c.** extrordinary
  **d.** ecstraordinary

**33.** The investigator gave his _____ that the report would be completed on time.
a. asurrance
b. assurance
c. assurence
d. assureance

**34.** The purpose of the law was debated _____.
a. frequently
b. frequintly
c. frequentlly
d. frequentley

**35.** The _____ was placed on scientific evidence.
a. enphasis
b. emphisis
c. emphasis
d. emfasis

**36.** When officers arrived, the victim was in a _____ state.
a. delirious
b. dilerious
c. delireous
d. delirous

**37.** Each of the new officers had the same _____.
a. asspiration
b. asparation
c. aspirration
d. aspiration

**38.** The young man wished to _____ his right to speak with an attorney.
a. excercise
b. exercise
c. exersize
d. exercize

**39.** The veteran officer and the rookie were a _____ pair.
a. compattible
b. compatable
c. compatible
d. commpatible

**40.** In many states, road tests require _____ parking.
a. paralel
b. paralell
c. parallal
d. parallel

**41.** The paramedics attempted to _____ the victim.
a. stabilize
b. stablize
c. stableize
d. stableise

**42.** Prosecutors argued that testimony concerning the past behavior of the accused was _____.
a. irelevent
b. irelevant
c. irrelevant
d. irrelevent

**43.** The mayor pointed to the _____ crime rate statistics.
a. encouredging
b. encouraging
c. incurraging
d. incouraging

**44.** The patient will have a _____ hearing on Friday.
   a. commitment
   b. committment
   c. comittment
   d. comitment

**45.** The prisoner's alibi seemed _____ on the face of it.
   a. rediculous
   b. rediculus
   c. ridiculous
   d. ridiculus

## Part Four: Reading Comprehension

Following are several reading passages, each accompanied by three or more questions. Answer each question based on what is stated or implied in the preceding passage.

DNA is a powerful investigative tool because, with the exception of identical twins, no two people have the same DNA. In other words, the sequence, or order of the DNA building blocks, is different in particular regions of the cell, making each person's DNA unique. Therefore, DNA evidence collected from a crime scene can link a suspect to a crime or eliminate one from suspicion in the same way that fingerprints are used. DNA can also identify a victim through the DNA of relatives if a victim's body cannot be found. For example, if technicians have a biological sample from the victim, such as a bloodstain left at a crime scene, the DNA taken from that evidence can be compared with DNA from the victim's biological relatives to determine if the bloodstain belongs to the victim. When a DNA profile developed from evidence at one crime scene is compared with a DNA profile developed from evidence found at another crime scene, they can be linked to each other or to the same perpetrator, whether the crime was committed locally or in another state.

**46.** What is the primary purpose of this paragraph?
   a. to show that DNA is a powerful investigative tool
   b. to illustrate how the unique characteristics of DNA make different types of comparisons and eliminations possible
   c. to teach the reader that identical twins have the same DNA
   d. to show how laboratory technicians develop DNA profiles

**47.** All of the following are true EXCEPT
   a. everyone, except for identical twins, has different DNA.
   b. the sequence of DNA building blocks is the same in particular regions of the cell, making comparisons possible.
   c. DNA can be used for comparisons or eliminations of offenders from different states.
   d. DNA from relatives can be used to identify victims.

**48.** According to the passage, DNA should be collected from a crime scene because
   a. it is better than fingerprints.
   b. there is DNA left at every crime scene.
   c. it can be used to eliminate potential suspects.
   d. DNA is a new investigative tool.

**49.** Which of the following conclusions can be drawn from the paragraph?
   a. DNA can be collected from sources other than blood.
   b. DNA can be collected from bloodstains only.
   c. DNA cannot be collected from bloodstains.
   d. DNA can connect crime scenes only if it is taken from bloodstains.

Stalking—the "willful, malicious, and repeated following and harassing of another person"—is probably as old as human society. But in the United States, until 1990, no substantive law existed to protect the stalking victim. The most that police officials could do was arrest the stalker for a minor offense or suggest the victim obtain a restraining order, a civil remedy often ignored by the offender. (One of the Orange County victims mentioned below was shot by her husband while carrying a restraining order in her purse.) Frightened victims had their worst fears confirmed: They would have to be harmed—or killed—before anything could be done.

In 1990, however, partly because of the 1989 stalker-murder of television star Rebecca Schaeffer, and partly because of the 1990 stalker-murders of four Orange County women in a single six-week period, California drafted the first antistalking law. Now most states have similar laws.

The solution is not perfect: Some stalkers are too mentally deranged or obsessed to fear a prison term. There is danger, however small, of abuse of the law, particularly in marital disputes. Most important, both police and society need better education about stalking, especially about its often sexist underpinnings. (The majority of stalking victims are women terrorized by former husbands or lovers.)

But the laws are a start, carrying with them felony penalties of up to ten years in prison for those who would attempt to control or possess others through intimidation and terror.

50. Which of the following best expresses the main idea of the passage?
   a. More education is needed about sexism, as it is the most important element in the crime of stalking.
   b. Stalking is thought of as a new kind of crime, but it has probably existed throughout human history.
   c. The new antistalking legislation is an important weapon against the crime of stalking, although it is not the complete answer.
   d. Today almost every state in the United States. has an effective, if not perfect, antistalking law.

51. Based on the passage, which of the following is likely the most common question asked of police by stalking victims prior to 1990?
   a. How can I get a restraining order?
   b. Does he have to hurt me before you'll arrest him?
   c. Why is this person stalking me?
   d. Is it legal for me to carry a weapon in my purse?

52. Which of the following is NOT mentioned in the passage as a weakness in the new antistalking legislation?
   a. The laws alone might not deter some stalkers.
   b. A person might be wrongly accused of being a stalker.
   c. Neither the police nor the public completely understand the crime.
   d. Victims do not yet have adequate knowledge about antistalking laws.

**53.** Based on the passage, which of the following is the main reason restraining orders are ineffective in preventing stalking?

   **a.** No criminal charges can be leveled against the violator.

   **b.** Until 1990, restraining orders could not be issued against stalkers.

   **c.** Law enforcement officials do not take such orders seriously.

   **d.** Restraining orders apply only to married couples.

**54.** Based on the information in the passage, which of the following did the murders of Rebecca Schaeffer and the Orange County women mentioned in the second paragraph have in common?

   **a.** The murders provided impetus for antistalking laws.

   **b.** The victims sought, but could not obtain, legal protection.

   **c.** The victims were stalked and killed by a husband or lover.

   **d.** The murders were the result of sexism.

**55.** Which of the following is NOT a stated or implied motive for stalking?

   **a.** to own the victim

   **b.** to terrify the victim

   **c.** to rob the victim

   **d.** to badger the victim

Criminology researchers who take a normative view on crime define it as a behavior that deviates from established norms, culture, and values. In this view, what is criminal is activity that is not normally engaged in or sanctified by society at large. The laws regarding the use of marijuana provide a good lens with which to understand the normative view. Prior to the twentieth century, it was not illegal to use or possess marijuana. In 1915, Utah passed the first law against marijuana use,

and through the years, the laws became more widespread and serious. In the 1950s, the Boggs Act and the Narcotics Control Act set mandatory sentences for drug crimes, including marijuana, which had a first-offense penalty of two to ten years in prison and a $20,000 fine. However, by the early 1970s, views on the use of marijuana were beginning to change. Many researchers attribute the change in views not to an increase in the medical or scientific understanding of the drug, but to the increased use of the drug for recreational and medicinal purposes by a larger segment of society. During this time, many states began to decriminalize the marijuana laws significantly, and by the late 1980s, individual states began to legalize the use of marijuana for certain medical conditions.

**56.** In what year did Utah pass a law against marijuana?

   **a.** 1970

   **b.** 1915

   **c.** 1956

   **d.** 1941

**57.** According to the passage, the view that crime is a behavior that deviates from established norms, culture, and values is the

   **a.** police view.

   **b.** criminology view.

   **c.** normative view.

   **d.** Boggs view.

**58.** Based on the passage, which of the following phrases best sums up the normative view's reason for the recent decriminalization of marijuana?

   **a.** societal acceptance

   **b.** moral depravity

   **c.** prison overcrowding

   **d.** gang violence

**59.** Based on the passage, which of the following is NOT correct?
  **a.** Societal views on marijuana began to change in the 1970s.
  **b.** Marijuana is often used for medicinal purposes.
  **c.** It is now legal to possess marijuana for recreational use.
  **d.** The Boggs Act set mandatory sentences for the possession of marijuana.

At 8:16 A.M., a police operator received a report of an accident on Morton Avenue near Farley Street from Helen Moreno of 1523 Morton Avenue. The caller said she had just arrived home when she heard the collision from her living room. Officer Rayburn arrived on the scene at 8:19. He saw that three vehicles, including an armored truck, were involved and that the driver of the green sedan was unconscious. He called for an ambulance and backup. He then checked the injured driver, saw that he was not bleeding, and covered him with a blanket provided by Mrs. Moreno. Martin Wilcox, of 1526 Morton, who was a passenger in the green sedan, identified the driver as Henry Woolf, also of 1526 Morton. Mrs. Moreno identified the third vehicle involved in the accident, a blue convertible, as her car. The ambulance arrived at 8:24. At 8:25, four officers, including Lieutenant Watts, arrived. Lieutenant Watts assigned Officers Rayburn and Stein to blocking off both streets and controlling traffic, Officer Washington to security on the armored truck, and Officer Parisi to examination of the skid marks on Farley Street. Mr. Wilcox told Lieutenant Watts that Woolf had stopped at the "T" intersection and then turned left onto Morton. Wilcox said the driver's side was struck almost immediately by the truck, which was skidding down Morton. The impact caused the Woolf vehicle to strike Mrs. Moreno's convertible. Frank Burroughs, the driver of the armored truck, told Officer Washington that he was due at Security Bank at 8:10 and that his brakes had failed. After checking with Lieutenant Watts and Officer Parisi, Officer Washington cited Burroughs for speeding, failing to obey a stop sign, and giving false information.

**60.** Who was the first person to view the accident scene?
  **a.** Lieutenant Watts
  **b.** Officer Washington
  **c.** Officer Rayburn
  **d.** the police operator

**61.** Which of the following can be concluded about the Morton Avenue–Farley Street intersection?
  **a.** There were at least two stop signs there.
  **b.** Farley Street is a one-way street.
  **c.** Morton Avenue runs north and south.
  **d.** No cars were parked near the intersection.

**62.** Which of the following best represents the order in which the accident occurred?
  **a.** The Woolf vehicle struck the Moreno vehicle, which struck the armored vehicle.
  **b.** The armored vehicle struck the Woolf vehicle, which struck the Moreno vehicle.
  **c.** The Moreno vehicle struck the armored vehicle, which struck the Woolf vehicle.
  **d.** The armored vehicle struck the Moreno vehicle, which struck the Woolf vehicle.

**63.** Who examined evidence relating to Frank Burroughs's claim that his brakes failed?
  **a.** Officer Rayburn
  **b.** Officer Stein
  **c.** Officer Washington
  **d.** Officer Parisi

**64.** Which vehicle had been traveling on Farley Street?
a. the green sedan
b. the blue convertible
c. the armored truck
d. the ambulance

**65.** Which of the following can be concluded about Helen Moreno's vehicle?
a. It was parked on a steep incline.
b. It was parked across the street from the Moreno residence.
c. It was struck by the armored truck.
d. It was unoccupied at the time of the accident.

## ▶ Book Two

This is a test of your reading ability. In the following passages, words have been omitted. Each numbered set of dashed blank lines indicates where a word has been left out; each dash represents one letter of the missing word. The correct word should not only make sense in the sentence, but also have the number of letters indicated by the dashes.

Read through the whole passage, and then begin filling in the missing words. Fill in as many missing words as possible. If you aren't sure of the answer, take a guess.

Then mark your answers on the answer sheet as follows: Write the **first letter** of the word you have chosen in the square under the number of the word. Then blacken the circle of that letter of the alphabet under the square. **Only the blackened alphabet circles will be scored.** The words you write on this page and the letters you write at the top of the column on the answer sheet **will not be scored**. Make sure that you blacken the appropriate circle in each column.

Some people say there is too little respect for the law. I say there is **1)** _ _ _ much respect for it. When people **2)** _ _ _ _ _ _ _ the law too much, they will **3)** _ _ _ _ _ _ it blindly. They will say, the majority has decided on this **4)** _ _ _; therefore, I must heed it. They will not **5)** _ _ _ _ to consider whether or not the law is fair. If they do think the law is **6)** _ _ _ _ _, they think it is even more wrong to **7)** _ _ _ _ _ _ _ it. They **8)** _ _ _ _ _ _ _ that people must not break the law but must live with it until the majority has been persuaded to **9)** _ _ _ _ _ _ it. For example, many people in Birmingham, Alabama, knew that the laws that made black people **10)** _ _ _ _ up their seats on **11)** _ _ _ _ _ to white people were unjust. However, it was not **12)** _ _ _ _ _ Rosa Parks (an otherwise law-abiding **13)** _ _ _ _ _ _ _) refused to stand up and so **14)** _ _ _ _ _ _ the law that change came about. I am not saying that we should **15)** _ _ _ _ _ laws because they are inconvenient to **16)** _ _. I am saying that we must listen **17)** _ _ our consciences first. Only **18)** _ _ _ _ should we follow the law. If we know in our **19)** _ _ _ _ _ _ that the law is wrong, it is **20)** _ _ _ duty to break it.

*(continued on page 274)*

Americans like to believe that a juror's race **21)** _ _ _ _ _ absolutely no part in reaching a verdict. It **22)** _ _ becoming increasingly clear, however, that this is not always **23)** _ _ _ _. In fact, there seems to be a trend toward **24)** _ _ _ _ _ _ _ _ influenced verdicts, at least in certain urban areas with large **25)** _ _ _ _ _ _ _ _ populations. Some observers deplore this **26)** _ _ _ _ _. Others, however, argue that the trend is the latest manifestation of **27)** _ _ _ American tradition of jury nullification. Jurors do have the power, affirmed by the Supreme **28)** _ _ _ _ _ a hundred years ago, to set aside the law in favor of their own opinions **29)** _ _ _ _ they believe the law is wrong. Because the Constitution forbids trying a person twice for the **30)** _ _ _ _ crime, an acquittal cannot be overturned on the grounds that the jury ignored the **31)** _ _ _. American colonists used this principle before the Revolution **32)** _ _ acquit fellow **33)** _ _ _ _ _ _ _ _ of crimes against the Crown. Later, in the nineteenth **34)** _ _ _ _ _ _ _, antislavery jurors would acquit people who sheltered runaway **35)** _ _ _ _ _ _ even though doing so was a **36)** _ _ _ _ _. Some observers say that **37)** _ _ _ _ nullification is a legitimate weapon for black people to **38)** _ _ _ in a legal system **39)** _ _ _ _ they see (often with good **40)** _ _ _ _ _ _) as biased against them.

# ▶ Answer Key

## Book One
## Part One: Clarity

1. **b.** *Woman* is singular and requires a singular possessive (*her*) and a singular verb (*was*).

2. **a.** The words that pertain to *Malinda and Ilsa* are all plural to agree with the plural subject. Choice **c** is incorrect because *apart* is mistakenly used for *a part*.

3. **c.** In choice **a**, *a mayor* does not agree in number with *they*. Choices **b** and **d** spell *cities* incorrectly for this sentence's intended meaning. Choice **d** also incorrectly lowercases *United States*.

4. **a.** Choices **b**, **c**, and **d** each contain one or more grammatical or tense errors.

5. **d.** Use *number* with nouns that can be counted, such as the number of summonses or number of cars. Also, *summonses* is the correct plural of the noun *summons*. In addition, *was* is the proper verb to use with the singular *number*.

6. **a.** The correct word is *severity*; *severeness* is not a word. *Trooper Gana's* is the proper possessive form; *Ganas* is not a possessive, and *Ganas'* is plural possessive.

7. **d.** The compound noun requires a plural verb and plural object.

8. **b.** No connecting word is needed to relate the first half of the sentence to the second. Connecting words in the other choices turn them into sentence fragments.

9. **b.** In choices **a**, **c**, and **d** the pronoun reference is ambiguous—who's in the hospital? Choice **c** also contains a misplaced modifier, *When in the hospital*, which seems to refer to *a phone call*.

10. **d.** The other answers contain unnecessary shifts in person from *I* to *one*, *you*, and *a person*.

11. **a.** The subject, *Lieutenant Jenny Crabtree*, and verb, *has written*, agree in number; in the other choices, subject and verb do not agree in number.

12. **b.** This is the only choice that does not contain a sentence fragment.

13. **d.** *However* is the clearest and most logical transitional word for these two ideas; the other choices contain less logical transitional words.

14. **a.** Choices **b** and **c** are sentence fragments. Choice **d** represents confused sentence structure as well as lack of agreement between subject and verb.

15. **d.** The correct verb form is *had drunk*.

## Part Two: Vocabulary
16. **b.**
17. **a.**
18. **d.**
19. **c.**
20. **c.**
21. **d.**
22. **b.**
23. **c.**
24. **a.**
25. **d.**
26. **a.**
27. **b.**
28. **b.**
29. **c.**
30. **d.**

## Part Three: Spelling
31. **d.**
32. **a.**
33. **b.**
34. **a.**
35. **c.**
36. **a.**
37. **d.**

**38. b.**

**39. c.**

**40. d.**

**41. a.**

**42. c.**

**43. b.**

**44. a.**

**45. c.**

## Part Four: Reading Comprehension

**46. b.** This choice most completely summarizes the primary purpose of the paragraph. The other choices are all supporting details in the passage.

**47. b.** See the second sentence of the passage: "The sequence or order of the DNA building blocks is *different* in particular regions of the cell . . ."

**48. c.** The passage states that DNA collected from crime scenes can either link or eliminate a suspect.

**49. a.** The passage states, "If technicians have a biological sample from the victim, such as a bloodstain . . ." From this statement, you can infer that DNA is collected from biological samples, of which bloodstains are one example.

**50. c.** See paragraphs 3 and 4. The other answer choices are mentioned in the passage but are not the central argument.

**51. b.** See the last sentences of paragraph 1, which discusses the stalking victim's "worst fear."

**52. d.** All of the other choices are mentioned in the third paragraph. The victim's knowledge or lack of knowledge about antistalking laws is not discussed in the passage.

**53. a.** As discussed in the first paragraph, a restraining order is a civil remedy that is often not taken seriously by the stalker.

**54. a.** See the second paragraph. Choices **b** and **c** apply only to the Orange County woman; choice **d** cannot be shown to apply to any of the women.

**55. c.** All three of the other choices are mentioned in the final paragraph.

**56. b.** The answer is found in the fifth sentence.

**57. c.** This is the main idea of the entire passage, as explicitly stated in the first sentence.

**58. d.** The passage mentions the "increased use of the drug for recreational and medicinal purposes by a larger segment of society."

**59. c.** The passage states, "By the late 1980s, individual states began to legalize the use of marijuana for certain *medical* conditions."

**60. c.** Officer Rayburn was on the scene first; the other officers arrived later, and the police operator was never on the scene.

**61. a.** The Woolf vehicle had stopped at the "T" intersection before turning on to Morton, so there must have been a stop sign on Farley. Burroughs was cited for failing to obey a stop sign on Morton.

**62. b.** Mr. Wilcox told Lieutenant Watts that the armored truck struck the car he was riding in, driven by Mr. Woolf, and that the Woolf vehicle subsequently hit Mrs. Moreno's car.

**63. d.** Officer Parisi examined skid marks, which show that the armored truck was braking.

**64. a.** The green sedan, with Mr. Woolf driving, had been driving down Farley before turning on to Morton at the "T" intersection.

**65. d.** Mrs. Moreno was in her house at the time of the accident.

## ▶ Book Two

1. too
2. respect
3. follow
4. law
5. stop
6. wrong
7. disobey
8. believe
9. change
10. give
11. buses
12. until
13. citizen
14. defied
15. break
16. us
17. to
18. then
19. hearts
20. our
21. plays
22. is
23. true
24. racially
25. minority
26. trend
27. the
28. Court
29. when
30. same
31. law
32. to
33. colonists
34. century
35. slaves
36. crime
37. jury
38. use
39. that
40. reason

## ▶ Scoring

To pass the California POST test, you need a *score* of 70%. But that doesn't necessarily mean that you need to answer 70 questions right. The number of correct answers you need for a score of 70% changes each time the test is given. It depends on how many questions the test contains. A good estimate of a passing score is 70%, or 74 questions right.

If you didn't do as well as you would like, analyze the reasons. Did you run out of time or feel rushed so that you made careless mistakes? Then you should work on pacing yourself through the exam. Did you do pretty well on some areas of the test and less well on others? Then you know where to concentrate further study. Did you have plenty of time but just not do well on any parts of the exam? Then you might need to spend a lot more time studying before you take the test. A refresher course in reading and writing skills at your local high school or community college might be in order.

What comes next? Here's what you should do based on your total number of correct answers on this test.

| WHAT'S NEXT | |
| --- | --- |
| IF YOU SCORED: | YOUR NEXT STEP SHOULD BE TO: |
| Below 70 | Do some concentrated work in the areas you're weakest in. Use some of the additional resources listed in Chapters 18–25 |
| 70–80 | Review all of the instructional material in this book and perhaps get some additional help from a smart friend or teacher—just to be on the safe side. |
| Above 80 | Relax. You're prepared. Review this book again before the exam if it will make you feel better. |

# 27 ▶ The Physical Ability Test

## CHAPTER SUMMARY

This chapter presents an overview of what to expect on the physical test you'll take on the way to becoming a police officer. It also offers specific advice on how to get in shape for this often demanding exam—and how to stay in shape.

Physical fitness testing, otherwise known as the physical ability or physical agility test, is a staple in the law enforcement selection process. In an attempt to measure your ability to perform successfully the duties of a law enforcement officer or to complete the training to perform those duties, an agency will in all probability require you to perform a test or series of tests that will physically challenge you. The timing as well as the makeup of the test are dictated to a certain extent by legislation that protects against potentially discriminatory practices. The goal of this chapter is to identify the types of tests you are likely to encounter and to provide you with some instruction—so that you can run and jump and push and pull your way through the selection test.

Tests to measure your physical ability to be a law enforcement officer generally take one of two forms: what's known as "job task simulation" and physical fitness. Physical fitness tests are widely used and favored for their validity and predictability. A battery of tests measure your physiological parameters, such as body composition, aerobic capacity, muscular strength and endurance, and flexibility. Physical fitness tests also hint at your medical status and, perhaps more important, they reveal your ability to perform the potentially hundreds of physical tasks required of a law enforcement officer.

Job task simulation tests, on the other hand, while they may tax your physiological fitness, are designed for the most part to illustrate your ability in a handful of job areas. Typically these tests also challenge your motor skills: balance, coordination, power, speed, reaction time, and agility.

## Physical Fitness Tests

Physical fitness testing typically takes place in a group setting, most often at a gymnasium, track, or athletic field—remember, these are "field tests." Attire for a day of testing is usually casual—sweats and running shoes—unless it occurs on the same day as other screening activities, such as a written exam. The time between events and the duration of the test vary according to the number of candidates and the number of test events.

Be prepared for the test. Bring water, nonperishable, easily digested "fuel foods" such as fruits, grains (bagels or bread), nutrition bars, and a change of clothes in the event locker and shower facilities are available. At least one positive picture identification, black ballpoint pens, and writing paper should also be in your bag.

Physical fitness test events typically include some *aerobic capacity test*, which measures your cardiorespiratory system's ability to take in and use oxygen to sustain activity. A field test, such as a one-and-a-half-mile run or a 12-minute run, give an indication of your ability to participate in sustained activities such as walking a patrol, foot pursuits, and subject control and restraint. The most common standards here are "time to complete the distance" and "distance covered in the allotted time."

Flexibility, the ability to freely use the range of motion available at a given joint in your body, is frequently tested because it impacts upon many movements and activities. Sitting for long periods at a dispatching center or behind the wheel of a patrol car or bending over to lift a handcuffed subject—all will affect or be affected by your flexibility. *Sit and reach tests* to evaluate lower back and hamstring flexibility require you to sit with straight legs extended and to reach as far forward as possible. The performance standard for this commonly used test is to touch or to go beyond your toes.

Another staple of fitness tests are muscular strength and endurance measures. Muscular strength, the ability to generate maximum force, is indicative of your potential in a "use of force" encounter, subject control, or other emergency situation. *Bench press* and *leg press tests* to measure upper and lower body strength are commonly used and require you to lift a percentage of your present body weight. A maximum effort is required after a warm-up on the testing machine/apparatus.

Dynamic muscular endurance, on the other hand, is the ability to sustain effort over time. This very common element of fitness tests is related to sitting or standing for long periods of time as well as to the incidence of lower back pain and disability. *Sit-up, pull-up,* and *push-up tests* are frequently timed events lasting one to two minutes that involve military push-ups, pull-ups and traditional or hands-across-the-chest, knee-bent sit-ups.

Finally, it is not uncommon to encounter a test that estimates the amount of fat compared to lean tissue or total body weight. *Body composition* is an indication of health risk status, and the results are usually expressed as a percent. Normal ranges for healthy young adults are 18–24% for females and 12–18% for males. A skinfold technique that measures the thickness of the skin and subcutaneous fat at sex-specific sites is the most common field test to estimate overall percentage of body fat.

## Job Task Simulation Tests

Job task simulation tests use a small sample of actual or simulated job tasks to evaluate your ability to do the job of a law enforcement officer. This type of test is used because of its realistic relationship to the job and law enforcement training and because of its defensibility as a fair measure of a candidate's physical abilities.

Because courts of law have found it unreasonable to evaluate skills that require prior training, general job-related skills are tested at the applicant level. It's unlikely that you will be required to demonstrate competency with a firearm or handcuffs, for example. But climbing through a window, over barriers, and up stairs, and simulating "use of force" situations, such as a takedown or simulated application of handcuffs, are common tasks.

Simulation tests are often presented as obstacle courses, with the events performed one after another and linked by laps around the gymnasium or athletic field. Frequently, the requirement is to complete the course or each event successfully in a given amount of time. The test may be given on an individual or small group basis. Candidates performing a job task simulation test may be walked or talked through the first run or allowed to practice certain events prior to actual testing.

A job task simulation test is typically held during one of two periods, subject to labor and anti-discrimination legislation. Testing can legally occur at the very beginning of the process, alone or in combination with a written test, to establish an applicant's rank. Or it can take place after a written test but before a conditional offer of employment. In some cases, it may also occur following a conditional offer of employment. If this is the case, you can reasonably expect a medical examination prior to participating in the test, which may also serve as an academy selection test. Because of the variability in the timing of the test, it is advisable to ask about physical standards as early in the selection process as possible.

## Important

Regardless of the type of physical test you take, you need to be reasonably fit to complete the test successfully. Because the selection process, law enforcement training, and lifestyle of law enforcement officers are all stressful, it is essential to achieve fitness early and to maintain it for the duration of your law enforcement career.

## Training Tips

In preparing for a physical fitness test, you must plan ahead, taking into account both the timing and the content of the test. The short-term objective, of course, is to pass the test. But your greater goal is to integrate fitness into your lifestyle so that you can withstand the rigors of the career you want in law enforcement.

The first order of business is to determine the type of fitness test you'll have to complete. What you have to accomplish on the test naturally will guide your training program. You can tailor your training to simulate the test and to train for the test events. Even if you're facing a job task test, you may want to include physical fitness test events, such as push-ups and sit-ups, in your training regimen. It's unsafe and inadequate to use skill events as your only training mode. If you're unfit, it won't allow for a slow progression, and if you are fit, it may not represent enough of a challenge for you.

Following some basic training principles will help you create a safe and effective training program. Steady progress is the name of the game. Remember, you didn't get into or out of shape overnight, so you won't be able to change your condition overnight. To avoid injury while achieving overall fitness, balance in fitness training is essential. Work opposing muscle groups when doing strength or flexibility training and include aerobic conditioning as well as proper nutrition in your total fitness program.

To achieve continued growth in fitness, you must overload the body's systems. The body makes progress by adapting to increasing demands. With adaptation, your systems are able to overcome the physical challenge, resulting in a higher level of fitness.

Finally, don't forget rest. It allows the body and the mind to recover from the challenges of training—and to prepare for another day.

FITT stands for Frequency, Intensity, Type, and Time. FITT simplifies your training by helping you plan what to do, when, how hard, and for how long. Because the four FITT "variables" are interrelated, you need to be careful in how you exercise. For example, intensity and time have an inverse relationship: As the intensity of your effort increases, the length of time you can maintain that effort decreases. A good rule of thumb when adjusting your workout variables to achieve optimum conditioning is to modify one at a time, increasing by 5–10%. Be sure to allow your body to adapt before adjusting up again.

The following presents some FITT guidelines to help you plan your training program:

### Frequency
- 3–5 times a week

### Intensity
- Aerobic training—60–85% of maximum effort
- Resistance training—8–12 repetitions
- Flexibility training—Just to slight tension

### Type
- Aerobic—Bike, walk, jog, swim, aerobic classes at a local gym
- Resistance—Free weights, weight machines, calisthenics
- Flexibility—Static stretching

### Time
- Aerobic—20–60 minutes
- Resistance—1–3 sets, 2–4 exercises/body part
- Flexibility—Hold stretched position 8–30 seconds

## 12 Weeks to the Test Date

Your primary goal when faced with a short window of preparation is to meet a given standard, either physical fitness or job task simulation. Therefore, "specificity of training"—training for what you will actually be asked to do on the test—is the rule.

If you're training for a physical fitness test, then the performance standards are your training goals. You should make every attempt to use or to build up to the standards as the training intensity level. If you are unable to reach the standards right away, approximate them and increase the intensity 5% per week until you achieve them.

If you're training for a pre-academy test, try to determine what the academy's "PT" curriculum

entails, use these as your modes of training, and test yourself with the standards every two to three weeks.

On the other hand, if the short-term goal is to meet a job task simulation test standard, particularly one that is used for pre-academy selection, you should determine the content of the PT curriculum and use it as the training model. At the same time, practice the skills required on the test once every two weeks in lieu of a training day.

## Six or More Months to Go

The training program when there are six or more months to prepare is essentially similar to the one just described. However, the longer time frame means that your goal can become making permanent, positive changes in your lifestyle rather than simply applying

## Sample Calisthenics

Here are some recommended calisthenics to help get you in shape:
- Jumping jacks
- Half squats
- Heel raises
- Push-ups
- Stair climbs
- Stomach crunches

And for the more advanced:
- Diamond push-ups
- Bent leg raises

training principles to pass a test. Reasonable and gradual changes in your lifestyle will help to ensure that the behavioral and physical changes are permanent.

This extended timetable also reduces the likelihood of injury and allows for more diversity and balance in your training program and lifestyle. If you're preparing for a physical fitness test, you have the opportunity to set (and meet) performance goals that may be 25–50% greater than the standards themselves. On the other hand, if you have more than six months to prepare for a job task simulation test, you may want to avoid practicing any of the skills required for the first three months to avoid injury. Instead, consider incorporating sports activities into your conditioning routine; this will provide an enjoyable opportunity to train the necessary motor skills. After three months, you could begin practicing the physical test skills one day every two to four weeks.

### A Sample Exercise Program

All of the information in this chapter about training principles and practices is put into action on the gym floor. A page taken from the police academy physical fitness training book will help to get you fit and ready to excel in the physical test.

Physical training begins with a warm-up to increase your core body temperature and to prepare you for the more intense conditioning to follow. Brisk walking or jogging, in place or around a gymnasium, or jumping rope are good start-up options and should be conducted for three to five minutes. This is followed immediately by a period of active head-to-toe stretching to prevent injury.

Basic conditioning in the academy frequently is achieved with calisthenic exercises (such as squats, sit-ups, chin-ups, etc.). Beginners can do sets of ten on a "two count" and those of intermediate or advanced fitness can begin on a "four count" (1, 2, 3, 1; 1, 2, 3, 2; etc.). Running in formation typically follows 'cals' and is done at about a 9–10 minute per mile pace. Marine Corps cadences played on an MP3 player may help to put you in the mood for academy runs! For those who are just beginning to prepare for the fitness test, 8–12 minutes of running is a safe start; those more fit may begin with 25 or more minutes. A three-to-five-minute cool-down period to recover and some gentle, static stretching from the floor, focusing on the lower legs, will complete your workout and prepare you for the showers! Remember to drink plenty of fluids during and after workouts, especially water.

# 28 ▶ The Personal History Statement

## CHAPTER SUMMARY

Paperwork tells the tale in police work—you get only one shot at this document. This chapter explores the quirks, subtleties, and realities of the most critical phase of the application process. Ignore the advice here and chances are you'll be reading a letter of rejection!

The personal history statement is exactly that—a detailed personal statement of your life history. You may hear it called many things—the application, the applicant history statement, and background questionnaire being the other common terms. No doubt you will come up with a few of your own by the time you finish this project. Although the paperwork may go by different names, the reason for jumping through these hoops is the same. The purpose of the statement is to provide law enforcement background investigators with the material for a panel, an individual, or a personnel department to make a sound decision about hiring you.

### Not for the Faint of Heart

When you take your first look at the personal history statement, you might want to be sitting down, or at least have a chair handy. This document can be a black hole for the unprepared. All of your precious time, energy, and resources will be sucked into the void if you aren't prepared to be asked for the tiniest details of your life. Although not all departments require the same level of detail, don't be surprised to find yourself madly hunting for the address of that kindergarten you once attended.

Some departments aren't so demanding. They'll ask you to start out this tale of your life with your high school days and work forward. It's best to expect the worst, though. As one investigator told an applicant to the Austin Police Department in Austin, Texas, "By the time I'm through going through the information in this document, I'll know whether or not you were breast-fed as a child." He was.

## This Size Fits All

No matter where you choose to apply, this chapter may be the helping hand you need to make your background investigation go as smoothly as possible. It will serve as a guide to help you present an accurate, honest summary of your past and present life. After all, the personal history statement—how you complete it, what you reveal, and what you don't reveal—can determine whether or not you get the opportunity to convince an oral board you are worth hiring.

You may not make the connection between the oral interview board and the personal history statement at first. The connection is there, and it's strong. What you reveal—and what you fail to reveal—in your personal history statement will come back around to help or haunt you at your oral board. Background investigators will rustle around in your life's basement using this document as a flashlight. They'll illuminate the good things and the bad things for all the oral board members to see and to use in their questioning. You're forewarned, however, and you are ready.

## Different Methods—Same Results

One of the more frustrating aspects of searching for that perfect law enforcement job is realizing that every department, even within the same state, has its own way of doing business. Yes, you may have applied yesterday to one police department 20 miles away from the one you are applying to today, but the process will usually be entirely different. Law enforcement agencies rarely have the same priorities, budgets, or staffing, so

the process, right down to the people they may want to hire, won't match up.

Be flexible. No matter how the application process is designed, no matter what order you handle each task given you, information you will need to supply each department remains the same. They all want to know about your past, present, and potential.

## No Need to Wait

Even if you haven't decided which departments you will grace with your applications, you can start work now. Beginning with the day you were born, make a list of every address where you've lived up to the present. If you are 34 years old and normally change addresses twice a year, you can pause a moment now to groan aloud. Make this list and keep plenty of copies. You'll need to do this only once instead of every time you apply to a different department if you are careful to keep copies of your efforts. Because your crystal ball works like everyone else's, you can't be too sure what's in the future. The CIA, FBI, or other agency may lure you from your dream department one day and you'll wish you'd kept up the list.

Addresses aren't the only project you can work on ahead of time. Create a list of every part-time, full-time, and some-time job you've had since your working life began. Once again, not every department will use the same jump-off point to investigate your job history. Many forms ask you to list the jobs you've held during the past ten years, some during the past five years, and the others want your history from the moment you received your first check.

## And There's Always . . .

Tickets. Here's yet another project to work on before applying to a police agency. Research your driving history. You'll be asked by some departments to list every traffic ticket you've ever received in any state or country, whether on a military post or on civilian roadways. Some may ask you to list only the moving violations (these include speeding, running red lights, unsafe lane changes, etc.), while other departments want to see moving violations and tickets for things like expired license plates, failure to wear seat belts, and most certainly expired automobile insurance.

One agency may ask for you to tell them about the tickets you've received in the past five years, while others want to know your driving history from the moment your foot first touched an accelerator. Do your homework. And don't leave off tickets you think they won't find out about, because that kind of ticket doesn't exist. Tickets leave paper trails, and paper trails are the easiest kinds to follow.

### Dig These Up ASAP

Your pre-application preparations wouldn't be complete without a list of documents you'll need to have handy. This list does not include *every* form you may have to cough up, but it's almost a dead certainty your department will want to see the following:

- birth certificate
- Social Security card
- DD 214 (if you are a veteran)
- naturalization papers (if applicable)
- high school diploma or GED certificate
- high school transcripts
- college transcripts (official and unofficial)
- current driver's license(s)
- current copies of driving records
- current consumer credit reports

If you don't have certified copies of these documents, start calling or writing the proper authorities **now** to find out what you need to do to get them. If you've sucked your Social Security card up in the vacuum cleaner and haven't seen it since, run down to the Social Security office in your community and arrange for a new one. Legal documents often take anywhere from six to eight weeks for delivery, but you probably won't be able to wait that long if you have already received and started on your personal history state-

ment. Most departments have a deadline for filling out and returning personal history statements so you may have to tap dance a bit.

If time runs out and you realize you won't be able to turn the personal history statement in with all the required documents, *ask* the powers-that-be what you should do. Many departments will tell you to attach a memo to your application outlining your problem and what you have done about it. For example, you've ordered a copy of your birth certificate, but either the postal service is using it for scratch paper or your request is mired in the bureaucratic process. Attach a letter of explanation to your application detailing when you requested a copy of your birth certificate, where you asked for the copy to be sent, and when you expect to receive the document. If you have it, attach all copies of correspondence you sent out requesting a copy of your certificate. That'll show that you are making all the right moves.

### Check First

You have a little homework to do before rounding up all of these documents. Check with as many departments as you can to find out what rules they have for how certain documents are submitted—college transcripts, for instance. Departmental officials may require you to have the school send the documentation directly to their recruiting office instead of to you at home via regular mail. The same goes for credit reports or copies of driving records. It's best to call the recruiting department, explain to them that you are trying to round up all of your documentation, and ask them how they accept these documents so you'll know what to do.

Other questions you need to ask are the following:

- Do you need photocopies or original documents?
- Will you return my original if I send it?
- How recent does the credit history have to be?
- What's the most recent copy you will accept of my college transcript?

The answers to these questions can save you lots of money on antacids and postage. You'd be surprised at the number of ways each department can come up with for you to chase paper.

## Ready for Action

So, you're as prepared as you can be. You've made your decision on where you are applying and let's even assume you are at the point in the application process where you've received the personal history statement. *Before* you set pen to paper, make a copy of this form. Do not write on it, breathe on it, or dare to set it down on the coffee table without having two copies made FIRST. After you have two copies, then put away the original for now. (You'll be using the photocopies as working drafts and a place to make mistakes.) Eventually you will transfer all the information you have on your practice copy onto the original. You may be spending lots of time on this project and using more money on copying before this is all over, but it'll be time and money well spent. Especially if the *unthinkable* happens. And the unthinkable usually goes like this:

> Your phone rings. It's your recruiter. "Gee, Fred, this is Officer Jones at Friendly P.D. recruiting and I have a little bad news. We can't seem to put a finger on that application you sent. Isn't that the darndest thing? Could you make us a copy from the one you have at home and send it out right away?"

Don't think it doesn't happen. Be sure to make copies of the application and accompanying documentation you submit and keep them in a safe place. And hold on to these copies! You need to review this document before the oral board gets ahold of you, not to mention the possibility that you may need this information to complete other applications for other adventures years down the road.

Personal history statements may vary from department to department, but the questions most applicants ask about these tedious documents have not changed over the years. Following are a few questions and comments made by actual applicants as they went through application processes across the United States. The responses made to these questions and comments will allow you to learn from someone else's mistakes, thereby giving you an advantage over the competition—and having an advantage in this highly competitive field can never hurt!

## "What do you mean you don't accept resumes? It cost me $60 to get this one done!"

A formal resume like one you may prepare for a civilian job is usually not much good to a law enforcement agency. Although criminal justice instructors in many colleges suggest to their students to have a resume made, it's always best to call and ask a recruiter whether or not to bother. Why go to the expense if the agency is going to throw away the resume upon receipt? Most agencies will rely upon their personal history statements to get the details of your life, education, and experience, so save yourself time and money when you can. The extra money will come in handy at the copy machine when you make backup copies of your personal history statement!

## "I didn't realize the personal history statement would take so long to complete and the deadline for turning it in caught me by surprise. I got in a hurry and left some things blank."

The letter this applicant received in the mail disqualifying her from further consideration probably caught her by surprise as well. As you know from reading this chapter so far, a personal history statement requires planning, efficiency, and attention to detail. Most departments demand accuracy, thoroughness, and timeliness. There are entirely too many applicants to choose from who have taken the time necessary to fill out an application properly for a busy background investigator to bother with an applicant who has left half of the form blank and isn't quite sure what should go in the other half. In fact, many departments will tell you up front in their application instructions that failing to respond to questions or failure to provide requested information will result in disqualification.

### "I read *most* of the instructions. I didn't see the part that said I had to print."

Read *all* of the instructions. Every sentence. Every word. And please do so before you begin filling out your practice copy of the personal history statement. In fact, you need to read the entire document from the first page to the last page before you tackle this project. Have a notepad next to you and as you read make notes of everything you do not understand. You'll be making a phone call to your recruiter AFTER reading the entire document to ask questions. It's important to read the whole document because the questions on your pad may be answered as you read along. It's a bit embarrassing to call with a question that the recruiter answers by saying "Well, as you would have found out by reading the next sentence, you should . . . "

### "No one is going to follow up on all this stuff anyway. It'd take way too long and it's way too involved."

Good background investigators live for the opportunity to follow up on the details of your life. That's their job. When all is said and done, they must sign their name at the bottom of the report documenting their investigation. It's not wise to assume people will put their career at risk by doing a sloppy job on your background investigation. A thorough investigator will take as much time as it takes to do a good job. The good news is that you can earn brownie points by making that investigator's job as simple as possible. Give them as much information as you possibly can and make that information right. When you write down a phone number, make

sure it's correct. For example, if you used to work at Jumpin' Jacks Coffee Parlor four years ago and you still remember the phone number, call that number to make sure it's correct before you write it down. Nothing is more irritating to a busy investigator than dialing wrong number after wrong number. If that's the only number you have and you discover it's no longer in service, make a note of this so the investigator doesn't assume you are being sloppy. Phone numbers get changed and businesses go under every day.

When you turn in a personal history statement, you are building on the reputation you began forming from the moment you first made contact with recruiting staff. An application that is turned in on time, is filled out neatly and meticulously, and that has *correct*, detailed information that is easily verified says a lot about the person who filled it out. Not only will an investigator have warm fuzzy thoughts for anyone who makes his or her job easier, he or she will come to the conclusion that you will probably carry over these same traits into your police work.

The investigator, the oral board, and the staff psychologist all will be looking at *how* you filled out the application as well as what information is contained in the application. Police officers will build a case for hiring you (or *not* hiring you) based on facts, impressions, and sometimes even intuition. With this in mind, *every detail is worth a second look* before you call your personal history statement complete. Ask yourself:

- Is my handwriting as neat as it can be?
- Did I leave off answers or skip blanks?
- Do my sentences make sense?
- Is my spelling accurate?
- Are my dates and times consistent?

**"I figured you could find out that information easier than I could. That's why I didn't look up that information. After all, you're the investigator."**

And this applicant is probably *still* looking for a job. The personal history statement is a prime opportunity for you to showcase your superb organizational skills, knack for detail, and professionalism. Do as much of the work as you can for the background investigator. Make your extra credit points where you can. For example, let's say you worked for Grace's High Heels and Muffler Emporium. The business went under after a few months, much to everyone's surprise, and you moved on to other employment. You're not sure what happened to Grace, your immediate supervisor and owner of the business, but you do know a friend of hers. Contact that friend, find out Grace's address and phone number, and give this information to your investigator. Yes, the investigator probably would find her on his or her own, but you went the extra mile, you showed the initiative, and you are going to get the brownie points.

It's not uncommon for a major police department to get thousands of applications per year. Most of the applicants have the same credentials to offer as you do. Do all you can do to stand out from the crowd. Nothing gets noticed faster than efficiency, professionalism, and accuracy. Well, that's not quite right. Inaccuracies, sloppiness, and laziness usually win first notice.

**"I know I got disqualified, but it's only because I misunderstood the question. I didn't want to ask about it because I didn't want to look dumb."**

If you do not understand a question, *ask* someone. By not making sure you know how to properly answer a question, you run the risk of answering it incorrectly, incompletely, or not at all. Any one of these mistakes can lead to your disqualification if an investigator thinks that you are not telling the truth or that you are unwilling to provide the information requested. Don't take chances when a simple question will clear up the problem.

**"You know, I didn't have any idea what that question meant so I just guessed."**

Never guess. Never assume. This advice can never be repeated too often—if you don't know, find out. *Ask questions.* Answering them is part of the job for recruiters or background investigators.

**"I lied because I thought if I told the truth, I'd look bad."**

Never lie about *anything.* As far as police departments are concerned, there is no such thing as a harmless lie. Supervisors don't want people working for them who cannot tell the truth, other officers don't want to work with partners whom they can't trust, and communities expect *criminals* to lie, not police officers. Your credibility must be beyond reproach.

Let's look at an example. One applicant told his recruiter that the reason he didn't admit to getting a ticket for failing to have his car registered was that he thought the department would think he wasn't organized and couldn't take care of business. Which would you prefer for a potential employer to know about you—that you lie instead of admitting to mistakes or that you make mistakes and admit to them readily? The fact is, telling the truth is crucial if you want to do police work. You will not be hired if you lie or have a history of deception.

**"I listed John Doe as a personal reference because he's the mayor and I worked on his campaign. Why did my investigator call and make me give another reference?"**

Choose your personal references carefully. Background investigators do not want to talk to people because they have impressive credentials. They want to talk to them so they can get a feel for how you are as a person. Investigators will know within minutes whether or not a reference knows you well. Personal references are important enough to warrant their own in-depth discussion later in this chapter, so read on.

## How to Read and Answer Questions

Reading questions and instructions carefully is critical to completing the personal history statement successfully. Certain words should leap off the page at you. These are the words you should key in on:

- all
- every
- any
- each

If you see these words in a question, you are being asked to include all the information you know. For example, you may see the following set of instructions in your personal history statement:

List **any** and **all** pending criminal charges against you.

This doesn't mean list only the charges facing you in Arizona, but not the ones from that incident in Nevada last week. This department wants to know about every single criminal charge that may be pending against you no matter what city, county, parish, village, country, or planet may be handling the case(s). Do not try to tap dance your way around instructions like these for any reason. If your fear is that the information you list might make you look bad, you may have some explaining to do. And you may have perfectly good explanations for your past and your present. If you lie or try to make yourself look good, chances are you'll be disqualified in short order, and no one will get the opportunity to consider those explanations.

Another question you may see is:

Have you **ever** been arrested or taken into police custody for **any** reason?

The key words are **ever** and **any**. This department means at any time in your life, beginning at your moment of birth, up to and including the split second that just went by. If you don't know what is meant by the term *arrested*, then call your recruiter or investigator and *ask*. Do not play the well-no-one-put-handcuffs-on-me-so-I-wasn't-really-under-arrest game. When in doubt, list any situation you think has a ghost of a chance of falling into the category you are working on. The best advice, though, is ASK IF YOU DON'T KNOW! Let your background investigator decide if your incident is important or not.

Here's a request for information that includes several eye-catching words.

List **all** traffic citations you received in the past five (5) years, in this or **any** other state (moving and nonmoving) **excluding** parking tickets.

In this example, the department leaves little doubt that what you should do here is make a complete list of every kind of violation you've been issued a citation for, no matter where you got it and no matter what the traffic violation was for within the past five years. They even let you know the one kind of citation they don't need to know about—parking tickets. If you aren't sure what a moving violation is or what a nonmoving violation is, call the department and have them explain. Keep in mind that when the officer issued you a citation on a single piece of paper, you may have been cited for more than one violation. Most citations have blanks for at least three violations, sometimes more. For example, last year you were pulled over for speeding. The officer discovered you had no insurance and your car license plates were expired. She told you she was writing you three tickets for these violations, but handed you only one piece of paper. Did you get one citation or three? You got three.

Once again, *ask* if you don't know. No one will make fun of you if you are unfamiliar with terminology such as *moving violation.*

## Personal References

Your personal references are the people who will be able to give the background investigator the best picture of you as a whole person. Some personal history statements ask you to list at least five people as references and some ask for only three. You also may be given a specific time limit for how long you may have known these people before listing them. Your instructions may direct you to list only those individuals whom you've known for a minimum of two years, for example. Pay close attention to the instructions for this section, if there are any. Selecting the people for this area is not something you should take lightly for many reasons.

Earlier, you read that by making the investigator's job easier you make your investigation run smoother, you get brownie points, and your background is finished quickly. The personal references section is one area where you really want to make it easy. You'll want the investigator to talk to people who know you well—who can comment on your hobbies, interests, personality, and ability to interact with others. Try to choose friends who will be honest, open, and sincere. When an investigator calls a reference and figures out quickly that the person he or she is talking to barely has an idea of who you are, the red flags will come shooting up. Investigators are suspicious people by nature. Most police officers are. The investigator will wonder why you listed someone who doesn't know you well. Are you trying to throw them off the track? Are you afraid someone who knows you too well will let out information you don't want known? This is how an investigator will look at the situation. And, at the very least, you'll get a phone call requesting another reference because the one you listed was unsatisfactory.

Most investigators expect for you to tell the personal references that you listed them and that they will be getting a phone call or a personal visit from the investigating agency. Get the *right* phone numbers, find out from your references what times they are most accessible, and *especially* find out if they have any objections to being contacted. You don't need a reluctant personal reference. They often do more harm than good.

Tell your references how important it is for them to be open and honest with the investigator. Let them know that if they do not understand a question, they should feel free to tell the investigator they don't understand. It's also wise to let them know that there are no right or wrong answers to most of these questions. Investigators do not want to have a conversation with someone who is terrified about saying the "wrong thing." And that's what your personal references should expect to have with an investigator—a conversation, not an interrogation. Your goal here is to let the investigator see you as a person through the eyes of those who know you best.

## Looks Aren't Everything—Or Are They?

You've filled out at least one practice copy you made of the personal history statement, made all your mistakes on that copy, answered all the questions, and filled in *all* the blanks. Now you're ready to make the final copy.

Part of the impression you will make on those who have the hiring and firing decisions will come from how your application looks. Is your handwriting so sloppy that investigators pass your work around to see who can read it? Did you follow the instructions directing you to print? Were you too lazy to attach an additional sheet of paper instead of writing up and down the sides of the page? Did you spell words correctly? Do your sentences make sense to the reader? (A good tip here is to read your answers out loud to yourself. If it doesn't make sense to your ear, then you need to work on what you wrote.)

*Every* contact you make with the hiring agency makes an impression. The written impression you make when you turn in your personal history statement is one that can follow you through the entire process and into the academy. In fact, it can have a bearing on whether or not you even make it into the academy because most departments have a method of scoring you on the document's appearance.

Make sure you fill in every blank on the application. If the particular question does not apply, write "N/A," or "Does Not Apply," or place a dash in it. Never leave any question unanswered or blank. If something needs further explanation, use another sheet of paper and number the response the same as the question. Again, a neatly prepared document that is fully filled out will gain you subtle and unconscious points with the reviewer, whether or not he or she is aware of it.

Here are some items you might find useful as you work on your application:

- a dictionary
- a grammar handbook
- a good pen (or pencil—whatever the directions tell you to use)
- a screaming case of paranoia

The paranoia will ensure that you check your work, check it again, and have someone you trust check it yet again **before** you make your final copy.

You now have the information you need to make the personal history statement a manageable task. This is not a document to take lightly, especially when you are now aware of the power this document has over your potential career as a police officer. Remember, it's important that you

- follow instructions and directions.
- take your time to completely, accurately, and neatly fill in every blank and answer every question.
- be honest and open about your past and present.
- provide **accurate** information.
- choose excellent personal references.
- turn in presentable, error-free documentation.
- turn in documents on time.
- make copies of everything for your records.

A recruiting department can ask for nothing better than an applicant who takes this kind of care and interest in the application process. And you will get all the credit!

# 29 ▶ The Oral Interview

## CHAPTER SUMMARY

This is the next best thing to having someone do your oral interview for you. The oral interview process is demystified in these pages with a down-to-earth look at the ordeal. Read on for tips, suggestions, and advice on what not to do.

**M**unicipal police departments nationwide depend on some form of oral interview to help them choose suitable police candidates. In Los Angeles, California, a panel of one civilian and one sergeant or detective questions applicants for 15 to 20 minutes about their qualifications. In Austin, Texas, applicants can expect to be grilled by a panel of five higher-ranking police officers and a civilian psychologist for more than an hour. And that's if you keep your responses short and to the point.

The oral interview board, no matter what form it takes, is unlike any oral job interview you will ever experience. The questions are pointed, personal, and uncompromising. Vague, plastic responses will usually goad a panel of veteran police officers into rougher questioning techniques until they get the honest response called for by the circumstances. The information you are about to receive will show you how to prepare for the oral board from the moment you decide to apply to a department until the moment the board chairperson thanks you for your participation.

## Hire Me, Please!

If you're like most people, you've had some experience asking someone for a job. So, it's not unrealistic to expect that the police oral interview board will be similar to a civilian oral interview—is it? Yes and no. There are a few similarities. Both prospective civilian and police employers are looking for the most qualified person for the job—reliable, honest men and women who will work hard and be there when they are needed.

## "Hire" Expectations

Civilian employers, as do police employers, expect applicants to show up on time for their interview, dressed professionally, and showing off their best manners. When you step into a police oral interview board, however, you will realize that the people who are interviewing you have more than a surface interest in you and your past experiences. And the board will have more than a two-page resume in their hands when the interview begins.

Exactly who is going to be using the details of your personal and professional life to interview you? More than likely, it will be a panel of two, three, four—maybe more—individuals with one purpose in mind: to get to know you well. The board members will most likely be supervisory-level police officers who have several years' experience on the force. Some departments use civilian personnel specialists to sit on their boards, but most interview boards will be made up of experienced police officers.

These board members will be using information you have provided on your application and information investigators discover during your background investigation. Investigators will provide board members with a detailed report on your past and present life history. Yes, you'll be asked questions when board members already know the answer and when they don't know the answer. You'll be asked to explain why you've made the decisions you've made in your life—both personal and professional. You'll also be asked questions that don't have right or wrong answers. In short, you can expect an intense grilling from men and women who don't have the time or patience for applicants who walk into their interview unprepared.

## Tell What You Know, Know What You Tell

Before you reach the oral interview board stage of the application process, you will have had to fill out a detailed personal history statement often referred to as the applicant history statement, the personal history statement, or simply the application. Terminology differs from department to department. Unless you are skipping around in this book, you've probably read about it by now. Call it what you want—just don't underestimate its role in the oral interview.

The personal history statement guides the oral board through your past and present life. You must be willing to open your life up to the board by giving them an informative, accurate tour of where you've been in your life and who you are.

Because the personal history statement is what background investigators use to conduct investigations and what a final report to the board is built on, it follows that you should make that document your life when you are filling it out. Members of the oral board generally are given a copy of your personal history statement and then a copy of the investigators' final report on you. While you are answering questions for the board, most board members will be shuffling through the pages of your life—checking what you say against what they see on paper. Naturally, you'll want to remember what information you gave them. Instead of tossing and turning the night before your interview, your time will be well spent reading and rereading your personal history statement so that you know what they know about you.

How much effort you put into the personal history statement will have a direct impact on how difficult your oral interview will be. If board members have an accurate, detailed picture of you as a whole person from the information you have supplied, your time under the microscope will be less than the applicant who turned in a vague, mistake-laden account of his or her past and present life. If the thought of the oral interview board makes your palms sweat, then pay close attention to the chapter on how to handle the personal history statement. You'll feel better afterward.

## There's Plenty of Time, Right?

Preparation for the oral interview board begins when you make the decision to apply. From the moment you first make contact with a police department, everything you say and do will be potential fuel for the oral interview board. Even walking through the doors of the recruiting office to pick up an application, you have the opportunity to make a lasting impression. You are dealing with professionals who are trained to notice and *remember* people and details.

If you show up to pick up an application wearing your favorite cutoff ratty jeans and beer-stained T-shirt from those college party days, you may be in for a shock several months later when a board member asks you why you chose to make that particular fashion statement. Dress neatly and as professionally as possible each and *every* time you make contact with the department where you want to work.

Same goes for telephone contacts—if you call a department to request an application, you will make an impression on the person who answers the phone. If all you want is an information packet and/or application and you do not have any specific questions to ask, do *not* take this opportunity to tell the recruiter your entire life story from the moment of conception.

Not only are you probably the 100th person to request an application that day, the recruiter has no way, or reason, to remember the details of your life at this stage of the process. Remember, though, you have to give out your name and address to this person who will be responsible for mailing your application, so the potential for connecting your name to the impression you make on the phone is high.

As silly as it may make you feel, it's a good idea to practice what you say *before* you dial the phone. In fact,

it's not a bad idea to write down what you'd like to say before you call. This will give you control over the impression you make and eliminate the possibility of the first words out of your mouth being: "Uh . . . hi . . . I . . . uh . . . wanna . . . uh . . . Can you mail me a . . . uh . . . one of those . . . uh . . . I wanna be a cop but I need a . . . application! Yeah, that's it!"

Do the same for any questions you may have. Make a list and, as you ask each question, listen carefully to the response without interruption. Above all, never ask a question that is designed to show off how much you know. The chances of you knowing more about law enforcement than the person who is already working in the field is slim. Your opportunity to impress the department will come later in the appropriate setting—the oral interview board.

## Self-Awareness—Don't Show Up without It!

You wouldn't want to show up for a car race on a tricycle, any more than you would want to try putting out a fire with gasoline. Using this same logic, you'd be safe to say you'd never want to sit down in front of a panel of professionals who have the power to offer you a career dealing with people without a good measure of self-awareness.

Self-awareness is knowing yourself—being aware of what you do and why you do it. Many of the questions you'll hear from the board are designed to reveal how well you know yourself and how honest you can be about your talents and your shortcomings.

## Big Tip!

Do *not* pay any attention to consultants or books suggesting that you downplay, or do not admit to, weaknesses. If you can remember only one piece of advice from this chapter, please let it be this! If an oral board member asks you to list the weaknesses you believe you have and you can't think of any, they will be more than happy to bring up a few instances in your life to illustrate the weaknesses you aren't able to identify.

You should be able to list your weaknesses with the same unhesitating manner with which you list your strengths. And you should be able to tell the board what you are doing to correct or compensate for your weaknesses. If you truly aren't aware of your failings, ask trusted friends and relatives for their input. Write down what you think your weaknesses are and then compare your list with what your friends and family have said. Don't forget to ask them about your strengths as well. Some applicants find talking about strengths as difficult as talking about weaknesses. You must be able to do both.

## Don't You Remember? You Put It on Your Application!

Part of being self-aware is knowing what others know about you. Hardly any of the questions during your oral board interview should come as a surprise to you if you have taken the copy of your application that you made *before* turning it in and studied it.

Before showing up for the board, you must take the time to go back over your application and carefully think about each piece of information in this document. The questions put to you by the board are generated mostly from the information you write in the personal history statement. As you review your copy of the statement, think about the questions such information could generate.

For example, if one of the questions on the application directed you to list any instances where you've been fired from a job, think about how you would answer the question, "Mr. Smith, can you tell the board why you got fired from Tread Lightly Tire Shop in 1993?" Although you may have told the investigator why you were fired during an earlier conversation, the board will want to hear it for themselves.

## Help Yourself!
## Tame Public Speaking Fears

Being interviewed by a group of people is a lot like having one of those dreams where you show up to work in nothing but a pair of socks. You experience anxiety, sweaty palms, and a burning desire to be some place else. Public speaking classes will go a long way toward easing your fear of talking to groups.

Strongly consider taking a speech class at a nearby community college or through an adult education course. At the very least, have a friend ask you questions about yourself and have them take notes about any annoying mannerisms you may exhibit while speaking. Then practice your speaking and learn to control those mannerisms.

Practice is one of the keys to success on an oral board. If you've ever truly practiced something—batting a ball, for instance—you know that once you have the motion down you can rely on your muscles to "remember" what to do when it comes time to play the game. The same rationale holds true for practicing oral board answers.

One effective technique is to place yourself mentally in a situation and visualize how you want to act or respond when the pressure is on. Some police officers call this mental exercise "What if" and they use this technique to formulate a plan of action for those times when split-second decisions rule the moment. Visualizing a successful performance ahead of time can help trigger that response once you're in the actual situation. This technique will work for you if you practice, practice, practice.

## Right on Time? Tsk, Tsk!

Show the board how much you want this job. They'll check to see when you arrived for your board. An early arrival means you planned ahead for emergencies (flat tires, wrong turns, etc.), that you arrived in enough time to prepare yourself mentally for what you are about to do, and that you place a value on other people's time as well as your own.

## Packaging Sells Product

You may feel like you don't have much control over what happens to you in an oral interview setting, but this is one area where you have total control. The initial impression you make on board members is up to you, and this is the perfect opportunity to score points without ever opening your mouth. The way you dress sends a signal to the people who are watching you walk into the room.

Jeans and a "nice shirt" tells the panel you wouldn't mind having the job if someone wouldn't mind giving it to you. Conservative business suits (for men and women) tell them you *want* this job, you take this interview seriously, and there's nothing casual about the way you are approaching it.

If you don't own businesswear, borrow it. Rent it. Buy it. Wear it! Chances are you've already invested time and money into the education necessary to get most criminal justice jobs. This is not the time to balk at spending money on appropriate clothing. Just go get the suit any way you can.

## Make Your Family Proud

After you've earned bonus points with your professional appearance, it's time to earn more with your manners. Most law enforcement agencies are paramilitary organizations—your first clue should be the uniforms and the rank structure. In the military, it's customary to address higher-ranking men and women with courtesy. "Yes, ma'am" or "yes, sir" or "no, ma'am" or "no, sir" is expected from military personnel. If you have military experience, you will be ahead in this area.

If you are not accustomed to using these terms of courtesy, practice them! Make a conscious effort to use them. It's rarely considered rude to simply respond "yes" or "no" to a question, but you'll *always* be on shaky ground if "yeah" or "uh-huh" are your customary responses.

Location is important. If you've flown from New York to Texas to apply for a job, you definitely do not want to say "yeah" or "what?" in your oral board. People in the South raise their children to say "yes, ma'am" and "no, sir," and hearing "huh?" or "yeah" is at best an irritant to southern ears. This may not be an issue in

other parts of the nation, although it'd be a safe bet to assume many board members have either been in the military at some point in their lives or like the paramilitary structure of law enforcement. You won't go wrong with "yes, sir" instead of "yeah," or "Could you repeat the question?" instead of "what?"

No doubt you realize that an oral board sees many, many applicants when a department is in a hiring phase. Most oral boards typically schedule five or six applicants in one day for interviews. Some departments schedule boards for one day during the week and some departments have oral boards set for every day of the week. The point here is that you are talking to people who are more than likely quite tired of listening. That means the "little things" take on an extra importance.

## Yes, It All Matters

What you've read so far may seem inconsequential. This is far from the truth. You walk a fine line when you appear before an oral board. They want you to appear self-confident and poised, but not cocky or arrogant. You're expected to be nervous, but not so nervous that you can't communicate beyond an occasional grunt or nod. You're expected to be polite, but you're not expected to fawn all over the board. Above all, you are expected to be yourself and not who you *imagine* the board might want. Which brings up another point— what exactly *is* the board looking for in an applicant?

## People Talent—Gotta Have It

Today's departments expect officers to attend neighborhood meetings, get to know the people living and working in their patrol areas, and be accessible to the public. This concept is known as community policing. Community policing is embraced by most medium-to-large police agencies and is designed to get the cop out of the squad car and back into the community. The days of riding around in a car waiting for the next call to come out are over for most officers.

Officers nationwide feel community policing is simply a return to the basic idea behind policing—

public service. Leaving the theory debates up to the intellectuals, oral interview boards are faced with the formidable task of hiring men and women with the skills and talents equal to the demands of modern policing.

The men and women most highly sought after by police departments are those who can handle the demands placed on them by advanced technology and changes in policing concepts. Computers are absolutely an essential part of your job. If you haven't already, now's the time to brush up on your typing skills and sign up for a computer class.

Then there's the liability issue. Lawsuits and threats of lawsuits have law enforcement agencies scurrying to find applicants who have specific qualities and skills that will keep them out of the headlines and civil courtrooms.

## Show Your Stuff

Yes, law enforcement agencies want it all. There's *always* room for men and women who can leap tall buildings and do the speeding train thing, but even if your cape isn't red, you can still compete if you can convince the board you have the following qualities:

- Integrity
- Maturity
- Common sense
- Good judgment
- Compassion
- Honesty
- Reliability
- The ability to work without constant supervision

These qualities aren't ranked in order of importance because it would be hard to say which should come first. They are all of importance in the eyes of the board, and your task in the oral interview setting is to convince them you have these qualities. Because you are in an obvious question-and-answer setting, you'll do your convincing through how and what you say when you respond to questions.

## Youth and Inexperience—Plus or Minus?

The question here is will an oral board think you have enough life experience for them to be willing to take a chance on hiring you. Law enforcement agencies have never been as liability conscious as they are today. Incidents such as the Rodney King trial and subsequent Los Angeles riots, not to mention the O.J. Simpson trial, and the Rampart scandal have heightened the awareness of city legal departments around the country.

This concern ripples straight through the department and eventually arrives to haunt recruiters, background investigators, oral boards, and everyone who has anything to do with deciding who gets a badge. The first question you hear when trouble hits a police department is "How did that person get a job here anyway?" As a result, police departments are scrutinizing applicants even more closely than ever before, and they are clearly leaning toward individuals who have proven track records in employment, schooling, volunteer work, and community involvement.

Youth and inexperience are not going to disqualify you from the process. You should be aware that if you are 21 years old, have never held a job, and have never been responsible for your own care, feeding, and life in general, you will have a more difficult time getting hired on your first try at a larger police department than someone who is older, has job references to check, and who is able to demonstrate a history of reliability, responsibility, and community involvement.

Maturity is a huge concern with police departments. They can no longer afford to hire men and women who are unable to take responsibility for their actions or the actions, in some cases, of those around them. Although maturity cannot be measured in the number of years an individual has been alive, departments will want to see as much proof as possible that you have enough maturity and potential to risk hiring you.

### Get Out in the World

Make it as easy as possible for the oral board to see how well you handle responsibility. Sign up for volunteer work *now* if you don't have any experience dealing with people. If you are still living at home with parents, be able to demonstrate the ways in which you are responsible around the home. If you are on your own, but living with roommates, talking to the board about this experience and how you handle conflicts arising from living with strangers or friends will help your case.

You may want to work extra hard on your communication skills before going to the board. The more articulate you are the better you will be able to sell yourself and your potential to the board if you are young. Your need to open up and let the board see you as a worthy investment will be greater than an older applicant who has plenty of personal and business history to pore over.

### Older and Wiser Pays Off

Being older certainly is not a hindrance in police work. Oral boards are receptive to men and women who have life experience that can be examined, picked apart, and verified. Maturity, as mentioned before, is not necessarily linked with how old you are. Older applicants can be either blessed or cursed by the trail they've left in life. Many applicants have gone down in flames because they were unable to explain incidents in their past and present that point to their immaturity and inability to handle responsibility.

Applicants of any age who have listed numerous jobs and have turned in personal history statements too thick to run through a stapling machine should be extra vigilant about doing homework before the oral board stage. If you fall into this category, you should carefully pore over the copy of the application your background investigator used to do your background check. Be fully aware of the problem areas and know what you will most likely be asked to explain. And decide now what you are going to say. Prepare, prepare, prepare.

### Don't Leave the Meter Running

The longer your history, the longer you can expect to sit before an oral board. If a board is not required to adhere strictly to time limits, you may be required to endure a longer session than other applicants simply because there's more material to cover. The more you know about yourself and the more open you are about your life, the smoother your interview will run. This advice holds true for *all* applicants.

## ▶ The Nitty-Gritty

Questions. What kind of questions are they going to ask? Isn't that what everyone is really worried about when they are sitting and outside of the interview room waiting to go inside? You will hear all kinds of questions—personal questions about your family life, questions about your likes and dislikes, questions about your temperament, your friends, and even a few designed to make you laugh so you'll get a little color back into your face. Don't look for many questions that can be answered with simply "yes" or "no" because you won't get that lucky. Let's look at the types of questions you are likely to hear.

### Open-Ended Questions

The open-ended question is the one you are most likely to hear. Here is an example of an open-ended question:

Board member: "Mr. Jones, can you tell the board about your Friday night bowling league?"

Board members like these questions because it gives them an opportunity to see how articulate you can be and it gives them a little insight into how you think. This is also a way for them to ease into more specific questions. Example:

Board member: "Mr. Jones, can you tell the board about your Friday night bowling league?"

Jones: "Yes, ma'am. I've been bowling in this league for about two years. We meet every Friday night around 6 P.M. and bowl until about 8:30 P.M. I like it because it gives me something to do with friends I may not get to see otherwise because everyone is so busy. This also gives me time to spend with my wife. We're in first place right now, and I like it that way."

Board member: "Oh, congratulations. You must be a pretty competitive bowler."

Jones: "Yes, ma'am, I am. I like to win, and I take the game pretty seriously."

Board member: "How do you react when your team loses, Mr. Jones?"

That one question generates enough information for the board to draw a lot of conclusions about Mr. Jones. They can see that he likes to interact with his friends, he thinks spending time with his wife is important, and that competition and winning are important to him. Mr. Jones's answer opens up an avenue for the board to explore how he reacts to disappointment and how he is able to articulate his feelings and reactions, and they'll probably get a good idea of his temperament.

Open-ended questions allow the board to fish around for information, granted, but this is not a negative situation. You should seize these opportunities to en up to the board and give them an idea of how you s a person.

## Obvious Questions

This is the kind of question boards ask when everyone in the room already knows the answer. Example:

Board member: "Mr. Jones, you were in the military for four years?"

Jones: "Yes, sir, I was in the Marines from 1982 until 1986."

Board member: "Why did you get out?"

The obvious question is used most often as a way to give the applicant a chance to warm up and to be aware of what area the board is about to explore. It's also a way for the board to check up on the information they've been provided. Board members and background investigators can misread or misunderstand information they receive. Understanding this, board members will usually be careful to confirm details with you during the interview.

## Fishing Expeditions

The fishing expedition is always a nerve-racking kind of question to answer. You aren't certain why they are asking or where the question came from and they aren't giving out clues. Example:

Board member: "Mr. Jones, in your application, you stated that you've *never* been detained by police. (Usually, they will pause a few seconds and then get to the point.) You've *never* been detained?"

If your nerves aren't racked by this kind of questioning, someone probably needs to check you for a pulse. In this example, if the applicant has been detained by police and failed to list this on his application, then he'll be wondering if the board *knows* this happened. The odds are sky-high that the board does know the answer before asking the question. If the applicant has never been detained, then paranoia is certain to set in. Did someone on his or her list of references lie to the background investigator? Did someone on the board misread his or her application? Did . . . . These questions race through the applicant's mind as the board scrutinizes him or her.

Chances are, the board is simply fishing to see what he'll say. In any event, don't let these questions cause you a dilemma because, if you are honest, there can be no dilemma. You simply *must* tell the truth at *all* times in an oral board. Your integrity is at stake, your reputation, and, not least of all, your chance to become a police officer is at stake. Don't try to guess at *why* the board is asking a question. Your job is to answer truthfully and openly.

## Situational/Ethics Queries

Who doesn't dread these? You hear the words "What would you do if . . . ," and your heart pounds wildly. Example:

Board member: "Mr. Jones, assume you are a police officer, and you are on your way to back up an officer who is on the scene of a burglary alarm at a clothing store. You walk in just in time to see him pick up a small bottle of men's cologne and put it into his pocket. What do you do?"

Some oral boards are almost exclusively one situational question after another. Other departments may ask one, and then spend the rest of the interview asking you about your past job history. Your best defense here is to decide ahead of time what your ethics are and go with how *you* honestly feel. The only possible correct answer is *your* answer. If the board doesn't like what they hear, then you may be grilled intensely about your answer; however, you *cannot* assume that you've given the "wrong" answer if the board does begin questioning you hard about your answers. Boards have more than one reason for hammering away at you, and it's never safe to assume why they are doing it.

Keep in mind, too, that it's not uncommon on police boards for one board member to be assigned the task of trying to get under an applicant's skin. The purpose is to see if the applicant rattles easily under pressure or loses his or her temper when baited. The person assigned this task is not hard to spot. He/she will be the one you'd love to push in front of a city bus after you've had to answer such questions as: "Why in the world would we want to hire someone like *you*?"

Expect boards to jump on every discrepancy they hear and pick apart some of your comments—all because they want to see how you handle pressure. Not all departments designate a person to perform this function, but someone is usually prepared to slip into this role at some point in the interview.

## Role-Play Situations

Answering tough questions is stressful enough, but doing it under role-play conditions is even tougher. Many departments are using this technique more and more frequently in the oral board setting. A board member will instruct you to pretend you are a police officer and ask you to act out your verbal and/or physical responses. Example:

Board member: "Mr. Jones, I want you to pretend that you are a police officer and you are chasing a fleeing suspect. The suspect is running from you now and I want you to stand up and instruct him to stop by yelling, "Stop! Police!"

Board members may set up a bit more elaborate role-playing scenes for you. Try to enter into these situations with a willingness to participate. Most people are aware that you are not a professional actor or actress, so they are not looking for Academy Award–winning performances. Do the best you can. Role playing is used heavily in almost all police academies and training situations today, so expect to do a lot of role playing during your career as a law enforcement professional. Shy, reserved people may have difficulty working up enthusiasm for this kind of interaction. Practice how you'd handle this scene, and prepare yourself mentally as best you can.

## They Can't Ask Me That, Can They?

"They" are the members of the oral board and they can indeed ask you just about any question that comes to mind. Applying for a job in public safety puts you in a different league from the civilian sector applicant. Yes, federal and state laws may prohibit civilian employers from seeking certain information about their applicants. But law enforcement agencies are allowed more freedom of movement within the laws for obvious reasons.

For example, you'll rarely find a space for an applicant's birth date on an application for employment in private industry. This is the result of age discrimination litigation. Law enforcement agencies, as well as other agencies dealing with public safety, need such information to perform thorough background investigations and do not have many of the same restrictions. You will be expected to provide your date of birth and identify your race and your sex before you get very far in the application process for any police department. You are applying for a sensitive public safety job and must expect information you may consider highly personal to come to light.

In short, law enforcement agencies can ask you any question that may have a bearing on your mental stability, your ability to do the physical tasks common to police work, your integrity, honesty, character, and reputation in the community. There's not much left to the imagination after all of this is covered. If some of the questions are probing and perhaps even offensive, it is because you are being held to a higher standard by both the courts who allow these questions to be asked and the departments who want to hire you to protect life and property.

## Answers—How Many Are There?

While you are sitting in the interview hot seat, you may feel like only two kinds of answers exist—the one you wish you had given and the one you wish you could take back. There isn't a law enforcement officer in uniform today who doesn't have a war story about the one thing he wishes he hadn't brought up in his oral interview board. And this is to be expected. Nerves, pressure, and that random attack of stupid often conspire at the most inappropriate times. To help you be on guard for these moments, let's look at the mysterious "wrong" and "right" answer.

## The Wrong Answer

The wrong answer to any question is the answer you think you should say because that's what you've been told the board wants to hear. Do not take well-meant advice from friends or officers who haven't been before an oral board in the last five years and can't remember much about the one they did go through except that it made them nervous. Boards will often overlook answers they don't "like" if they feel you have good reasons for what you say and if you are being honest with them.

If the board fails you, it will not be because you gave the wrong answer. It will be because you are not the kind of person they are looking for, *or* there are some things you need to work on about your life or yourself and the board feels you need some time to work on these matters before they consider you for a job in law enforcement.

## The Right Answer

The answers the board wants to hear are the ones only *you* can give. They want *your* opinion, *your* reasons, *your* personal experiences, and they want to know what *you* would do under certain circumstances. Nothing else matters but you and how you present yourself in the oral interview. If you try to say what you think the board wants to hear, you will almost certainly give them a shallow, unsatisfying response to their question.

## What *Do* I Say?

It's not so much *what* you say as *how* you say it. The best way to answer *any* question is with directness, honesty, and brevity. Keep your answers short, but give enough information to answer the question fully. The board won't be handing out prizes for conserving words, but they also don't want to have to pull answers out of you like an old country dentist pulling teeth just so that they can get enough information.

There are a few ways you might want to avoid answering questions. Try not to play "if you ask the question *just* the right way, I'll give you the right answer" with the board. Here's an example:

Board member: "Mr. Jones, I see you've been arrested once for public intoxication while you were in college? Is that true?

Jones: "No, sir."

Board member: "Really? That's odd. It says here on page seven that you were arrested and spent the night in the city jail."

Jones: "Yes, well, I wasn't exactly *arrested* because the officer didn't put handcuffs on me.

Don't play word games with the board. You won't win. In this case, the applicant clearly knows that the board is aware of his arrest record, but he's trying to downplay the incident by trying to duck the question.

Then there's the "you can have the answer if you drag it out of me" technique, which you also want to avoid. For example:

Board member: "Mr. Jones, tell the board why you left the job you held at Tread Lightly Tire Shop."

Jones: "I was fired."

Board member: "Why were you fired?"

Jones: "Because the boss told me not to come back."

Board member: "Why did the boss tell you not to come back?"

Jones: "Because I was fired."

Board member: "What happened to cause you to be fired?"

Jones: "I was rude."

Board member: "Rude to whom and under what circumstances?"

You get the picture. This question could have been answered fully when the board member asked Jones why he left the tire shop job. The board would prefer that you not rattle on and on when you answer questions, but they would also appreciate a little balance here. This applicant also runs the risk of being labeled a smart aleck with this kind of answer. An oral board's patience is usually thin with an applicant who uses this answering technique.

Let's not forget the "you can have any answer but the one that goes with your question" technique. Avoid it, too. Example:

Board member: "Well, Mr. Jones, we know about some of the things you are good at, now tell us something about yourself that you'd like to improve."

Jones: "I'm really good with people. People like me and find it easy to talk to me for some reason. I guess it's because I'm such a good listener."

If he is a good listener, Mr. Jones didn't demonstrate this quality with that answer. It's important to listen to the question and answer directly. If you duck the question, then the board will assume you have something to hide or you are not being honest. If you don't understand how to answer the question, tell the person who asked it that you don't understand. They will be happy to rephrase the question or explain what they want. Be specific, and above all, answer the question you are asked, not the one you wish they'd asked instead.

## Reality Check

By now, you should have a reasonable idea of what an oral board is looking for and how best not only to survive the experience, but to come out ahead on your first board. You've had a lot of material to absorb in this chapter. Read the following scenarios illustrating the wrong way and the right way to tackle an oral interview. As you read, try to put yourself in the shoes of the oral board member who is asking the questions.

## Scenario #1

Mary Smith is sitting before the Friendly Police Department oral interview board. She is wearing a pair of black jeans, loafers without socks, and a short-sleeve cotton blouse. As the questions are being asked, she is tapping her foot against the table and staring at her hands.

Board member: "Ms. Smith, can you give the board an example of how you've handled a disagreement with a coworker in the past?"

Smith: "Nope. I get along with everybody. Everyone likes me."

Board member: "I see. So, you've never had a disagreement or difference of opinion with anyone you've ever worked with."

Smith: "That's right."

Board member: "Well, I see by your application that you were once written up by a supervisor for yelling at a fellow employee. Can you tell us about that situation?"

Smith: "That's different. It was his fault! He started talking to a customer I was supposed to wait on, so I told him off."

Now read the second situation.

## Scenario #2

Mary Smith is sitting before the Friendly Police Department oral interview board, dressed in a gray business suit. She is sitting still, with her hands folded in her lap and she is looking directly at the person asking her a question.

Board member: "Ms. Smith, can you give the board an example of how you've handled a disagreement with a coworker in the past?"

Jones: "Yes, sir. I can think of an example. When I was working at Pools by Polly, I had an argument with a coworker over which one of us was supposed to wait on a customer. I lost my cool and yelled at him. My boss wrote me up because of how I handled the situation."

Board member: "I see. How do you think you should have handled the situation?"

Smith: "If I had it to do again, I'd take James, my coworker, aside and talk to him about it in private. If I couldn't work something out with him, I would ask my supervisor to help out."

Board member: "What have you done to keep this sort of thing from happening again?"

Smith: "I've learned to stop and think before I speak and I've learned that there is a time and place to work out differences when they come up. I haven't had a problem since this incident."

So, which scenario left the best taste in your mouth? In scenario #1, the applicant is obviously unwilling to accept responsibility for her actions, she isn't showing any evidence that she is mature, and she isn't honest with herself or the board members when she said everyone liked her and she's never had disagreements with coworkers.

On the other hand, in scenario #2, the applicant is able to admit her mistakes and take responsibility for her part in the incident. Although she may have wished she could present herself in a better light, she did illustrate maturity by being honest, open, and straightforward in talking about the disagreement. In scenario #2, the applicant may have had to endure a long, hard interview in order to sell herself, but she was able to articulate what she did to correct a fault.

On the other hand, you can bet she had a very short interview and a "we're not interested, but thanks" from the board in scenario #1. Let's not even talk about the way the applicant was dressed in scenario #1 or her irritating mannerisms!

These two situations may seem exaggerated, but unfortunately applicants all over the country are making these mistakes as you read.

## What Do *You* Think?

Now that you are all warmed up, read the following situation. Pick from choice A, B, or C—decide which response you think is most appropriate for the question.

Alfred Wannabe's oral interview board is today at 9 A.M. at the police academy. He's parked in a chair outside of the board room by 8:40 A.M. awaiting the call.

When it comes, Alfred is ushered into the room and introduced to all of the board members. He sits where he's told and waits. It begins.

Board member: "Mr. Wannabe, what would you like for us to call you this morning?"
Wannabe: (A) "I don't know. It doesn't matter. Alfred is okay, I guess."
(B) "Alfred is fine, sir."
(C) "I go by Al."

Board member: "Why do you want to be a police officer?"
Wannabe: (A) "I don't know. I guess because it's fun and you get to help people. I want to be there when somebody needs something."
(B) "I'd like to be a police officer because I'm very interested in the work. I love to be around people. I like the variety of duties. And I like the challenge of trying to figure out what's really going on in a given situation."
(C) "Police work is what I've always wanted to do."

Board member: "I see. Well, we have a few standard questions for you, and I know a few others will crop up as we go along. First, can you tell us about your personality? What are you like to be around on a social basis?"
Wannabe: (A) "Oh, I don't know. I'm okay, I guess. My friends like me."
(B) "My friends tell me I'm usually fun to be around. I'm not particularly shy. I'd say I'm outgoing. I like meeting new people, talking, and I can be a pretty good listener, too. I am even-tempered. I get mad sometimes, but if I do, I get over it quickly. I have a good sense of humor and don't mind being teased as long as I get to tease back."
(C) "I'm easy to talk to, friendly, very social—I like being around lots of people—and I'm laid-back."

Board member: "I see here that your background investigator found that you once got thrown out of a friend's house during a party because you were picking fights with the other guests. Tell us about this experience."

Wannabe:

(A)    "Well . . . that was just that once. I had a little too much to drink I guess. I walked home from there."

(B)    "That happened about five years ago in my very early college days. I had just discovered beer, and I don't think I handled myself well at all in those days. At that party, I kept trying to get everyone to agree to switch the stereo to another station and was quite a jerk about it. My friend asked me to leave so I walked home. I was a jerk again the very next weekend and had to be asked to leave again. That wised me up. I realized I didn't need to be drinking like that, so I did something about it."

(C)    "Yes, that did happen. I got into an argument with friends over what music we'd listen to. I had been drinking. My host asked me to leave. I did."

Board member: "What steps have you taken to make sure this type of situation doesn't happen again?"

Wannabe:

(A)    "I guess I just watch how much I drink. I don't go to that guy's house anymore, either."

(B)    "I learned to eat before I went to parties where there was alcohol being served and then carried around the same drink for a while. I limited myself to two beers during an evening. I went home happy that way and so did all my friends. I still follow the same rules for myself today."

(C)    "I limit myself to two beers at a party and I don't drink much any other time. I'm responsible about the way I drink now."

All of the choices you read are responses candidates have made in oral board situations—not verbatim, but awfully close to it. If you chose Answer A for all your responses, you will be guaranteed to grate on the last nerve of every board member. It's not hard to see why. Phrases like "I don't know" and "I guess so" and "I think so" tell the listener that the speaker isn't sure of himself. It says the speaker probably has never thought about what you asked and is giving the answer without bothering to think about it now.

Answer A does not give the board much to go on. The answers don't offer explanations, although the open-ended question gives the applicant all the necessary room to do so. The board would be left with a wishy-washy impression of this candidate at best.

If you liked Answer B, you've kept yourself awake for most of this chapter. Answer B shows the applicant has manners, but he doesn't go overboard. He is direct, but not so direct that he comes across as blunt. He has either thought about the kinds of questions that will surface in the interview, or he thinks about what he wants to say before he speaks.

He comes across as confident, willing to discuss his past life, and not ashamed to admit mistakes. He also has a detailed explanation for how he's handled the drinking situation and the potential for future problems. It's at this point the applicant needs to be the most vocal. Board members are especially interested in how you handle your life in the present and what you will most likely do in the future.

If Answer C is what you chose, you probably won't blow the interview, but if you pass, it will be a squeaker. He's not rude, but he walks a thin line. He should elaborate more on how he feels about police work, because this is one of his opportunities to show the board how well he can express himself. People have different reasons for wanting to go into police work. Some are good and some are marginal, but for the most part, this question is designed to warm you up and let the board warm up, too.

It'd be hard to come up with a truly wrong answer for this question, although people have managed to do so. ("I love to shoot guns" would not win extra points here.) The board gets a feel for how you are going to be as an interviewee with this standard question. You don't have to deliver the Gettysburg Address, but give them *something* to go on. By now, you shouldn't have to think about this response anyway. It's a freebie.

Answer C is the type of response quiet, self-assured people often tend to give. They don't use up a whole lot of words and usually answer questions with directness. The danger here is that this applicant may not say enough to convince the board that he will deal well with the public and with other officers and supervisors.

These kinds of answers will most often force the board to switch to different kinds of questions that will force the applicant into lengthier responses. Don't make them work too hard getting the answers, though, unless you want a *really* short interview.

## Pulling It All Together

Chances are the postal service is looking pretty good right about now. But don't let all of this information become overwhelming. Make yourself step back and look at the big picture. You know what kind of overall impression you are most likely to make. If you don't, you should. And cut yourself a little slack. The people who interview you aren't perfect and have no real desire to hire someone who is, considering they may have to work with you some day.

Keep your sense of humor intact while you're going through this process. No, don't go into the board cracking jokes, but if you can keep your sense of humor close at hand, you might actually be able to come out of interview shock long enough to react if the board

jokes with you about something. It wouldn't be unusual for this to happen. Most law enforcement personnel like to tease or joke around to relieve stress. Let the board lead the way in this area, though.

Self-confidence is key. Relax, believe in yourself, and let it all come out naturally. If you feel like you are "blowing it" during the interview, show the board your self-confidence by stopping yourself. Take a deep breath and tell them that's not exactly what you'd like to say, then tell them what you'd like to say. Now *that's* self-confidence. Be firm if a board member tries to rattle your cage. "Firm" doesn't mean inflexible—change your mind if you need to—just don't do it every other sentence. There's always the wishy-washy label to consider—and avoid.

## Ready, Set, *Go*

You are as ready as you'll ever be if you follow these suggestions. There are no secrets to give away when it comes to oral interview boards. You can't change your past, your job history, or your educational status at this point in the process, nor can you change your personality or go back and do a more thorough job on your personal history statement. And you can't fake maturity if you are not a mature individual. But you can put your best foot forward, fight for your cause, and be as well prepared as possible.

Many police officers you see on the street today failed on their first attempt to be hired by their department's oral board and then passed the board after working on shortcomings and correcting problems. Your goal, of course, is to make it through the process on the first try. If that doesn't happen and you decide to try again, you owe it to yourself to come fully prepared the next time around.

If you follow the tips you've read so far, you should keep from making many mistakes that tend to eliminate otherwise well-qualified candidates. You will certainly be ahead of the applicant who has the same qualifications you have, but doesn't have a clue as to how to prepare for an oral interview board. Good luck.

# Some Final Words of Advice

Dr. Rick Bradstreet is a 17-year veteran psychologist for the Austin Police Department in Austin, Texas. He holds a law degree from Stanford University and a PhD in counseling psychology from the University of Texas in Austin. His specialty is communication skills and conflict resolution. Throughout his career with APD, Dr. Bradstreet estimates that he's sat on about 250 to 300 oral interview boards and has had plenty of opportunity to observe applicants in oral interviews. He offers the following advice to those who see an oral board in their future.

- Make eye contact. Applicants who fail to make eye contact with interviewers can expect a negative reaction from the board. Making eye contact makes the speaker feel like what he or she is saying is being heard and is being taken seriously.

- Sit erect in your chair, but not so stiffly that you appear to be ripe for the woodsman's axe. You should not have the same posture that you would have if you were sitting at home in your living room, yet you want to appear somewhat relaxed and alert.

- Keep your hands in your lap if you have a tendency to wring your hands together when agitated. Wringing hands are generally perceived as a sign of nervousness.

- Try not to drum your fingers on the table. Although this behavior is most often interpreted more as a sign of someone who has excess energy and is not necessarily seen as nervous behavior, it can be distracting to those around you.

- Feel free to shift positions periodically. It's perfectly natural to move around as you speak and is expected during normal conversation. An oral board is not meant to be an interrogation, so you are not expected to sit frozen in place for the duration.

- Speak up. If a board member lets you know you are mumbling, then project your voice. Speaking in a voice so soft that no one can hear you does nothing to enhance the image you want to project—that of a self-confident, take-charge person who knows what you want.

- Focus on explaining how you are as a person and not on responding to questions defensively. Once again, this is not an interrogation. Try to have a normal, respectful conversation with the board members and your body language will take on a more natural, confident look.

- Get out of the self-conscious mode. Your goal is to let the board see you and your experiences as unique. Do not try to mold your experiences and answers to questions according to what you "think" the board may want.

# 30 ▶ The Psychological Assessment

## CHAPTER SUMMARY

The psychological assessment, which includes an interview and testing, is an important step in the police officer selection process. The following chapter describes what to expect and how to prepare for it.

**P**sychologists can have a fearsome reputation. Whenever there's a terrorist or serial killer, someone sticks a microphone in a psychologist's face to ask, "Why did he do it? What's he like? When will he do it again?" In court, psychologists are asked to describe a stranger's past state of mind: "Was the defendant insane when he committed the murder two years ago?" All of this gives the impression that psychologists have special powers to predict the future and travel into the past, and that they can make accurate diagnoses of people they haven't even met. The media enjoy this dramatic image, and play it up—which makes many people believe it.

But the truth is psychologists are neither fortune tellers nor mind readers. They are just skilled professionals who make educated guesses about people based upon known traits, recognizing that they cannot know everything about anyone. They try to produce fair evaluations based on their training and experience and all the available information.

During your assessment, it may be helpful to remember that, more than anyone else, psychologists recognize that everyone has weaknesses and makes mistakes (including themselves). In fact, they're less interested in your specific mistakes than in how you handled them—for example, did you learn from them, keep repeating them, and/or blame them on other people?

The point of the psychological assessment is not to criticize or "nail" you; no one expects you to be perfect or even wonderful. Your value as a human being is not on the line here. The goal is only to discover whether your individual pattern of good and bad points matches the profile of most police officers, which says nothing about how successful you may be in other areas and careers.

## ▶ Psychological Testing

Testing is part of the assessment process. Most police departments use some form of the Minnesota Multiphasic Personality Inventory (MMPI), which has 560 simple true/false questions, together with perhaps one other, shorter test. Both are designed to produce a general psychological profile and to detect extremes in attitudes and behaviors. The results may or may not be explained to you, depending on the policies of the department; explanations are very time-consuming and thus impossible to do for everyone.

You cannot study for a psychological test. Besides, you already know the subject matter better than anyone else. You are the world's foremost expert on your own feelings, attitudes, and behaviors, and that's what the testing is about. But even though you can't study, there are ways to prepare yourself for it.

One is to remember that testing is only one piece of the picture. You've already filled out a lengthy application and had a background check and probably at least one interview—if you were totally unfit for police work, you wouldn't have gotten this far! If the test results raise any questions, your meeting with the psychologist enables you to answer them face to face. So try to relax as much as possible, because tension can make it difficult to concentrate (a few deep breaths will help).

It is crucial to be honest in your answers. Don't try to figure out the "right" answer or what each question is getting at. The tests are designed to make this difficult, so you'll only waste time and make yourself more nervous in the process. If you fake your answers, someone is sure to notice (you won't add up right). Besides, if you don't give a true picture of yourself, you may begin a career for which you are poorly suited. And this is not in anyone's best interest, least of all yours.

## ▶ The Psychological Interview

It's important to show up for your interview on time and be neatly dressed. Respond politely to the questions, but don't volunteer too much information—this is not a social event where you can get loose and friendly. The psychologist (or psychologists—some departments use a team) may spend a few initial moments breaking the ice, but the rest of the 60–90 minutes will be focused and businesslike.

It may feel strange to discuss personal things with strangers. It's almost like going to a medical doctor, where you may feel embarrassed about sharing certain information, but must do it for your own good. In the same way, being evasive or defensive in the psychological interview will not do you any good at all.

And yes, you are expected to be nervous. Who wouldn't be? This is a hurdle you have to jump on the way to your goal. At some time in their lives, most people wonder whether or not they're crazy, and you may be afraid that this psychologist will finally confirm it. Even though it's a myth, that all-powerful, all-seeing shrink image may come to mind. For these and other reasons, it's normal to be nervous. And if you are, it's a good idea to admit it, for it shows honesty and mature self-acceptance. If you are nervous and try to deny it, this suggests a lack of confidence and a tendency to be dishonest, neither of which will gain you any points.

Remember that the psychologist who interviews you is not interested in your full history, only what's relevant to being a police officer. And don't be surprised if the questions are more personal than in other job interviews you've had. One simple reason is that this job comes with a gun—in other words, when public safety is on the line, the courts allow interviewers to get really nosy.

So you may be asked about your childhood, relationships/marriage(s), and military and high school experiences. Expect questions about which supervisors you liked and didn't like on jobs you've had; this shows how you deal with authority. If you've jumped around from job to job but had good reasons for it, be ready to explain them if asked.

You may be asked how you feel about getting into a physical force situation with someone, or if you could shoot someone.

Of course you'll be asked why you want to be a police officer. It's easy to tell a good answer from a bad answer on this one. Good answers: "I want to help people." "I want a secure job with a pension." "My relative (friend) is a cop and I think the work is interesting." Bad answers: "I want to have power over people." "I like excitement and danger." "I can't wait to put all those jerks in jail." Answers that are rehearsed or not really "you" will be obvious, so, once again, just be honest.

Last but certainly not least, don't try too hard to sell yourself. Nervousness is fine, but desperation is not. If you are right for this profession, you must be able to meet challenges with confidence—including the challenge of a brief psychological assessment.

## Special FREE Offer from LearningExpress

**LearningExpress guarantees that you will be better prepared for, and score higher on, the California police officer exam**

 Go to the LearningExpress Practice Center at www.LearningExpressFreeOffer.com, an interactive online resource exclusively for LearningExpress customers.

Now that you've purchased LearningExpress's *California Police Officer Exam*, you have **FREE** access to:

- A **full-length California police officer practice test** that mirrors the official California police officer exam
- **Multiple-choice questions** covering memory, verbal expression, written comprehension, spatial orientation, and judgment and problem-solving skills
- **Immediate scoring** and **detailed answer explanations**
- A **customized diagnostic report** to benchmark your skills and focus your study

Follow the simple instructions on the scratch card in your copy of *California Police Officer Exam*. Use your individualized access code found on the scratch card and go to www.LearningExpress FreeOffer.com to sign in. Start practicing online for the California police officer exam right away!

Once you've logged on, use the spaces below to write in your access code and newly created password for easy reference:

Access Code: _____     Password: _____